THE SAINT BARTHOLOMEW'S DAY MASSACRE

MANCHESTER
1824

Manchester University Press

THE SAINT BARTHOLOMEW'S DAY MASSACRE

THE MYSTERIES OF A CRIME OF STATE

(24 AUGUST 1572)

ARLETTE JOUANNA

Translated by
Joseph Bergin

Manchester University Press

Copyright © Editions GALLIMARD, Paris 2007

The right of Arlette Jouanna to be identified as the author of this work has been asserted by her in accordance with the Copyright, Designs and Patents Act 1988.

Published by Editions GALLIMARD 2007, *La Saint-Barthélemy: Les mystères d'un crime d'etat (24 août 1572)*

First English-language edition published in 2013 by Manchester University Press
Altrincham Street, Manchester M1 7JA, UK
www.manchesteruniversitypress.co.uk

British Library Cataloguing-in-Publication Data is available

Library of Congress Cataloging-in-Publication Data is available

ISBN 978 0 7190 9755 3 *paperback*

This paperback edition first published 2015

The publisher has no responsibility for the persistence or accuracy of URLs for any external or third-party internet websites referred to in this book, and does not guarantee that any content on such websites is, or will remain, accurate or appropriate.

Printed by Lightning Source

CONTENTS

TRANSLATOR'S NOTE

This book first appeared in a well-known French series originally entitled 'The thirty days which made France', although in the recent and still unfinished re-make of the series – which led to the present book being written – the limitation to thirty days has been removed. In this context, the French word 'journée' (and not 'jour') for a 'day' has itself to be understood quite loosely. From the coronation of Charlemagne to the fall of the Bastille and beyond, such 'days' dot the landscape of French history, so that they should be seen in terms of 'moments' or 'turning points' in history. An understanding of this initial editorial format will help readers of this translation to see better why the book is shaped as it is and why the author raises, especially in the introduction and the conclusion, explicit questions about the significance of the Massacre.

Likewise, the book's original title – *La Saint-Barthélemy* – makes immediate sense in French, rendering the words 'day' and 'massacre' of the English title quite redundant. It is the word 'la' which makes the difference here, but it has no functional equivalent in English. Rather than peppering the pages that follow with the rather cumbersome phrase 'The Saint Bartholomew's Day massacre', I have translated it, wherever possible and where no ambiguity might arise from doing so, simply as the Massacre, while using the word 'massacre(s)' to describe individual cases of massacre, including elements of the Massacre itself. The term 'crime d'état' of the original sub-title jars much less in French than 'crime of state' does in English, but alternative translations (e.g. 'political crime') would have unduly diluted the meaning that it conveys. Finally, in a subject which has generated endless speculation since 1572, especially over the motives of those involved, it is important, but often quite difficult, to distinguish known fact from supposition when writing about them. The elegant, and extremely economical, French use of the conditional tense when wishing to convey the uncertain or the assumed (e.g. 'Charles IX *aurait* dit') cannot be directly reproduced in English, so I have resorted, depending on context, to circumlocutions such as 'reportedly', 'supposedly', or 'people thought that', and so on, to convey the nuances of the original text.

In my efforts to render the meaning of the original French as faithfully as possible, I am greatly indebted the author, who carefully read my efforts, making valuable suggestions for improvement, as well as spotting mistakes and omissions. Needless to say, anything lost in translation is my sole responsibility.

Joseph Bergin
Manchester, September 2012

AUTHOR'S ACKNOWLEDGEMENTS

I wish to express my gratitude to all those who assisted me in writing this book, especially Jacques Frayssenge, Nicolas Fornerod and Myriam Yardeni. I also wish to thank Ran Halévi for his careful reading of the manuscript, as well as Philippe Bernier.

Arlette Jouanna

ABBREVIATIONS

AGS	Archivo General de Simancas
BEC	*Bibliothèque de l'École des chartes*
BHR	Bibliothèque d'Humanisme et Renaissance
BnF	Bibliothèque nationale de France
BPU Genève	Bibliothèque publique universitaire de Genève
BSHPF	*Bulletin de la Société de l'histoire du protestantisme français*
CSP	*Calendar of State Papers*
HES	*Histoire, Économie et Société*
MS Fr	Manuscrit français
RH	*Revue historique*
RHD	*Revue d'histoire diplomatique*
RHMC	*Revue d'histoire moderne et contemporaine*
SCJ	*The Sixteenth Century Journal*

GLOSSARY OF FRENCH TERMS

The following French terms have been retained in the text. They are italicised on their first occurrence.

bailliage/bailli	local royal law-court and area of jurisdiction in northern France, presided over by a bailli
cour des aide	royal court dealing with fiscal questions
grand	a member of the titled aristocracy
ligueurs	adherents of the Catholic League
parlement/parlementaires	a 'sovereign' high court of appeal and its magistrates
présidial	a law-court below a parlement and above a bailliage
prévôt des marchand	mayor of Paris
sénéchal/sénéchaussée	equivalent of bailliage (see above) in southern France
taille	the principal royal tax levied on property

INTRODUCTION:
THE ENIGMAS OF SAINT
BARTHOLOMEW'S DAY

Sunday 24 August 1572 was the feast of Saint Bartholomew. The streets of Paris were wet on that day, 'as if it had rained a lot', according to a bourgeois from Strasbourg who was passing through the city.[1] But it was with blood, not rain that the streets glistened.

Before dawn a troop of soldiers of the duc de Guise, the Catholic hero, came to kill Admiral Gaspard de Coligny, the military leader of the Protestants, in his residence on the rue de Béthisy. At the Louvre palace, the Admiral's principal lieutenants were pulled from their beds, disarmed, and then cut to pieces in the courtyard by the pikes of the Swiss and French guards. All of this was done with the consent of the King, Charles IX, a consent that the King was pressured into giving by circumstances whose elucidation continues to divide historians.

The day began with scenes of slaughter. Wearing a cross on their hats and white armbands, symbols of the purity which they believed they had lost, Catholics scoured the city and pursued the 'heretics' in the name of God. Armed gangs systematically searched houses; Protestants were hauled outside and executed without judgment; corpses, stripped of their clothes and often mutilated, were dragged towards the Seine; some of them had previously been piled up in the squares or at crossroads and then transported in carts. The river was red with blood, so much so that the Parisians, according to a Calvinist from Millau, 'remained for a long time without eating fish, on account of the corruption of the water and the stench from the bodies'.[2] Those massacred in the faubourg of Saint-Germain were dumped into *le puits aux Clercs* (the Clercs' Well) where it was customary to throw the carcasses of dead animals.

Children, women, the elderly – nobody was spared. Babies were snatched from their mothers' breasts and thrown into the river; children were killed with their parents, and servants alongside their masters. The dwellings of the victims were sacked and pillaged. Before dawn, the tocsin of Saint-Germain l'Auxerrois church bellowed out its harrowing sound, and was soon imitated by the bells of nearby churches. The air was thick with the protests of those being murdered, the shouts of the assassins and the noise of the shootings. Panicked by the scale of the murderous fury, the King lay low in the Louvre, while the orders he gave to end the Massacre were openly ridiculed. The city had fallen into the hands of the Catholics most determined to eradicate heresy; in a state of terror, other people remained indoors, not daring to go outside. Groups of lookouts were established in most streets, controlling the comings and goings, identifying those fleeing and turning them over to the murderers. Anyone wishing to leave the city had to show a valid passport. For three whole days, the gates of Paris remained closed; the chances of escaping the trap set for the prey were tiny. Although resolutely hostile to the Protestants, a Catholic doctor from Mantua, Filippo Cavriana, recounts the fear which the frightful spectacle that he witnessed engendered in him:

> One saw only naked bodies pierced by a thousand stabs in the streets; the river transported just as many bodies. No distinction was made for sex, age or the status of people ... people fled through the streets, with others pursuing them and shouting, 'kill, kill', so that it was a real massacre. What should be underlined is the stubbornness of some people, both men and women, who, although they had a knife to their throats and the possibility of saving their lives by abjuring, nevertheless wished to become martyrs of the devil and so lose both their soul and their body because of their obstinate ignorance ...
>
> We do not remark such joy and jubilation among Catholics that we were accustomed to previously, because the spectacle was truly horrible and pitiful. ... All of them wear the white cross in their hats, because when the feast-day was celebrated, people put a shirt-sleeve on their left arm. And the password was 'Long live God and the King', in order to recognise our people and distinguish them from the others.[3]

This account suggests that the choice of abjuring in order to save their lives was offered to the Protestants, but other accounts make no mention of it, merely recording the savagery of the killings. Some Huguenots were taken to prison, only to be executed there during the night. Whole families were exterminated. The Massacre lasted a week. The number of murders fell after the frenzy of the first three days, but they were still happening until Saturday 30 August. On Thursday 28th, the bourgeois of Strasbourg witnessed the killing of a young, heavily pregnant woman, a countess 'of great beauty' who was expensively attired. Despite her appeals, she was stripped of her clothes, deprived of her jewels, pierced with blows and thrown into the Seine. 'And while she was falling, one could see her child still stirring' in her breast, wrote the bourgeois. Shortly afterwards, he saw a silversmith, who was trying to escape via the rooftops, felled by a shot from a musket. On Saturday, the bodies of three people just killed were dumped in the river before his eyes.[4]

This murderous fury decimated the Protestant community of Paris, which, although a minority in a city that was massively Catholic, still comprised before the Massacre several thousand persons. How many perished during this bloody week? The estimates made by contemporaries cannot be accepted – they varied, depending on confessional affiliation and polemical intent, between 1,000 and 100,000 people. We know how much the grave-diggers of the Holy Innocents cemetery were paid for burying the bodies which the Seine carried as far as Chaillot, Passy, Auteuil and Saint-Cloud; the number of bodies involved has been estimated at 1,825.[5] This figure represents only a fraction of the number of victims in the capital. An estimate of the order of at least 3,000 people killed is plausible. Massacres subsequently occurred in about fifteen provincial towns, bringing the total figure for the kingdom as a whole to around 10,000.

Women disembowelled, old people with their throats cut, children thrown into the river, men emasculated, murderers drunk on blood – such is the memory transmitted by contemporary accounts of 24 August 1572. So does the picture by François Dubois, a Parisian painter who took refuge in Switzerland after escaping the massacre, and which depicts atrocious scenes of violence, hatred and barbarity.[6]

BEFORE THE CARNAGE, THE FESTIVITIES

Yet if we rewind the clock to just a week before the killings, we encounter a radically different spectacle, in which Paris offers the observer images of joy and union.

On 18 August the marriage of Marguerite de Valois, sister of Charles IX, to her cousin, Henri, the young King of Navarre and hope of the Protestants, was celebrated. This union was designed to consolidate the peace agreed in 1570 at Saint-Germain after the Third War of Religion. On that day, all Parisians were able to observe the progress of the wedding, which was blessed by Cardinal Bourbon on a platform erected outside the doors of Notre-Dame cathedral. The ceremony brilliantly illustrated the determination to reconcile the hostile confessions. Apart from the fact that a Catholic princess was marrying a Protestant leader, it was conducted, as one anonymous chronicler put it, according to 'a formula which both sides did not disapprove of' – that is, in a manner acceptable to both camps.[7] This was not self-evident because, in Protestant theology, marriage, contrary to Catholic doctrine, is not a sacrament. To overcome this obstacle, the King and his mother, Catherine de Medici, needed considerable perseverance in their desire to consolidate a peaceful yet fragile co-existence, as they also did by agreeing that the groom need not attend the Mass in the cathedral, but could wait for it to end in the nearby episcopal residence, along with the nobles of his retinue. The King even ignored the absence of a papal dispensation needed both for the degrees of consanguinity and for the difference of religion between the young couple, a dispensation which Pope Gregory XIII had not sent.

Sumptuous feasting followed the wedding, during which Protestant and Catholic nobles mingled together. After the ceremony, a banquet was organised in the Cité palace, followed by a ball and finally, a masquerade, the high point of which was a procession of golden and silver chariots decorated with nautical motifs. On the biggest chariot the King of France sat beside Neptune, god of the sea, while the King's brothers, Henri d'Anjou and François d'Alençon, and then, without distinction of religion, the King of Navarre, his cousin Prince Henri de Condé, the dauphin Prince François de Bourbon, duc Henri de Guise and the chevalier of Angoulême, sat on the others. 'Such was the intermingling of Protestants and Catholics', wrote the chronicler quoted above.

Union and concord: this was also the theme that ran through the celebrations that continued for the following three days. The masquerade of 20 August in the great hall of the Petit-Bourbon residence struck people very forcibly. It presented themes borrowed from both ancient mythology and the novels of chivalry, as was common at the time for these types of entertainment. The King and his two brothers were stationed by the door of an enclosure representing 'paradise' and beat off the attack of 'errant cavaliers', led by the King of Navarre, and turfed them into 'hell'. Then, after the intervention of Mercury, Cupid and twelve nymphs, they released them. This scenario was designed to glorify the chivalrous courage of the three brothers, but also to celebrate their power of mercy and pardon. The message was clear: by ordering the release of the nobles imprisoned in hell – the other participants in the combat, who were, it should be noted, a mixture of Catholics and Protestants – the King saved them from the forces of evil, undesirable passions and the temptations of violence. He thus engineered the triumph of concord through the reconciliatory magic of his omnipotence. This point should not be obscured by the jousts organised on the 21 August, which had Protestants dressed as Turks, the enemies of Christianity, fighting against the King and Henri d'Anjou disguised as Amazons. These 'turqueries' were often part of court entertainments.[8] No particular significance should be attached to the disguises worn by Protestant nobles, whose turbans and long robes did no more than add a dash of exoticism to events. The celebrations organised for the marriage were all programmed to illustrate the peace-inducing powers of music, song and dance, bringing together the now-pacified antagonists in a shared joy, under the auspices of a unifying king.

No greater contrast could be imagined between these rejoicings and the bloody fury unleashed a few days later. And this is the principal enigma of the massacre of Saint Bartholomew's Day. How can such a reversal be explained?

It is, of course, true that between 18 and 24 August there was the failed attack of 22 August against Admiral Coligny, which wounded him in the right hand and the left arm. This event, and the conjectures that it spawned as to the motives and identity of its instigator, suddenly revived the latent distrust between Catholics and Protestants. But can this episode of itself explain the chasm which separates, in less than a week, the marriage festivities and the

Massacre? The first reactions of the most seasoned observers reveal their bewilderment. Many of the King's subjects would have shared the incredulity, for example, of the leading citizens of Limoges when they heard 'the more than strange news of such a sudden and unexpected change' from the envoy of a Limousin nobleman returning from Paris.[9] This sudden turnaround has troubled contemporaries and historians alike. Interpretations of it were developed in due course, but if one surveys them, one realises that many of them reach their conclusions only at the cost of denying, or underestimating, the contrast between 18 and 24 August – which says much about the opacity of the mystery.

THINKING THE UNTHINKABLE

The need to make sense of the events was particularly intense among the survivors of the Massacre and their co-religionists, who were powerfully confronted with the difficulty of recounting, or even imagining, what had happened. Théodore de Bèze, Calvin's successor in Geneva, was one of the first to express the almost literally unthinkable character of the event. On 4 September he confided to a correspondent: 'overwhelmed by grief as I try to imagine these sad events, I write nothing; meanwhile the news is brought to me – news which, as it is presented, cannot even be grasped by the mind. Even less can one explain it in any way, either in speech or in writing.'[10] The horror of the killings was, of course, the principal cause of the kind of dumbstruck state into which de Bèze had lapsed, but there was also an incapacity to comprehend its suddenness.

However, the Protestants soon felt the necessity to make sense of things, and to render the Massacre intelligible by placing it within a chain of causality whose logic could be deciphered. After the first shock had passed, the process of interpretation was kick-started among them, with a view to providing not an impossible justification, but at least a 'readability' for events that were beyond the ordinary. The solution that they adopted was the suppression, pure and simple, of the inexplicable discrepancy between the marriage of 18 and the carnage of 24 August. They thus erased any contradiction between these two events by considering the first as a trap designed to lure the victims of the second; it was the execution of a carefully premeditated plan by the King, the Queen Mother, and their most resolute advisors. This is what we find in the Protestant pamphlets and treatises written after the event, most of which were collected later in the *Mémoires de l'Estat de France sous Charles neufiesme*, published in 1576–77 by the pastor Simon Goulart. In their interpretation, the King organised his sister's wedding in order to bring to Paris a large number of Protestant nobles and have them opportunely assassinated there. Once the marriage was completed, the attack on Coligny aimed to provoke the Protestants' fury and lead them into making threats of reprisals; Charles IX could then use this pretext to accuse them of sedition against him and to carry out the extermination plan that he had been contemplating since at least 1565 – that is, since his interview in Bayonne with the Duke of Alba, the King of Spain's chief military commander and a fierce enemy of the Protestants. The successive peace agreements signed since the beginning of the troubles (Peace of Amboise in 1563 after the first war, peace of Longjumeau in 1568 after the second, and finally that of Saint-Germain in 1570) were no more than 'valois peaces' – namely, acts of treachery designed to lull the mistrust of the victims.[11]

This thesis is remarkable for its simplicity and coherence; although it heightens the horror of the Massacre itself, its logic has the advantage of making it *thinkable* and a clear object on which one could take up a position; to some extent, it frees those holding it from the anguish of the incomprehensible. Among Protestants, it triggered a full re-evaluation of events between 1564 and 1572, which were reinterpreted as so many *signs* that demonstrated the perverted enterprise of the King and his mother.

The paradox is that this thesis was first diffused by Catholics. Although it quickly became accepted by ambassadors, both English and Italian, it was a nobleman from the papal court, Camillo Capilupi, who did most to broadcast it by composing a work entitled *Lo stratagema di Carlo IX, Re di Francia, contro gli Ugonotti rebelli di Dio e suoi*, and published in Rome.[12] This author obviously wrote from a completely different perspective to that of the victims of the Massacre. He marvelled at the cleverness of the 'stratagem' employed by Charles IX to exterminate the heretics. The explanation by premeditation has the advantage of being usable by both camps: it only has to be ticked by them as either negative or positive. The Protestants lost no time in appropriating it, publishing Capilupi's book in Geneva in an edition containing both the Italian text and a French translation. Simon Goulart included part of it in the *Mémoires de l'Estat de France*.

Later historians were also confronted with the enigma of the contrast between the marriage and the Massacre.[13] Gradually, through a historiographical process which it would take too long to recount here, a standard account developed which solved the mystery, not by suppressing the contradiction, but by attenuating and reducing it to a psychological confrontation between Charles IX and Catherine de Medici, albeit at the cost of underestimating the religious and political stakes involved. The contradiction between the two events mirrored the one dividing the two royal figures then in power. In this version, the desire for concord and peace was the King's, and the perfidious initiatives designed to serve personal interests were his mother's. Thus, it was out of jealousy that Catherine de Medici desired the attack of 22 August on Coligny, whose ascendancy over the King had become too great for her liking; then, panicked by its failure and by the consequences of her action, and with the help of her advisor, Albert de Gondi, comte de Retz, she brought such pressure to bear on her terrorised son that he apparently ended up saying – 'kill them all, so that there is no one left to reproach me for it'.

In order to reinforce the credibility of this interpretation it was necessary to seriously blacken the character of the Queen Mother. Her Florentine background facilitated the risky deduction that she was influenced by the Florentine Machiavelli; from her taste for magic, her talent as a poisoner was inferred; from her desire for power came the conclusion about her manipulative dishonesty. This is how, for example, Jean Mariéjol, in the classic history of France edited by Ernest Lavisse at the beginning of the twentieth century, describes the sequence of events:

> Catherine had not planned anything in the event of the attack on Coligny failing; she was caught in her own trap. The Protestants were threatening, and the population of Paris was beginning to stir; the Guises were arming to defend themselves. If the duc de Guise spoke out to defend himself, if he named his accomplice, or if the enquiry got side-tracked in her direction – she would have a lot to fear. She foresaw the exodus of thousands of nobles from Paris and a new war led by an implacable commander. It was thus in a mind panicked by fear and without scruples that (unless it was suggested to her by Gondi) the idea of killing all Protestant leaders took shape.[14]

This reconstruction of events has the advantage of explaining the volte-face between 18 and 24 August, of which it offers a novel-like reading, which is probably the reason for its longevity in the collective memory. It was reiterated notably in the two short and stylish books written about the Massacre in 1968 and 1987 by Janine Garrisson, who portrays a Catherine de Medici who was responsible for the attack on Coligny and who 'harassed' her son in order to obtain his consent to the Massacre – an interpretation that Garrisson subsequently revised in a book on the later Valois kings.[15] The problem is that this version is based on the accounts of memorialists of dubious value.

More recently, research has moved towards other possible solutions to the enigma. Drawing partly on the work of Lucien Romier, Jean-Louis Bourgeon searched for its coherence in the theory of premeditation. But, in contrast to the Protestant theses, he completely absolved the King and the Queen Mother, whom he portrays as unwillingly drawn into the tragedy and forced to adapt to the situation.[16] According to Bourgeon, the massacre was the result of a 'vast and ingenious international Catholic conspiracy against France' planned by the King of Spain and the Pope, and put into operation by the Guises, its 'docile executors', and by the Parisian bourgeoisie and magistrates of the *parlement*, who had for a long time prepared their own revolt against a monarch whom they judged to be at once tyrannical and too favourable towards heretics.[17] The extermination of the Protestants by the Catholics was, in this view, the consequence of an uprising of the latter against the King to force him to abandon his policy of concord. 'The Saint Bartholomew's Day massacre was conceived and planned by moderate, responsible people; it was cleverly crafted in order to force the King to yield, but not to discredit him.'[18] This planning was visible from the beginning of the marriage celebrations, whose unifying character-istics could not hide the bad omens: 'behind this official façade designed to create an illusion, the tragedy was being prepared'. In short, if we follow Bour-geon, the clash between the marriage festivities and the killings that followed them was merely apparent; the conspiracy had been launched on 18 August.

This argument is interesting; it convincingly stresses the seditious aspect of the generalised carnage that followed the elimination of the Huguenot leaders, since the orders given by the King to stop it were not obeyed. But Bourgeon makes no distinction between the execution of Coligny and his followers and the bloody fury that followed. Furthermore, the thesis of a plan organised by Spain is invalidated by a careful reading of the documents preserved in the Simancas archives, while the complicity of the Guises is based only on conjec-ture.[19] A variation of this thesis was presented by Thierry Wanegffelen in his biography of Catherine de Medici, where he claimed to see the hand of Spain in the attack of 22 August against Coligny, and discharged the King of all respon-sibility for the Massacre, which is attributed to the dukes of Anjou and Guise.[20] In a wide-ranging and stimulating book, Denis Crouzet has also reduced the opposition between the marriage and the subsequent violence, but in a very different manner. For him, the execution of the Huguenot leaders was actually 'a crime of love', which corresponded, as much as did the royal marriage, to Charles IX's desire to reunite his subjects in a state of concord; it was in order to lift the threat which Coligny and his allies represented to the royal dream of union that the King had them executed, hoping that this violent remedy would save what could be saved of the peace, and which the marriage of his sister and the King of Navarre symbolised.[21] This interpretation is based on a learned study of the Neoplatonic ideals then fashionable at court, and which had apparently seduced both the King and his mother, impelling them to do everything to protect the cohesion of the kingdom in the harmony of love; the murderous frenzy of the Paris population, viewed as the mystical ardour of a people who saw themselves as God's armed right hand, destroyed that hope. This analysis rightly brings into play the force of the *imaginaire* in the reactions of the King and his entourage. However, by deliberately locating it in the field of representation, Crouzet posits the impossibility of finding a reliable logic for the succession of events; his approach resolutely proclaims itself as a 'chronicle of incertitude'.[22] Indeed, according to the author, it would be pointless to try to solve the mystery and the ambiguity, both of which were essential characteris-tics of the Renaissance political system.

More recently, in a book on Catherine de Medici, Crouzet returned to the mystery of the contradiction between the royal desire for concord and the carnage.[23] He explains it in terms of the notion of 'necessity', the centrepiece of the art of politics which imposed the solution of a temporary recourse to violence on the King in order to prevent the unleashing of evil passions; but this apparent discontinuity, for all its real painfulness, still functioned as part of the objective of restoring union among the King's subjects. Dramatic and unforeseen circumstances, it is argued, forced the King and his mother to adopt a 'schizophrenic' type of behaviour which, in reality, revealed their submission to God's will. An event unwillingly endured, the tragedy of 1572 was accepted, with absolute confidence in the unfathomable providence of God, by a monarchy that was perpetually in search of a 'life-giving communion between the world down here and the celestial sphere'.[24]

POLITICS AND RELIGION

Crouzet's insistence on the aspect of 'love' in the crime of St Bartholomew's Day is valuable because it also draws attention to a second enigma. The decision to execute those Huguenots regarded as the most dangerous was accompanied by a desire, explicitly proclaimed by the King, to preserve the Edict of Pacification promulgated at Saint-Germain in 1570 – as if it was somehow possible to reconcile these two apparently irreconcilable objectives and to believe that eliminating the Protestant leaders would guarantee the peace.

This was in remarkable and paradoxical contrast with earlier instances of royal changes of mind. Precedents – some of them spectacular – were not lacking. In January 1562, the edict granting partial freedom of worship to the Protestants was followed, as early as March 1562, by a war – the first of many – against them; the Edict of Longjumeau of March 1568 was followed in September by that of Saint-Maur, which deprived the Protestants of all right to hold services. After the Saint Bartholomew's Massacre, there would be the reversal of 1574, which would undermine the Peace of Boulogne and prefigure the fifth war; in 1585, there would be a more considerable shift, with Henri III, after five years of peace, suppressing not just freedom to worship, but also freedom of conscience.

The entire history of the Wars of Religion is punctuated by more or less sudden shifts in royal policy between Catholic inflexibility and the acceptance of confessional duality. These oscillations arose out of the choices that alternatively faced the King, the Queen Mother and the leading members of their entourage. For these Catholics, there were only two conceivable solutions to the religious division. The first was to temporise, which meant the provisional acceptance of peaceful co-existence between the two confessions until the hoped-for reconciliation could come about by peaceful means within the bosom of the Roman church; all of the edicts of pacification, including that of Nantes, which brought the religious wars to an end in 1598, reveal the hope that one day God's grace will permit the reunion of souls, even if this outcome is envisaged in the undetermined future. The second solution was the eradication of heresy by violent means. Each of these options was defended in the royal council by distinct groups which did not form parties in the modern sense but were shifting political constellations that reshaped as events unfolded. The champions of extirpation were those intransigent Catholics who recognised themselves in the charisma of the Guise family of Lorraine origin; they found powerful support in the expanding Tridentine reform, as well as in the financial support and the manoeuvres of the King of Spain. The others began to be labelled from 1568 onwards as 'politiques'.[25] No less fervent Catholics than the former groups, they nevertheless sought, however provisional it might be, a legal way out of religious division. They were mostly men of the robe, magistrates and jurists imbued with ideas of peace, and who had supporters at court, such as Jean de Morvillier or François de Montmorency.

Charles IX was divided between these two positions. On the one hand, his humanistic education fostered in him the dream of an enduring concord between his subjects; on the other, the distrust that he felt towards the Protestant leaders made him see them as potential rebels. This is why the two 'parties', that of the intransigent Catholics and that of the 'politiques', successively found in him an attentive listener, depending on whether the internal or external situation favoured – or not – the credibility of their arguments. It was in the mind of the King and his entourage – and doubtless that of his mother too – that the differences between the two opposing positions were to be found.

But in each of the reversals just alluded to, the direction followed was relatively clear; none of them exhibits the paradox of St Bartholomew's Day, whose objective was *both* a recourse to violence and the continuation of peaceful co-existence between the confessions. It is now well established that there was no intention to exterminate all the Protestants of the capital, and even less so of the kingdom, but only to eliminate the 'war-making Huguenots', who threatened to drag their co-religionists into insurrection with them. Yet how was it possible to believe that a limited execution of presumed criminals was compatible with the preservation of the Edict of Pacification? Invoking the incoherence of a decision taken in a state of urgency and panic is a rather limited explanation. The historian has to examine more closely this combination of rigour and clemency. The former concerned rebellion, which was to be repressed without pity; the latter dealt with religious dissidence, which could be reduced by gentler methods. But did this duality of approach not involve a wish to separate two spheres of action hitherto closely correlated? We can discern, in the arguments used by Charles IX and his publicists when seeking to legitimate the decision taken in the night of 23–24 August, the precursor signs of a 'reason-of-state' logic, one that was activated, it should be said, as an extreme remedy imposed by circumstances, rather than as a philosophy of government. But it did betray the desire to affirm the all-powerfulness of monarchical sovereignty, which would be free to impose a form of 'exceptional' justice when facing an exceptional situation. In this sense, the literature justifying the execution of the Protestants needs re-reading: it represents without doubt an important stage in the evolution of the conceptions of power.

Finally, and this is the third enigma of the St Bartholomew's Day Massacre: why did the partial liquidation of the Protestant leaders degenerate into a generalised massacre, not just in Paris but also in several cities in the kingdom? Could the King have foreseen that the elimination of Coligny and his lieutenants would unleash the murderous fury of those Catholics known as the *zélés*, and for whom the oscillations of the royal attitude towards the heretics were neither explicable nor tolerable? In the eyes of these intransigents, whose indignation was fanned by the angry sermons of excited preachers, the option of civil concord seemed intolerable. And they were particularly numerous in the capital. Here we observe yet another division, one which separates the 'political' vision of those in government – 'political' in the sense that they fumbled in search of temporary solutions for the confessional division – from the purely religious vision of the fervent Catholics. Between these two readings of the conflict there is a profound gulf, a fundamental misunderstanding which was brutally revealed on the morning of 24 August, when these Catholics interpreted the execution of the Protestant leaders as a miraculous sign that the King had authorised the extermination of all Protestants.

But can religious passion alone suffice to explain the duration, the extraordinary brutality and the systematic, organised character of the Paris massacre? Should we remain satisfied, as previously, with references to 'mystical aggression', or even a 'pogrom' – as if these killings were no more than the consequence of an irrational release of archaic urges? On the contrary, many of its aspects point to well-considered and orderly action. Historians have not sufficiently stressed that the Parisians regarded the Protestants not simply as heretics but also, and especially, as dangerous agitators who threatened their lives and property, and who were all the more deadly because they were located in the heart of the city itself. Against such enemies 'within', they needed methodically to take in hand their own defence and conduct the war of eradication themselves, since the King refused to do so.

The contrast between the marriage celebrations and the killings; the apparent contradiction between the execution of Protestant leaders and the will to maintain the Edict of Pacification; the scale and duration of the massacre despite the royal orders: these are the three enigmas which still make the Saint Bartholomew's Day Massacre an exceptional historical subject, one whose mystery it is difficult to identify and catalogue. The event was experienced as a major upheaval; all of the protagonists felt that something irreversible had taken place and that nothing would be the same again. In a letter of 29 August to the French ambassador in Madrid, Catherine de Medici spoke of a 'mutation';

the same word was used by the vicomte d'Orthe, governor of Bayonne.[26] Saint Bartholomew's Day irrevocably defined the Catholic destiny of the kingdom of France; by dramatising the debate on the nature of the royal institutions, it also accelerated their evolution towards absolute power.

IN SEARCH OF SOURCES

To write the history of this mutation and the circumstances surrounding it, the sources are relatively abundant, but their interpretation is problematic. Eyewitnesses are few in number. Those who escaped it and left descriptions did not see very much, since they owed their survival either to flight or to having remained hidden. One of these was Maximilien de Béthune, future duc de Sully, then ten and a half years of age, who managed to find refuge in the college of Burgundy, where the principal hid him; another was Charlotte Arbaleste, future wife of Philippe Duplessis-Mornay, who found four successive hiding-places before fleeing dressed as a lower-class woman. The narrative of the bourgeois of Strasbourg, who confided it to a notary on 7 September 1572 on returning to Heidelberg, is short. On the Catholic side, that of Doctor Cavriana is very useful, as is that of the Florentine Tomasso Sassetti, who was absent from Paris during the events but who seems well informed. The dispatches and reports of diplomats, in particular those of the Florentine Petrucci, the Venetians Cavalli and Michiel, the nuncio Salviati, the Spanish ambassador Zuñiga, all supply precious but partial information. The letters of the King, his mother and their councillors present only the official version of events. Many contemporaries, paralysed by the fear of giving offence, dared only to 'half-write', as Blaise de Monluc says in his *Commentaires*.[27]

The Protestant accounts written *a posteriori* are very polemical, but we can profit from them in order to learn the names of victims and killers. Simon Goulart, for example, appealed for witnesses in the first edition of the *Mémoires de l'Estat de France*, which enabled him to expand his lists in the second edition.[28] As for memoirs such as those of Marguerite de Valois, Gaspard de Saulx, seigneur de Tavannes, Michel de la Huguerye or Jean de Mergey, they were written long after the Massacre, which makes it difficult to use them. The same point applies to the work of historians such as Henri de la Popelinière or Jacques-Auguste de Thou.[29]

Yet if we wish to advance beyond the somewhat polemical challenge of Denis Crouzet, who sees in St Bartholomew's Day 'an event without a history' and 'a history without an event', we must assume the risks of configuring these events in an intelligible framework, despite the fragmentary and biased character of the sources. A reading of the correspondence and the collections held in the Manuscripts Department of the Bibliothèque nationale de France, some of which have been only partly studied, and the use of the documents preserved in the archives of Simancas, are of considerable help in illuminating many aspects of the tragedy, its gestation and its consequences.[30] The possibility of a plausible reconstruction remains open, but on condition of recognising that the criteria of plausibility used by historians are necessarily influenced by the time and the place where they work; and also on condition of giving up on establishing an hour-by-hour account of the events that occurred between the evening of 23 August and early the following morning, given the discrepancies between the unreliable evidence. The evidence collected can benefit from being placed alongside comparative studies, which are increasingly numerous in contemporary historiography, on massacres committed during human history.[31] Thus, despite the difficulties, it is possible to analyse the conditions which permitted the Coligny execution and the carnage that followed; to examine both their processes and their presentation in the royal declarations; and finally to measure the scale of the reactions among Protestants and Catholics, both at home and abroad, in order to understand how the convulsion of Saint Bartholomew's Day – that dramatic and bloody 'day' – altered the history of France.

NOTES

1 Rodolphe Reuss, ed., 'Un nouveau récit de la Saint-Barthélemy par un bourgeois de Strasbourg', *BSHPF*, 23 (1873), p. 378.

2 Jean-Louis Rigal, ed., 'Mémoires d'un calviniste de Millau', *Archives historiques du Rouergue*, 2 (Rodez, 1911), p. 236.

3 *Négociations diplomatiques de la France avec la Toscane*, ed. Abel Desjardins, 6 vols (Paris, 1859–86), vol. 3, 1855, pp. 818–820, anonymous letter (from Filippo Cavriana) to secretary Concini, Paris, 27 Aug. 1572.

4 R. Reuss, 'Un nouveau récit', p. 378.

5 Nathanaël Weiss, 'La Seine et le nombre des victimes parisiennes de la Saint-Barthélemy', *BSHPF*, 46 (1897), pp. 474–481.

6 The picture is in the Musée cantonal des Beaux-Arts of Lausanne.

7 'Relation du massacre de la Saint-Barthélemy', in Louis Cimber et Charles Danjou, eds, *Archives curieuses de l'histoire de France*, 1st series, vol. 7 (Paris, 1835), p. 79.

8 Ivan Cloulas, *Henri II* (Paris, 1985), p. 357.

9 *Registres consulaires de la ville de Limoges*, ed. Émile Ruben and Louis Guibert (Limoges, 1867–97), vol. 2, p. 388, quoted by Michel Cassan, *Le Temps des guerres de Religion. Le cas du Limousin (vers 1530–vers 1630)* (Paris, 1996), p. 253, n. 101.

10 Théodore de Bèze, *Correspondance*, eds Alain Dufour and Béatrice Nicollier, vol. 13 [1572] (Geneva, 1988), p. 179–180, quoted by Cécile Huchard, *D'Encre et de sang. Simon Goulart et la Saint-Barthélemy* (Paris, 2007), p. 314, n. 26.

11 The name was used in a dialogue in verse that figured in the Protestant work published under the name of Eusèbe Philadelphe (for Nicolas Barnaud?), *Le Réveil-le-Matin des François*, Edinburgh (but Geneva?), 1574.

12 On the context of this publication, see Robert M. Kingdon, *Myths about the St. Bartholomew's Day Massacres, 1572–1576* (Cambridge, Mass., 1988), p. 43. The premeditation thesis was detailed in the report by the Venetian ambassador, Michiel:

William Martin, ed., *La Saint-Barthélemy devant le Sénat de Venise. Relations des ambassadeurs Giovanni Michiel et Sigismondo Cavalli* (Paris, 1872), pp. 34–35. According to the French ambassador, La Mothe-Fénelon, it was quickly accepted by the English court: *Correspondance diplomatique de Bertrand de Salignac de La Mothe-Fénelon*, ed. Charles Purton Cooper, 7 vols (Paris and London, 1838–40), vol. 5, p. 116.

13 For historians' treatment of the massacre up to the mid-twentieth century, see Henri Dubief, 'L'historiographie de la Saint-Barthélemy', in *L'Amiral de Coligny et son temps*, (Paris, 1974), pp. 351–365.

14 Jean-H. Mariéjol, *La Réforme et la Ligue. L'édit de Nantes (1559–1598)*, in *Histoire de France des origines à la Révolution*, ed. Ernest Lavisse, 1st ed. Paris, 1904; new ed. (Paris, 1983), p. 146.

15 Janine Garrisson, *Tocsin pour un massacre, ou la saison des Saint-Barthélemy* (Paris, 1968); eadem, *La Saint-Barthélemy* (Paris, 1987); eadem, *Les Derniers Valois* (Paris, Fayard, 2001). The present tendency is to reject completely the 'black legend' of the Queen Mother. See the biographies by Jean-François Solnon, *Catherine de Médicis* (Paris, 2003), and Thierry Wanegffelen, *Catherine de Médicis. Le pouvoir au féminin* (Paris, 2005). For a less flattering presentation of the character of Catherine, see Robert Knecht, *Catherine de' Medici* (London, 1998).

16 Jean-Louis Bourgeon, *L'Assassinat de Coligny* (Geneva, 1992), and *Charles IX devant la Saint-Barthélemy* (Geneva, 1995); Lucien Romier, 'La Saint-Barthélemy. Les événements de Rome et la préméditation du massacre', *Revue du seizième siècle*, 1 (1913), pp. 529–560.

17 Bourgeon, *Charles IX devant la Saint-Barthélemy*, pp. 36–37.

18 Bourgeon, *L'Assassinat de Coligny*, p. 34.

19 Bourgeon acknowledges that in constructing his thesis on Spain's role he did not read the Spanish sources 'for want of linguistic competence', *ibid.*, p. 92, n. 4.

20 Wanegffelen, *Catherine de Médicis*, pp. 357–358.

21 Denis Crouzet, *La Nuit de la Saint-Barthélemy. Un rêve perdu de la Renaissance* (Paris, Fayard, 1994).

22 *Ibid.*, p. 10.

23 Denis Crouzet, *Le Haut Cœur de Catherine de Médicis. Une raison politique aux temps de la Saint-Barthélemy* (Paris, 2005).

24 *Ibid.*, p. 9. On the apparent 'schizophrenia' of royal policy, see also pp. 10, 399, 547.

25 The use of the word 'politique' as a substantive designating a group with vague contours but recognisable by its will to establish at least temporary peaceful co-existence among the confessions can be dated from this year. Previously it had been an adjective that could describe this or that individual. Remonstrances attached to a letter sent to the King by the Prince of Condé on 23 August 1568 state that the intransigent Catholics were beginning to criticise those who wanted peace, saying that they 'were Politiques who were worse and more dangerous than heretics'. See letter and remonstrances published in the *Memoires de la troisieme guerre civile*, at the end of the 1578 edition of Simon Goulart, *Mémoires de l'Estat de France sous Charles neufiesme*, vol 3, p. 128.

26 *Lettres de Catherine de Médicis*, ed. Hector de La Ferrière, 10 vols (Paris, 1880–1909) vol. 4, p. 114 ; BnF, MS. Fr. 15555, fol. 47r, letter from vicomte d'Orthe to the King, Bayonne, 30 Aug. 1572.

27 Blaise de Monluc, *Commentaires, 1521–1576*, ed. Paul Courteault (Paris, 1962), p. 835.

28 Simon Goulart, ed., *Mémoires de l'Estat de France* (1577 ed.), vol. 1, p. 411, quoted by Huchard, *D'Encre et de sang*, p. 257.

29 On the problem of sources, see N. M. Sutherland, *The Massacre of St. Bartholomew and the European conflict, 1559–1572* (London, 1973), chs 17–18, as well as the article by Marc Venard, 'Arrêtez le massacre', *RHMC*, 39 (1992), pp. 645–661. Marc Venard is rightly critical of the hyper-criticism and writes: 'the sources for the Saint Bartholomew's Day massacre are no more suspect than those which support any historical analysis; they are obviously partial and of uneven value, but historical sources always are'.

30 Among the sources insufficiently used by historians we can cite the letters in which Geoffroy de Caumont wrote of his desperate flight from the faubourg Saint-Germain (BnF, Ms. Fr. 15553, fols 197r, 199r and 201r), or the *Memoires d'Estat* of Jean de Morvillier (BnF, Ms. Fr. 5172). The archives of Simancas were explored by Pierre Champion, *Charles IX. La France et le contrôle de l'Espagne*, 2 vols (Paris, 1939), and more recently by Valentin Vásquez de Prada, *Felipe II y Francia. Política, religión y razón de Estado* (Pamplona, 2004). But their full implications for the comprehension of the massacre have not been explicated by these authors.

31 For an overview of this research, see the stimulating presentation by Jacques Sémelin, 'Analyser le massacre. Réflexions comparatives', *Questions de recherches/Research in question*, 7 (2002), pp. 1–42, available online at http://www.ceri-sciences-po.org.

PART I

THE FRAGILITY OF CONCORD

1

TRIAL BY SUSPICION:
THE PEACE OF 1570

To understand the genesis of the tragic events of August 1572, we must return to the conditions under which, after three bloody civil wars, peace was restored and signed on 8 August 1570. The Edict of Saint-Germain, which made it official, granted the Protestants a limited liberty of worship. They could do so only in places where it had been established on 1 August 1570; elsewhere, it would be on the outskirts of two towns in each of the twelve governorships that constituted the kingdom – that is, in twenty-four listed towns. Lords possessing the right of 'high' justice were also allowed to hold services in their houses for an attendance limited to their own family and up to ten 'friends'. These terms recapitulated, but also altered, those of the edicts of January 1562, March 1563 and March 1568. However, the Edict of Saint-Germain contained one remarkable novelty. In the very first article, it called on people to forget the past:

> That the memory of all past things on both sides and since the beginning of the troubles in our kingdom, and on account of them, remain extinguished and laid to rest as if they had never happened. And neither our procurators-general nor any other person, public or private, shall be authorised, at any time or in any circumstance whatsoever, to mention them nor start lawsuits or investigations into them in any jurisdiction.[1]

What was being asked of the French required real heroism: they were voluntarily to forget the wars which had pitted them against each other and *behave as if they had never happened*. It was a question of winding the clock back to the fatal moment when the violence erupted, and of re-knitting the thread of their history from that point forward by avoiding, this time round, any breach of the peace. The second article presented the objective which should henceforth guide them: 'to live peacefully together as brothers, friends and fellow-citizens'. This formulation suggests that the ties of fellow-citizenship should trump, temporarily at least, confessional bonds. In this edict, there began to appear the idea, which had been sketched somewhat timidly at the beginning of the 1560s in the speeches of the former chancellor, Michel de l'Hospital, that peaceful co-existence between Catholics and Protestants was based on the distinction – which did not mean the separation – of politics and religion, a distinction which would provide adversaries with civic reasons for mutual acceptance.[2]

But what could this lofty ideal achieve when faced with the still-open wound of recent sufferings and, especially, the persistent distrust that each camp displayed towards the other?

THE DIFFICULTIES OF FORGETTING

Forgetting meant, first of all, erasing the memory of the atrocities committed by both sides. The effort it required was all the more demanding because these atrocities had been particularly bloody in the recent war, in which each side responded to the other with pitiless reprisals. Thus, on 1 May 1569, the capture of Mussidan in Périgord by the Catholic army led by the duc de Montpensier ended in a bloodbath; the victors, wrote the duke to the King after the event, 'attacked and took the town and castle, cutting to pieces everything they encountered, so that nobody escaped alive.'[3] On 25 June, the Huguenots took revenge when they won the battle for La Roche-l'Abeille in the Limousin: they took no prisoners and massacred all the survivors. Coligny's soldiers then moved into the Périgord and found themselves faced with a fierce guerrilla war conducted by the peasantry, led by their parish priests; the exasperated Admiral seized over two hundred of these improvised soldiers, locked them into a room of the castle of La Chapelle-Faucher, and had them executed. When Brantôme later asked him what the reasons for this were, Coligny replied that he had to punish the Perigourdins for their harassment tactics, which in the previous year had caused the massacre of the Provençal soldiers of the Huguenot Paul de Mouvans and their commander.[4] Voluntary amnesia was the only real means to break the dreadful spiral of violence and vengeance.

If the military encounters of the third civil war reached this degree of ferocity, it was because each side had mobilised energetically, both militarily and religiously. At this point the Protestants still possessed the dynamism which, since the introduction in the 1520s of the Lutheran reformation and, especially, in the 1530s of the Calvinist reformation, had attracted nearly two million disciples, approximately 10 per cent of France's population. Their numbers were especially strong in what was called 'the Huguenot crescent', extending from the Lyonnais to Aunis and Poitou via the Dauphiné, Upper Provence, Languedoc, Gascony and Guyenne; they were also well entrenched in Normandy and the Ile-de-France; in the kingdom of Navarre and the principality of Béarn, the Reformation had been imposed from above by Queen Jeanne d'Albret. Artisans, merchants, lower magistrates and members of the 'liberal professions' (lawyers, solicitors, notaries, teachers, doctors, booksellers, printers) were over-represented among the converts by comparison with their presence across the kingdom. Amongst other social groups, the nobility were also relatively numerous, principally in Normandy, Quercy, Guyenne, Gascony, Gévaudan and Upper Provence; the regular clergy provided many recruits, as did the episcopate, with two archbishops out of fourteen (Aix and Arles) and nine bishops out of 101 (Montauban, Pamiers, Nevers, Troyes, Beauvais, Gap, Apt, Uzès and Riez). Only the peasantry remained massively faithful to the traditional religion, with the exception of the Cévennes valleys and, out of necessity, Béarn and Navarre. However, in the Agenais, Périgord, Quercy, Rouergue, Gévaudan and Velay, Forez and the Dauphiné, some peasants did follow their landlords in converting to Protestantism.

The Protestants fought for their faith, convinced that the Roman church had betrayed the Gospel, whose true meaning they had themselves rediscovered. Christ, they argued, had instituted only two sacraments, baptism and the eucharist; the other five – penance, confirmation, marriage, extreme unction and the sacrament of priestly orders – all had to be rejected. Nowhere, they added, did the Scriptures mention purgatory, so there was no point in praying for the souls of the dead, who went straight to hell or to paradise. In their view, Catholics were guilty of idolatry by worshipping saints in a manner too similar to that which should be reserved for God alone; they venerated relics which were nothing more than bits of wood and cloth, or fragments of bones whose provenance was more than dubious. Worse still, by believing that at the moment of the eucharistic consecration during the Mass the bread of the host and the wine of the chalice became the body and blood of Christ, they showed a credulity which seriously misunderstood God's transcendence. According to Théodore de Bèze, Calvin's chief disciple, the body of Christ 'is as far removed from bread and wine as the highest heaven is from the earth'.[5] It was also in the name of transcendence that the Protestants were indignant at the sin of pride which, in their view, Catholics committed by conceding to human free will the capacity to co-operate in one's own salvation through good works; in doing so, they denied the sovereign liberty of God, who saves those whom he wishes; Catholics refused to recognise that man is a wretched creature, irredeemably corrupted by original sin and whom grace alone can rescue from the abyss.[6]

This conception of the Gospel's message was exposed with brilliant clarity in Calvin's *Institutes of the Christian Religion*, first published in Latin in 1536 and then translated by its author into French in 1541. Inspired by his teaching, French Protestants were sure that their struggle was that of the Gospel itself; they fought so that what they believed to be the only Truth should be finally recognised, and they dreamt of overthrowing the institutions of the Roman church, which they compared to the great prostitute of Babylon portrayed in the Apocalypse of Saint John – corrupt, rapacious and hungry for domination. They were also convinced that it was urgent to restore free access to the word of God to the faithful, by providing them with vernacular translations of the sacred texts and by restoring worship to its original purity. The temples where their religious services were held were bereft of pictures and statues; the pastors who preached there did not constitute a clergy, but were a body of men devoted to the service of the churches and assisted by a council – the consistory – made up of elders and 'deacons'.

The strength of the Protestants also derived from their organisation in both the kingdom and the provinces. Their first national synod met clandestinely in 1559; it brought together delegates of the churches 'established' since 1555, who adopted a confession of faith inspired mainly by Calvin's ideas. Little by little, a pyramid of assemblies took shape: at local level, the consistory; in the 'provinces' that gradually emerged, the provincial synod brought together the delegates of the churches twice a year; at the level of the kingdom, the national synod, whose frequency was more uncertain. A further body, the colloquy, located between the local churches and the provincial synods, was created once the churches had become sufficiently numerous.

This structure was used for military mobilisation when the conflicts began. From very early on, the churches and provinces sought armed protection from the nobility. The military leaders whom they designated recruited among their friends and dependents, who were tied to them by the duty of reciprocity arising from the exchange of services between neighbours and relatives. These solidarity networks worked perfectly in the raising of troops at the beginning of each conflict; on the eve of the battle of La Roche-l'Abeille, in June 1569, the numbers amounted to 25,000 men.[7] During the third war, however, the Protestant forces suffered two major defeats, the first at Jarnac on 13 March 1569, the second at Moncontour on 3 October following. But during the spring of 1570, Coligny's army, reinforced by units from Périgord, Quercy, Rouergue and Béarn, went on a destructive march through southern France, returning up through the Rhône valley, slipping past the royal army commanded by marshal Cossé at Arnay-le-Duc on 27 June, before reaching La Charité-sur-Loire and alarming the Parisians. Thus, when the peace was made, the Protestants obtained favourable conditions, but these were no more than a half-way house; they remained hopeful that one day their Protestant worship would be accepted everywhere, and without limitation, across the kingdom, even though defections had already begun gradually to erode their numbers. To forget the wars and behave as if they had not happened, as the first article of the Edict of Saint-Germain required of them, was tantamount to abandoning their long struggle for the triumph of the Gospel, admitting that they would never be more than a minority, and compromising with the powers of darkness.

The mobilisation of the Catholics was no less vigorous. Most of them were scandalised by the upheavals proposed by the Protestants, which wounded them in their most intimate religious selves. They were horrified by the idea of ceasing to pray for their dead, who perhaps were in urgent need in the other world, or of giving up their devotion to the Virgin Mary, who consoled to them in suffering, or again to saints such as Saint Roch, who protected them against the plague. For them, the Protestants misunderstood the fact that the Truth was not just in the Scriptures, but also in the tradition which the church transmitted under the inspiration of the Holy Spirit, and which was expressed in the teachings of the theologians and the councils. Doctrinally, Catholic orthodoxy had been defined by the Council of Trent, which ended in 1563.[8] But dogmatic reaffirmations mattered less for the immense majority of the faithful than did the visceral dread that the Protestants aroused in them. In their eyes, these heretics who defied the magisterium of the pope and the bishops rejected the religion of their ancestors; in doing so, they undermined society as a whole and threatened the traditional order. The dreadful pollution which they imported into the kingdom threatened, therefore, to provoke God's wrath, and it was thus absolutely essential to eliminate it. Such themes were expounded by vehement preachers, among them Simon Vigor, parish priest of Saint-Paul in Paris, who knew how to communicate their repulsion of heresy. Writings in the same vein by Artus Désiré, Antoine de Mouchy and Claude de Sainctes spread the message of sermons and incited their readers to use sacred violence against the impure.[9]

The zealous Catholics exulted when the King's brother, the duc d'Anjou, won the battles of Jarnac and Moncontour against the Huguenots; panegyrists like Ronsard celebrated the young hero who would deliver France from the hydra of heresy. They were bitterly disappointed on discovering that, once again, negotiations with their adversaries were taking place at Saint-Germain, and that they were offered a partial freedom of worship. Blaise de Monluc, an old warrior seasoned by campaigns in the King's service, expressed their rancour: 'We defeated them over and over, yet despite that they had such good credit in the king's council that the edicts were always favourable towards them; we won the battles, but they triumphed via these diabolic documents.'[10] How could such iniquity be acceptable? Like Monluc, many thought that the blame lay with the moderate Catholics who, like duc François de Montmorency or the keeper of the seals, Jean de Morvillier, enjoyed important positions in the royal council in 1570 and, more particularly, with the artisans of the peace talks, Armand de Gontaut-Biron and Henri de Mesmes. In short, they blamed the lukewarm and the traitors who preferred peace to the restoration of religious unity. A parish priest from Provins, Claude Haton, berated these peace makers as 'temporisers'; without their pernicious influence, he felt, Admiral Coligny and his friends 'would have been exterminated through the rigour of the royal and catholic armies'.[11] Peace with one's enemies in such conditions was shameful; far from deserving the name of peace, bellowed Simon Vigor from his pulpit on Ascension Day in 1570, 'it is a torch that once it catches fire will consume the entire kingdom of France'.[12] The forgetting demanded by the Edict of Saint-Germain was nothing more than a betrayal of the faith.

Faced with the passions expressed on both sides, the Utopia of voluntary amnesia was sustained only by those seeking a path towards a *via media*, equidistant from the diehards in both camps and open to all Christians of goodwill. In the late 1560s, it was the Catholic 'moyenneurs' who still hoped to reach a doctrinal compromise. This hope having failed in the short term, others of a more realistic bent sought to organise the legal framework of the unavoidable co-existence between hostile confessions, but without abandoning the dream of a subsequent reunion. As we saw, the zealous Catholics began around 1568 to stigmatise them with the polemical label of 'Politiques', who were 'worse and more dangerous than heretics, because they want to preserve the peace and are the enemies of conflict'.[13]

The identity of the men so labelled is difficult to define with precision, because they shared a sensibility rather than a doctrine, while their motivations were quite diverse. If we can believe the indications provided by the text quoted above, these 'Politiques' included Cardinal Bourbon, the Chancellor Michel de l'Hospital (who would be disgraced in September 1568) and the marshals of France François de Montmorency and his cousin, Artus de Cossé. In fact, these men were the go-betweens that the 'Politiques' could count on at court.[14] We find in the letters of the Catholic magistrate Étienne Pasquier around 1567–58 an evocation of the milieu of the 'zealots for peace', who were members of the sovereign courts like himself or Christophe de Thou, and humanist diplomats like Arnaud du Ferrier.[15] Moderate Protestants like Charles de Téligny, son-in-law of Coligny, or François de la Noue, were ready to support their efforts. Understanding the calamities that the civil wars brought on France, these men grasped the urgency of restoring order. With the ending of the third war, hopes for pacification and voluntary forgetting rested on them, but their influence, if already significant in government circles, was not yet preponderant across the kingdom.

RESTORING PUBLIC ORDER

The will to erase past conflicts from the collective memory could not dispense with the need to review the conflicts left over from the war and capable of making the confrontations recur. After such bloody encounters, the task was not easy. Commissioners, who were frequently leading nobles supported by magistrates, were despatched to the provinces to settle disputes. The men 'of the robe' did remarkable work on these missions. Sometimes covering as many as 2,000 kilometres, they listened to the complaints of the inhabitants of the towns and the nearby villages which they visited; decided on new places for Protestant worship wherever the edict did not allow for a sufficient number; restored the Mass where it had been suppressed; resolved the difficult questions of cemeteries and the decoration of Protestant houses on the routes of Catholic processions; banned or limited the bearing of arms; and obliged yesterday's adversaries to negotiate with a view to making agreements, thus contributing effectively to reinforcing royal authority and sketching the outlines of a public space in which the two confessions could co-exist.[16] The Peace of Saint-Germain may have been derided as 'lame and badly seated', since its principal negotiator, Armand de Gontaut-Biron, limped, and the second negotiator, Henri de Mesmes, was lord of Mal-Assise ('Bad-Seat'), but the crown did everything it could to ensure that it lasted. It should be noted that the edict of August 1570 was said to be 'perpetual and irrevocable', contrary to the earlier edicts of pacification, and that, unlike them, it was sealed with green wax, the symbol of everlastingness, and not with yellow.

But, despite their zeal, the efforts of the King's envoys did not always succeed in eliminating every source of tension. A particularly thorny problem was the restoration of lands and houses confiscated from the Protestants and sometimes sold off, which supposed that the purchasers would be indemnified. Coligny, for example, repeatedly complained about the problems he encountered in recovering his own property. He informed the King on 12 September 1570 that he was told not to reopen past quarrels and hostilities, an argument which infuriated him. 'If by such means they hope to deny me the benefit of the edict, I will be done a manifest injustice, and my enemies will be treated better than me.' To accept such spoliation, he added, 'would be at the expense of my honour and reputation, which I regard far more than mere property'.[17] He did not hesitate to strongly demand – even though, as a Protestant he was, in principle, hostile to church benefices – the lucrative abbeys held by his brother, Odet de Châtillon, who had died on 24 March 1571 and who, although he had converted to Protestantism, had kept his title of cardinal: 'I am also assured, Sire, that your Majesty has agreed that I should have my proper share of the benefices held by the late Cardinal Châtillon, my brother, but so far I also see relatively little effect of this'.[18]

The Coligny case attracts attention because of his status as a former military leader, but many other, more obscure individuals faced serious obstacles. In Picardy, the duc de Longueville, governor of the province, did not know what to do, as he explained in a letter to the King on 26 July 1571: he wished to satisfy the Protestants of Calais, Boulogne and other places who wished to recover their houses, but the governors of the towns in question opposed their return there.[19] The unwillingness of Catholics to restore property to the exiles was not based purely on confessional hatred: they could feel insulted simply for having to return what they thought they had legitimately acquired.

It was also necessary, as the Edict of Saint-Germain allowed, to readmit the Protestants to all the offices they had held before the wars, especially in the sovereign courts of justice and finance; and once readmitted, they had to face hostility from their Catholic colleagues, who viewed unfavourably the return of these purveyors of heresy. Tensions that were difficult to pacify resurfaced.

Amnestying acts of war was even more problematic. In this respect, the monarchy found a remarkable way of legitimating the acts perpetrated by former belligerents, and in doing so it recognised that the conflicts were not rebellions but civil wars pitting Frenchmen against each other. It was critical to distinguish these confrontations from riots or private crimes, which remained subject to punishment. Thus operations conducted on the orders of a recognised commander, for example the Prince of Condé or Admiral Coligny, were amnestied; payments made to the treasuries of the Protestant party were validated; Protestant taxpayers who paid their taxes to collectors from their side were exempted from paying them again.[20] It was also necessary to demobilise the forces recruited by the different sides, which generated resentment. The Catholics, for their part, accepted with difficulty that the King should for the first time grant the Protestants four 'places of security', as they were called – La Rochelle, Montauban, Cognac and La Charité-sur-Loire – as a guarantee of the full implementation of the peace edict, and which were to be handed back after two years.

This patient work of reconstruction encountered all the more difficulties, as the monarchy was financially weakened. The third war had been very expensive and the soldiers recruited for the royal armies were numerous – up to about 70,000 men. It has been calculated that the expenses involved amounted to 18 million *livres* per year for each of the two years of the conflict.[21] Total royal revenues in normal times amounted to 13–14 million, but the wars had prevented tax revenues from being paid as usual. To cope with the deficit, the King increased the *taille* in 1571, when it rose to 9.5 million *livres*, whereas its average total for the years 1561 to 1576 was 7 million. The King also resorted to other expedients – borrowing, taxes on cities, the sale of new offices. All of these stratagems provoked discontent; the parliament of Paris, in particular, protested against the creation, in the autumn of 1570, of forty offices of royal secretaries and of additional presidents and councillors in the Court of Monies.[22] The clergy were also required to contribute – in a contract with the monarchy that was renewed in 1567, they promised to provide 630,000 *livres* a year.

Despite this search for financial resources, Charles IX found it impossible to pay regularly the soldiers of the companies or garrisons which remained under arms. Complaints flooded in to Paris. The duc de Longueville informed the King on 25 July 1571 that the soldiers in charge of the fortified places in Picardy were ready to disband because they had not been paid for two years.[23] On 10 August, Colonel Alphonse d'Ornano deplored the non-payment of his Corsican companies; they were on the point of dispersing, which, he added, 'would really break my heart … as they are composed of men as good as anywhere in the world'.[24] The vicomte d'Orthe, governor of Bayonne, declared on 20 March 1572 that 'his credit was exhausted': for three years he had received no money, and he was owed 38,000 to 40,000 *livres* of arrears for his salary and pensions.[25] On 28 July 1572, Ludovic Birague, governor of Saluces, begged the King to have his oldest companies, which were 'reduced to extreme poverty and necessity', paid.[26] The King's own guards were no better off. All of these delays fostered a latent dissatisfaction among the King's soldiers.

One of the most acute problems was the payment of the mercenaries, German reiters or Swiss Catholics commanded by Ludwig Pfyffer, recruited by Charles IX during the war. A special tax was to be levied for that purpose, but the Protestants were loath to pay it, as these soldiers were raised to fight them. Coligny made this known to the King in no uncertain terms:

> There is another point – if you do not discharge the Protestants from contributing what is being imposed on them for the payment of your Swiss and reiters, apart altogether from the fact that they cannot pay what they are obliged to pay, you should not hope to obtain their support for anything that you might undertake, as much for the discontent they feel as for things being made impossible for them. In this regard, Sire, since I know the people whom I am dealing with, I will not hide anything of the truth from you, so that later on I will not be accused of having hidden or dissimulated things from you.[27]

Discontent: the term used by Coligny is harsh. Under the pretext of frankness, the Admiral raised the possibility of a refusal to obey. Certainly, he let it be clearly understood that he was not in full control of the mood of his most spiteful co-religionists, but the tone of his letter suggested that he regarded their reasons for being irritated as legitimate.

CHARLES IX FACES THE DANGERS

With so many difficulties to face, the King's task was not easy. Yet his determination to make peace – which he called 'his' peace – triumph was unmistakable. He was twenty years old in 1570 and determined to impose his authority.

Charles IX had a lofty idea of the royal dignity, an idealised image of which was provided by his entourage. He was raised in the cult of the ancient virtues by his tutor, Jacques Amyot, the learned translator of Plutarch's *Moral Works*. He took seriously his role of protector of letters and the arts, as attested by the support given to the Academy of poetry and music founded by Jean-Antoine de Baïf and Joachim Thibault de Courville, whose statutes he approved in November 1570 and whose meetings he honoured with his presence on numerous occasions. He was also open to the appeal of Neoplatonic philosophy, which was then in vogue in cultivated circles, especially among poets like Baïf, Ronsard or Pontus de Thyard; painters like Antoine Caron; and musicians like Claude le Jeune or writers like Louis Le Roy. This current of thought exalted a monarchy based on love and concord.[28] But did Charles IX really identify with the magnified portrait which the adepts of Neoplatonism painted for him? No document in his hand allows us to be certain.[29] His mother, Catherine de Medici, who was Florentine by her father but French by her mother, was doubtless more influenced than he was by the exquisite refinements of Neoplatonic ideas on monarchy; the court ceremonies that she inspired translated, both visually and musically, the harmonious conception of a pacified world, in which the King's wisdom made justice reign in the image of that of God.[30]

As for Charles IX, he was primarily driven by the desire to have his power respected, at the end of a war which had shaken that power. His correspondence reveals his obsession with being seen as a weak king whose authority was flouted. The letter he wrote in December 1571 to Claude Marcel, *prévôt des marchands* of Paris, concerning the disturbances over the cross of Gastines, reveals this clearly:

> Seeing myself so badly obeyed and my commands, in this as in other cases, despised on all sides, I don't know whom to blame except those who have authority over others, such as you have. It seems that when I give an order, everyone asks himself whether he should obey me or not, whether he should seek security from elsewhere but from me, and fears displeasing troublemakers of every kind. In behaving this way, they are flanking me with a double; they fear giving offence to someone else more than to me; and they are mistaking who they are. I see myself despised and my orders as scorned as those of Charles VI.[31]

The memory of the unfortunate Charles VI (1380–1422), who went mad and was incapable of preventing civil war and an English invasion, was well made to obsess Charles IX. Most of the foreign ambassadors at the French court were, in their despatches, unforgiving about his capacity to enforce obedience to his person. The Tuscan ambassador, Giovanni Maria Petrucci, frequently spoke with pity of this 'poor kingdom' and 'this poor king'. In November 1571, he observed, 'the poor king would like to pacify everything in order to live in peace, and I do not know if he will succeed, but to his cost, he is neither obeyed nor followed by many people, if by anyone.'[32]

In such circumstances, the desire of the touchy Charles IX to declare on every possible occasion that he was the sovereign and that his orders should be implemented is understandable. On 12 March 1571, he haughtily reminded the parlement of Paris, which was resisting the registration of edicts designed to procure financial resources for him, of its duty: 'I wish that, having declared my intention to you, you obey without picking an argument with me, who am your king and master, who knows better than you what ought and can be done for the good and necessity of my state, the affairs of which I will not allow you to take cognizance of, and which I reserve to myself alone.'[33] Such energetic language clearly indicates his ambition to be a king who did not share power.

At the same time, he showed himself anxious to be loved by his subjects. The model that he chose for himself was the traditional one of the king who resembles the father of a family who 'embraces with paternal affection' all his children and has compassion for them for the evils they have suffered.[34] These were the reasons why, as he wished his ambassador in Spain, Raymond de Fourquevaux, to explain to Philip II, he had negotiated the Peace of Saint-Germain: the war could continue no longer, he argued, 'without the complete ruin of his subjects and kingdom, since the evils that it had produced were so extreme and so full of violence, especially for his poor people, that they were exhausted, ready to go under and fall into despair'.[35]

But to be either respected or loved, Charles IX needed to ensure public order. This concern is the key to his attitude towards the Protestants. His Catholicism was sincere, but the ferocity of the last war and the seriousness of the disorders it spawned had convinced him of the necessity of peaceful co-existence between the contending confessions, which he doubtless viewed as temporary, and capable, at a later date and through peaceful methods, of restoring the community of faith. He explained it to Raymond de Fourquevaux in order to justify the peace: 'I believe that by this means I did much to reduce my said subjects to the obedience that they owe me, and this is a first step towards bringing them back, step by step, like my other subjects, to the Catholic religion.'[36] Meanwhile, he demanded that the Protestants behave above all like obedient subjects. He did not hesitate to transmit to the King of Spain the complaints of Huguenot merchants whose goods had been seized by Spanish pirates from the ships that were carrying them: 'even though they belong to the new religion, by obeying me as they do, they are my subjects like the others; on condition that they do not break the laws and statutes of the countries which they frequent, I wish that they be protected and not be treated any worse than the Catholics'.[37] The firmness of this declaration towards his powerful and very Catholic neighbour is evidence of the sincerity of his wish to ensure the security of the Protestants.

Unfortunately for him, his margin of manoeuvre was very narrow. All his doings were observed with suspicion, not just by the radicals on both sides within the kingdom, but also by neighbouring sovereigns. For the latter, the ultimate religious direction of France could still seem uncertain. In the early 1570s, Europe was divided by the influence of two antagonistic camps: the Catholic camp, on the one side, led by the King of Spain, Philip II; the Protestant camp on the other, in which the Queen of England, Elizabeth I, enjoyed great prestige. If France were to tip towards the one or the other, the balance of European power would collapse. Philip II was the most anxious and the most active, and did not hesitate to spend money, mobilise the influence of his ambassadors, and establish spy networks in order to be informed and to ensure that the balance would tip in ways that he wanted. The Guises, on whom he counted in order to advance the Catholic cause in France, were temporarily in disgrace during the negotiation of the Peace of Saint-Germain. But he had other go-betweens at court, especially Albert de Gondi, comte de Retz, the Queen Mother's favourite, and his cousin, Jerome, who was in charge of introducing the ambassadors of foreign powers in France.[38]

Under such surveillance, Charles IX needed to avoid giving grounds for suspicion. This was all the more difficult for him, as the court was a stage where he was permanently exposed to observation. His smallest gestures or words were interpreted and commented upon, and then repeated in letters and reports by courtiers and ambassadors. It was a suffocating form of surveillance, and it is understandable that the King often sought to escape it by engaging in hunting, of which he was a genuinely passionate professional, and in which he could regain some of his freedom. At court, observers remarked that he sometimes kept his eyes fixed downwards, in fear, no doubt, that a badly controlled expression would become a pretext for tendentious suppositions.[39] Both camps were quick to cry injustice and treason, and such recriminations could always trigger the worst outcomes. In this regard, Catholics and Protestants were equally dangerous.

In such a situation, Charles IX sought to distribute his favour equitably to each confession. To the Catholics and in response to a request from the university of Paris, he granted an edict banning the Protestants from holding 'primary schools, principalships and colleges', and reiterating that every book should be presented for prior approval by the Faculty of Theology before publication.[40] To the Protestants, in April 1571 he granted the right to hold a national synod at La Rochelle. This was the 'synod of the princes' because it was attended by Queen Jeanne d'Albret, her son Henri de Navarre, and her nephew, Henri de Condé, son of Prince Louis killed at Jarnac. But this policy of equilibrium was not easy to understand; it generated perplexity and disarray, sentiments that were perfect for encouraging suspicion.

THE BURDEN OF MISTRUST

The Protestants were undoubtedly the most mistrustful, since they had felt it necessary to obtain fortified towns as a guarantee until all of the clauses of the Edict of Saint-Germain were fully implemented. The fear, which they had experienced at the end of the previous conflict, that the peace was merely a trap designed to secure their goodwill in order to exterminate them, now obsessed them again.[41] Later on, François de la Noue would write in a chapter of his *Discours politiques et militaires* devoted to the third war, that the accord which ended it was for many Protestants 'a disguised peace ... and this made some people so bitter that they always think there is poison hidden beneath the brilliance of such gold'.[42]

Coligny acted as spokesman for the suspicions of his co-religionists. In the long and remarkable letter already quoted of 8 May 1571, written from La Rochelle to the King, he referred to a royal letter which his son-in-law, Téligny, had just brought to him; he claimed that it had relieved him of the disquiet that he felt on account of the 'infinite suspicions and mistrusts' which the Protestants harboured, '… and this [fear] had such credibility and good reason that I will not deny, Sire, that I might myself have joined them in it'. The assurances given by Téligny, he added, had enabled him to prevent 'this same distrust from growing so strong in many parts of the realm that it might have produced the greatest misfortune possible'.

Why such mistrust? Coligny alleged that there was a 'plan ready to raise an agitation and general insurrection across the kingdom, as the Count of Olivares (who had come from Spain to Blois to congratulate Charles IX on his recent marriage) did not fear to put it when he passed through here recently'. We see here an echo of one of those fear-induced rumours, leading the Protestants to believe that a Catholic conspiracy was in preparation and orchestrated by Spain. The Admiral pleaded with the King to 'remove all suspicion and mistrust', first of all by the exemplary punishment of all violations of the peace, especially at Rouen and at Orange, where there had been disturbances, but also by giving clear signs that he favoured Protestant nobles as much as Catholic ones. This request was formulated in peremptory terms:

> otherwise people will think that you say the opposite of what you wish, or that you wish what you cannot do, and both will be a matter of shame for you. But as such ambitions cannot be achieved without considerable support, it will be difficult to believe that you wish things to go well until it is clear that you are attracting the leaders to you. If you do not do so, you will go down as the most despised king for a very long time. Excuse me for this freedom of expression, as it is exclusively my zeal for your service and the success of your affairs which makes me adopt it.[43]

There can be no doubt: this was not an appeal, it was a warning to Charles IX, who, in turn, can only have been cut to the quick by this barely veiled accusation of dissimulation or impotence.

Yet Coligny was right to invoke the King's service and the success of his affairs. Several times he was indignant at the calumnies that were circulating against him; it was said that he was threatening the King's life; that he was under arms and on campaign; that he had authorised the destruction of [Catholic] statues and places of worship. It was also rumoured that a conspiracy to place La Rochelle under the domination of the Holy Roman Empire had been foiled.[44] These fabrications were capable of endangering the peace. The Admiral's advice to put an end to them was appropriate: it was urgent that the King let everyone at court, where every sign was closely scrutinised, *see* the confidence that he wished to show in the Protestant leaders.

The most obvious way for Charles IX to do this was to welcome Jeanne d'Albret, Henri de Navarre and Coligny to his side. Their presence was indispensable in order to negotiate the marriage that was projected between Prince Henri and Marguerite de Valois; in addition, the King needed the Admiral if he desired, as he was tempted to do, to assist the rebellious subjects of the King of Spain in the Netherlands.[45] But before that he had to overcome the mistrust of the Huguenot leaders. Since the second war, they no longer felt secure anywhere except in La Rochelle, where they could also engage in lucrative piracy which the King, inundated with complaints from pillaged Spanish merchants, was incapable of preventing.[46]

Invited by Catherine de Medici to come and visit her, the Queen of Navarre replied: 'I am of a suspicious disposition, Madame'; she feared the favour of her enemies, whom she regarded as sufficiently powerful to modify the good intentions of her counterpart.[47] Long negotiations had to be undertaken over the marriage of her son before she finally agreed to go to Blois in early March 1572. As for Coligny, he was for a long time held back by the anxieties of his friends who feared a murder trap. When he finally agreed to go to court, it was on eleven conditions which amounted to a genuine contract with the royal family. He requested that the King, the Queen Mother and the ducs d'Anjou and d'Alençon promise him that he could come to court in total serenity; he would begin his journey once he had received from each one of them a separate letter to that effect. Orders should also be given to the same effect to marshal Montmorency, his brother, Damville, and Filippo Strozzi, colonel of the infantry, and to the captains of the guards. Four of the conditions concerned the good relations that were to be restored between the Admiral and Catherine de Medici. The other clauses had to do with implementing the 1570 edict. On the question of the restitution of the four 'security towns' as expressed in article 39, Coligny demanded and obtained, on the pretext that he needed the agreement of the Protestant leaders, that the decision to return them promptly should be made by an assembly of his co-religionists composed of one deputy per province. The least that one can say is that these demands expressed substantial suspicion.[48]

Having obtained the assurances he asked for, Coligny arrived at Blois, where the court resided, on 12 September 1571, accompanied by marshal Cossé and fifty Huguenot nobles. If we can believe Petrucci, the Tuscan ambassador, the King's initial welcome was somewhat reserved, but things then improved. The Admiral was admitted to the council. Restored to all his offices and dignities, he received money to rebuild his house at Châtillon, 150,000 *livres* for his services, the revenues for a year of his late brother the Cardinal's benefices, and even an abbey worth 20,000 *livres* a year; the number of soldiers in his bodyguard was raised from thirty to fifty.[49] These favours should be taken for what they were – gestures to reassure the Protestants; they do not allow us to construe the King's real feelings towards Coligny. Later, the Protestants would exaggerate the friendship shown him by Charles IX, the better to show the blackness of the royal heart. As for Catholic accounts, it was indignation which made them overestimate the influence of Coligny: the Spanish ambassador and the Paris parish priest Jehan de la Fosse both claimed that the Admiral dominated the King.[50]

The fears on both sides were intensified by some strange rumours. Ambassador Petrucci reported that the Admiral had proposed certain changes in Protestantism to the King in order to bring it closer to Catholicism; the Protestants would recognise the sacrament of confession, accept the invocation of the saints, and consent to a Mass in each church in the kingdom, but on condition that the priests – who would be nobles and have at least 150 *livres* in revenue – could not demand money for saying Mass. That would amount, according to Petrucci, 'to adopting the same regime as in Germany'.[51] News like this was perfect for stirring up tension, as much in the Protestant as in the Catholic camp. Among the most intransigent Catholics, distrust reached alarming proportions: did not the presence of the Protestant leader in the royal entourage mean that the King would make intolerable alterations to the traditional faith? One witness reported that the population at large believed that the King was 'on the point of becoming a Huguenot'.[52] Many Catholics must have thought what Philip II did not hesitate to write to his ambassador in France: the only good reason for bringing Coligny to court would have been to arrest and execute him. But, the Spanish King added, Charles IX did not have the courage to do that.[53]

Coligny's first stay at court was short lived, since the court soon dispersed. Charles IX went off hunting, and the Admiral left Blois on 19 October 1571 to retire to his house at Châtillon. The King's intention was to recall him quickly, but an impediment of a completely different kind soon appeared, one just as dangerous to the peace as confessional dissensions: namely, the threat to public order from the desire of the Guises to avenge the death of duc François, killed in February 1653 by a pistol shot fired by a Protestant noble, Poltrot de Méré.

THE GUISES' REVENGE

The Guises were firmly persuaded that Coligny had commissioned the murder of François de Guise, since Poltrot de Méré accused him of it during his interrogation. Family honour bade them to punish what they considered to be a cowardly assassination. Against all the rules of chivalry, the fatal shot was fired from behind a hedge as the victim was returning to his house on the eve of the attack that the royal army was to mount against Orleans. This thirst for vengeance seemed all the more dangerous, as the Guises, powerful nobles enjoying high-ranking offices – duc Henri of Guise was governor of Champagne, his uncles Aumale and Cardinal Lorraine were governor of Burgundy and archbishop of Reims respectively – were able to enlist numerous clients, followers and dependents willing to promise under oath to serve their objectives. We can see the force of such ties in the document signed on 16 August 1563 by one of the Guises' clients, Guy de Daillon, seigneur du Lude, in which he promised to do everything possible to avenge duc François:

> I, the undersigned, promise and swear by the living God to give every obedience and loyal service to Monsieur the duc de Guise, to Messieurs the cardinals his uncles and Madame, his mother, as I promised to the late Monsieur de Guize, both in order to recover what is owed to him and to avenge the death of the late Monsieur de Guize until the fourth generation of those who ordered or provided support for the said homicide.[54]

Sensing the danger, in January 1564 Catherine de Medici had secured a reconciliation among the adversaries, which was then confirmed in January 1566 by a judgment of the Paris parlement declaring Coligny innocent. But this was a fire badly dowsed. When the Admiral returned to Blois, the Guises ostentatiously left. Charles IX set about recalling all of them to court to compel them to confirm their reconciliation. At that point, in November 1571, news arrived of a suspicious gathering of soldiers summoned by the Guises at Troyes, and rumours spread that they would besiege Coligny in his house. The King had to order everyone involved to stay put.

It is very difficult to grasp the real purpose of the Guise mobilisation. Henri de Guise claimed that he was merely organising his solemn entry into Troyes as governor of Champagne. But for Coligny there was no doubt that his life was in danger. His reaction was that of a noble whose honour was threatened. In a letter of 13 December, he thanked the King for having saved him 'through his forces', which seems to suggest that Charles IX had sent soldiers to protect him. But he added that he feared that the obligation of inactivity in which he found himself would prove shameful for him. 'And were it not, Sire, for the promise that I made to Your Majesty when I left Blois, I had the means of sparing those said to be coming to besiege me in my house all that trouble, as I could have gone to meet them half way, without either challenging or threatening them.' For the Admiral, to suffer a challenge like the duc de Guise's without reply was contrary to the noble ethic. He warned the King that, as a precaution, he had alerted his 'friends', meaning his dependents and clients, to be ready to come to his assistance if he was attacked.[55]

This episode shows the capacity of the great nobles to mobilise their private clienteles in support of their own disputes. Here we encounter one of the major limitations of royal power, one which rendered even more difficult the resolution of confessional conflicts. A noble might feel more bound to obey a patron whose service he entered than to give the submission he owed to the King as a subject. Lineal forms of solidarity also came into play: although he was a

Catholic, duc François de Montmorency nevertheless warned the King that if his cousin Coligny (son of his aunt, Louise) was attacked, he would find himself obliged to assist him.[56] Petrucci reported that Jeanne d'Albret had offered to send troops to the Admiral to defend him, while on other side, Catholics collected money in Paris and Toulouse on behalf of the duc de Guise. The disabused Tuscan ambassador commented on this news: 'it takes very little to provoke new disorders in this kingdom'.[57]

A declaration issued by Charles IX on 27 March 1572 reaffirmed Coligny's innocence, and in May, Henri de Guise agreed to acknowledge it publicly. But not every threat had been removed; Cardinal Lorraine, who was then absent, was not party to the accord, while the duc d'Aumale's attitude remained ambiguous. What is more, when the Admiral returned to court, on 6 June 1572, an English diplomat noted that duc Henri and he did not speak to each other.[58] The Guises' behaviour thus weakened the symbolic value that the King desired Coligny's presence at his side to represent; as a result, the Catholics could feel their distrust correspondingly reinforced.

CATHOLIC INDIGNATION

Three events with serious consequences further intensified tensions during 1571. In each case, violence provoked by Catholics was severely punished, giving rise to complete incomprehension and profound bitterness among those punished, who believed that they had done only what was right.

The first occurred at Orange. On 3 February 1571, the town's Huguenots made an unsuccessful attempt to seize the town castle. The Catholics' reaction was fierce: they drove back the aggressors, besieged them in the houses where they had taken refuge and massacred everyone who fell into their hands. The survivors complained to Prince William of Orange and his brother, Louis of Nassau, but also to Coligny. Pressed by Coligny to intervene, Charles IX had Orange handed over to a governor chosen by William of Orange, who exacted merciless repression. The leaders of the Catholic riposte were executed, and many others were hanged in effigy; among the latter were all the superiors of the religious orders of mendicants, images of whom, dressed in their clerical robes, the inhabitants could see swinging on the gibbet – an ideal spectacle for fanning the indignation of the faithful.[59]

In Rouen, it was confessional divergences over the real presence of Christ in the consecrated host that sparked disturbances. On Sunday 18 March 1571, a group of 500–600 armed Huguenots travelled to the sermon in the faubourg of Bondeville. A priest bringing the host to a dying person happened to pass by; along his route, the Catholics knelt down and removed their hats, but the Protestants refused to do so and even uttered some jeers. Guards tried to intervene but were driven back. Rumours of the scandal spread quickly and, on leaving the sermon, the Protestants were greeted with shouts of 'let's get the Huguenots' and attacked by the crowd. Forty of them were said to have been killed. An inquiry was conducted, and five authors of the 'Bondeville massacre' were arrested, but their friends freed them immediately. The King then sent a commission led by duc François de Montmorency which had armed backup. Sixty-six sentences of death and heavy fines were imposed. But these measures were ineffective: the condemned succeeded in fleeing or obtained a pardon from the King, in which case they returned to Rouen nursing a grudge at having been punished for what they saw as their desire to defend the honour of the Holy Sacrament.

The most serious events occurred in Paris in late autumn 1571. During the recent war, a secret Protestant religious service in a house belonging to Huguenot merchants Philippe and Richard de Gastines on the rue Saint-Denis was discovered. The Gastines were condemned to death, their house razed to the ground and a pyramid topped by a cross erected on the site. When peace was made, the Protestants believed that the pyramid was going to be demolished; article 32 of the Edict of Saint-Germain expressly decreed that, in order to extinguish the memory of past divisions, all trace of the executions that had been decreed should be effaced, and that places where 'demolitions and razings' had occurred would be returned to their owners. Convinced of their rights, the Protestants, with Coligny's support, requested and, on 7 October 1571, obtained royal letters patent ordering the demolition of the pyramid and the cross. But the Catholics viewed this monument as the symbol of their victory over heresy. The city authorities began to resist the move; when, on 12 October, the royal letters were delivered to the Châtelet court, the destruction of the cross could not be carried out because Claude Marcel, the prévôt des marchands of Paris, who had retired to his house in Nantouillet, refused to come back to Paris.[60] For its part, the parlement was also evasive. The King became angry; on 6 November he added the following furious postscript to a letter to marshal Cossé: 'Marshal, I ask you to head to Paris for my service and, among other things, I want you to have the pyramid removed and make people obey me, because the time has come to do it.'[61] A delegation of *parlementaires*, merchants and doctors of the Faculty came to negotiate with Charles IX. A compromise was finally found: the pyramid would not be destroyed, but moved to the Cemetery of the Holy Innocents.

That did not suffice to calm the anger of the Parisians. Each night, the work of the men digging the foundations in the cemetery was undone. Armed men guarded the place from then on, but during the night of 8 December they were attacked by the crowd and had to flee under an avalanche of stones. Despite the precautions taken by the authorities to avoid disorder, Protestant houses were pillaged on 9 December, among them the one called the 'Golden Hammer' on Notre-Dame bridge, which belonged to the niece of Philippe de Gastines and her husband, Claude Le Mercier. The removal of the pyramid finally occurred during the night of 19–20 December, igniting a new outburst of violence: the 'Golden Hammer' and its neighbour, known as 'the Pearl', were looted and their furniture hurled into a bonfire; a house belonging to the heirs of the Gastines was burned down.[62] During the same month, marshal Montmorency, governor of Paris, informed the King, according to a report by Petrucci, that numerous noble supporters of the duc de Guise had rented lodgings in the capital, where they were stockpiling arms and holding mysterious night-time assemblies.[63] On Charles IX's orders, order was restored by Montmorency, who had one of the rioters hanged and others prosecuted.

The issue at stake here was very clear for the Catholics, who had been indoctrinated by the sermons on the subject by Simon Vigor and a pamphlet by the parish priest of Saint-Eustache, René Benoist. The cross, Benoist argued, is the symbol of the Passion of Christ; by this sign true Christians are distinguished from heretics and infidels. It was for having sought to preserve the cross on the pyramid that the faithful were condemned. The feeling of injustice was all the stronger because, if we believe the parish priest Jehan de la Fosse, the Gastines were thought to have 'helped to demolish altars and other things'.[64] In such circumstances, it is possible to see why the erection of the cross of Gastines was a form of reparation for the Catholics; therefore, it seemed incomprehensible to them that God would have tolerated its transfer elsewhere. René Benoist explained it to them: God had used this to punish the sins of his people, who did not obey his Word with sufficient zeal. There was no point, he continued, in blaming magistrates and princes or in provoking 'stirrings of the people, which are not always worthwhile'; they should instead try to appease God's wrath through tears and penances. However, in a disturbing passage in his pamphlet he added that if all, great and small, are equally sinners, 'scripture says that the great will suffer more than the others, because when they do not avenge things done against God, they are often punished by God, who puts power in the hearts and stones in the hands of the coarse and feeble populace, who become the executor of his just sentence'.[65] Eager readers could thus feel authorised to act as the armed hand of God's violence when they judged that the iniquity of the Prince was becoming intolerable.

For his part, Charles IX seemed largely oblivious of the anxiety that the riots over the Gastines cross symbolised. On 14 October 1571, in recounting to Raymond de Fourquevaux the difficulties he had in being obeyed, he expressly accused the Spanish ambassador, Don Francés de Álava, of stirring up disturbances and inciting 'some factious people whom he has always known in order to get the little people to rebel, if he can', with the intention of perpetuating divisions among the French, preventing the restoration of royal authority and destroying the peace.[66] For the King – at least this was how he wished his ambassador to present it to the King of Spain – the sedition was the work of 'a few troublemakers, thieves and other layabouts, who created disorder to prevent the pyramid being put in its proper place, and who tried to use this as a pretext for pillaging and ransacking houses, some of which they set on fire'.[67] The accusation against Francés de Álava was not without substance, as he maintained an entire network of agents and spies in Paris, the South-West and on the Atlantic coast.[68] Exasperated by his activities, Charles IX renewed his request to Philip II for his dismissal, a dismissal that he had already requested in his instructions to Fourquevaux on 2 August. Don Francés did leave the French court on the night of 13 November, without even taking leave of the King or his mother.[69]

However, should we see in the events of autumn 1571 the signs of a vast conspiracy orchestrated by Spain, utilising the Guises and aiming to destabilise both Charles IX and Elizabeth of England – a conspiracy whose objective, in France, was to increase the power of Henri d'Anjou, the King's brother, who was the hope of the Catholics, and, in England, to free Mary Stuart, the Queen of Scotland, who was Elizabeth's prisoner? This hypothesis has been advanced, based on the concomitance of the Guise troop movements at Troyes, the Parisian disturbances over the Gastines cross, the dismissal of Álava and the expulsion from the English court, in mid-December, of the Spanish ambassador, Guérau de Spes, accused of complicity in the conspiracy of the Florentine banker Roberto Ridolfi and the Duke of Norfolk to organise from the Netherlands a Spanish invasion of England.[70] The simultaneousness of these events is indeed disturbing. But if it is probable that Philip II was disposed to assist the Ridolfi and Norfolk conspiracy against the English Queen, on condition that the forces recruited by the conspirators were adequate, he did not himself organise it. Moreover, as his correspondence attests, the King of Spain had too little confidence in the perseverance of the French to think of implicating some of them in the project, despite their desire to fight against heresy.[71]

Other events, of lesser symbolic consequence, showed the fragility of the peace during the first half of 1572. At Orleans on 14 June, the feast of Corpus Christi, the mayor and the town councillors narrowly diverted the anger of the Catholics, which was on the verge of exploding against the Protestants who had not decorated their houses with hangings for the procession of the Holy Sacrament; at Troyes on 10 August, Huguenots returning from their service were assailed with stones, one of which killed a newly baptised baby.[72] Orleans and Troyes were towns where the massacres following the Parisian Saint Bartholomew's Day were particularly violent.

Nevertheless, the determination of Charles IX to have the Edict of Saint-Germain respected was not weakened, as was clearly demonstrated during the months preceding 24 August 1572. Two of his interventions attest to this. On 22 June, he ordered the governor of Metz, on the question of readmitting Protestants to public offices, to make 'no distinction between those of the new religion and those of the Catholic religion'.[73] At the beginning of August, confronted by the repugnance of the Parisian *parlementaires* to receive as a master of requests Arnaud de Cavaignes, a well-known Protestant close to Coligny, the King commanded them to obey; on the 13th, having received their remonstrances on the subject, he would allow them to defer the candidate's reception only on condition that the reasons for it had nothing to do with religion.[74]

The King solemnly reaffirmed his desire for peace in a circular letter of 4 May 1572 to the provincial governors. Noting that the Protestants had recently returned the places of security that had been provisionally given to them, the King rejoiced in seeing that people seemed ready to 'put a stop to all occasions of mistrust which, considering the things which had previously occurred, could have remained present in the minds of his subjects'.[75] He added: 'there is nothing that I am more anxious for in this world than to see my said subjects living with each other in true union, peace and tranquillity, with such an oblivion of things past'. Repeating the words of the edict, he ordered his governors to enjoin on all French people, 'both Catholics and those of the new religion, to continue to live according to his edict of pacification in good peace, union and friendship among themselves, as good brothers and co-citizens'. In this way his kingdom would be restored to its 'pristine splendour'.

This desire for concord was part of a much grander project, which was both matrimonial and international, of which the marriage of Marguerite de Valois and Prince Henri de Navarre was to be the consecration. Absorbed in the realisation of this project, the King badly misjudged the growing distrust which ranged the radicals of both sides both against him and against each other. Over against the omnipresence of suspicion and the violence of the antagonistic commitments in play, the Utopia of voluntary amnesia, in which he desperately wished to believe, was in increasing danger of becoming unattainable.

NOTES

1   *Édits des guerres de Religion*, ed. André Stegmann (Paris, 1979), p. 69. In the Edicts of Amboise (March 1563) and Longjumeau (March 1568), the appeal for voluntary forgetting and concord among 'brothers, friends and fellow-citizens' was left to the end (*ibid.*, pp. 36 and 57). See Mark Greengrass, 'Amnistie et oubliance: un discours politique autour des édits de pacification pendant les guerres de religion', in Paul Mironneau and Isabelle Péray-Clottes, eds, *Paix des armes, paix des âmes* (Paris, 2000), pp. 113–123.

2   In a speech of 3 Jan. 1562 before an assembly representing France's parlements at Saint-Germain, Michel de L'Hospital proposed a distinction between the citizen and the Christian: Michel de L'Hospital, *Œuvres complètes*, ed. P. J. S. Duféy (Paris, 1824–26), vol. 1, p. 452. L'Hospital only made this distinction 'the better to place the

former in the service of the latter': see Loris Petris, *La Plume et la Tribune. Michel de L'Hospital et ses discours, 1559–1562* (Geneva, 2002), p. 311.

3 Montpensier to Charles IX, 1 May 1569, quoted by Stéphane-Claude Gigon, *La Troisième Guerre de Religion. Jarnac-Moncontour (1568–1569)* (Paris, 1911), p. 229.

4 Pierre de Bourdeille, seigneur de Brantôme, *Œuvres complètes*, ed. Ludovic Lalanne, 11 vols (Paris, 1864–82), vol. 6, pp. 18–19.

5 Bèze stated this at the colloquy of Poissy, on 9 Sept. 1561, to the assembled Catholic theologians with whom he and his twelve fellow Protestants were to debate. See Alain Dufour, 'Le Colloque de Poissy', in *Mélanges d'histoire du xvie siècle offerts à Henri Meylan* (Geneva, 1970), pp. 127–137.

6 On these questions see Jean Delumeau and Thierry Wanegfellen, *Naissance et affirmation de la Réforme*, 8th ed. (Paris, 1997), esp. chs 5–6.

7 Jean de Pablo, 'Contribution à l'étude de l'histoire des institutions militaires huguenotes. II. L'armée huguenote entre 1562 et 1573', *Archiv für Reformationgeschichte*, 48 (1957), pp. 192–216.

8 See Alain Tallon, *La France et le concile de Trente* (Rome, 1997).

9 Their ideas are analysed by Denis Crouzet, *Les Guerriers de Dieu. La violence au temps des troubles de Religion, vers 1525–vers 1610*, 2 vols (Seyssel, 1990), vol. 1, pp. 416ff.

10 Monluc, *Commentaires*, p. 800.

11 Claude Haton, *Mémoires*, ed. Laurent Bourquin, vol. 2 (Paris, 2003), p. 346.

12 Quoted by Crouzet, *Les Guerriers de Dieu*, vol. 1, p. 428.

13 Remonstrances attached to Condé's letter to the King, 23 Aug. 1568, quoted above, p. 14, no. 25.

14 Recent historiography has contested the application of the label 'Politique' to Michel de L'Hospital. See Denis Crouzet, *La Sagesse et le malheur. Michel de L'Hospital, chancelier de France* (Seyssel, 1998), and Loris Petris, *La Plume et la Tribune*.

15 Étienne Pasquier, *Les Lettres*, in *Œuvres* [1723] (reprint Geneva, 1971) vol. 2, livre XIX, col. 559.

16 Jérémie Foa, 'Making peace: the commissions for enforcing the pacification edicts in the reign of Charles IX (1560–1574)', *French History*, 18 (2004), pp. 256–274.

17 BnF, MSS 500 Colbert 24, fol. 420r, Coligny to the King, 12 Sept. 1570.

18 BnF, MSS Français 15553, fol. 111r, Coligny to the King, 1 July 1571.

19 *Ibid.*, fol. 137r, Duke of Longueville to the King, Calais, 26 July 1571.

20 On these questions, see Pierre-Jean Souriac, *Une guerre civile. Affrontements religieux et militaires dans le Midi toulousain, 1562–1596* (Seyssel, 2008).

21 James B. Wood, *The King's army. Warfare, soldiers and society during the wars of religion in France, 1562–1576* (Cambridge, 1996), p. 285.

22 On these aspects, see Pierre Chaunu, 'L'État de finance', in Fernand Braudel and Ernest Labrousse, eds, *Histoire économique et sociale de la France*, vol. 1 (Paris, 1977), tome I, p. 172; Jean-Louis Bourgeon, 'La Fronde parlementaire à la veille de la Saint-Barthélemy', *Bibliothèque de l'Ecole des Chartes*, 148 (1990), pp. 17–89.

23 BnF, MSS Fr. 15553, fol. 137r, Longueville to the King, Calais.

24 *Ibid.*, fol. 159r, Ornano to the King, Valence.

25 BnF, MSS Fr. 15554, fol. 38r, letter from Vicomte d'Orthe, Peyrehorade.

26 BnF, MSS Fr. 15555, fol. 17r, Ludovic Birague to the King, Saluces. The marquisate of Saluces was then a French possession.

27 BnF, MSS 500 Colbert 24, fol. 415v, Coligny to the King, La Rochelle, 8 May 1571.

28 On this point see Crouzet, *La Nuit de la Saint-Barthélemy*, pp. 213ff.

29 Garrisson, *Les Derniers Valois*, pp. 57–58, found the text of a contract with an alchemist signed by the King. But if this reveals the 'magical universe' inhabited by the sons of Catherine de Medici, is it evidence of the influence of Neoplatonism?

30 Crouzet, *La Nuit de la Saint-Barthélemy*, pp. 240ff. See also Crouzet's fascinating analyses of the magical powers of the spoken word as an instrument of government for Catherine de Medici, in Crouzet, *Le Haut Cœur de Catherine de Médicis*, pp. 23ff.

31 BnF, MS Dupuy 775, fol. 26, quoted by Bourgeon, 'Pour une histoire, enfin, de la Saint-Barthélemy', *Revue historique*, 282 (1989), p. 120, n. 65. On the Gastines cross affair, see p. 36.

32 *Négociations diplomatiques avec la Toscane*, vol. 3, p. 728, Petrucci to Francesco de Medici, Blois, 20 Nov. 1571.

33 King's speech at the 'royal session' of 12 March 1571, quoted by Bourgeon, 'La Fronde parlementaire', p. 40.

34 The expression, 'I have embraced them all in paternal affection', figures in a circular addressed to provincial governors on 4 May 1572: BnF, MS. Fr. 16104, fol. 46r.

35 *Lettres de Charles IX à M. de Fourquevaux, ambassadeur en Espagne, 1565–1572*, ed. Charles Douais (Montpellier, 1897), p. 300, letter of 13 Aug. 1570, Saint-Germain-en-Laye.

36 *Ibid.*, p. 281, letter of 7 Feb. 1570, Angers.

37 *Ibid.*, pp. 345–346, letter of 8 April 1571, Paris.

38 V. Vásquez de Prada, *Felipe II y Francia*, pp. 37–70.

39 *La Saint-Barthélemy devant le Sénat de Venise*, p. 54 (Ambassador Michiel's despatch).

40 *Recueil général des anciennes lois françaises*, ed. F. A. Isambert and Decrusy, vol. 14 (July 1559–May 1574), pp. 230–231 (the edict, dated 4 Oct. 1570, was registered by the Parlement on 20 Nov.).

41 N. M. Sutherland, *The Massacre of St. Bartholomew and the European conflict, 1559–1572* (London, 1973), pp. 125–126.

42 François de La Noue, *Discours politiques et militaires*, ed. F. E. Sutcliffe (Geneva, 1967), p. 784.

43 BnF, MS 500 Colbert 24, fols 415r–416r, Coligny to the King, 8 May 1571, La Rochelle (this passage in partially quoted by Liliane Crété, *Coligny* (Paris, 1985), pp. 391–392).

44 BnF, MS. Fr. 15553, fol. 3r, letter to Queen Mother, 2 Jan. 1571; *ibid.*, fol. 84 r, letter to the King, 16 May 1571; *ibid.*, fol. 107r, 17 June 1571, anonymous report on the La Rochelle conspiracy; MS 500 Colbert 24, fol. 420r, Coligny to the King, 12 Sept. 1570.

45 On the Netherlands affair, see below, ch 2.

46 *Lettres de Charles IX à M. de Fourquevaux*, pp. 342–347, letter of 8 April 1571, Paris. On the piracy in question, see Martine Acerra and Guy Martinière, eds, *Coligny, les protestants et la mer* (Paris, 1997).

47 Jeanne d'Albret to Catherine de Medici, 3 Jan. 1571, in *Lettres de Catherine de Médicis*, vol. 4, p. 22, n. 1.

48 *Négociations diplomatiques avec la Toscane*, vol. 3, pp. 698–701, Petrucci to Francesco de Medici, Paris, 10 Aug. 1571, which includes a copy of these conditions.

49 *Ibid.*, p. 706, Petrucci to Francesco de Medici, Blois, 19 Sept. 1571.

50 Champion, *Charles IX*, vol. 1, p. 409; Jehan de La Fosse, *Les 'Mémoires' d'un curé de*

Paris (1557–1590), ed. Marc Venard (Geneva, 2004), p. 103.

51 *Négociations diplomatiques avec la Toscane*, vol. 3, p. 706, Petrucci to Francesco de Medici, Blois, 19 Sept. 1571.

52 Luc Geizkofler, *Mémoires de Luc Geizkofler, tyrolien (1550–1620)*, ed. Edouard Fick (Geneva, 1892), p. 56.

53 Champion, *Charles IX*, vol. 1, p. 405, n. 3, letter to Francés de Álava, 14 Sept. 1571.

54 Quoted by Mark Greengrass, 'Functions and limits of political clientelism in France before Cardinal Richelieu', in Neithard Bulst, Robert Descimon and Alain Guerreau, eds, *L'État ou le roi. Les Fondations de la modernité monarchique en France (XIVe–XVIIe siècles)* (Paris, 1996), p. 79.

55 BnF, MS. Fr. 3193, fols 25r–26r, Coligny to the King, 13 Dec. 1571, Châtillon, published in *BSHPF*, 21 (1872), p. 460ff.

56 *Négociations diplomatiques avec la Toscane*, vol. 3, p. 743, Petrucci to Francesco de Medici, Amboise, 24 Dec. 1571.

57 *Ibid.*, p. 738, Petrucci to Francesco de Medici, Blois, 4 Dec. 1571.

58 Sir Henry Middlemore to Lord Burghley, 17 June 1572, quoted by Crété, *Coligny*, p. 419.

59 Marc Venard, *Réforme protestante, Réforme catholique dans la province d'Avignon, xvie siècle* (Paris, 1993), p. 542.

60 BnF, MS 500 Colbert 7, fol. 357r, magistrates of the Châtelet to the King, 17 Oct. 1571.

61 BnF, Ms. Fr. 3193, fol. 23r–23v, the King to marshal Cossé, 6 Nov. 1571.

62 Barbara Diefendorf, 'Prologue to a massacre: popular unrest in Paris, 1557–1572', *American Historical Review*, 90 (1985), pp. 1087–1089.

63 *Négociations diplomatiques avec la Toscane*, vol. 3, p. 743, Petrucci to Francesco de Medici, Amboise, 24 Dec. 1571.

64 La Fosse, *Les 'Mémoires' d'un curé de Paris*, p. 85.

65 René Benoist, *Advertissement du moyen par lequel aisément tous troubles et differens tant touchant la Croix, de laquelle y a si grande et si dangereuse altercation en ceste ville de Paris, que autres concernans la Religion*, in Simon Goulart, ed., *Memoires de l'Estat de France sous Charles IX*, 2nd ed. (Middlebourg, 1578), vol. 1, fol. 91v.

66 *Lettres de Charles IX à M. de Fourquevaux*, pp. 364–365, letter of 14 Oct. 1571, Blois.

67 *Ibid.*, p. 374, letter of 26 Dec. 1571, Amboise.

68 Vásquez de Prada, *Felipe II y Francia*, pp. 49–55. See also Serge Brunet, 'Anatomie des réseaux ligueurs dans le sud-ouest de la France (vers 1562–vers 1610)', in Nicole Lemaître, ed., *Religion et politique dans les sociétés du Midi* (Paris, 2002), pp. 153–191.

69 Vásquez de Prada, *Felipe II y Francia*, p. 200.

70 The hypothesis of a Catholic conspiracy in autumn 1571 was presented by Sutherland, *The massacre of St. Bartholomew*, pp. 211–213.

71 *Correspondance de Philippe II sur les affaires des Pays-Bas, publiée d'après les originaux conservés dans les archives royales de Simancas*, ed. Louis Gachard, vol. 2 (Brussels, 1851), pp. 185–187, 191–192 and 198–202, royal letters of 14 July, 4 Aug. and 14 Sept. 1571.

72 Crouzet, *La Nuit de la Saint-Barthélemy*, p. 502.

73 BnF, MS 500 Colbert 7, fol. 415r, letter of 26 June 1572.

74 Bourgeon, 'La Fronde parlementaire', pp. 57–58.

75 BnF, MS. Fr. 16104, fol. 45r, circular to provincial governors, 4 May 1572. Of the four places of security in question, the restitution of La Rochelle remained purely theoretical.

2

POLITICS MATRIMONIAL
AND INTERNATIONAL

In order to consolidate the fragile peace obtained thanks to the Edict of Saint-Germain, other means besides repression or pious exhortation were available to the monarchy. The first was the traditional one of marriages, as no treaty was conceivable at that time without one or more such unions, which were held to translate and guarantee the newly found concord. Luckily, princes of a marrying age were numerous: the young Protestant leaders, Henri de Navarre and Henri de Condé, the King himself and his brothers Henri d'Anjou and François d'Alençon. The marriages of the first two were intended as a bridge between the two rival confessions, while those of the royal brood would serve to consolidate France's position in Europe. It was thought that the forces of division, once hemmed in by the web of marital bonds, could not but be snuffed out.

Such grand matrimonial manoeuvres belonged to the classic mainsprings of diplomacy. The far-reaching plan which accompanied them appeared more ambitious – that of contracting alliances with Protestant rulers against the over-powerful Spanish neighbour, whose possessions in the north (the Netherlands), the east (Franche-Comté) and south (Roussillon) dangerously surrounded the kingdom. It would also mark the return of the policy inaugurated by François I and Henri II, which gave priority to the realist search for external support over dealing with confessional divisions. This policy would help to weaken Philip II by assisting his Calvinist subjects in the Netherlands in revolt against him.

In this project of intervening to assist the Dutch rebels, was there a way of uniting Catholics and Protestants in the service of a common objective which would overcome their dissensions and turn their warlike humours against a foreign enemy? Coligny believed there was. Charles IX allowed himself to be seduced for a while by an enterprise in which he could hope for territorial gains. It was a high-risk aspiration, as the dangers of discord concealed in it equalled at least the prospects of reconciliation that it offered; it could also provoke war between France and Spain. Some historians have explained the assassination attempt of 22 August against Coligny, the principal champion of this policy, in terms of the Spanish desire to prevent its realisation.[1] We must, therefore, try to see if one of the keys to the Massacre lies in the contemporary matrimonial and international conjuncture.

THE WEB OF ALLIANCES

Marrying adversaries and uniting opposites – the seductive power of this ideal derived from the place it held in the predominant world-view of the sixteenth century. In the cosmological imagination of the time, the miraculous equilibrium of the universe was based on the conjunction of dissimilar elements – water, earth, air and fire – with 'light things prevented by the heavy ones from rising upwards, and heavy ones correspondingly suspended lest they fall', according to the jurist and philosopher Louis Le Roy.[2] Similar rules were thought to govern the human community, whose structure – reflecting that of the cosmos – resulted from hidden correspondences. Among mankind, marriage in particular was designed to seal the rapprochement of opposites. This idea drew on Christian sources: the sacrament creates an indissoluble bond, sanctified by the grace of God, and capable of overcoming every rift-inducing factor. It was also anchored in the prevailing lineal conception of society at the time: the union of two people also made allies of their lineages, or even their states, calming possible conflicts. The pacifying virtues of marriage were vaunted in mythological disguise by the poet Jean Dorat, on the occasion of Charles IX's marriage. Relating how Cadmos, the legendary introducer of civilisation into Greece, married Harmony, the daughter of Mars and Venus, Dorat made her the symbol of concord restored.[3] In this way, he celebrated the role of conciliator attributed to the wife, who formed the bond between the families of her father and her husband, and became the arbiter par excellence of the differences that might pit them against each other.

Charles IX inaugurated the series of marriages destined to consolidate peace both outside and inside the kingdom. On 26 November 1570, at Mézières, he married Elisabeth of Austria, younger daughter of the Emperor and whose elder sister, Anne, had married the King of Spain. Matrimonial links were thus established with the Empire, restoring those which had united France and Spain by the marriage of Philip II and Elisabeth de Valois, sister of Charles IX, and which were ended by the premature death of Elisabeth in 1568. The Parisians were associated with the festivities during the solemn entries of the sovereigns. The King's entry was held on 6 March, the Queen's on 29 March 1571. In both cases, the theme of the paintings and sculptures which adorned the ephemeral monuments on the route of the royal cortèges was that of friendship between France and Germany. Enlisted to comment in verse on the paintings which the spectators could see, Ronsard saw in it an opportunity to revive the old legend, which nobody believed in anymore, of the Trojan origins of the Franks by adding that of their German descent, which historians had accredited since the early sixteenth century. He thus presented the royal marriages as the return of that original unity:

> Heureux le siècle, heureuse la journée
> Où des Germains le sang très ancien
> S'est remeslé ici avec le sang troyen
> Par le bien-faict d'un heureux Hymenée
> [Happy the age and the day when
> The ancient blood of the Germans
> Mingled again with that of Troy
> Through the blessing of a joyful union.][4]

In these celebrations, Catherine de Medici personified the woman as pacifier, since Elisabeth was still too young and too recently arrived in France to play such a part. The Queen Mother was represented during the King's entry both as a woman holding up a map of Gaul with her arms and as Juno, the tutelary goddess of marriage, accompanied here by a rainbow, the biblical symbol of reconciliation between man and God.[5] Her and her son's victory over war was symbolised by the chains that shackled the god Mars and the spider's webs that rendered his weapons harmless.

These marriages seem to confirm that France was anchoring itself in the Catholic camp. It was thus necessary, in accordance with the notion of counterweights which seemed essential to Europe's equilibrium, to oppose this orientation by one in the direction of the Protestant camp. France turned naturally towards England, whose Queen, Elizabeth, was not married. But which suitor should be offered to her? The idea of proposing the King's brother, Henri d'Anjou, originated with Cardinal Châtillon, as Catherine de Medici confided to the ambassador, La Mothe-Fénelon – an idea which the Queen Mother initially greeted with some reticence before fervently embracing it.[6] Some Huguenots also supported this project enthusiastically. A letter from one of them, Jean de Ferrières, vidame of Chartres, describes the effects of such a union on the peace of Europe in astonishingly idyllic colours. If the marriage were to happen, he reasoned, the House of Austria would be facing 'two brothers, each as powerful as the other, as counterweights to its ambition'; while Charles IX, also allied to the German Protestant princes and the Prince of Orange, would recover Flanders, which had previously been under French suzerainty. And the King's other brother, François d'Alençon, could obtain the duchy of Milan and perhaps the kingdom of Naples: 'by these means', the vidame explained, 'the queen would have the great pleasure of seeing all her children kings'. More than that, in a surprising passage Ferrières dreamt that the Gallican church would be led to purge itself of Roman corruption and, in union with the English and German churches, would initiate a huge movement to bring Europe back to the purity of the faith – the Protestant one, that is.[7] It was Utopian reverie, but its fervour tells us much about the passing euphoria that took hold in certain Huguenot circles following the 1570 peace, encouraged by moderates in the royal entourage such as François de Montmorency, to whom the letter was written, and who were capable of resisting the current of distrust which enveloped many Protestants.[8]

When Catherine de Medici adopted the idea of her son Henri's marrying Elizabeth of England, it was not with the intention of breaking with the Pope; of the vidame of Chartres' arguments, she embraced only that of the necessity of counterbalancing Spanish power and the advantage of securing a crown for the duc d'Anjou, if necessary by marriage. Charles IX saw in it an opportunity to get his brother out of the way, as he took umbrage at his popularity, derived from the victories at Jarnac and Moncontour. The Queen of England was not hostile to the project, despite the difference in age – in 1570, she was thirty-seven and the duc d'Anjou was nineteen that September – and the English negotiators, Francis Walsingham, Thomas Killigrew and Thomas Smith, appreciated the diplomatic advantages which such a union could bring. But, after many vicissitudes, the discussions foundered on the difference of religion: neither Elizabeth nor her councillors were ready to concede the public exercise of his religion to her future spouse, who, being close to the Guises and attached to his religion, was in no way disposed to make concessions on this point. Pressure was exerted on Henri d'Anjou, urging him not to commit himself, and one can imagine the fierce struggle within his entourage between the factions hostile or favourable to the English match; the assassination, on 10 December 1571, of his favourite, Lignerolles, who was an agent of Cardinal Lorraine and a fierce opponent of the marriage, was perhaps a bloody episode in this struggle.[9] In any case, the Catholic manoeuvres, strengthened by Spanish support and, no doubt, money, won the day. By the summer of 1571, it was clear to all that the marriage would not take place. The Queen Mother then proposed a substitute, François d'Alençon, who was sixteen years old in March 1571 and who was thought to be less intransigent than his brother Henri over the exercise of his religion. But this plan proved no more successful, although it would long remain a subject of diplomatic discussion between France and England. These extended negotiations were not entirely fruitless: on 19 April 1572, the two countries signed a defence treaty, the realisation of a major aspect of the policy of counter-balances pursued by the French monarchy.

It was also necessary to take in hand the marriage of the two young cousins, Henri de Condé and Henri de Navarre. Princes of the blood, they stood in line to the throne, a possibility all the more worrisome because they were Protestants who, by virtue of their birth, were the natural leaders of their co-religionists: hence the importance of finding the right marriages for them. On 10 August 1572, at Blandy-en-Brie, Condé married Mary of Cleves, brought up as a Protestant by Jeanne d'Albret, but who was also sister of Catherine, who had recently married duc Henri de Guise, in the autumn of 1570, and of Henriette, wife of the duc de Nevers, another fervent Catholic. Thus Condé became brother-in-law to two powerful defenders of the opposite confession.

The most difficult objective – to draw Henri de Navarre into the inner royal family – still remained. His fiancée was to be Marguerite de Valois, sister of the King. Obstacles to it were not lacking. The two young people were not well matched; she, the 'pearl of the Valois', was coquettish, refined and cultivated; by comparison, Navarre appeared uncouth. Yet, they were of the same age – both were born in 1553, she on 14 May and he on 13 December – and they had had the opportunity to take the measure of each other during their childhood, since Henri had lived at court from 1557 to 1568; obtaining their consent to marry was not expected to be difficult.[10] They were cousins to the third degree, which meant that it would be necessary to obtain a papal dispensation not just for their consanguinity, but also – and most of all – for the difference of religion between them. On this point, the obstacle might be insurmountable.

The reasons which Catherine de Medici and Charles IX indefatigably put forward to justify their plan were all based on the benefits that would follow for both public concord and the Catholic religion. The planned union would be the sign and the means to the restoration of harmony. Its accomplishment, Charles IX wrote on 28 September 1571 to Raymond de Fourquevaux, ambassador to Spain, 'will be the bond and the establishment of peace in this kingdom, and will render the union among my subjects enduring, something which I desire more than anything else in the world'. For her part, the Queen Mother pleaded with the Grand Duke of Tuscany on 8 October 1571 that 'nothing can make us hope more for the full increase of our religion and the universal peace of this kingdom than the marriage of my daughter and the prince of Navarre'.[11] The hope that drove Catherine was that her future son-in-law would be gradually drawn to convert or, at least, would not behave as a rebel towards his brother-in-law, the King. Imbued with the generally held idea that without leaders the 'people' were incapable of sustained initiatives, she confided to the Florentine ambassador, Petrucci, that once Condé and Navarre had been 'won' and secured by the bonds of marriage, the remainder of their forces would resolve to obey.[12]

However, religion was not the only issue in the Navarre marriage; it also had vital geostrategic importance for the French monarchy. The Albret family had accumulated a considerable number of possessions in south-west France, the most important of which were the kingdom of Lower Navarre, the sovereign principality of Béarn, the duchy of Albret, the counties of Foix, Bigorre and Périgord, and the vicomté of Limoges. In 1527, Marguerite d'Angoulême, sister of François I and widow of the duc d'Alençon, on marrying Henri d'Albret, added to this collection the possessions of her late husband, namely the counties of Armagnac, Fézensac and Rodez, as well as the vicomtés of Lomagne and Fézenzaguet. The marriage in 1548 of their only daughter and heiress,

Jeanne d'Albret, to Antoine de Bourbon, added the duchy of Vendôme, which belonged to the husband. It was this accumulation of fiefs that the young Henri de Navarre, son of Jeanne and Antoine, would inherit on his mother's death on 9 June 1572 (his father had died in 1562 from a wound sustained during the siege of Orleans). As a result, he was lord of an impressive number of lands. Drawing on the wealth they provided, and leader of the Huguenot party, he was in a position, consequently, to mobilise troops both from his feudal clientele and from among the faithful of the Protestant cause; in addition, as sovereign in his kingdom of Navarre and principality of Béarn, Henri was clearly what Anglo-Saxon historians call an 'over-mighty subject' of the King of France. In attempting to bind him more tightly to the royal family, Charles IX and his mother were behaving exactly like their predecessors, who had utilised the instrument of marriage – those of Marguerite d'Angoulême and Antoine de Bourbon – to draw the Albret family into the royal orbit. The idea of this union was an old one, having been proposed as early as 1557.[13]

But it was difficult to persuade the Catholic camp to accept this matrimonial solution. Parisian preachers thundered against such an unnatural union and execrable coupling.[14] Pope Pius V, who had energetically expressed his disapproval during the negotiation of the Peace of Saint-Germain – 'we are certain that Satan and the sons of the Light have nothing in common', he wrote to Catherine de Medici – saw the marriage of Marguerite de Valois to a heretic as an 'insult to God' and a 'danger for souls'.[15] In mid-January he sent Antonio Maria Salviati as nuncio to France with the mission of dissuading Charles IX from his objective; he also sent as legate to the French court Cardinal Alessandrino, who suggested in vain a revival of an earlier marriage project for Marguerite with King Sebastian of Portugal. Philip II was not inactive either: he convinced the general of the Jesuits, Francisco Borgia, to support the papal envoys. Borgia arrived in Blois on 9 February, two days after the legate.[16] But to no avail – Alessandrino left, discouraged, as early as 25 February.

Some of the French prelates did support the views of the King and his mother. When Salviati tried to intervene with Cardinal Bourbon, Henri de Navarre's uncle, who was being pressed to receive the consent of the future spouses and celebrate the nuptial Mass, he found him inflexibly optimistic, if we can believe the account of the interview sent to the Duke of Alba on 9 April 1572, by the secretary Pedro de Aguilón, who acted as representative of the King of Spain while awaiting the arrival of the successor to Francés de Álava. The Cardinal, he said, answered the anxious questions of the nuncio that 'everything would be done for the service of God and the good of the kingdom'; if it proved impossible to induce the Béarnais [Henri] to become a Catholic, at least his children would be Catholics; Cardinals Lorraine, Guise and Pellevé would be persuaded to give their consent; moreover, the nuncio's interlocutor added, 'since Lorraine is presently excluded [from royal favour], he would sell his soul to the devil to return to favour and play a role in government.' As for the Pope, it would be a bad move by him if, by reason of his intransigence, the King of France was obliged to go ahead with the marriage by doing without the dispensation.'[17] A few days after this discussion, Salviati found even greater enthusiasm in a letter from the Bishop of Mâcon, Giovanni Battista Alamanni, almoner to Catherine de Medici: according to the prelate, Navarre would certainly convert and, with peace thus consolidated, the kingdom would, little by little, be reconciled in the unity of the Catholic faith; and France would owe its happiness to the pacifying action of Catherine de Medici, assisted by divine grace.[18] During the infectious euphoria characteristic of April 1572, Petrucci, the Florentine ambassador, also celebrated the 'voluntary concord' which was about to unite the House of Navarre and that of Valois.[19]

Little by little, this optimism crumbled because the eagerly awaited papal dispensation was not forthcoming. Hope was briefly revived with the death of Pius V on 1 May 1572, but it was short lived, because his successor, Gregory XIII, proved equally inflexible: he would grant a dispensation for consanguinity only if Henri de Navarre converted to Catholicism. Cardinal Lorraine, who was then in Rome, attempted – energetically, it seems – to bring the new Pope around to more conciliatory dispositions; as Cardinal Bourbon had sensed, Lorraine desired to return to favour and saw in the success of his efforts a way of achieving it. The letters that he wrote on 1 August to the King and Queen Mother evince a certain bitterness, as he was obliged both to admit his failure and challenge the suspicion of having exercised little zeal in the negotiations which he had conducted; it was not without a certain cynicism that he declared to Catherine de Medici that only a fool would wish to oppose the will of the King and her own:

> So, Madame, please do not believe that I was so badly counselled as to displease you and act against your service, even if it had been in my nature and I had desired to do so. Madame, I think that, on the price of my salvation, if you yourself had been here, you would not have done better than I did in soliciting the dispensation for the marriage of Madame, your daughter, and the king of Navarre; there is no kind of artifice that I did not try in order to achieve it; and if I had been able to do it, believe me that I would have been proud to despatch it to you and would have welcomed acquiring such glory.[20]

The support given by Cardinal Lorraine to the Navarre marriage seems, therefore, to have been real, even if the terms of his letter half suggest that he did so against his will. The French ambassador in Rome, François de Ferrals, certified to the King that the prelate did not economise with his 'fine, learned and customary remonstrances' in order to convince the Pope.[21] The scruples of Cardinal Bourbon, who, frightened by the absence of the papal dispensation, lost the strong optimism of April that year, were successfully countered by the Queen Mother. The bishops who disapproved of the planned union dared not voice their views openly.[22] Ultimately, those in the Catholic camp whose hostility was most to be feared were, apart from the King of Spain and the Pope, the preachers and the majority of the people of Paris. In order to conciliate them, Catherine de Medici, using the comte de Retz as intermediary, requested the opinion of the Paris theology faculty in order to see if the marriage could be celebrated in a Catholic manner. According to Petrucci, many of the theologians replied negatively and only a few positively. Things rested so, as if it sufficed for the King to claim that he had requested the opinion of the Sorbonne.[23] But such cover seemed rather flimsy.

It was also necessary to convince the Protestants. The discussions with Jeanne d'Albret were long and difficult; the Queen of Navarre was subject to contradictory pressures because her entourage was very divided over the prospect of an alliance with the royal family. During the difficult negotiations conducted with her by the King's and the Queen Mother's agents, she bargained hard for every possible guarantee for herself (especially the return of Lectoure, capital of the county of Armagnac) and for her party.[24] The negotiations were not focused solely on the marriage of her son, but also on an eventual action in support of the Dutch rebels. It was probably the prospect of obtaining royal support for their oppressed co-religionists which was the most decisive in gaining the consent of the Queen of Navarre and Henri, which was virtually assured by November 1571.[25]

The same hope influenced the decision of Coligny, who was perhaps the slowest to be persuaded. The Admiral felt that Henri de Navarre, once married to Marguerite de Valois, ran too great a risk of being led into abjuring his faith, and would have preferred to see him marry the Queen of England. But he understood well the importance of not opposing the enterprise of the Netherlands, to which he was strongly attached. By the autumn of 1571 the two questions – those of the marriage and of aiding the subjects of the King of Spain in revolt – appeared inextricably linked to each other.

THE LIBERTY OF THE 'BEGGARS' OF THE NETHERLANDS

The revolt of the Netherlands broke out in August 1566, at the same moment as a widespread iconoclastic movement began in the towns of western Flanders and then spread throughout most of the country. The causes of this insurrection were numerous. The Calvinists, who were numerous in Antwerp and the textile centres of the south-west, reacted badly to the repression that they had to endure; in addition, many nobles, such as William of Orange and his brother, Louis of Nassau, or others like the Counts of Egmont and Horn, protested against the authoritarian nature of the government, which they accused of violating their privileges and of serving exclusively the interests of Spain. On 5 April 1566, discontented nobles, who had come to present their grievances to the governor, Margaret of Parma, half-sister of Philip II, were treated as 'beggars' by one of her councillors. Espousing the insult as a badge of honour, they met on 8 April at a banquet, dressed as beggars, each one with two bowls on his belt and a bag on his shoulder, and adopted 'Long live the Beggars' as their rallying cry.

Fierce repression ensued. In 1568, the Duke of Alba, despatched by Philip II, established a special tribunal, the Council of Troubles; over 12,000 people were tried and over 1,000 executed, among them the Counts of Egmont and Horn. Numerous refugees fled to France. The emotion aroused among France's Protestants was intense, while the execution of Egmont and Horn sparked the solidarity of the great noble families, because the victims were connected by friendship and kinship with the Montmorencys and the Châtillons (Horn was a Montmorency-Nivelle). Flemish fugitives fought in the Huguenot ranks during the second civil war. The ties between the Calvinists on both sides of the frontier were further reinforced during the summer of 1568, as in August a treaty of alliance was negotiated between Louis de Condé (who was to die at Jarnac the following year) and Gaspard de Coligny, on the one side, and William of Orange, on the other. Claiming that 'evil counsellors' had pressed their respective sovereigns to 'exterminate the true religion, the nobles and other good people, without whom Kings cannot be maintained in their kingdoms', the parties promised to defend 'the glory of God, the profit and service of their kings, the public good, and the liberty of religion'.[26] The document added that each party to this 'holy alliance' should assist the other if it was threatened, with the party thus assisted being liable to 'pay' its debt later. This treaty was probably not signed, but the course of subsequent events showed its validity, since, during the third civil war, the troops of Orange and Nassau entered France to support the Huguenots.

This alliance reveals the close connection established by its authors between noble and religious liberty; it was sealed by the ideal of the reciprocity of service, the basis of the networks of friendship and solidarity so common among nobles. With the conclusion of the peace, Coligny found himself constrained, since the rules of honour obliged him to repay the princes of Orange and Nassau for the assistance that he had received from them during the third war; his sense of duty was closely linked to the demands of his faith. At the beginning, it seems that he mainly envisaged acting with England as his sole ally,[27] but he gradually allowed himself to be persuaded by the idea that the aid which he was bound to provide could, if he was supported by Charles IX, take the form of a war between France and Spain, a war that would have the advantage of uniting Catholics and Protestants against a foreign enemy and leading them to forget, momentarily at least, their own differences.

But Coligny was not the first to push the King in that direction. If the project of a French intervention in the Netherlands probably first emerged in December

1570, it took shape only in April 1571, during discussions between, on the one side, Louis of Nassau and the Dutch exiles and, on the other, Charles de Téligny, son-in-law of the Admiral, and Huguenot nobles such as François de la Noue or François de Beauvais, seigneur de Briquemault, discussions in which duc François de Montmorency soon became involved.[28] Charles IX was requested to act. Louis of Nassau perhaps first met him at the château of Lumigny, which belonged to La Noue's wife, but certainly at Fontainebleau between 28 and 30 July 1571. A plan for the partition of the Netherlands was proposed to the King. One of the key preconditions for the success of the project was England's participation in it, and, according to Ambassador Walsingham, who was informed by Nassau, France was to receive Flanders and Artois; England would gain Holland and Zeeland; the Prince of Orange would gain Brabant, Guelders and Luxemburg, all of three of which belonged to the Holy Roman Empire.[29]

What effect did such fabulous projects have on the King? It should first be remembered that Flanders and Artois were, at the beginning of the century, under the suzerainty of the French kings, from which they were removed by the calamitous treaty of Madrid, extracted from François I during his captivity and explicitly confirmed by the treaty of Cateau-Cambrésis in 1559. It could, therefore, seem legitimate to Charles IX to attempt to recover them. The international scene in 1571 seemed favourable. The negotiations with England over the marriage of Elizabeth to Henri d'Anjou offered the possibility of a treaty of alliance; Gaspard de Schomberg, despatched in May to the German princes, was negotiating for their support; Hubert Languet worked for a rapprochement between the Elector of Saxony and France.[30] Cosimo de Medici, a friend of the Montmorencys and enemy of the Guises, who was crowned as Grand Duke of Tuscany by the Pope in February 1570, to the fury of the King of Spain, was in favour of French action in the Netherlands. Catherine de Medici allowed herself to be seduced by the project for a while, before becoming totally hostile to it: in a letter of 2 August 1571, she expressed her sadness at the reticence of her son Henri in relation to the English marriage, amazed that nobody had been able to make him understand 'the grandeur that this marriage could bring him, as well as the friendship with the German princes, which would enable him to conquer the Netherlands and acquire sovereignty over them'.[31]

Charles IX was more imbued by the desire to attach his name to a great enterprise than by that of territorial gains. He had read Plutarch's *Lives of Illustrious Men*, translated by his preceptor, Jacques Amyot; the Florentine ambassador, Petrucci, judged him to be desperate for greatness.[32] On his entry to Paris, he saw on the summit of an arc of triumph the effigy of his father, Henri II, as 'protector of German liberty' – an allusion to the victorious campaign of 1552 undertaken on the pretext of liberating Metz, Toul and Verdun from the 'tyranny' of Charles V. According to the account of the celebrations left by the chronicler Simon Bouquet, this figure showed how Henri II, when asked for help by the Germans, 'immediately showed himself prompt and diligent to rescue them, having preserved them in their German liberty by his presence'.[33]

Liberty: the emotional resonance of the word was strong in France, where writers explained that the word 'Franks' meant 'free', which they had deserved by emancipating themselves from the yoke of Emperor Valentinian.[34] Now the revolt of Philip II's subjects offered Charles IX the opportunity to equal his father by gaining the title of protector of the liberty of the Netherlands, the spell under which his brother François would himself later fall. All of the books and pamphlets which orchestrated the resistance of the rebels focused on the theme of the liberty of their 'patria', enslaved by Spanish oppression.[35] There can be no doubt that Louis of Nassau evoked it during his negotiations. The French agent in Brussels, Claude de Mondoucet, constantly exhorted Charles IX to act; the rebels themselves, he claimed, implored his help, arguing that it was for the King of France to defend their country, which was the legitimate possession of the infantas, who were his nieces (daughters of the late Queen of Spain, Elisabeth de Valois), and whose natural protector he was.[36]

Charles IX was, indisputably, tempted. In the summer of 1571, he awarded a pension to Nassau and Orange.[37] On 27 April 1572, he wrote to Nassau – very imprudently, as the letter fell into the Duke of Alba's hands – saying: 'the sieur de Téligny, the bearer of this letter, has informed me several times and in detail of the considerable resources available to engage in a good enterprise for the liberty of the Netherlands, at present oppressed by the Spaniards ... a thing truly worthy of compassion and in which every noble and Christian prince should deploy the forces and resources that God has given him, which for my part is something that I am determined to do, whenever the opportunities and disposition of my affairs will permit me'.[38]

But for all that, was it worth risking a conflict with Spain?

WAR SUSPENDED

From May 1571 onwards one of the questions that most agitated and fascinated European diplomatic circles was whether the King of France would break with his Spanish neighbour. On two occasions, these anxieties became quasi-certainties. A first wave of rumours circulated in the spring of 1571: on 10 May, the Florentine ambassador, Petrucci, thought that everything was ready in France for a clash; the King seemed full of military ardour; the Huguenots were in favour of it; the great and the small desired war with Spain.[39] The second wave spread in the spring of 1572. In early April, the Queen Mother admitted to the Spanish embassy secretary, Aguilón, who had complained about them, that 'rumours of a break' between France and Philip II were circulating almost everywhere; and she seemed to Aguilón to be 'trembling in fear' over them.[40] At the end of that month, the French ambassador in Rome, François de Ferrals, declared that those around him believed a French attack was imminent; two months later, on 30 June, he informed the King of 'the great rumour which is spreading more and more of a collapse of the peace and a war between Your Majesty and the King of Spain'.[41]

This suspense has influenced the historiography of the Massacre until today. Since Coligny appeared as the principal instigator of the offensive to help the Dutch rebels, some historians deduced that 'in order to kill the war, Coligny had to be killed'.[42] In trying to discover who wished to stop the war, some historians pointed to Catherine de Medici, and others to Spain, as being behind the attack of 22 August against the Admiral.[43] These deductions resemble each other in taking seriously the rumours of conflict. But before being swayed by them, we should first ask the following question: did the war really need to be 'killed' by those who, for one reason or another, desired the preservation of peace? In other words, is it necessary to see in the noises about war anything more than a clever game of dissuasion which, on the contrary, aimed at avoiding a breakdown in relations?

It is true, as François de Ferrals said in his letter of 29 April, that many facts 'sorely intrigued' observers. The defence of France's borders was actively organised. In August 1571 the King ordered the transfer of companies stationed at Saint-Jean-d'Angély and Angoulême and inactive since the peace with the Huguenots, to the fortresses of Picardy, which he ordered to be reinforced in September; in March 1572, artillery was moved there from the Paris Arsenal; by mid-July, seventeen companies were stationed on the Picardy frontier.[44] Troop recruitment occurred in the Dauphiné, while the fortifications of Marseille were improved.[45]

The Spaniards themselves were not idle. They also fortified the Netherlands along their southern frontiers. They raised troops in Catalonia and Roussillon and, as Guillaume de Joyeuse informed the King in a letter of 9 June 1572, they stored in Perpignan 'eight or nine canon, a large quantity of shot, barrels of powder, with many soldiers in heavy armour and pikemen'. The result was, Joyeuse added, that 'merchants no longer go as readily as before to the fairs, and that a great number of your subjects who were in Spain, have left and are leaving daily, with everyone there saying that war is already declared'. The King, he concluded, should urgently equip the fortresses along the coast and the castles situated on the Pyrenees frontier.[46] It was also in order to be ready for every eventuality that, on 20 May 1572, Philip II ordered his half-brother, John of Austria, not to allow his ships to leave Messina to link up, as had been planned, with the Levant fleet organised against the Turks; when he rescinded this ban, on 4 July, he asked him to remove a number of galleys for an expedition to the Bizerta area under the command of Gian Andrea Doria. In both cases, according to the French ambassador in Rome, it was a question of having forces available to head for the coast of Provence in case of a French attack in Flanders.[47]

However, all of this hubbub was dominated by the principle of precaution. Monsieur de Rieux, on his return from an information-gathering mission to Montferrat and Catalonia, confirmed on 13 April 1562, in a letter to the Queen Mother, that the Spaniards were reinforcing their frontier defences; but, he added, 'they fear having war much more than they want it'.[48] Everything led to the conclusion that they were only observing the rule of prudence formulated on 27 June 1572 by the new Spanish ambassador, Diego de Zuñiga, by virtue of which one had to 'keep the sword in one's hand' to deal with every eventuality.[49]

On both sides, the essential objective was deliberately to sustain the fears of the adversary. The fleet assembled on the Atlantic coast by Philippe Strozzi, cousin to Catherine de Medici, is a good example of this. Merchant ships were fitted out as war-ships under his command in Bordeaux, La Rochelle and Brouage. From the outset, a thousand guesses were hazarded about the fleet's destination. Where should it sail to? Brantôme, who knew Strozzi well, claimed that he wished to head 'for the islands of Peru'.[50] The information seemed credible, and many nobles who fancied adventure sought, at the risk of their lives, to make themselves famous through a prestigious conquest somewhere. Thus the son of Blaise de Monluc, Captain Peyrot, who, as his father says in his *Commentaires*, 'projected a maritime enterprise to Africa to conquer something', died in 1566 in Madeira, while Strozzi himself died miserably in 1582 on an expedition to the Azores. Petrucci, for his part, thought that the assembled ships would sail for the coast of Africa in the hope of lucrative pillage.[51] But many Spanish observers were convinced that the French armada was preparing to help the rebels. In June, an English agent spread the rumour that Strozzi had transported 6,000 men to the Netherlands.[52]

What is remarkable about this is the concomitance between the publicity given to the naval preparations, of which everyone was aware – even in Geneva Theodore de Bèze wondered, like many others, about them – and the well-concealed mystery as to their objective.[53] The evasive answers given by the French to Spanish questions was that it was designed to fight against piracy in the Atlantic. One thing was sure: Charles IX, having authorised the outfitting of the ships, left them for a long time without permission to weigh anchor, so much so that in Rome jokes were made about this fleet 'which lord Philippe Strozzi kept immobile, going neither forwards nor backwards'.[54] The key to the enigma lies without doubt in the letter which the King wrote, on 11 May, to his ambassador in Constantinople, the bishop of Dax:

> All my desires are at one in making me oppose the power of the Spaniards, and I consider how to do so the most dexterously possible ... I have had a good number of vessels fitted out in the ports and harbours of my kingdom, raising a naval army of 12,000–15,000 men which will be ready to sail where we wish by the end of this month on the pretext of protecting my harbours and coasts from depredation, but in reality in order to keep the Catholic king in a state of apprehension and to encourage

those Low Countries' beggars to action, as they have already done by taking all of Zeeland and weakening Holland, in such a way that the problems that the Spaniards will have there will suffice, I believe, to divert them from other enterprises.[55]

Unsettle the King of Spain and 'keep him guessing': this objective was fully achieved. The Spanish spy networks were mobilised in order to uncover the secret of the French mobilisation.[56] In Rome, on 24 July, Ambassador Ferrals noted that the destination of the ships was what he was most frequently asked about, 'with more passion and conjectures than could be otherwise possible'.[57] Every means seemed worthwhile, for the King of France, to inspire 'boldness in those Beggars from the Netherlands to bestir themselves' and thus weaken his Spanish neighbour by keeping his forces occupied. But the assistance given was indirect, nothing more. In the same vein, Philip II was willing to encourage, via his agents and his money, the actions of the intransigent Catholics, which could keep Charles IX worried.

In reality, in the situation which obtained in late 1571 and the first half of 1572, neither king was willing to take the risk of appearing to promote war. A major event occurred on 7 October 1571 – the brilliant victory over the Turks by the forces of the Holy League between the Pope, the King of Spain and Venice, under the leadership of Don John of Austria. This victory was celebrated as the sign of the renewal of Christendom. In this context, how could anyone wish to shatter the unity of Christians faced with the Infidel, which is what the prince who first declared war on his neighbour was bound to be appear to do? Every temptation to go to war had to be resisted, as yielding to it would cost dearly in terms of one's international reputation. Philip II was conscious of the dilemma involved: 'I see clearly', he affirmed on 17 July 1572, 'the spirit and desire that the French have, and it can be said that, in essence, they wish the world to believe that they want peace and I want war'.[58] He did in fact have the feeling that he was under the eyes of the 'whole world'. European opinion – that is, the diplomatic circles and the courts – which was shaped by ambassadors and their spy networks, constituted a powerful sounding-board ready to magnify or vilify the image of princes; for this reason, it undoubtedly influenced their decisions. In this respect, Rome was the nerve-centre where rumours were magnified and from where they were diffused. François de Ferrals, for example, thought that his main duty there was to defend the 'reputation' of his master.[59] That of Philip II was also at stake there, and he was particularly keen to enjoy the glory of the defender of Christendom.[60] The struggle against the Turks was an important element in this; if he was obliged to fight against the King of France, as he confided to his ambassador in Rome, he would not be able to supply the forces that he wished 'for the affairs of the Levant'.[61]

As for Charles IX, he was keen not to worsen the reproaches made against him: he was widely accused for not joining the Holy League, being an ally of the Turks and, by troubling the King of Spain, delaying John of Austria's fleet – in short, 'for each day doing a disservice to peace and union'.[62] Moreover, in late June the Pope informed him via Ferrals that war against Spain would immediately end his hopes of a dispensation for his sister's marriage to Henri de Navarre.[63] The King also knew from the information reaching him that both his northern and southern frontiers were still vulnerable, despite his efforts to fortify them. He understood the obstacles which hampered his desire to work for the 'liberty of the Netherlands'. In the letter already quoted to Louis of Nassau on 27 April, in which he expressed this aspiration, he pointed out that he would defend the rebels 'as much as the opportunities and the disposition of his affairs allowed'. The situation was worsening. It became increasingly clear that England would not support France in case of an attack on the Netherlands: on 26 June, Elizabeth declared to her council that in no circumstances would she break with the Catholic King – which did not prevent her envoys from diffusing propaganda among the inhabitants of the Flanders towns declaring the wish of the Queen to liberate them from 'the miserable tyranny of the duke of Alba'.[64] The Grand Duke of Tuscany, Cosimo de Medici, took Alba's side. The German princes, for their part, only offered vague assurances of friendship without real substance.[65]

For Charles IX, the solution consisted of worrying his adversary, secretly supporting every initiative capable of stimulating the rebels and, especially, encouraging the Huguenots to send help to their co-religionists – while at the same time taking care not to admit it. He had to proceed wearing a mask, even to the point of denying clear evidence, and to such an extent that the real question for the King of Spain was this: would Charles IX drop the mask? The correspondence between Philip II and his agents is punctuated by this obsessive expression – 'removing the mask'. It was essential not to be forced into open war. For that, it was better that the King of France kept his mask on, because if he was obliged to drop it, and thus openly recognise the offensive actions of his subjects against Spanish interests, Spain would be forced into war in order to respond to this official challenge and defend its interests.[66] This explains the orders given: as the Duke of Alba advised Ambassador Zuñiga, we have to envelop with sweetness the complaints made to the King and his mother about the Netherlands, so that they do not lose their 'verguença' – that is, 'good face' – in the eyes of observers.[67] If that happened, Charles IX would be constrained to avow the assistance given to the rebels, which would constitute a manifest *casus belli* for Spain, one it could not avoid without a loss of honour.

Hence the subtle game in which each side knew perfectly well what the other knew. But Charles IX still went on publicly denying the encouragements he gave to the Dutch rebels and Philip II diligently pretended to believe him. On 1 June 1572, the King of Spain explicitly ordered Zuñiga that 'for as long as the king and his mother keep the mask on, we should not drop ours, but lead them to think that we believe them, and proceed with the same dissimulation as they do, insofar as they give us no greater and more overt reason for behaving differently'. On 2 August, he was even more explicit: 'they must believe that we believe their external demonstrations' until such time as the success which God will not fail to give Spanish arms in Flanders will force them to abandon their policy of duplicity and their support of rebellion which will have become useless. He had, he continued, ordered Don John of Austria to remove a regiment from his army to send it to the duchy of Milan; but Zuñiga was to say to the King of France that it was absolutely not intended to offend him.[68]

All of this was a game of pretence, mutual complicity in dissimulation and denial offered and accepted. On both sides there emerges the 'readability' of policies which have too often been described, on the French side, as uncertain and erratic, but which, in fact, reflect the clear recognition by Charles IX of the narrowness of his room for manoeuvre.[69]

From April 1572 onwards, the difficulty of this position became fully clear. On 1 April, the Sea Beggars seized the port of Brill, at the mouth of the Meuse, and that success was quickly followed by the capture of Flushing. The revolt soon swept through the coast of the north-west Netherlands, from Zeeland to Frisia. Galvanised by these events, Louis of Nassau went to recruit supporters in France; he secretly left Paris, bearing the famous royal letter of 27 April. But at the same time, faithful to his tactic of dissimulation, Charles IX sent to his ambassador in Madrid a copy of a written order he had given the Prince of Orange's brother to disarm his ships, so that he could show it to Philip II.[70] On 4 May 1572, he wrote a circular letter to the provincial governors in which he declared his wish to live in good friendship with his neighbours, and especially the King of Spain, 'expressly forbidding all subjects, residents and inhabitants of our kingdom from contravening it, either directly or in an underhand way, and from favouring or assisting their enemies and rebels, even those who have rebelled in the Netherlands against the Catholic king, my good brother'.[71]

On 23 and 24 May, Nassau led an army of Flemish exiles and Huguenot volunteers, among whom were François de la Noue and Jean de Hangest, seigneur de Genlis, which seized Valenciennes, and then Mons. Valenciennes was retaken on the 29th by the Spaniards, who then besieged Mons. These events had significant repercussions on the European stage. It was now clear that French subjects had crossed the frontier and fought alongside the rebels. Thus began for Charles IX a long series of denials. To Zuñiga, who expressed the Duke of Alba's indignation, he replied that he disapproved of the capture of Mons and was pleased with the Spanish reconquest of Valenciennes.[72] It is true that he was disappointed by the meagre success of the rebels so far: 'the affairs of the Beggars are going ever worse', he confided on 16 June to Vulcob, gentleman-in-ordinary of his chamber, 'and those in Mons are currently besieged on all sides, with little hope of escaping being captured when the said town is reduced to obedience by the duke of Alba, which is all that one can expect from such unfortunate enterprises, and the just judgment of God towards those who rebel against their prince.'[73] The last part of this sentence derived from more than just a wish to dissimulate: it also betrays the ambivalence of the King's own sentiments. The struggle of the Netherlands for their liberty may have captured his sympathy, but he perceived increasingly clearly its subversive aspects, which could contaminate his Huguenot subjects and incite them to take up arms against him.

On 5 June, the duc de Longueville, governor of Picardy, admitted his confusion to the King. Some of the French troops going to help Mons claimed to be 'avowed by persons who had been authorised by His Majesty'; their commanders had come to see him, and he did not know how to reply to them, because some were Catholic and some were Protestant.'[74] This information is not without interest, not merely because it reveals Charles IX's secret encouragement of these recruits, but also because it suggests how much the Netherlands enterprise could appear so exciting to many nobles, independently of their confessional affiliation. Petrucci noted the enthusiasm of those who joined in it: these young people were enthusiastic, 'avid for novelty, and so fond of action as to be unable to remain inactive.'[75] On the English side, a similar phenomenon was observed – many rushed to Flushing 'of their own accord', without being overtly authorised by the Queen.[76]

Genlis succeeded in escaping the Spanish pincer and came to Paris to raise new troops. According to the Spanish ambassador, he received 60,000 *livres* from Charles IX. The King and his mother, wrote Zúñiga to the Duke of Alba, would continue to aid the Huguenots; they even hoped to cut the Spanish army's supply line by sea and procure its death by starvation. But in his view, this would be done secretly; they would never admit it.[77]

THE HIGH-RISK HOPES OF COLIGNY

There was one man, however, who could not be satisfied by this policy of secrecy – Admiral Coligny. For many reasons, he wished the King to commit himself openly in the Netherlands. Firstly, he felt a keen sense of confessional solidarity with his oppressed Calvinist brethren; in his religious fervour, he saw himself as a 'warrior of God' fighting against what he called, in a letter to Lord Burghley, the 'henchmen of Satan' and devoting his life to the triumph of the Reformation.[78] Concern for national reconciliation was doubtless also important to him, as was the loyalty he felt towards his sovereign and which he hoped – if Charles IX gave his approval – to square with the assistance to the rebels. Walsingham summarised for Burghley the tenor of his discussions with Coligny: 'he asked me to tell you, my lord, that it is not his personal interest which makes him act, but … the great peril which threatens all those who profess the Gospel ... in the state things are in, and foreseeing as he does the misfortunes that will follow, he would betray God and his country, he says, and would be ungrateful towards his king, if he did not do whatever he could to prevent such disastrous results'.[79] In addition, he needed to repay his debt, contracted during the third civil war, to the Prince of Orange. He needed to take advantage of every opportunity to have the King declare his position explicitly.

But in the royal entourage opposition was strong. Between 19 and 26 June, at the King's request, three of his most influential councillors, Jean de Morvillier, Gaspard de Saulx-Tavannes and Louis de Gonzague, duc de Nevers, composed memoranda outlining their views; all disapproved strongly of war with Spain. Coligny, too, put his arguments in writing, very probably using a young nobleman – Philippe Duplessis-Mornay – whose first appearance on the political stage this was.[80] Debate over their viewpoints occurred during several council meetings between the end of June and 12 July;[81] the outcome was to determine officially France's policy of preserving the peace.

Coligny's desire to ignore this was the occasion of an extraordinary episode related by the Spanish ambassador. On 13 July, Zuñiga informed Philip II that, the day before, the Admiral 'had stayed a long time with the king, keeping his hat on his head. In the middle of the conversation, he removed it and made deep bows, giving to understand that the king had accepted his request.'[82] We should picture the impact of such a mini-drama in a milieu where individuals' smallest movements were spied and commented on. As nobody had heard the words exchanged during this encounter, Coligny resorted to these gestures to project an interpretation of them that was favourable to him. Keeping his hat on was undoubtedly not a show of insolence on his part; where decorum and external respect for the King were concerned, the relaxed attitude of the French court still astonished foreign observers.[83] Not immediately removing his hat was probably a way for the Admiral to make even more spectacular its subsequent removal and his 'great reverences'. Some of those present concluded that the King had authorised him to leave for the Netherlands with the troops he had recruited. It was probably this scene which enabled Walsingham to claim, in his letter of 10 August already cited, that 'although he had not obtained everything that was necessary for the cause, he still obtained part of it'. It was essential for the Admiral to make people *believe* in the King's consent, which was vital for his credibility among those whom he was recruiting. But there is no proof that that assent was really given. In any event, Zuñiga did not believe it had been: 'I believe that as things are in this kingdom, the king will not give it, and if he did so, it would be with the same dissimulation that he has observed hitherto.' Charles IX, he concluded, will not 'remove the mask', and the men of Mons 'will pay the price they have to pay'.

This price the Huguenots were soon to pay. On 17 July reinforcements brought from France by Genlis were routed at Saint-Ghislain, near Quiévrain, by the Duke of Alba's son, Don Fadrique. Genlis was taken prisoner, and papers compromising Charles IX were found on him, notably the letter of 27 April to Nassau.[84] However, the King was ready to deny everything, and as early as 6 June he had ordered his ambassador in Spain, Saint-Gouard, to reply, if anyone mentioned the seized letters, that they were 'impostures and calumnies, as he had never written such letters to the said count on such matters'.[85] So he decided to congratulate the father of the victor, though not without showing his anger at the arrogant manner in which Alba had gloated over it.

According to the Venetian ambassadors, Michiel and Cavalli, Coligny made a final effort in early August – profiting from the absence of Catherine de Medici, who had left to meet her daughter Claude, duchesse de Lorraine, and calculating perhaps on the suppressed rancour of Charles IX towards Spain. He began recruiting openly, with the connivance of François de Montmorency. And the King let him do so. Cavalli reports having witnessed the joy caused by these levies among 'everyone, Catholics and Huguenots'.[86] Rumours of war instantly increased. The French agent to the Duke of Savoy, Pierre Forget de Fresnes, reported disturbing rumours: it was being said in his circle that, indignant at the execution of the prisoners arrested at Saint-Ghislain, Charles IX envisaged selling some of the clergy's property, as he had done in 1563, 1568 and 1569, to finance a war against Philip II. Forget de Fresnes did his best to stop such suspicions from circulating. But he reproached the King, in barely concealed terms, for leaving him without instructions – which says much about the difficulty Charles IX had in keeping to his chosen tactic and overcoming the annoyance that he felt over Spain's success.[87]

Alerted to this, the Queen Mother returned in haste. A full-dress council met on 9 August (prepared no doubt by one on the 8th), about which Zuñiga was informed by Jerome de Gondi. 'The principal men of the long and short robe of the kingdom' were present, wrote the ambassador in a letter of 10 August. Coligny offered to lead 4,000 cavalry and 15,000 infantry for the Netherlands enterprise, but was unsuccessful, since the council clearly reaffirmed France's wish to keep the peace. Zuñiga asked Gondi if the King had authorised the Admiral to help the Prince of Orange, to which Gondi replied in the negative. He assured Philip II that everything suggested that Charles IX would not commit himself publicly, a view that he only slightly modified in his letters of 20 August. If the King were to commit himself, it would be in the following spring; until then he would make war, using England as his proxy, and await its outcome before committing himself – a highly improbable hypothesis.[88]

Despite his failure, Coligny continued to mobilise. He informed William of Orange that he would join him with a force of 12,000 infantry and 3,000 cavalry.[89] Ambassador Petrucci mentions two other armies raised at the Admiral's request – one, commanded by the Marquis de Rethel, would cross Lorraine with 3,000 infantry and 1,000 cavalry; the other, led by Briquemault, would bring 3,500 infantry and 600 cavalry into Picardy.[90] Even if these estimates were inflated, the forces raised by Coligny were considerable. And they were levied at his own initiative, which the King was not really able to control. There was doubtless some truth in the Queen Mother's evasiveness in her response to the Spaniards' irritated questions: she assured them that the soldiers levied in Champagne had been dispersed, but added that the survivors of the Genlis expedition could not be punished, as her son was not 'obeyed in this kingdom as she would like or was actually necessary.'[91]

In reality, the troops thus raised had, at best, only the King's tacit permission. Zuñiga was entitled to believe that, even if Charles IX had given the authorisation, he would have given it in the same spirit of dissimulation – namely, that the Admiral would be disavowed as were Nassau and Genlis, and that the official position would remain as had been determined by the July and August council meetings. Coligny, therefore, did not appear either to the Spaniards or to any other observer, as capable of leading France into an open conflict – which amounts to saying that there was no need to 'kill him in order to kill the war'.

Indeed, a close reading of Zuñiga's letters shows that, on the contrary, Coligny acted as a real brake against open war. We find in them the following argument: if Charles IX has not removed the mask, it is precisely because of the Admiral, since a publicly assumed war would make him a threat to the King's authority, given the numbers of troops that he had recruited. This is what the ambassador wrote to Philip II on 23 August, the day after Maurevert's attack, explaining to him that it would be better for the Admiral to survive. For as long as he lived, Charles IX would be obliged to stick with the convenient solution of duplicity, because the official opening of hostilities would enshrine Coligny's position as a military leader, at the head of a large army which would be difficult to control. 'If', wrote Zuñiga, 'the king and his mother had not yet revealed their position openly, it might be out of fear that the Admiral, along with his heretics, gained more power than the king.'[92] This argument is repeated even more clearly in the ambassador's letter of 31 August, after the Massacre, to Alba:

> [The King and his mother] were not free to do what they wanted, because if they had been, I believe that they would have dropped the mask in order to do what they could against these States [the Netherlands]. Although the Admiral was the one who urged them to go to war, they dared not trust him, as it seemed to them that if war began, he would become the master.[93]

With Coligny dead, Zuñiga continued, an open commitment could now be feared. This argument apparently convinced the Duke of Alba, since he asserted, on 13 October 1572, that it is *now* that we should fear the King of France.[94] This judgement was doubtless not well founded, but it proves that the analysis, according to which Charles IX did not declare himself because that would have made the Admiral too powerful, seemed perfectly plausible.

Coligny's death could thus seem to the Spaniards to be inimical to their current interests; far from preventing a conflict, it threatened, as they saw it, the opposite – eliminating the reticence of the King of France to take the decision. Such a realisation finally renders implausible the idea that Spain viewed the assassination of Coligny as the only way of preventing a war.

Everything, therefore, leads us to believe that on the eve of the marriage of Henri de Navarre and Marguerite de Valois a break with Philip II was simply not on the agenda of the King and his mother; in preparing to celebrate his sister's wedding, Charles IX hoped above all to benefit from the peace in order to strengthen the union that he hoped to see reign among his subjects.

A 'TRIUMPHANT' MARRIAGE

However, clouds obscuring the royal hopes were not lacking. The first major setback was the death of Jeanne d'Albret. She managed to conclude the negotiations which led, on 4 April, to an agreement to marry her son and, on 11 April, to finalising the contract. But, weakened by tuberculosis and exhausted by the difficulties encountered during the negotiations, she died on 9 June, aged forty-three. After her death, there were discussions about conducting the marriage 'in mourning', discreetly and without festivities, out of respect for her, but the political meaning attached to this symbol of concord was too great to renounce celebrating it brilliantly. It would, therefore, be a marriage 'in triumph'.[95]

The persistent refusal of the Pope to grant the dispensation that was needed both for the consanguinity of the future spouses and the differences of religion, was another source of worry. The marriage of Henri de Condé and Mary of Cleves on 10 August at Blandy-en-Brie made it possible to measure the resistance which the absence of a papal dispensation could produce among the most intransigent Catholics. Zuñiga reported that when the marriage contract was signed, Cardinal Bourbon accosted the future husband, his nephew, asking him how he could dare marry in Huguenot fashion and, secondly, without a dispensation, since his fiancée was his first cousin (her mother, Marguerite de Bourbon, was sister of Louis de Bourbon, Henri's father). The Prince replied that he needed no other dispensation than the King's, whereupon the Cardinal turned heel on him. Duc Louis de Montpensier, head of the junior branch of the Bourbons and a fervent Catholic, said 'grave words' to Charles IX before leaving, followed by the ducs de Nevers and Guise; the King attended the wedding, but the leaders of the Catholic faction failed to show.[96] The Parisians worried about the massive exodus of the Huguenots at court to Blandy: what were they going to discuss among themselves there? Petrucci thought they had a secret objective, while hoping that it would not start new troubles.[97]

It was believed for a time, on the basis of an imprudent promise by the French ambassador in Rome, that the dispensation for consanguinity between

Henri de Navarre and Marguerite de Valois would finally be granted, but this did not last long.[98] However, the Pope's refusal was a conditional one, since he made his consent subject to the King of Navarre's conversion, even it was kept secret for the time being; so long as this refusal was not absolute, a narrow margin of manoeuvre remained and it was possible to give the impression that negotiations were continuing.[99] Thus, on 14 August, Catherine de Medici gave orders to stop all couriers from Italy until the 18th, in order to deal with the possibility of the despatch of a categorical refusal, which would destroy the crown's patient efforts.[100] This amounted to presenting Gregory XIII with a fait accompli, in the hope that he would regularise the situation after the event. It was a dangerous gamble: the prelates who consented to attend the wedding would be exposed to excommunication and would be obliged to request a papal dispensation afterwards. Cardinal Bourbon, whom his nephew Henri wanted absolutely to conduct the wedding, was terrified. He locked himself away in his abbey of Saint-Germain-des-Prés, which panicked Charles IX, and it required visits from the Queen Mother, Gaspard de Saulx-Tavannes, Armand de Gontaut-Biron and, finally, the secretary of state Villeroy, for Bourbon to agree *in extremis* to return to the court.[101]

The wedding ceremony itself, on 18 August 1572, reflected these problems. A platform was erected at the doors of Notre-Dame that was sufficiently high for everyone to see what was happening; access was though a gallery leading from the episcopal palace nearby. A magnificent cortege of princes of the blood, marshals of France and the *grands* of the kingdom, conducted the future spouses, whose consent was received by Cardinal Bourbon. An anonymous Protestant account says that Charles IX, his brothers, the King of Navarre and Prince of Condé were all dressed, as a sign of fraternity, in the same pale yellow satin clothes embroidered with silver and adorned with pearls and precious stones, but the bridegroom's Huguenot retinue wore 'ordinary' clothes, in tacit disapproval of the splendour of the Catholic nobles who were covered in 'gold, silver and precious stones'.[102] Henri de Navarre did not attend the mass that followed and retired with his retinue to the episcopal palace. During the ceremony, Marguerite, dressed in a violet velvet dress decorated with fleurs de lys and a heavy royal mantle of the same cloth, was accompanied by her brother, the duc d'Anjou. Among the attendance, the absence of nine of the twenty-two ecclesiastics who were at court and had been invited was noted.[103] The presence of parlementaires is not recorded in the Paris city registers, which should have included such a reference, although that does not necessarily prove that the magistrates did not attend.[104] Doubts remain, too, about the diplomatic corps. The Spanish ambassador stayed away, but claimed that the representatives of Ferrara, Florence and Venice were present, which the testimony of Giovanni Michiel contradicts.[105]

Many observers regarded the wedding with hostility. The author of the Protestant account already cited did not hide his aversion for the 'mixture' of religions which resulted, 'at which many people were as astonished before as after the massacres.'[106] Indignation was even fiercer among most Parisian Catholics, who had bitter memories of the Gastines cross affair, while the virulence of the preachers fanned their resentment against this 'mongrel marriage'.

City tensions had other contributing elements too. That of the Paris parlement's magistrates had serious political consequences. As early as the autumn of 1570, they had clashed several times with royal authority. They did not wish to be reduced to the role of administering justice; having the duty to register edicts, they claimed the right to examine them beforehand to see if they conformed to the kingdom's traditions and, where necessary, to submit remonstrances; this gave them the right to block legislation, which often angered the King, who then had to break them by unilaterally imposing his will. The parlementaires mobilised against the fiscal expedients thought up by Charles IX to cope with his financial penury, especially against the sale of new offices, which devalued the existing ones, or increases in taxation. The religious problem poisoned these conflicts: many magistrates disapproved of the civil tolerance observed since the Peace of Saint-Germain. Their discontent peaked on 16 August 1572, two days before the Navarre wedding, when the parlement was forced to register a fiscal edict which affected the solicitors (*procureurs*).[107]

The worsening of the fiscal burden also provoked irritation among the Paris militia, which had been reorganised in June 1562 and was composed of the capital's heads of families; in case of danger, it was mobilised for active service and complemented the professional soldiers who guarded the city. The militia had a violent hostility towards the Huguenots. It was also exasperated by the multiplication of taxes on the city: in 1571, a 'free gift' of 300,000 *livres* (reduced finally to 250,000) was demanded; in April 1572, the King announced that he still expected 200,000 that year, and 100,000 for 1573.[108] The irritation was all the greater, since, in principle, the money was collected to pay the reiters, but also served, people believed, to finance a war with Spain – that is, to weaken the fight to support the Catholic religion.

The intensity of the summer heat on the date of the royal wedding also contributed towards exciting the people. So did problems with the food supply during August, when the 'gap' between the harvests of 1571 and 1572 looked a difficult one. The price of cereals rose dangerously high: a *setier* of wheat (1.56 hectolitres) rose from 7.50 to 9.33 *livres* between 2 July and 20 August.[109] The run-of-the-mill obsession with their 'daily bread' was thus added to the Parisians' anxiety that the unity of the faith was irreversibly compromised.

One might be surprised by the contrast between these bad omens and the splendour of the festivities accompanying the marriage. Were the latter a sign of blindness and a misreading of the dangers? The King and his mother spared no expense over the luxury of the ceremonies. Observers all noted the magnificence of the balls and banquets, the sumptuousness of the decors and costumes which enriched the allegorical representations, the beauty of the songs and poems which charmed their ears, and the ingenuity of the machines which enchanted the eyes. Everything was designed to transport the imagination: richly adorned chariots carrying sea gods or the gods of Parnassus; the great wheel turning the twelve signs of the zodiac, the seven planets and an infinity of stars; the Elysian garden planted with flowers and inhabited by nymphs; Paradise defended by valiant warriors and separated from hell by a river on which Charon's bark sailed. All of these artifices created a dream-world.

Such prodigality, however surprising in a time of financial crisis, corresponded to a precise objective, which was artistic, political and metaphysical As with all Valois ceremonies, Marguerite's wedding was a carefully crafted work of art, using the combined resources of music, poetry, painting, architecture and dance; they evince the good taste of a court society which advertised its aesthetic enjoyment and its cultural rapport with the artists whom it patronised (members of the royal family and the major courtiers were actors as much as spectators). They were also the expression of a pedagogical intention. The chosen themes illustrated the King's clemency and his desire to see concord triumph: this was particularly apparent in the representation given on 20 August in the hôtel de Bourbon, when the King and his brothers acted as guardians of Paradise and delivered from hell the 'errant cavaliers', both Catholic and Protestant, led by Henri de Navarre. A world of harmony was presented to the participants, in which religious passions and political quarrels were obliterated, where hierarchy and precedence were respected, and where all were united in the same values. The luxury on display had itself a didactic purpose: the King attempted to persuade people that he was rich. According to a commonly held idea, spending without counting the cost was a sign of grandeur and power. Such munificence was meant to impress foreign spectators, rebuild the monarchy's symbolic capital and stimulate feelings of allegiance among the nobility, since it was honourable to serve a lavish master.

Moreover, the marriage celebrations had a magical purpose, which was undoubtedly the most important of all. The entertainment of 20 August was perhaps composed by Jean-Antoine de Baïf and Joachim Thibault de Couville, who, with Charles IX's support, had founded the Academy of poetry and music. They conducted learned research on poetry 'in antique measures', in which the syllables of the verses and the notes of the accompanying music matched each other. The coincidence between poetic and musical rhythms was expected to affect the listener in ways similar, it was believed, to ancient music, especially that of Orpheus. Composers, imbued with the theories of Marsilio Ficino, the great Florentine champion of the Neoplatonic revival, also thought that music 'in ancient form' was capable of harnessing the power of the stars by imitating the harmony believed to emanate from the rotation of the heavenly spheres. The great wheel bearing the planets which turned so spectacularly above the Champs-Elysées on 20 August was not just an entertaining artifice; it evoked the celestial melody to which responded the voice of Étienne Le Roy, the famous castrato who played the role of Mercury; it also symbolised the influx of the stars which needed to be intercepted. The harmony between the 'measured' poetry, music, the geometric figures of the ballets and the circular movement of the stars acted as a vast talisman capable of attracting beneficial influences to France.[110]

The ceremonies of the marriage, therefore, did not mean ignoring contemporary difficulties. On the contrary, they were a means of exorcising, by the magic of art, negative forces. They were the product of a wager on the possibility of making reality submit to the incantatory power of festive practices in which elements of Christian culture and mythology were inextricably mixed.

Faced with the accumulation of dangers, such a gamble could seem fragile. However, it revived the confidence of moderate Catholics and even of many Protestants. In February 1572, the Protestant jurist François Hotman, then in Bourges, labelled the announcement of the royal wedding 'a great joy for good people.'[111] A Huguenot from Troyes, Nicolas Pithou, expressed the satisfaction of his co-religionists after 18 August, because they witnessed 'the accomplishment of the marriage of the king of Navarre and the daughter of France, in the hope of perfect prosperity in the future and the advancement of the reformed churches, as it was (in appearance) proof of the benevolence of the king towards the Protestants.'[112] The marriage rejoicings may have aroused passions, but they also awakened hope.

NOTES

1 See the chapter 'Madrid ou Bruxelles? Deux capitales pour un crime', in Bourgeon's *L'Assassinat de Coligny*, pp. 45–59.

2 Louis Le Roy, *Les Politiques d'Aristote* (Paris, 1568), pp. 60–61.

3 Frances A. Yates, *Astraea. The Imperial theme in the sixteenth century* (London, 1975), pp. 142–143.

4 Simon Bouquet, *Brief et sommaire recueil de ce qui a esté faict et de l'ordre tenuë a la joyeuse et triumphante Entrée de Charles IX de ce nom en sa bonne ville et cité de Paris* (Paris, 1572), fol. 29v.

5 Yates, *Astraea*, pp. 134–135.

6 *Lettres de Catherine de Médicis*, vol. 4, pp. 6–10, Catherine de Medici to La Mothe-Fénelon, 20 Oct. 1570.

7 *Ibid.*, Ferrières to the Duke of Montmorency, Oct. 1570, published as a footnote to his letter to Catherine de Médicis.

8 This euphoria is reflected in the correspondence of Hubert Languet, a French Protestant in the service of the Elector of Saxony: see Béatrice Nicollier, *Hubert Languet, 1518–1581. Un réseau politique international, de Melanchthon à Guillaume d'Orange* (Geneva, 1995), pp. 256–259.

9 The most contradictory rumours circulated about this assassination: see Nicolas
   Le Roux, *La Faveur du roi. Mignons et courtisans au temps des derniers Valois (vers
   1547–vers 1589)* (Seyssel, 2000), pp. 111–114.

10 Éliane Viennot, *Marguerite de Valois. Histoire d'une femme, histoire d'un mythe*
   (Paris, 1993), p. 42.

11 *Lettres de Charles IX à M. de Fourquevaux*, p. 361, letter of 28 Sept. 1571, Blois;
   Lettres de Catherine de Médicis, vol. 4, p. 76, letter of 8 Oct.

12 *Négociations diplomatiques avec la Toscane*, vol. 3, p. 719, Petrucci to Francesco de
   Medici, Paris, 15 Oct. 1571.

13 Nancy Lyman Roelker, *Queen of Navarre. Jeanne d'Albret, 1528–1572* (Cambridge,
   Mass., 1968) p. 102.

14 *Tocsain contre les massacreurs* (1577), in Cimber and Danjou, eds, *Archives curieuses
   de l'histoire de France*, 1st series, vol. 7 (Paris, 1835), p. 43; Bourgeon, *L'Assassinat de
   Coligny*, p. 32.

15 Nicole Lemaitre, *Saint Pie V* (Paris, 1994), p. 283.

16 Vásquez de Prada, *Felipe II y Francia*, pp. 202–203.

17 AGS, Estado, K 1526, no 32, Pedro de Aguilón to Duke of Alba, Blois, 9 April 1572.

18 *Négociations diplomatiques avec la Toscane*, vol. 3, pp. 763–766, Giovanni Battista
   Alamanni to Salviati, Blois, 15 April 1572.

19 *Ibid.*, p. 771, Petrucci to Francesco de Medici, Paris, 22 April 1572.

20 *Lettres du cardinal Charles de Lorraine (1525–1574)*, ed. Daniel Cuisiat (Geneva,
   1998), p. 771, letter of 1 Aug. 1572, Rome.

21 BnF, MS. Fr. 16040, fol. 166r, Ferrals to the King, Rome, 10 Aug. 1572. The historiographical tradition, according to which the Cardinal of Lorraine did everything
   possible behind the scenes to prevent the Pope from granting the dispensation,
   seems to be badly founded.

22 Salviati relates the final hesitations of the Cardinal Bourbon: *Correspondance en
   France du nonce Antonio Maria Salviati (1572–1578)*, ed. Pierre Hurtubise, vol. 1
   (1572–1574) pp. 195–196, letter of 18 Aug. 1572. See *ibid.*, p. 196, note 11, for the list of
   nine members of clergy (of the twenty-two who had been invited) who manifested
   their disapproval by not attending the marriage.

23 *Négociations diplomatiques avec la Toscane*, vol. 3, p. 748, Petrucci to Francesco de
   Medici, Paris, 24 March 1572.

24 Roelker, *Jeanne d'Albret, pp.* 354–383. Marguerite de Valois was to have a dowry of
   300,000 écus, with her mother giving her 200,000 *livres* and each of her brothers
   50,000 *livres*.

25 Sutherland, *Massacre of St. Bartholomew*, pp. 168–169.

26 Text published by Guillaume Groen van Prinsterer, ed., *Archives ou correspondance
   inédite de la maison d'Orange-Nassau*, 1st series, vol. 3, (Leyden, 1836), pp. 282–286.

27 N. M. Sutherland, *The Huguenot Struggle for Recognition* (New Haven and London,
   1980), p. 189.

28 Vásquez de Prada, *Felipe II y Francia*, p. 198; Sutherland, *Massacre of St. Bartholomew*, pp. 145–146 and 168.

29 Francis Walsingham to Lord Burghley, 12 Aug. 1571, in Dudley Digges, *The Compleat
   Ambassador* (London, 1655), quoted by Sutherland, *Massacre of St. Bartholomew*,
   pp. 169–170.

30 Nicollier, *Hubert Languet*, pp. 247–262.

31 *Lettres de Catherine de Médicis*, vol. 4, pp. 62–63.

32 Garrisson, *Les Derniers Valois*, p. 58; *Négociations diplomatiques avec la Toscane*, vol. 3, p. 648, Petrucci to Francesco de Medici, 22 Feb. 1571.

33 Bouquet, *Brief et sommaire recueil*, fol. 6v.

34 Jacques Poujol, 'Étymologies légendaires des mots France et Gaule pendant la Renaissance', *Publications of the Modern Language Association of America*, 72 (1957), pp. 900–914.

35 Martin van Gelderen, *The Political thought of the Dutch Revolt, 1555–1590* (Cambridge, 1992), p. 126.

36 Claude de Mondoucet to the King, 26 Dec. 1571, quoted by Louis Gachard, *La Bibliothèque nationale à Paris. Notices et extraits des manuscrits qui concernent l'histoire de Belgique*, vol. 2 (Brussels, 1877), p. 511.

37 Sutherland, *Massacre of St. Bartholomew*, p. 174.

38 Quoted by Joseph Kervyn de Lettenhove, *Les Huguenots et les Gueux*, vol. 2 (Bruges, 1884), p. 433.

39 *Négociations diplomatiques avec la Toscane*, vol. 3, pp. 669–670, Petrucci to Secretary Concini and Francesco de Medici, both 10 May 1571.

40 Vásquez de Prada, *Felipe II y Francia*, p. 204.

41 BnF, MS. Fr. 16040, fol. 74, Ferrals to the King, 29 April 1572; *ibid.*, fol. 152, same to same, 30 June 1572.

42 P. Champion, *Charles IX*, vol. 2, p. 82, who used the same word 'abattre' to indicate the preventing of war and killing Coligny.

43 Catherine de Medici is accused by Ivan Cloulas (*Catherine de Médicis* (Paris, 1979, p. 283) and Spain by Champion and Bourgeon (*L'Assassinat de Coligny*, p. 47). See the more recent questions raised by Serge Brunet: 'did the alerts by Philip II's agents decide the Spaniards to have Coligny assassinated, cutting short, and rapidly, the drift to war?' in Brunet, *'De l'Espagnol dedans le ventre!' Les catholiques du sud-ouest de la France face à la Réforme, vers 1540–1589* (Paris, 2007, p. 511).

44 BnF, MS. Fr. 15553, fols 250r and 251r, for the transfer of the companies from Saint-Jean-d'Angély and Angoulême; *ibid.*, fol 193r, letter to Duke of Longueville, 14 Sept. 1571; Sutherland, *The Massacre of St. Bartholomew*, p. 223; Bourgeon, *Charles IX devant la Saint-Barthélemy*, pp. 115–116.

45 BnF, MS. Fr. 15554, fol. 160r, M. de Coudres to the King, Grenoble, 5 June 1572, and *ibid.*, fol. 174r, Count of Tende to the King, Marseille, 6 June 1572.

46 BnF, MS. Fr. 15554, fol. 176r, Joyeuse to the King, Loudun, 9 June 1572.

47 BnF, MS. Fr. 16040, fol. 152r, Ferrals to the King, 30 June 1572; *ibid.*, fol. 179r, same to same, 18 Aug. 1572. Fernand Braudel, *The Mediterranean and the Mediterranean world in the age of Philip II*, 2 vols (English trans., London 1973), vol. 2, pp. 1116–1117, showed that Bizerta was not just a pretext , since Philip II wished to secure his fortresses in North Africa.

48 BnF, MS. Fr. 15554, fol. 58r, Rieux to the King, Narbonne, 13 April 1572.

49 Zuñiga to Philip II, 27 June 1572, quoted by Vásquez de Prada, *Felipe II y Francia*, p. 210.

50 Brantôme, *Œuvres complètes*, vol. 4, pp. 297–298.

51 *Négociations diplomatiques avec la Toscane*, vol. 3, p. 772, Petrucci to Francesco de Medici, 2 May 1571, Paris.

52 *CSPF*, vol. 4, p. 130, Morgan to Burghley, 16 June 1572, Flushing, quoted by Sutherland, *Massacre of St. Bartholomew*, p. 245. But a letter from Strozzi to the King of 25 July shows that he was at Bordeaux. He says that he has finally received the order

to be ready to sail, but did not yet know what his destination would be. Another letter, dated 29 August and written from Brouage, indicates that he should have left on 24th (he does not say where to), but that bad weather had prevented him. He claimed to be short of supplies and demanded reinforcements. His forces were finally employed against La Rochelle (see his letters in Henri-Léonard Bordier, *La Saint-Barthélemy et la critique moderne*, Geneva, 1879, pp. 87–89).

53 De Bèze, *Correspondance*, vol. 13 [1572], pp. 135–138, letter to Bullinger, Geneva, 17 June 1572.

54 BnF, MS. Fr. 16040, fol. 152r, Ferrals to the King, 30 June 1572.

55 Letter published by Emmanuel de Noailles, *Henri de Valois et la Pologne en 1572* (Paris, 1867), vol. 1, p. 9.

56 Brunet, 'De l'Espagnol dedans le ventre', pp. 495–506.

57 BnF, MS. Fr. 16040, fol. 155r, Ferrals to the King, 29 July 1572.

58 AGS, Estado, K1529, letter of 17 July 1572, quoted by Champion, *Charles IX et l'Espagne*, vol. 2, p. 48.

59 BnF, MS. Fr. 16040, fol. 16r, Ferrals to the King, 15 Jan. 1572.

60 The royal secretary Zayas in a letter of 16 March 1572 regretted that Philip II could not, for reasons of reputation, be on good terms with England (AGS, Estado, K1529, quoted by Braudel, *Mediterranean*, vol. 2, p. 1107).

61 Quoted by Vásquez de Prada, *Felipe II y Francia*, p. 212, n. 74. The Duke of Savoy, who closely observed the situation, believed that Philip II would go to war only if Charles IX did so first (BPU, Geneva, MS. Fr. 90, fol. 156v, letter of the French agent Pierre Forget de Fresnes, 20 July 1572).

62 Ferrals relayed these reproaches from Rome (BnF, MS. Fr. 16040, fol. 154r, letter of 30 June 1572).

63 BnF, MS. Fr. 16040, fol. 142r, Ferrals to the King, 20 June 1572.

64 Sutherland, *Massacre of St. Bartholomew*, p. 268; *CSPF, reign of Elizabeth, 1572–1578*, London, Longman, 1876, no. 532, p. 169, Ralph Lane to the burgermeister of Neuport, 18 Aug. 1572.

65 Bernard Vogler, 'Huguenots et protestants allemands vers 1572', in *L'Amiral de Coligny et son temps*, pp. 182–183.

66 This is the meaning of the questions raised by Zuñiga in a letter of 4 June 1572 to Alba, whether Philip II should be asked to pretend that he believes the denials of Charles IX and to dissimulate 'until such time as he can no longer do so for the good of his reputation' (AGS, Estado, K1529, no. 75).

67 AGS, Estado, K1529, Duke of Alba to Zuñiga, 24 June 1572, quoted by Vásquez de Prada, *Felipe II y Francia*, p. 209.

68 ASG, Estado, K1530, no. 5, Philip II to Zuñiga, 2 Aug. 1572, partially quoted in Vásquez de Prada, *Felipe II y Francia*, p. 209.

69 Bourgeon's analyses of this point are penetrating, even though he did not grasp the full meaning of the game of masks between Charles IX and Philip II ('Pour une histoire, enfin, de la Saint-Barthélemy', p. 123).

70 Sutherland, *Massacre of St. Bartholomew*, p. 229–236.

71 BnF, MS. Fr. 16104, fol. 46r, letter to provincial governors, 4 May 1572.

72 AGS, Estado, K1529, no. 68, Zuñiga to Alba, 31 May 1572, quoted by Vásquez de Prada, *Felipe II y Francia*, p. 206.

73 BnF, MS. Fr. 3318, fol. 23v, King to Vulcob, 16 June 1572, quoted by Jules Delaborde, *Gaspard de Coligny, amiral de France* (Paris, 1882), vol. 3, p. 388.

74 BnF, MS. Fr. 15554, fol. 158r, Longueville to the King, 5 June 1572, Amiens.

75 *Négociations diplomatiques avec la Toscane*, vol. 3, p. 771, Petrucci to Francesco de Medici, Paris, 22 April 1572.

76 *Correspondance diplomatique de Bertrand de Salignac de La Mothe Fénelon*, vol. 5, p. 471, letter to the King, 24 May 1572, London.

77 AGS, Estado, K1529, no. 105, Zuñiga to Alba, 29 June 1572.

78 Coligny to Burghley, 27 May 1572, published by Hector de La Ferrière, *Le XVI* siècle et les Valois d'après les documents inédits du British Museum et du Record Office* (Paris, 1879), pp. 314–315; Crouzet, *La Nuit de la Saint-Barthélemy*, p. 347.

79 *Mémoires et instructions pour les ambassadeurs, ou lettres et négociations de Walsingham, ministre et secrétaire d'État sous Élisabeth, reine d'Angleterre, traduit de l'anglois* (Amsterdam, 1700), p. 275, Walsingham to Burghley 10 Aug. 1572, Paris.

80 Hugues Daussy, *Les Huguenots et le roi. Le combat politique de Philippe Duplessis-Mornay* (Geneva, 2002), pp. 64–80.

81 On the dating of these meetings, see *ibid.*, p. 72; Zuñiga mentions a council debate on breaking relations with Spain as early as 26 June (letter of 27 June quoted by Vásquez de Prada, *Felipe II y Francia*, p. 210).

82 AGS, Estado, K1529, no. 124, Zuñiga to Alba, 13 July 1572.

83 Marc Smith, 'Familiarité française et politesse italienne au xvi° siècle. Les diplomates italiens juges des manières de la cour des Valois', *RHD*, 102 (1988), pp. 193–232, at p. 202, for example, 'in 1572, a Roman cleric was shocked, among other things, at seeing the King's eschanson make only a simple bow and keeping his hat on when serving him'.

84 Kervyn de Lettenhove, *Les Huguenots et les Gueux*, p. 498.

85 Gachard, *La Bibliothèque nationale à Paris*, vol. 2, pp. 373–374.

86 *La Saint-Barthélemy devant le Sénat de Venise*, p. 9 (Michiel's report) and p. 80 (Cavalli's report).

87 BPU, Geneva, MS. Fr. 90, Pierre Forget de Fresnes to the King, 9 Aug. 1572, f. 158v.

88 AGS, Estado, K1530, no. 13, Zuñiga to Philip II, 10 Aug. 1572, and no. 19, résumé of letters from Zuñiga to the King, 20 Aug. 1572. On the date of the council meetings, for which other sources give 9 and 10 Aug., see Vásquez de Prada, *Felipe II y Francia*, p. 215, n. 89.

89 As William of Orange wrote to his brother, John, on 11 Aug., in a letter published by Groen van Prinsterer, *Archives ou correspondance inédite de la maison d'Orange-Nassau*, pp. 490–491).

90 *Négociations diplomatiques avec la Toscane*, vol. 3, p. 798, letter of 15 July 1572; Sutherland, *Massacre of St. Bartholomew*, pp. 261–262.

91 This was her reply to Gomicourt, envoy of Alba, who complained of troop recruitment: Gomicourt to secretary Zayas, Paris, 18 Aug. 1572, AGS, Estado, K1529, no. 17, quoted by Vásquez de Prada, *Felipe II y Francia*, p. 215. Zuñiga is ironic about this kind of evasion in his letters of 20 Aug. already quoted.

92 AGS, Estado, K1530, no. 20, Zuñiga to Philip II, 23 Aug. 1572 (a copy wrongly dated 22 Aug.: the ambassador talks about the attack which occurred 'yesterday' and the guards stationed 'this night' around the Admiral).

93 *Ibid.*, no. 29, Zuñiga to Alba, 31 Aug. 1572. Here Zuñiga hypothesises that, with Coligny dead, Charles IX will seek to reconnect with Orange and Nassau – but without success, he predicts, since they will distrust him.

94 *Correspondance de Philippe II sur les affaires des Pays-Bas*, vol. 2, pp. 286–287, Alba to the King, 13 Oct. 1572, Tongues.

95 Hector de La Ferrière, *La Saint-Barthélemy, la veille, le jour, le lendemain* (Paris, 1892), p. 61.

96 AGS, Estado, K1530, no. 13, Zuñiga to Philip II, 10 Aug. 1572. Pierre Champion wrongly attributes the scene to Henri de Navarre: *Charles IX*, vol. 2, p. 72.

97 *Négociations diplomatiques avec la Toscane*, vol. 3, pp. 802–803, letter to Francesco de Medici, Paris, 9–13 Aug. 1572.

98 BnF, MS. Fr. 16040, fol. 166r, Ferrals to the King, 10 Aug. 1570.

99 *Ibid.*, fols 159r and 189r: the Pope's first four conditions were reduced to three (that Henri de Navarre confess the Catholic faith to the papal nuncio, that he himself request the dispensation for consanguinity, and restore their titles and benefices to the clergy of Navarre and Béarn).

100 *Lettres de Catherine de Médicis*, vol. 4, pp. 109–110, letter to M. de Mandelot, 14 Aug. 1572.

101 *Correspondance en France du nonce Antonio Maria Salviati*, pp. 195–196, letter of 18 Aug. 1572.

102 *Mémoires de Luc Geizkofler*, pp. 52–54; *Relation du massacre de la Saint-Barthélemy*, pp. 78–79. Marguerite de Valois, in her *Mémoires* written much later, indicates that the King of Navarre's entourage had, like him, 'left mourning aside and changed into very rich and beautiful clothes'. A case of the embellishment of memory? (Marguerite de Valois, *Mémoires et autres écrits*, éd. Éliane Viennot (Paris, 1999), p. 90).

103 The list is provided by Pierre Hurtubise in *Correspondance en France du nonce Antonio Maria Salviati (1572–1578)*, vol. 1, p. 196, n. 11.

104 Barbara Diefendorf, 'La Saint-Barthélemy et la bourgeoisie parisienne', *Histoire, Économie et Société*, 17 (1998), p. 345.

105 AGS, Estado, K1530, no. 13, résumé of letters of Zuñiga to Philip II, 20 Aug. 1572; report from Giovanni Michiel, 22 Aug., published in *Atti del regio istituto veneto di scienze, lettere ed arti*, 3rd series, 15 (1869–1870), quoted by Champion, *Charles IX*, vol. 2, p. 75, n. 1.

106 *Relation du massacre de la Saint-Barthélemy*, p. 80.

107 Bourgeon, 'La Fronde parlementaire à la veille de la Saint-Barthélemy'.

108 Robert Descimon, 'Paris on the eve of Saint Bartholomew: taxation, privilege and social geography', in Philip Benedict, ed., *Cities and social change in early modern France* (London, 1989), p. 78. A small proportion (50,000 *livres*) of the gift imposed in 1571 was collected in the form of a forced sale of *rentes sur l'Hôtel de Ville*, and the sums demanded for 1572 were reduced to 150,000 *livres*, also payable by the sale of *rentes*.

109 Michèle Baulant and Jean Meuvret, *Prix des céréales extraits de la mercuriale de Paris (1520–1698)* (Paris, 1960), vol. 1, p. 190; Garrisson, *La Saint-Barthélemy*, pp. 60–61.

110 The exorcising value of the Valois entertainments has been magisterially studied by Frances A. Yates, *The French academies of the sixteenth century* (London, 1947), pp. 236–274.

111 Letter to Heinrich Bullinger, Feb. 1572, published by Rodolphe Dareste, 'François Hotman. Sa vie et sa correspondance', *RH*, 2 (1876), p. 54.

112 Nicolas Pithou de Champgobert, *Chronique de Troyes et de la Champagne (1524–1594)*, ed. Pierre-Eugène Leroy, 3 vols (Reims, 1998–2000), vol. 2, p. 689.

3

THE ASSAULT ON PEACE

It was on the morning of 22 August 1572 that the obstacle that would shatter the dream of a durable peace appeared. Coligny was caught in a trap and wounded by a musket-shot on his way home. Contemporaries and historians ever since have been troubled by the proximity of this attack and the massacre which followed two days later. The Saint Bartholomew's massacres project their shadow onto the earlier event. It is hard to believe that the assassination of the Admiral, early on 24 August, was not the completion of the attack of two days earlier, and that the same responsibility cannot be identified in each of them. Yet the correlation between the two events is far from clear. In seeking to understand what happened, it is necessary to isolate the attack on Coligny and try to disentangle the relevant factors by provisionally ignoring the tragedy that followed, in order to set aside preconceived ideas which develop retrospectively out of knowledge of the subsequent events.

THE AMBUSH

The different accounts of the trap set for Coligny derive from sources that were not eyewitnesses, with the exception of Jacques Pape, seigneur de Saint-Auban, who was close to the victim when the shot was fired. But in his *Memoirs* written much later, this faithful companion remembered primarily the frantic but unsuccessful chase which he and René de Valsergues, seigneur de Séré, gave to the killer.[1] Fuller information is provided by the despatches of the diplomats then in Paris, such as nuncio Salviati, ambassadors Petrucci, Michiel and Zuñiga, the Florentine doctor Cavriana or the Spanish secretary Juan de Olaegui. A few useful indications can also be gleaned from the memoirs of individuals present in Paris when the crime was committed, such as the *Sommaire Mémorial* of the royal secretary, Jacques Gassot, the *Mémoires* of Jehan de la Fosse, parish priest of Saint Bartholomew's, or of the Tyrolese Luc Geizkofler, despite their accounts being written long after the events they describe. There is also value in the *Vie de messire Gaspar de Coligny*, whose author – probably François Hotman – claimed that his information came from a friend who held the arm of the wounded Admiral while Ambroise Paré operated on it.[2]

From the information provided by these sources a number of clear facts emerge, despite the inevitable divergences of detail. On the morning of 22 August, the Admiral left the Louvre after a council meeting presided over, in the King's absence, by Henri d'Anjou. He was on foot, reading a letter and escorted by twelve to fifteen nobles. It was around eleven o'clock when, having passed the Bourbon gate (between the hôtel de Bourbon and the duc d'Anjou's residence), he skirted a house on the rue des Poulies (now rue de l'Amiral-Coligny) which was part of the enclosure of the canons of Saint-Germain-l'Auxerrois.[3] The assassin was hiding here, positioned in a window and hidden from view by clothes drying on the washing-line.[4] A shot rang out. For a reason not well elucidated, Coligny made a sudden movement (according to Cavriana, it was to adjust one of his slippers; according to Jehan de la Fosse, to spit). So, instead of hitting him right in the chest, the shot severed a finger of his right hand and went through his left arm.[5]

The Admiral pointed to the window from where the shot had been fired. Men of his escort rushed inside, but the assailant fled by a door at the rear of the house, leaving behind his still-smoking musket. His escape was well prepared; a horse was waiting for him, and he galloped to the Saint-Antoine gate, where he changed horse – to a Turkish horse, Zuñiga notes – and made off.[6] Saint-Auban and Séré followed in hot pursuit, arresting an accomplice at Charenton who had prepared a relay horse for him. But they failed to capture the assailant, who took refuge in the fortified house of the sieur de Chailly, near Corbeil, whose raised drawbridge and flanks bristling with muskets dissuaded the pursuers.[7]

Who fired the shot? His identity remained mysterious for a while. According to Zuñiga, public rumour suggested he was either an archer in the King's guard or, according to Cavriana, a soldier of the Queen Mother's guard. However, suspicion quickly turned to Charles de Louviers, seigneur de Maurevert: the accomplice arrested was a servant of his uncle, Georges Postel, while Maurevert himself later boasted of having done the job. Maurevert was from a Hurepoix family of recent noble status. Relatively wealthy, he owned lordships and lands located within a triangle embracing Melun, Fontainebleau and Provins. His personal itinerary before the shooting of Coligny was that of an adventurer choosing his camp in terms of his immediate interests rather than confessional preferences. Initially a household page of duc François de Guise, he entered the service of the duc d'Aumale; then, after a murder incident which forced him to flee the kingdom, he enrolled among the troops of the Prince of Condé. A subsequent crime led him to change sides again. On 7 October 1569, during the third civil war, he shot Artus de Vaudray, sieur de Mouy, one of Coligny's lieutenants. According to historiographical tradition, his real target that day was the Admiral; having failed to execute him, he settled for someone close to him. It seems as if this was a premeditated crime and part of a private vendetta.

Mouy belonged to a group of nobles associated with a powerful Champagne family called Raguier, to whom Maurevert was connected by family ties. The Raguier family was wracked by religious divisions as well as by violent internal feuds.[8] Coligny apparently swore to avenge his lieutenant; Mouy's assassin was thus pushed into the Anjou and Guise camp.

Was Maurevert, on 22 August, attempting to prevent eventual reprisals against him by eliminating the Admiral, whose position in the council made him dangerous? The hypothesis is worth considering. It was defended by Pomponne de Bellièvre, who was entrusted after the massacre with exonerating the King before the Diet of Bâle, and who portrayed the killer as follows:

> He is a gentleman of substance, so it cannot be believed that he engaged in this enterprise in the hope of gain. He is known as a person of fierce resolution, direct and daring in action. It was he who killed the late sieur de Mouy in the presence of his soldiers. Since the recent peace, this gentleman was strangely persecuted in both his private life and his honour by the late Admiral ... via lawsuits that he concocted for him ... For a person of his resolution to be reduced to despair, there was no need of any advice from my lord of Guise or anyone else to convince him to undertake such vengeance, having already given sufficient proof by the audacious deed against the sieur de Mouy of what was in his belly.[9]

The consequences of the murder of Coligny's lieutenant finally caught up with Maurevert, who was mortally wounded, on 14 April 1583, by Mouy's son, who also died that day. In his *Journal* Pierre de l'Estoile penned a kind of funeral oration for him: 'Maurevert died the following night, regretted by none, hated by all; even the princes who, while he lived, had protected and looked after him, were happy to see such an assassin out of this world, since his death delivered them from both the fear and burden that he was for them.'[10]

Yet the logistics provided for the ambush of Coligny make an isolated act unlikely, and indicate that it was not a simple private matter. A servant girl and a lackey were arrested in the house from which the shot was fired, thanks to which it was discovered that it had been rented by canon Pierre de Piles de Villemur (then absent), formerly preceptor of Henri de Guise and household official of one of the Guise's followers, Cardinal Pellevé (then in Rome with Cardinal Lorraine). It was also discovered that the man who introduced Maurevert was François de Villiers, seigneur de Chailly, *maître d'hôtel* to Charles IX and superintendent of the affairs of the duc de Guise. It was in Chailly's house that the murderer took refuge, according to Saint-Auban. Villemur and Chailly were related – either half-brothers or brothers-in-law – and connected to the Raguiers; they also belonged to the Guise clientele.[11] A whole raft of presumptions seemed to point to the Guises as having commissioned the attack.

The Admiral was taken to his residence on the rue de Béthisy (replaced today by part of the rue de Rivoli). The famous surgeon, Ambroise Paré, came to treat his wounds; for a time it was thought necessary to amputate his left arm, but Coligny vehemently rejected this solution. The King was playing tennis with Henri de Guise when he heard of the attack and, according to Zuñiga and Michiel, turned white at the news; according to Pomponne de Bellièvre, he hurled his racket away in anger.[12] 'At that moment', writes Zuñiga, 'the captain of the guard arrived who, unusually, had kept the guard on duty; everyone was ordered out of the palace; the duc de Guise accompanied the King, escorted by the guards, to his room.' Security measures were taken; all but two of the city gates were closed and the prévôt des marchands and city councillors had them guarded by soldiers from the bourgeois militia. They launched an appeal for calm and ordered the shops which had been spontaneously closed on the announcement of the news to be reopened.[13]

The King of Navarre and Prince of Condé came to demand justice of Charles IX, who assured them that the crime would be punished and established an inquiry headed by the president, Christophe de Thou. In the afternoon, the King, then his mother, brothers and leading courtiers, visited the Admiral's bedside; he proposed to transfer him to the Louvre because he remonstrated with him that – according to François Hotman's account – 'it was to be feared that the people, who were already fully excited, might engage in sedition, or that in a city as enraged and turbulent as Paris, some kind of tumult would arise'.[14] Coligny declined, doubtless on the advice of the doctors, who judged it imprudent to move him. According to Cavriana, whose evidence is corroborated by Hotman's, he tried to persuade the King one final time to commit himself openly in the Netherlands, which he believed was the only way to avoid another civil war. But Charles IX remained silent on this point.[15]

The danger referred to in these accounts was real: in a city excited by the preaching of its parish priests and in high dudgeon against the Huguenots, the Admiral's situation was precarious. One might be surprised at his imprudence and the risks he took that morning by walking through the narrow streets of Paris with such a small escort. He should have known, when agreeing to return to the city on 6 June, that his life would necessarily be in danger there; when he did first return to court, on 12 September 1571, the peril was less acute, because the court was then at Blois and not in a major city full of hostile Catholics. Blaise de Monluc expressed his surprise and judged it a mistake for the Admiral to have 'imprisoned' himself in Paris. 'I am surprised that such a circumspect, wise man of the world made such a grave mistake; he paid a heavy price, as it cost him his life and that of many others.'[16] The Florentine ambassador, Sigismondo Cavalli, was of the same opinion: 'The Admiral, who passed for an old fox, showed himself a great idiot by letting himself be caught in the trap; but I know for certain that he believed that he had sufficiently won over the king to have nothing to fear.'[17]

Should we believe the reality of the warnings given in vain, according to several sources, to Coligny? Pierre de l'Estoile recounts the charming anecdote of a peasant-woman from Châtillon who threw herself at his feet as he was getting ready to mount his horse, begging him not to go to Paris, since he would die with those who accompanied him.[18] Jacques-Auguste de Thou writes that numerous warnings were passed on to Coligny to dissuade him from going to court, where the King, he was told, was preparing to ensnare him; but the Admiral replied to these sinister predictions with the unshakable faith that he had in Charles IX.[19] Protestant sources also mention these admonitions, which served to establish their thesis of the King's premeditation.

But it is difficult to know if these warnings were actually made. The accounts of the assassination of other major figures – the duc de Guise in 1588 or Henri IV in 1610 – also mention urgent warnings ignored by the victims. They correspond to a need to dramatise the narrative, in order to transform the violent death of extraordinary individuals into a tragic destiny and, in doing so, to increase the sense of reverential horror that it generates. This is the role that the warnings play in the accounts of the Admiral's death, especially in Protestant historiography. Hotman wrote in his *Vie de messire Gaspar de Coligny*: 'such was his confidence in the faith and goodwill of the king, which was constantly confirmed to him by his son-in-law Téligny, that from being so clairvoyant in everything, he was, through some destiny that I know not, blind in this one'.[20] The manner in which he is portrayed as disdaining the premonitions of his entourage makes him a sympathetic victim, his innocent confidence confronting the machinations of darkness. 'In these circumstances', Hotman adds, 'the Admiral, fearless and true to himself, and whose behaviour showed the same constancy and assurance in the king's goodness, could have no grounds for alarm.' However, in his *Mémoires* composed later, his fellow Protestant La Huguerye attributed to him an obscure premonition of what awaited him and his desire to give his life for the cause that he defended. 'He resolved to await what God would send him, assured that his blood, if it came to that, would serve his party more than his arms.'[21] He thus deliberately made the choice of martyrdom.

Hagiographical intent is pervasive here. But it is perfectly correct in evoking Coligny's 'faith' in the King. As Charles IX's guest, he knew that accusing him was to insult the sovereign; he could hope that respecting the laws of hospitality and the King's authority would suffice to protect him. But the King, apparently, was less sure of his capacity to control the crowd; he promised to have Coligny's residence protected by a guard of musketeers and ordered the quartermaster to house the principal Protestant nobles as close as possible to the Admiral.[22] He then despatched letters patent to the provincial governors announcing the attack, declaring his desire to punish its author and solemnly reaffirming his wish to impose the edict of pacification.[23] With these measures, 22 August 1572, a day full of dangers, ended.

THE ATTACK AND ITS UNIDENTIFIABLE INSTIGATOR

The brutality of the attack plunged observers into a state of perplexity. Their pens produced a host of hypotheses as to who had instigated the crime. The Admiral and his friends accused the Guises, an opinion which, according to Ambassador Giovanni Michiel, was shared by 'everybody'. In a letter to Ambassador La Mothe-Fénelon in England, Charles IX attributed it 'to the hostility between the house of Coligny and Guise', and added angrily that he would make sure that his subjects were not drawn into that private quarrel.[24] For his part, Zuñiga believed that Coligny was fired at on royal orders, but that it was the Queen Mother, whose face showed no emotion when she heard the news, who had planned it.[25] As for the duc de Guise, he saw in it one of the Duke of Alba's 'mines'.[26] The prudent Petrucci confined himself to reporting the different rumours: some said it was done under orders from the duc de Guise; others that it came from the royal palace, but without the King's knowledge; others again that the guilty party was Cardinal Lorraine, along with the Duke of Savoy, assisted by the comte de Retz and Spanish agents, but that the ducs de Guise and Aumale were not informed.[27] Petrucci also mentioned the possible role of Mme de Nemours, widow of François de Guise, to whom the house from where the shot was fired had been assigned and who had left it empty, thus enabling the assassin to move into it; her almoner, according to a source close to the duc d'Alençon, had knowingly brought the assassin into the building. Petrucci further mentions the possible involvement of Mme de Dampierre, mother-in-law of Retz, who may have acted on behalf of the court of Savoy. The Duke of Savoy, Emmanuel Philibert, husband of Charles IX's aunt, Marguerite de France, and a fervent Catholic, did not like Coligny, the Florentine ambassador wrote, especially since the remarriage of the Admiral to Jacqueline d'Entremont (the duke was in dispute with her over property she owned in Savoy and imprisoned her after her husband's death).[28] Cavriana echoed another supposition: 'the wisest heads', he insisted, saw the hand of Henri d'Anjou in the attack.[29] The Florentine Tomasso Sassetti, also pointed to Anjou, along with the King, the Queen Mother and Louis de Gonzague, duc de Nevers.[30]

The sheer number of names proposed without real proof is enough to show the uncertainty of the observers. The suddenness and audacity of the ambush opened the floodgates of suspicion and rumour; the events that followed, because of the violence of the emotions that they released and the scale of the stakes involved, would further obfuscate the facts by encouraging fantasy and dissimulation. Faced with such difficulties, the historian's only weapon in handling such elusive sources is the criterion of plausibility.

A superficial analysis could make the Guises responsible for the attack. Everything seems to point to them: the house from which the shot was fired and the fact that Maurevert, Villemur and Chailly were clients of theirs. Their motive also seems perfectly clear: to avenge duc François, whose assassination by Poltrot de Méré in 1563 they attributed to Coligny's machinations. But even the convergence of these clues is suspect; their very accumulation could have been prepared in advance to enrage the Huguenots against the Guises and thereby shatter the peace. As a recent biographer of Charles IX put it, 'the house of Villemur makes the Guises innocent rather than guilty'. Of course, the argument is two-sided: 'we could expect, on the contrary, that if there was a vendetta, the crime should be "signed" and leave no doubt as to its instigators'.[31] However, to exact vengeance at this particular moment would have been very risky for the Guises. This is a strongly common-sense view advanced by Ambassador Giovanni Michiel:

> It is claimed that as far as the shooting imputed to M. de Guise is concerned, he knew nothing about it, because as I have said, he would not have had the nerve to behave so audaciously towards the king, since the insult would have been directed at the latter; and even though the king would have pretended at first not to treat it as such, he would have remembered it later, to the considerable harm of Guise and his house, by excluding him from his service and favour.[32]

It should be remembered that when the Peace of Saint-Germain was signed, the Guises were in disgrace, and that their return to limited favour at court, in early 1572, was recent and fragile.[33] It would have been highly dangerous for them to jeopardise this situation by an action that would indubitably affront the King and which he, so concerned with royal 'majesty', could not have easily forgotten. On this point, the words attributed by Hotman to Charles IX seem true: the King allegedly said to Coligny that 'he had indeed been wounded, but his Majesty had been insulted'.[34] The suspicions about Cardinal Lorraine, then in Rome, are explicable in terms of the black legend attached to his name which, after the massacres of 24 August, gave rise to the macabre rumour recounted by Petrucci: 'I am informed by a good source that M. de Guise sent one of his equerries to Cardinal Lorraine with the head and hands of the Admiral.'[35] The head, which the bourgeois of Strasbourg describes as 'horribly shattered' by the defenestration of Coligny's body on the morning of 24 August – and in a condition which the summer heat cannot have improved – was in fact cut up and removed after the murder. Thinking that it might be sent to Rome, Charles IX ordered Mandelot, the governor of Lyon, to intercept it; he replied on 5 September that an equerry of Henri de Guise had passed through the city but, as the royal order had not yet reached him, he had not stopped him.[36] Forget de Fresnes, the French agent at the court of Savoy, mentions that 'someone called Cremonoys, a servant of certain courtiers, was heading for Rome', using four post-horses and keeping an unusually close eye on two large trunks, one of which might contain the head in question, but unfortunately he had been allowed to proceed without a search.[37] Another source suggests that the recipient of the gruesome package was the Duke of Alba in the Netherlands[38] ... It is surely risky to suppose that the presumed recipient of the hypothetical despatch of such a trophy was the instigator of the attack of 22 August.[39] As for Cardinal Lorraine, it is hardly likely that he would have wished to jeopardise the consolidation of his family's position at court, and his own wish to return to politics is clear from his letters and the evidence given by Cardinal Bourbon, as recorded by Pedro de Aguilón and already noted.[40] Whatever animosity Henri de Guise felt towards Coligny, he would surely not have wished to undo so perfidiously the public reconciliation to which, on the King's entreaty, he had recently agreed.

*   *   *

There is one weighty objection to this train of argument. The risks run by the Guises would have been completely removed if the instigation for the assault had come from higher authority. This argument is still used by historians who continue to see in the vendetta the immediate motive of the attack.[41] It raises the question of the Queen Mother's – and even the King's – responsibility.

Catherine de Medici has been accused of many things. She had been in the political frontline since Henri II's death in 1559; her eldest son, François, who was fifteen years old at his accession, ruled for just over a year, while Charles IX was only ten when he succeeded his brother. In 1572, the King, now an adult, was attempting to shake off her maternal guardianship. However, the ambassadors were not mistaken in seeing her as the predominant influence. Those Catholic observers who believed in a premeditated strike naturally believed that she was the only one capable of it. Here is the admiring portrait of her penned by the Venetian ambassador, Giovanni Michiel:

> With each passing day she increasingly shows that as far as liberty of mind and judgement are concerned, she is one of the most clever – if not the cleverest woman in living memory. She has such a perfect grasp of the politics, not just of France, but of all other kingdoms and rulers, as to need nobody to counsel her. She has so well manoeuvred during the disturbances of the civil wars, using the discord and hatreds between these two powerful houses across the realm – those of Guise and Bourbon (the latter related to Montmorency) – that she always retained the highest authority.[42]

It is not surprising that the Venetian, fascinated by the manipulative talents that he saw in Catherine de Medici, wrote to the Doge: 'Let your Serenity understand that this entire affair was, from start to finish, her doing – conceived, hatched and conducted by her, with as sole participant, her son duc Henri d'Anjou.'[43] Her presumed motive was hatred of the Huguenots, for whom she wished the same fate as Coligny.

Elegant as it may be, this reconstruction is implausible. It contradicts everything that we know about her role in the search for concord and peace, of which the marriage of her daughter with the King of Navarre was to be the culmination. Attacking Coligny would have been a denial of the aim of reconciliation of the King's subjects pursued since the Peace of Saint-Germain; it would have destroyed the policy pursued up to then.[44] On the eve of the ambush, Catherine de Medici was thinking only of the negotiations for the marriage of her son, François d'Alençon, to the Queen of England; she wrote on that day to Elizabeth to propose a rendezvous in the English Channel, half way between their two realms, 'on a fine day, between Boulogne, Calais and Dover'.[45] The serenity with which she evokes the interview reveals a pacific intent that corresponds to her persistent wish to harmonise and marry the opposed forces, rather than to thoughts of blood-letting. On the next day, 22 August, she was especially concerned about her own property, writing a letter to the Grand Duke of Tuscany about her rights to the Medici inheritance.[46]

Another motive has often been adduced to support the postulate of the Queen Mother's implication in the attack on Coligny – her jealousy towards him because he seemed to dominate the King. Maternal jealousy, it has been noted, is a historical fact in its own right, and concerns the historian's domain as much as the 'pride of Louis XIV or the ambition of Bonaparte'.[47] True enough, but we should be careful not to overestimate the role of Coligny in the King's decisions. The observers whose reports fed the 'jealousy thesis' (nuncio Salviati and ambassador Zuñiga) were taken in by the signs of favour which Charles IX heaped on Coligny, but which, in a court where signs had so much importance, were no more than the exterior show necessary to reassure the Protestants and attain the goal of concord. At certain moments, Catherine de Medici did become worried, but after the council meeting of 9 August and its clear decision to reject the interventionist policy proposed by Coligny for the Netherlands, it was plain that the King would not enter the war that his mother feared so much. The 'jealousy' of Catherine de Medici had no raison d'être at this moment; as Zuñiga himself wrote, she confided to Jerome de Gondi at the end of the council as to being reassured on that point.[48] If we stick with the documents and the known actions, there is no evidence for the theory of the Queen Mother's supposed culpability.

Was it, therefore, the King who authorised the ambush on 22 August? The same argument of implausibility undermines this hypothesis. The constancy of Charles IX's desire for concord since 1570 is no more in doubt than his mother's. We have noted his efforts to punish infractions against the edict of pacification and to have the Protestants' rights respected; as his principal aim was to reinforce his authority, he knew that the pacification of attitudes was a necessary precondition, and that the reconciliation of his subjects 'as good brothers and fellow-citizens' was indispensable to the restoration of the kingdom.[49] True, he harboured a latent distrust towards the Huguenots, which was based on the souvenir of past wars and was ready to resurface at the slightest alert; but since the Peace of Saint-Germain no serious alarm had come along to revive it. The King had committed himself deliberately to the cause of voluntary forgetting specified in the first article of the edict, in the belief that the measures taken to preserve peaceful co-existence would suffice to maintain order. At the moment when the marriage so long projected between his sister and Henri de Navarre had taken place and the poets and musicians employed for the wedding celebrations had praised the happiness of the refound harmony, it would have been totally incoherent for him to destroy the whole enterprise by having the Admiral killed.

Should we then look further afield, to Madrid or Brussels, to find the instigator of the attack? The thesis of the King of Spain's responsibility is based on an important argument. Since at least 1568 and, more recently, since early August 1572, Philip II openly hoped that Charles IX would have Coligny executed.[50] But the question which arises here is why he would have sought to realise this recurring wish himself by employing one of his agents (or the Guises) on 22 August precisely. His motive may seem clear – to stop the assistance that the Admiral was about to send to the Calvinist rebels in the Netherlands. This was indeed one of the consequences of the attack which Ambassador Zuñiga mentioned in his letter of 23 August to Philip II: Coligny, he concluded, would now leave aside his projects to aid his co-religionists in order to devote himself entirely to avenging the crime.[51] But for that to happen, he added, 'the rascal has to survive'.[52] If we accept the thesis of Spanish premeditation, that would suggest a volte-face on their part when confronted with the unforeseen turn of events. But this hypothesis is immediately negated by Zuñiga's next observation, when he says that if it were better for the Admiral to survive, it would be primarily because his survival would *prevent* the King from participating publicly in a conflict with Spain: according to the ambassador's explanation already analysed, Charles IX feared that, if war was declared, Coligny's authority would be a danger for him.[53]

From the Spaniards' perspective, whatever their hatred of the Huguenot leader and their wish to see him dead, his survival *at that precise moment in the summer of 1572* seemed necessary in order to maintain peace between the two countries; everything, as we saw, prompted Zuñiga to believe that as long as the Admiral lived, the King of France would 'not remove the mask' and would openly disavow his secret help of the Dutch rebels, thus enabling Spain to avoid having to respond to France's move to open conflict. There is no reason to think that the Duke of Alba – to whom Zuñiga wrote on 31 August presenting even more clearly the same argument – thought any differently.[54] There is no doubt that Coligny's death, on 24 August, represented for Alba's major enemy, the Prince of Orange, a crushing blow, as he put it.[55] But recent Spanish success against Genlis's expeditionary force had kick-started the process of reconquest, so that Alba could believe that the force of arms would suffice to eliminate the threat from Coligny's troops, without having to resort to the roundabout and uncertain instrument of assassination.

That leaves the Duke of Savoy, who, according to Pierre Forget de Fresnes, was surrounded by servants of Spanish interests and 'had a Spanish agent at his heels all the time'. However, the duke's secret advice to Charles IX in response to the rumour that he was preparing to sell off church property – advice mentioned by Forget in his letter of 14 August 1572 – contained no warning against Coligny; Emmanuel Philibert merely exhorted the King to act prudently and think seriously before undertaking a war – but which he hoped that the King would declare against England.[56]

None of the suppositions made by contemporaries as to the instigator(s) of the ambush presents proofs sufficiently strong to support them; all of them, on the contrary, are quite fragile. But before proceeding further, we should question the obstinacy with which the instigators of such a crime are sought among rulers and the elites. This preoccupation was comprehensible enough among contemporaries, for whom such a bold act as the work of minor individuals was inconceivable, but is much less easy to understand among historians in our time. History records enough examples of attacks conducted precisely at the moment when peace negotiations seemed ready for completion, with the intention of sabotaging them and relaunching war, for us not to imagine that that could have been true on 22 August 1572. To scuttle the peace so brilliantly – and so provocatively – celebrated by the marriage of Henri de Navarre and Marguerite de Valois, there was no need to seek the approval of a high-status figure; the murderous fury of the most inflamed Catholics of Paris was incitement enough to the authors of such an enterprise. The fact that Maurevert, Villemur and Chailly belonged to the Guisard networks only proves that these networks were functioning and provided the necessary logistical support.[57] Nothing indicates that Henri de Guise or his uncle Aumale were kept informed of the plot; and perhaps the intention was, by implicating them in it despite themselves, to force them out of the inaction which their supporters considered scandalous. The hatred of the Protestants would turn against the Guises and war would restart. This time it would involve the final eradication of heresy, as was hoped for by the most radical Catholics, the probable fomenters of the plot against the Admiral.

THE FERVOUR AND ANXIETIES OF PARIS

Understanding the motives behind the desire to kill Coligny requires some sense of what Paris was like in the early 1570s. A huge city, the most populated in Europe, it had in mid-century around 300,000 inhabitants. A political and economic centre, it was also home to intense religious activity, proud of its numerous converts, churches and theology faculty which the whole of Europe was in the habit of consulting. It was the object of virtually mystical veneration; frequently compared to Jerusalem, it seemed to its inhabitants to enjoy God's special protection.[58]

The devotion of the Parisians was revealed in spectacular fashion during the processions for the great liturgical festivals. Each parish had its particular festive rhythm, as the celebration of its own patron saints was added to the calendar of the universal church. The parish of Saint-Jacques-de-la-Boucherie, for example, which extended to both banks of the Seine, including part of the Île de la Cité and the commercial district of the right bank, had eight annual procession days, among which were those of the two saint Jameses – the 'Greater' and the 'Lesser'. Each procession had its own ornamentation and distinctive route through the streets, whose houses were decorated with tapestries, so that the areas concerned became a sacralised space. The most beautiful procession, that of the Holy Sacrament (also called the Fête-Dieu), occurred at the end of May, when the parish prepared three dozen red roses to adorn the cross and the monstrance in which the consecrated Host was exposed, as well as to decorate the heads of the clergy and laypeople accompanying them.[59]

Collective piety was particularly evident in devotion to Sainte Geneviève, protectress of the capital, which mobilised the Parisians whenever danger threatened. The cult of this saint enjoyed astonishing vitality during the sixteenth century; her relics were solemnly carried in procession forty-six times, compared to five times in the fifteenth, eleven in the fourteenth, seven in the seventeenth and twice in the eighteenth century; the greatest frequency was in the 1550s and 1560s, when anxiety arising from religious division preyed on the faithful.[60] Each time it was organised, the procession in honour of the patron saint of Paris saw several corteges converge – those of the parishes and the religious orders, that of the city officials setting out from the town hall; that of the sovereign courts processing from the Palace of Justice, and that of the bishop of Paris bringing the relics of Saint Marcel, another defender of the city, from Notre-Dame. Barefooted, dressed in white and wearing flowers, the canons of the abbey of Sainte-Geneviève escorted the reliquaries of both saints, flanked by a guard of honour of Châtelet officials.[61] The presence of the monarchical, urban and religious authorities underlined the spiritual and civic character of the ceremony, representing the close link between religious unity and civic cohesion, a unity that was well expressed by the motto engraved above the entrance of the town hall – 'one king, one faith, one law'.

The religious zeal of the Parisians was also expressed by membership of the confraternities – pious associations whose objective was to help their members to be good Christians and assist them materially in case of need. Confraternities of intercession, placed under the patronage of a saint, were the most numerous.[62] Conditions of membership were simple – attend mass in the chapel which the confraternity had built or decorated in the parish church, participate in the city processions, accompany the funeral corteges of deceased members, assist with their prayers and donations those afflicted by illness or poverty and share in the banquet which brought the members together each year. The most prestigious Parisian confraternity was that of Notre-Dame, founded in 1168 in the small church of Sainte-Marie-Madeleine in the centre of the Ile de la Cité and renowned for its members' distinction and piety. The trades' confraternities were more turbulent, to the point that François I wished to suppress them in 1539. But this measure was hardly implemented at all, and the artisans continued to see in their associations the proper framework for expressing both their solidarity and their faith. Another type of confraternity, more focused on devotion and asceticism, also appeared – for example, those dedicated to the Rosary (the roses of the mysteries of the life of the Virgin – white for the joyous, red for the painful and gold for the glorious mysteries). The confraternities of Penitents, which spread first from Genoa and later from the Florentine colony in Avignon, into Provence at the end of the fifteenth century, had not yet reached Paris.

This traditional piety was stimulated, from the 1530s and 1540s, by the rise of the Catholic Reformation, which expanded alongside, but also in opposition to the Protestant Reformation. In reply to the criticisms by disciples of Luther and, later, Calvin, Catholic theologians made real efforts to render accessible to as many people as possible the doctrines transmitted by the Roman church and reaffirmed by the Council of Trent (1545–63). A popular preacher like François Le Picart, dean of Saint-Germain-l'Auxerrois from 1549 until his death in 1556, devoted his life to exhorting the clergy to reform themselves and the laity to lead a virtuous life; he tirelessly explained the meaning of the sacraments, the necessity to pray for the dead and the validity of the cult of the saints. His sermons were published in 1566.[63] This concern for pastoral questions was also manifest in many books explaining, in French and a simple idiom, the points of doctrine attacked by the Calvinists. We can cite, among many others, the *Catéchisme ou sommaire de la foi et devoir du vray chrestien* by Gentian Hervet (Paris, 1561), the *Catéchisme ou Instruction populaire* of René Benoist (Paris, 1569) or *La Manière d'ouïr la messe avec devotion et fruict spirituel* by Edmond Auger (Paris, 1571). All of these works attempted to educate the faith of the Catholics in order to protect them against the temptation of heresy.[64] Their effectiveness was bolstered by the pedagogic activities of the Jesuits: approved by Paul III in 1540, the Company of Jesus had founded in Paris in 1564 the college of Clermont on the rue Saint-Jacques, which began to educate the future urban elites.

For all that, believers were not immune to the great waves of eschatological anxiety which every so often terrified people, leading them to discern the precursor signs of the end of time in the smallest of unusual events – climatic catastrophes, monstrous births, comets, supernatural wonders spread by rumour and inflated by fear.[65] They were no more immune to obsession with the devil, whose influence they could see in the revival of sorcery. 'During this time', wrote the parish priest Jehan de la Fosse in November 1571, 'there was much talk in France of sorcerers, male and female, of whom it was said there were more than 30,000, and that the men had a mark behind their ears and the women on their thighs.'[66] But these real fears did not hide the reassurance which the collective, ritualised manifestations of their devotion brought to Catholics, reinforcing their sense of community cohesion; nor did they undermine the confidence which they had in the capacity of intercessions of the saints, and especially of the Virgin Mary, to assist them in the trials of life and turn their repentance into God's mercy.[67]

It was precisely here, at the heart of their devotional practices, that one of the sharpest of the criticisms of the Calvinists, for whom the cult of the saints was mere superstitious idolatry, began to penetrate. The attack did not just take the form of a theoretical refutation, but was accompanied by spectacular destructions of images. From spring of 1560 to the end of 1562, the Huguenots mutilated or destroyed statues in numerous sanctuaries across France; in Paris, the church of Saint-Médard was pillaged on 27 December 1561, following a tumult triggered, it seems, by mutual provocation by Catholics and Protestants. Parisians had also realised in 1558, when the Protestants organised meetings from 13 to 19 May to sing psalms in the Pré-aux-Clercs, how far the Christian unity of the city had been rent and new ideas attracted the elites of city and court.

It is difficult to know the exact numbers of converts to Protestantism in the capital; they fluctuated with the alternation of persecution and civil tolerance, itself determined by the succession of wars and edicts of pacification. Although fervent and active, the Protestants were never more than a tiny minority within the huge population of Paris; they perhaps numbered between 10,000 and 15,000 on the eve of the Massacre.[68] But their visibility was heightened by the distinction of those constituting this minority. An analysis of the list of prisoners confined in the Conciergerie prison on charges of heresy between 1564 and August 1572 casts some light on the social make-up of the Parisian protestant community. Of the 528 suspects whose social status is known, 9 per cent were nobles with at least the title of 'esquire' or 'lady'; 4 per cent were royal officials of or above the rank of a *bailliage* lieutenant; 22 per cent were lower officials or members of the 'liberal' professions (professors, doctors, lawyers); 15 per cent were merchants or 'bourgeois'; 31 per cent were artisans, of whom almost half belonged to trades with a high degree of literacy (surgeons, apothecaries, printers, painters, musicians, silversmiths), and 34 per cent belonged to trades with average literacy levels (leather-workers, furriers or clothmakers, tailors, shoemakers). A small percentage (13) was made up of people of lower status – domestics, soldiers, day-labourers, or people 'of no estate'; students represented 5 per cent and the clergy 1 per cent.[69] This shows, as other studies have noted, the correlation between adherence to Protestantism and a relatively high degree of education and technical skills – and which rendered the division all the more visible, and doubtless all the more scandalous, to those who remained in the traditional faith. It was the urban notables themselves who had destroyed religious union.

PEACE ASSASSINATED

Confronted with the anguish provoked by religious division, it was the desire to eradicate Protestantism which, fuelled by nostalgia for the age of unity, surfaced most frequently. For the most intransigent Catholics, peace was a synonym for resignation, surrender and, therefore, cowardice. Worse still, peace was capable of corrupting the faithful and endangering the collective salvation of the kingdom, since it was thought that the heretics would not fail to take advantage of the respite granted to them in order to infect other souls. An impassioned preacher like Simon Vigor, parish priest of Saint-Paul, did not hesitate to say of the Edict of Saint-Germain: 'this is not peace, but blasphemy', or 'this is not peace but a bone of contention; not a settlement but a shame [*non est pax, sed fax; non est foedus, sed foedum*]. It is a disgusting and filthy thing which will infect and contaminate your kingdom, your city, your wives and children'.[70] Only war was just, as it alone could eradicate the pollution of heresy.

In the eyes of Parisians, it was Coligny who, by virtue of his metamorphosis from rebel leader to royal counsellor, symbolised the peace and personified the notion of treason they attached to it. The transfer of the Gastines cross to the Holy Innocents cemetery, the marriage of the King of Navarre with Marguerite de Valois and the risk of war with Spain were attributed to his advice. He also embodied in their eyes the incoherence of royal policy. The capital's population could not forget that a few years earlier, during the third civil war, an edict was promulgated in March 1569 depriving him of his office of Admiral; a few months later, on 13 September, the Paris parlement put a price of 50,000 écus on his head and condemned him to be executed at the place de Grève or, if he could not be apprehended, to be burned in effigy there. The parish priest of Provins, Claude Haton, described the ritual of this execution which, although a fiction, had nevertheless struck the imagination of those watching it:

> A straw man was made and dressed in the colours the Admiral usually wore on his body and legs, with a face painted on it based on his portrait. It was brought from the Conciergerie prison and placed on a pallet, to which a horse was yoked in order to pull it, while another horse had [the Admiral's] coat of arms attached to its tail. Dragged through the city, the effigy was brought to the place de Grève, in front of the Paris town hall, where it was strung up by the public executioner and left until after the conclusion of peace, and where I saw it several times when I was in Paris.[71]

The fact that the effigy was not removed from the gibbet immediately after the peace of Saint-Germain is revealing of the hatred which many Parisian Catholics bore towards Coligny; his presence in the capital, in a place as frequented as the place de Grève, made it even more incomprehensible that the King had accepted a peaceful compromise with a man for whose execution a large reward had been offered only months previously. In such conditions, it is not surprising that the anxieties and anger of Parisians should have focused on the Admiral himself.

What was to be done about the apparent royal capitulation, which was so scandalous to the most impassioned Catholics? Some placed their hope in God's justice, which, they believed, always punished the impious. This conviction was expressed by Jehan de la Fosse in relation to the death of Jeanne d'Albret, that other symbol of the unacceptable pacification. The parish priest of Saint-Bartholomew saw in her premature death God's punishment for having despised one of the most cherished of Catholic collective devotions, the procession of the Holy Sacrament:

> Rumour had it that on the eve of the Holy Sacrament the said queen went to ask the king that the sacrament should not pass by her door, and in fact the procession did not go there, nor was the body of our God, which she called an idol, carried through the street where she lived; but on returning from asking the king to ensure no procession would pass through that street, illness overcame her and she died the Monday following.[72]

But in the case of Coligny, God was slow to show his hand, which therefore made it necessary to act as the instrument of divine justice. Simon Vigor worked hard to inculcate in the minds of his listeners the idea that it was legitimate to act. In a sermon preached on the second Sunday of Lent (3 March 1572), he argued that if the King ordered the Admiral's death, there would be no sin in obeying him. Then, invoking Saint Augustine as his authority, he added: 'there is a king who is above the law, who is God; if he bids a person to kill someone, as he ordered Abraham to kill his son, then that person must kill.'[73] Such a dangerous affirmation could justify the aberrations of any crank convinced that he was inspired by God; when directed, as here, against an 'impious' royal counsellor, it contained the seeds of tyrannicide. It is difficult to evaluate the influence of such language on audiences, but Jehan de la Fosse, when he mentions sermons delivered during the affair of the Gastines cross, some of which were directed against Coligny, claims that Vigor was keenly listened to.[74]

It is indispensable to take the full measure of the atmosphere in Paris after the King of Navarre's marriage in order to understand the significance of the attack of 22 August. Its organisers could believe that they were accomplishing God's revenge; subsequently the Catholic account of events entitled *Discours sur les causes de l'execution faicte es personnes de ceux qui avoyent conjuré contre le Roy et son Estat* explicitly assimilated the attack to divine punishment.[75] Coligny was attacked for who he was and for what he represented in the eyes of many Catholics; he was the scapegoat whose death was designed to restore the social and religious cohesion of the community.[76]

Yet the organisation of the ambush and the wish to implicate the Guises in it suggest that the aggressors aimed higher than the person of the Admiral. They tried not just to kill the King's evil counsellor, but to assassinate the peace itself. It was easy to predict that the Huguenots' desire for revenge would be directed against the Guises, who were so openly fingered by the circumstances of the attack. Jacques-Auguste de Thou reconstructed the argument which lay behind the crime; if we ignore the fact that he attributed its paternity to the King's advisers, we can retain as plausible the train of thought which he ascribes to its instigators:

> To implement this plan without risk or attracting the hatred that it was bound to generate, one could employ an assassin for the job; there are many who would do it in return for immediate recompense or some hope of future gain; and it would be easy for the murderer to escape on a fast horse which would be ready and waiting. The city's Protestants were bound to turn their suspicions on the Guises and, impetuous as they are, they will take up arms to avenge the death of Coligny by attacking the princes of this house. The Guises, who are more powerful than the Protestants, because they are supported by the people of Paris, will decimate this party; and perhaps the Montmorencys, who are little loved by the Parisians, will also be caught up in the massacre.[77]

Such a project could have been planned well in advance. Many observers had the feeling that it had been carefully organised. Petrucci wrote on 23 August: 'the case of the admiral was prepared for a long time'. 'It was a pre-meditated event', according to Zuñiga, who, as we have seen, regarded the King and Queen Mother as responsible for it.[78] The timing was well chosen: the concentration of Huguenots in the capital would pump up their anger and they would incite each other to action. It was probable that, faced with such a threat, the Guises would defend themselves; war would restart, permitting, as de Thou put it, the decimation of the heretics.

No doubt the prospect of the Admiral's being merely wounded was not foreseen. But this probably was of little importance compared to its anticipated effects. It is true that the consequences of the attack would have been insignificant if the King's authority had been firmer; the Protestants might, in this case, have believed in the royal promises to render even-handed justice and wait confidently for its effects to follow. But that was manifestly not so for the majority of them, who did not sufficiently trust the King's promise of rapid punishment of the aggressors. Prompted by Jean de Ferrières, vidame of Chartres, on 22 August some Protestant nobles envisaged fleeing immediately from Paris; but Coligny, supported by his son-in-law Téligny, refused, probably in the knowledge that a mass departure would be an insult to the King and virtually a declaration of war.[79] But the decision to remain in the capital increased the tension and disquiet of Coligny's friends; doubts grew among them as to Charles IX's capacity to exact revenge on the authors of the ambush.

The Florentines Cavriana and Sassetti, the nuncio Salviati, the royal secretary Jules Gassot mention 'swaggering' and 'threats' from the Huguenots.[80] Zuñiga reported that the Prince of Condé 'blustered terribly', while adding that Henri de Guise had written to his 'friends' to come and join him.[81]

Around midday on 23 August, the ducs de Guise and Aumale went to the Louvre, perhaps with the intention of exonerating themselves; they may have asked for, and obtained permission to leave court.[82] But, having given the impression of leaving the capital, they changed their mind and retreated to one of their residences. Their situation was extremely awkward. By all accounts the King believed in their guilt, yet they could not leave unanswered the challenge which talk of vengeance by their adversaries represented. They sensed that their protégés and followers had their eyes fixed on them; they also knew that for the most fervent Catholics they symbolised the defence of religious orthodoxy. Since at least 1524–25, their house had, thanks to the works of devoted historians and publicists, built up a prestigious 'capital of identity', which was that of a 'lineage divinely chosen to accomplish great deeds and acts in defence of the traditional religion'.[83] There can be no doubt that preserving that identity mattered as much to them during these critical days as did their resentment towards Coligny. Leaving Paris would not only have seemed like fleeing in the face of the enemy, but would have been a cowardly desertion, abandoning the capital to the power of heresy.

The attack of 22 August has often been described as a 'failed crime', a verdict that is correct if only Coligny is considered. But as far as the peace was concerned, it was perfectly executed. The ambush of the Admiral wrecked, in every respect, the policy of Charles IX and Catherine de Medici, for whom it was a terrible accident, at once predictable and unexpected. It was predictable, since they could imagine the reactions which their dream of reconciliation between Catholics and Protestants, as symbolised by the marriage of Marguerite de Valois and Henri de Navarre, were bound to trigger. It was unexpected in that they had reasons to believe in the success of their project of uniting opposites in the extravagant celebration of rediscovered concord. They failed to appreciate how much the fermentation of attitudes, in a capital that was predominantly hostile to the Protestants, rendered these aspirations Utopian. Without really surprising them, the brutal eruption of violence nevertheless – and paradoxically – caught them unawares. The shock of the event would derail the fine mechanism so carefully designed to consolidate peace, provoking a tragic spiral of violence.

NOTES

1 *Mémoires de Jacques Pape, seigneur de Saint-Auban,* ed. Michaud and Poujoulat, 1st series, vol. 11 (Paris, 1838), p. 497.

2 *La Vie de messire Gaspar de Colligny, seigneur de Chastillon, admiral de France* (French trans. of *Gasparis Colinii Castellonii ... vita,* n.p., 1575) ed. Émile Telle (Geneva, 1987). This repeats elements of *De furoribus gallicis* (Edinburgh, 1573), also attributed to Hotman, but minimising its polemical tone.

3 Its present location is indicated by Jean-Pierre Babelon, 'Le Paris de Coligny', in *L'Amiral de Coligny et son temps* (Paris, 1974), p. 566.

4 This indication comes from Jules Gassot, who writes that 'wet clothes were placed to dry near the window', in *Sommaire Mémorial (1555–1623),* ed. Pierre Champion (Paris, 1934), p. 97. Other sources mention 'draperies'.

5 *Négociations diplomatiques avec la Toscane,* vol. 3, p. 812, anonymous letter (Cavriana) to secretary Concini, Paris, 27 Aug. 1572; La Fosse, *Les 'Mémoires' d'un curé de Paris,* p. 113. The Venetian ambassador, Giovanni Michiel, is the only one to mention the finger severed from the *left* hand and the *right* hand pierced: *La Saint-Barthélemy devant le Sénat de Venise,* p. 20.

6 AGS, Estado, K1530, no. 20, Zuñiga to Philip II, 23 Aug. 1572 (copy misdated 22 Aug.). Olaegui's report of 26 Aug. *(ibid.,* K1524, no. 79, a copy of which, with some differences, is in K1530, no. 24) includes an error on the date of the attack, which it assigns to Thursday (and not Friday) 22nd. A somewhat different report, full of implausible details, is in draft in K1524, no. 78, but is close to that of the chevalier de Gomicourt, the Duke of Alba's agent; it was published in Philippe Erlanger, *Le Massacre de la Saint-Barthélemy* (Paris, 1960), pp. 258–260.

7 *Mémoires de Jacques Pape,* pp. 497–498.

8 These details on Maurevert have been elucidated by Crouzet's research, in *La Nuit de la Saint-Barthélemy,* pp. 462–468.

9 Pomponne de Bellièvre, *Proposition faite aux Suisses* [...] *sur la mort de Monsieur l'admiral de Colligny et journee de St Barthelemy,* in BnF, MS. Fr. 18895, fols 214r–215r.

10 Pierre de L'Estoile, *Registre-Journal du règne de Henri III,* ed. Madeleine Lazard and Gilbert Schrenck, vol. 4, [1582–84] (Geneva, 2000), pp. 89.

11 Crouzet, *La Nuit de la Saint-Barthélemy,* p. 462–468.

12 *La Saint-Barthélemy devant le Sénat de Venise,* p. 21; Zuñiga to Philip II, 23 Aug.1572; Pomponne de Bellièvre, *Proposition faite aux Suisses,* fol. 221r.

13 *Registres des délibérations du Bureau de la Ville de Paris,* 15 vols, vol. 7 [1572–1576], ed. François Bonnardot (Paris, 1893), p. 10.

14 *Discours simple et véritable des rages exercées par la France,* Bâle [La Rochelle], French edition of *De Furoribus gallicis* by François Hotman, quoted by Bourgeon, *L'Assassinat de Coligny,* p. 74, n. 7. In *La Vie de messire Gaspar de Colligny,* p. 119, the comte de Retz says he fears 'some popular tumult'.

15 *Négociations diplomatiques avec la Toscane,* vol. 3, p. 814, anonymous letter (Cavriana) to secretary Concini, Paris, 27 Aug. 1572; *La Vie de Messire Gaspar de Colligny,* p. 118.

16 Monluc, *Commentaires,* p. 834.

17 *La Saint-Barthélemy devant le Sénat de Venise,* pp. 81–82.

18 Pierre de L'Estoile, *Journal pour le règne de Henri IV et le début du règne de Louis XIII,* ed. André Martin (Paris, 1960), p. 472 (appendix).

19 Jacques-Auguste de Thou, *Histoire universelle depuis 1543 jusqu'en 1607, traduite sur l'édition latine de Londres*, 16 vols (London, 1734), vol. 6 [1570–1573], pp. 370–374.

20 *La Vie de messire Gaspar de Colligny*, p. 104.

21 *Mémoires inédits de Michel de La Huguerye*, ed. Alphonse de Ruble, 3 vols (Paris, 1877), vol. 1, p. 95.

22 *Négociations diplomatiques avec la Toscane*, vol. 3, p. 814, anonymous letter (Cavriana) to secretary Concini, Paris, 27 Aug. 1572.

23 *Correspondance du roi Charles IX et du sieur de Mandelot, gouverneur de Lyon, pendant l'année 1572*, ed. Paulin Paris (Paris, 1830), pp. 36–37.

24 *Correspondance diplomatique de Bertrand de Salignac de La Mothe Fénelon*, vol. 7 (*Lettres de la cour à l'ambassadeur*), Charles IX to La Mothe-Fénelon, 22 Aug. 1572, p. 322.

25 AGS, Estado, K1530, no. 20, Zuñiga to Philip II, 23 Aug. 1572 (copy with erroneous date of 22 Aug.).

26 Accusation in the manuscript account of the massacre of 24 Aug. (*Discours particulier où est amplement descrit et blasmé le massacre de la St-Barthélemy*, in BnF, MS. Fr. 17529, fol. 112v).

27 BnF, MS. Fr. 17309, *Dessein de ceux qui soubz le nom et autorité de Sa Majesté ont faict le massacre*, fol. 58v.

28 *Négociations diplomatiques avec la Toscane*, vol. 3, pp. 807–808, Petrucci to Francesco de Medici, Paris, 23 Aug. 1572.

29 *Ibid.*, p. 813, anonymous letter (Cavriana) to secretary Concini, Paris, 27 Aug. 1572.

30 Tomasso Sassetti, *Brieve Raccontamiento del gran macello fatto nella città di Parigi il vigesimo quarto giorno d'agosto*, ed. John Tedeschi, in Alfred Soman, ed., *The Massacre of St. Bartholomew. Reappraisals and documents* (The Hague, 1974), p. 131.

31 Michel Simonin, *Charles IX* (Paris, 1995), p. 322.

32 *La Saint-Barthélemy devant le Sénat de Venise*, p. 36.

33 Jean-Marie Constant, *Les Guise* (Paris, 1984), pp. 68–69, who believes that the thesis of Guise responsibility for the attack of 22 August is without foundation.

34 *La Vie de messire Gaspar de Colligny*, pp. 118–119.

35 *Négociations diplomatiques avec la Toscane*, vol. 3, p. 855, Petrucci to Francesco de Medici, Paris, 2 Nov. 1572.

36 *Correspondance du roi Charles IX et du sieur de Mandelot*, Mandelot to the King, 5 Sept. 1572, pp. 55–58.

37 BPU, Geneva, MS. Fr. 90, fol. 162v, Forget de Fresnes to the King, 10 Sept. 1572.

38 Marguerite Christol, 'La dépouille de Gaspard de Coligny', *BSHPF*, 111 (1965), pp. 136–140, who relies on Henri Forneron, *Histoire de Philippe II* (Paris, 1881–1882), vol. 3, p. 206, who in turn cites an ambiguous letter from the Duke of Alba of Feb. 1573.

39 Bourgeon, *L'Assassinat de Coligny*, p. 47 believes that Alba was the recipient of Coligny's head and bases in part his conclusions as to the duke's responsibility on this.

40 See above, ch. 2, pp. 48–49.

41 Venard, 'Arrêtez le massacre!', p. 650.

42 *La Saint-Barthélemy devant le Sénat de Venise*, p. 61.

43 *Ibid.*, p. 34. The thesis of Catherine's responsibility has a long historiographical pedigree, which Cloulas in particular has revived in his *Catherine de Médicis* (Paris, 1979).

44 On this point, see the analyses of Crouzet, *La Nuit de la Saint-Barthélemy*, pp. 352–353.

45 *Lettres de Catherine de Médicis*, vol. 4, p. 111, 21 Aug. 1572.

46 *Ibid.*, p. 112.

47 Venard, 'Arrêtez le massacre!', p. 650.

48 AGS, Estado, K1530, no. 13, Zuñiga to Philip II, 10 Aug. 1572, 'the said Gondi told me that afterwards the Queen Mother informed him that it had been resolved not to go to war against Your Majesty, saying that she was disappointed to see in this council a substantial number of her enemies, but that in the end she had obtained from it what she wanted – that there would be no war'.

49 See above, ch. 1, pp. 38–39.

50 He mentioned this desire to the Spanish nuncio, Rossano, as the latter indicates in a letter to Cardinal Como of 5 Aug. 1572, quoted in Sutherland, *The Huguenot struggle for recognition*, p. 204. See *ibid.*, pp. 190 and 192 for earlier instances of this wish. Philipp II's letter to Alba of 4 May 1568, in which he expresses the hope that Charles IX will take advantage of the Peace of Longjumeau to cut off the heads of the rebellious Huguenot leaders, is published in *Archivo Documental Español. Negociaciones con Francia*, vol. 10 (Madrid, 1959), no. 1632, pp. 390–391.

51 AGS, Estado, K1530, no. 20, Zuñiga to Philip II, 23 Aug. 1572.

52 'I say to Your Majesty that at this hour it would be better if this scoundrel were to live' ['*Yo digo a V. M.d que a la hora de agora creo conviene que viva este vellaco*'].

53 This document has already been examined above, ch. 2, p. 62.

54 AGS, Estado, K1530, no. 29, Zuñiga to Alba, 31 Aug. 1572, analysed above, ch. 2, p. 62.

55 *Archives ou Correspondance inédite de la maison d'Orange-Nassau*, vol. 3, p. 503.

56 BPU, Genève, MS. Fr. 90, fol. 158r, Forget de Fresnes to the King, 30 July; fol. 158v, to same, 9 Aug.; fol. 160v to same, 14 Aug. 1572.

57 At least as concerns those networks composed of radical Catholics, as it would be mistaken to think that the Guise clienteles were confessionally uniform; paradoxically, they contained a number of Protestants: see Stuart Carroll, *Noble power during the Wars of Religion. The Guise affinity and the Catholic cause in Normandy* (Cambridge, 1998), p. 140.

58 Descimon, 'Paris on the eve of Saint-Bartholomew', p. 69.

59 Barbara Diefendorf, *Beneath the Cross. Catholics and Huguenots in sixteenth-century Paris* (New York and Oxford, 1991), esp. ch. 2, 'The most Catholic capital', which has a detailed analysis of Parisian piety.

60 *Ibid.*, p. 40.

61 *Ibid.*, p. 41.

62 Marie-Hélène Froeschlé-Chopard, *Dieu pour tous et Dieu pour soi. Histoire des confréries et de leurs images à l'époque moderne* (Paris, 2007).

63 Larissa J. Taylor, *Heresy and orthodoxy in sixteenth-century Paris. François Le Picart and the beginnings of the Catholic Reformation* (Leiden, 1999).

64 Diefendorf, *Beneath the Cross*, pp. 147–149; Louis Châtellier, *Le Catholicisme en France*, vol. 1, *Le xvie siècle* (Paris, 1995), pp. 160–161.

65 See the fears of the year 1524 analysed by Crouzet, *Les guerriers de Dieu*, vol. 1, pp. 106–112.

66 La Fosse, *Les 'Mémoires' d'un curé de Paris*, p. 104.

67 This double aspect of religious faith has been studied in two major works by Jean Delumeau, *Le Péché et la peur* (Paris, 1983), and *Rassurer et protéger* (Paris, 1989).

68 The merchant Jean Rouillé claimed that there were 5,000 abjurations in Paris after

the Massacre, in a letter of 22 Sept. 1572, published by Charles Pradel, 'Un marchand de Paris au xvie siècle (1560–1588)', *Mémoires de l'Académie des sciences, inscriptions et belles-lettres de Toulouse*, 9th series, vol. 2 (Toulouse, 1890), pp. 421–423. This estimate cannot be verified. But if it is accepted as a plausible order of magnitude and we assume that an equivalent number of people fled the kingdom, that would give a hypothetical total – taking account of the 3,000 massacred – of 13,000 in all.

69 See the analysis of Barbara Diefendorf, 'Les divisions religieuses dans les familles parisiennes avant la Saint-Barthélemy', *HES*, 7 (1988), pp. 55–77. The percentage for students given in this article (3) is corrected to 5 per cent in her book, *Beneath the Cross*, p. 109.

70 Simon Vigor, *Sermons catholiques sur les Dimenches et festes depuis l'octave de Pasques jusques à l'Advent* (Paris, 1587): sermon 'for the feast of Saint Magdalen [22 July 1570?] and for the day and feast of the Assumption of the glorious Virgin Mary' [15 Aug. 1570?], quoted by Jean-Louis Bourgeon, 'Quand la foi était révolutionnaire: les sermons d'un curé parisien, Simon Vigor, en 1570–1572', in *Mélanges offerts à Pierre Chaunu. La vie, la mort, la foi, le temps* (Paris, 1993), p. 477.

71 *Mémoires de Claude Haton*, vol. 2, p. 286.

72 La Fosse, *Les 'Mémoires' d'un curé de Paris*, p. 110.

73 Quoted by Bourgeon, *L'Assassinat de Coligny*, p. 38. See also B. Diefendorf, 'Simon Vigor: a radical preacher in sixteenth-century Paris', *SCJ*, 18 (1987), pp. 399–410.

74 La Fosse, *Les 'Mémoires' d'un curé de Paris*, p. 105.

75 *Discours sur les causes de l'execution faicte es personnes de ceux qui avoyent conjuré contre le Roy et son Estat* (Antwerp, 1572), fol. D 2v.

76 An interpretation that would illustrate the theories of René Girard on violence: see *La Violence et le sacré* (Paris, 1972).

77 De Thou, *Histoire universelle*, vol. 6, p. 382. Bourgeon cites this passage from the 1659 edition in *L'Assassinat de Coligny*, p. 61, n. 1, and compares it to the identical analysis to be found in English despatches: *CSP Rome*, vol. 2 [1572–1578] ed. J. M. Rigg (London, 1926), pp. 40–41.

78 *Négociations diplomatiques avec la Toscane*, vol. 3, p. 807, Petrucci to Francesco de Medici, Paris, 23 Aug. 1572; AGS, Estado, K1530, no. 29, Zuñiga to Alba, 31 Aug. 1572.

79 *La Vie de messire Gaspar de Colligny*, pp. 121, 124–125.

80 *Négociations diplomatiques avec la Toscane*, vol. 3, p. 813, anonymous letter (Cavriana) to secretary Concini, Paris, 27 Aug. 1572; Sassetti, *Brieve Racconta-miento*, p. 132; *Correspondance en France du nonce Antonio Maria Salviati*, p. 203, letter of 24 Aug. 1572; Gassot, *Sommaire Mémorial*, p. 102.

81 AGS, Estado, K1530, no. 20, Zuñiga to Philip II, 23 Aug. 1572.

82 This initiative is reported by de Thou, *Histoire universelle*, vol. 6, p. 394, and by Camillo Capilupi, *Le Stratagème, ou la ruse de Charles IX, Roy de France, contre les Huguenots rebelles à Dieu et à luy*, in Louis Cimber and Charles Danjou, eds, *Archives curieuses de l'Histoire de France*, 1st series, vol. 7 (Paris, 1835), p. 432.

83 Denis Crouzet, 'Capital identitaire et engagement religieux: aux origines de l'enga-gement militant de la maison de Guise, ou le tournant des années 1524–1525', in Joël Fouilleron, Guy Le Thiec and Henri Michel, eds, *Sociétés et idéologies des Temps modernes*, 2 vols (Montpellier, 1996), vol. 2, pp. 573–589.

PART II

SWORD OF GOD,
SWORD OF THE KING

4

SURGICAL STRIKE

Historians are in the habit of using just one term, the Saint Bartholomew's Day Massacre, to indicate what happened on 24 August 1572. This is misleading, as it risks confusing two quite different events – first, the 'execution' of the Huguenot leaders thought to be seditious, as decided by the King's council on the evening of 23 August; second, the extermination of all Protestants in the capital triggered by the explosion of anger among Parisian Catholics. It would be better to distinguish a first from a second massacre.[1] The problem of the correlation of the two events will be examined in the next chapter. Before that it is necessary to deal with the most complex of the enigmas raised by the tragedy of August 1572 – how to explain the sudden withdrawal of the favour shown to Coligny and which had been so publicly sustained until the afternoon of 22 August. Did Charles IX suffer a sudden panic attack? Did he experience irresistible pressures that forced him to adapt to a situation he did not control? Or should we not regard the council's decision as a defensive reaction by a state perceived to be endangered?

ROYAL MAJESTY WOUNDED

In exhorting the French people to practise voluntary forgetting in the first article of the Edict of Saint-Germain of August 1570, the King doubtless realised that he himself would have to make a considerable effort to achieve it. It should be remembered that during the previous conflicts the Huguenots had at several junctures provoked his anger and distrust. The hold over him of suspicion relating to them dated from at least the 'surprise of Meaux' on 26–27 September 1567, which sparked the second civil war. On 26 August, after four years of peace, the royal family and entourage, then at Monceaux, learned that a large force of Protestants was marching on Lagny. Gripped by fear, the King and his escort took refuge in Meaux; two days later, on 28th, they had to head for Paris at full speed under the protection of hastily summoned Swiss guards and under attack from clashes with the Prince of Condé's soldiers. Exasperated by infractions of the 1563 Edict of Pacification and despairing of

obtaining justice so long as their enemies dominated the council, the Huguenots aimed to seize the person of the King in order to bend royal policy to their
wishes. The failure of the plan was disastrous for them, and from that moment
onwards Charles IX and Catherine de Medici suspected them of being rebels
out to attack their authority. Distrust and a desire for concord now cohabited in
the royal minds; reconciliation among their subjects remained their basic goal
when circumstances were favourable, but their suspicions lay dormant, ready
to resurface if the Protestants' behaviour gave grounds for it.

The first major reversal of the reign occurred in late summer 1568, in conditions which in some ways prefigure those of 1572. That summer, the intransigent Catholic faction which dominated the council was worried by the
rapprochement between the Prince of Orange, Condé and Coligny following
the bloody repression of the Calvinist revolts in the Netherlands. They had
marshal Cossé decimate the small expeditionary force which a Huguenot
commander, François de Cocqueville, led in support of his oppressed co-religionists. Fearing for their lives, Condé and Coligny fled to La Rochelle; and
in September 1568 Charles IX issued the Edict of Saint-Maur, which removed
all freedom of worship for Protestants and ordered their pastors to leave the
realm within two weeks.

The preamble of the edict is a remarkable synopsis of the accusations of
subversion directed against the Huguenots. Having recalled the clemency with
which he had acted in granting them a limited freedom of worship at the end
of each previous war, the King denounced their latest uprising and launched a
blistering indictment of them:

> In which we, seeing them so often and so many times abusing our goodness and
> clemency, can no longer doubt of their wicked and damnable intent to establish
> and set up in this kingdom another sovereign principality to undo ours ordained
> and established by God, and to divide by such means our good subjects from us by
> means of the permission and toleration of their religion and the assemblies which
> they hold on the pretext of their sermons and communions, at which they collect
> money, enrol men, make oaths, associations, conspiracies, practices and designs,
> both within and without our realm, disturbing it with the arms which they have in
> their hands, dealing with us as with neighbours and not as obedient subjects, such
> as they declare by word and in their writings, but who behave as mortal enemies.[2]

The preamble highlighted the political reasons for the suppression of
'sermons and communions'; nowhere in it was the 'new opinion' described as
'heresy', although the Catholic religion was described as the only 'true' one. The
King preserved liberty of conscience in the hope, he asserted, 'that hereafter,
by divine inspiration and through the efforts that we shall make to ensure that
all the bishops and pastors of the church of our kingdom carry out their duties,
our said subjects of the so-called reformed religion will return and reunite with
us and our other subjects in the union of the holy Catholic church'. He granted

the Protestants a full amnesty and offered them his protection if they returned to obedience. Here the spheres of conscience and public order were clearly distinguished from each other. The King prescribed the methods of gentleness for action in the first, while for the second he proscribed all external manifestations of the reformed faith, suspected of providing occasions for revolt.

The charges laid against the Huguenots to justify the edict were nevertheless extremely serious. Creating a sovereign principality and behaving like 'neighbours' and not like 'subjects' – here was the desire to create a state within a state that was ascribed to them. Such accusations were based on the fear that the radical protestant minority had generated since March 1560, the date of the Amboise conspiracy mentioned in the 1568 edict. The profanation of the royal tombs at Cléry, Bourges and Orléans during the first war; the appeal to revolt against tyranny in works published in Lyon in 1562–63; the resurgence of the theme of a contract between king and subjects in the polemical writings published at La Rochelle in 1567–68 – all of these had rekindled anxieties, despite the disavowals made by many pastors of the most extreme theories.[3] Protestants seemed to be dangerous insubordinates vis-à-vis royal authority, and the Catholic intransigents who dominated the royal council exploited that fear in order to formulate the indictment included in the Edict of Saint-Maur. At the signature of the Edict of Saint-Germain in 1570, those favouring the immediate eradication of heresy were no longer in power, but their chillingly detailed denunciation of the subversive activities of the Huguenots lodged, without doubt, in a recess of the royal memory.

That Charles IX managed to repress his distrust until 23 August 1572 seems all the more remarkable in that Coligny, for all his desire to gain royal support, scarcely bothered to spare his sensitivities. We need but remember the brutal frankness with which the Admiral reminded the King, on 8 May 1571, that if he did not punish infractions of the peace edict, he would be regarded as saying the opposite of what he wished, or that he wished for more than he could attain, which would make him 'the most despised king for a long time'.[4] Nor did the Huguenot leader show much respect for the royal majesty in putting pressure on him for an open conflict with Spain. Several converging sources indicate the disturbing character of Coligny's pronouncements. One anonymous observer claimed to have himself heard Coligny's words in the King's study on 6 August 1572; by his account, the Admiral was in threatening mode:

> And I heard the late admiral Chastillon say, in the king's cabinet and in his presence on 6 August last, a propos of certain arguments that he was putting to him to make war against the king of Spain, that if he did not make war he would have in his kingdom the biggest troubles he ever had, which he himself could not see how to deal with. He said this twice in order to intimidate His Majesty into going to war with Spain rather than have one in his kingdom, something which he knew was quite odious for the king to listen to. Realising that he had threatened the king too

much, he repeated the same argument and explained what he meant, which was that, knowing that those of the religion, as he called them, were convinced that if the king of Spain defeated the prince of Orange, he would wish to take revenge on them, they would be forced to take up arms to defend themselves, something which would provoke the most considerable and cruel troubles so far.[5]

This argument, if it was actually formulated, was not without merit: Philip II, once his subjects' revolt had been put down, might wish to destroy the haunts of refugees and Huguenot sympathisers by authorising raids across the frontiers similar to those which had brought Genlis into his lands, which in turn might lead to the Protestants taking up arms. The Florentine ambassador, Petrucci, also attributes a similar argument to Coligny, and which, according to Petrucci, he had deployed somewhat earlier, in late June 1572.[6] The tone and insistence of these warnings may have been viewed as threatening by Charles IX. In his speech exculpating the King before the diet of Bâle, Pomponne de Bellièvre referred to the 'incredible insolence' of the Admiral's saying to the King in council 'that if His Majesty did not quickly agree to go to war in Flanders, he would surely have one very soon among his own subjects in France'.[7]

Another source, Giovanni Michiel, quotes statements that were undoubtedly perceived as hostile. According to him, during one of the council meetings which clearly rejected the hypothesis of an open war with Spain, a furious Coligny said to the King:

> Sire, since the opinion of these people has persuaded Your Majesty that you should not seize such a favourable opportunity for your service and grandeur, I can no longer oppose your will, but I am certain that you will repent of it ... I hope that Your Majesty will not find it amiss if, having promised support and assistance to the prince of Orange, I undertake to help him with all my friends, relations and servants, and even with my person, if need be.

Then, turning towards the Queen, he added: 'Madame, the king refuses to go to war. May God will that he does not have another which it may not be in his power to avoid.'[8]

It was rash to boast of being able to recruit many 'friends, relatives and servants' for an armed expedition rejected by the royal council. All of these accounts suggest that, on the eve of the tragedy, Coligny's behaviour contained gestures and statements which could be interpreted as provocations. It is perhaps to this that a contemporary alluded when saying that the King had been obliged, before 24 August, 'to swallow big and bitter chunks of indignity'.[9] And yet, until 23 August 1572, Charles IX had kept his resentment under control, such was his desire to achieve the pacification of attitudes and to see concord rule; peace remained his primary objective.[10] So what happened, during 23 August, for the fire smouldering under the embers to be suddenly rekindled and the King's distrust revived?

In his account of events, Tommaso Sassetti made a fundamental point: Téligny, Coligny's son-in-law, allegedly claimed when demanding justice from Charles IX on the day of the ambush that, if he did not obtain it, the supporters of his father-in-law would do it themselves; in saying this, writes Sassetti, he used words which 'attacked the king's dignity.'[11] Such language effectively rejected the royal monopoly of justice and amounted to a denial of royal sovereignty. The Huguenots' audacity grew on 23 August when, according to Sassetti, during a third deputation to court, one of Coligny's companions, Armand de Clermont, baron de Piles, behaved particularly threateningly. As we have seen, all the ambassadors mentioned the 'provocations' of the Huguenot leaders.

Rumours increased the seriousness of the views attributed to the Protestants. The Florentine ambassador, Giovanni Michiel, records that some of them were ready to go 'to the Louvre palace where Monsieur de Guise lived and to kill him in his chamber, *driving back the royal guard* and all those who might oppose them.'[12] Pomponne de Bellièvre, in the speech already quoted, went yet further: 'that same day [Saturday 23 August] a council was held in Coligny's residence and it was resolved that to gain revenge they should go to the Louvre and kill Monsieur de Guise, *even if it were at the king's feet*.'[13] For the Florentine doctor, Cavriana, as for the secretary of Cardinal Alessandro Farnese, Guido Lolgi, both present in Paris during the attack, the Admiral's supporters intended pursuing and assassinating Henri de Guise 'even if he was in the arms of the king himself.'[14] It is quite probable that their anger drove Coligny's companions to use such expressions, thus making them plausible to Charles IX. And they were particularly alarming – the wish to kill an enemy in the royal palace and, worse, before the monarch himself, amounted to planning an overt act of lèse-majesté. The offence to royal majesty which such talk represented could not but revive the worst anxieties.

It was at this point that the King's distrust and resentment burst out into the open, with a brutality which can be explained by the violence with which he had previously bridled his suspicions of the Protestant leaders. Bellièvre's evidence of Coligny's behaviour in the royal council throws some light on how this occurred: 'it was not long ago that the king, remembering such arrogance, said to some of his servants, of whom I was one, that when he heard himself threatened in this manner, the hairs stood up on his head. I saw it, I knew it, I heard it, I was there, I was frequently horrified by it.'[15] Bellièvre's vehemence in insisting that he saw this with his own eyes suggests the intensity of the process of 'recollecting' which was probably the consequence of the blustering of the Huguenots. The behaviour of the Admiral's companions on 23 August rekindled the memory of past humiliations in the mind of the King, whose rancour focused on the person of Coligny. With his capacity to mobilise without royal approval his 'friends, relatives and servants', Coligny would have seemed an 'over-mighty' and potentially dangerous subject to the King. The King's letter of 13 September to Schomberg contains the following revealing sentence: '[Coligny] was more powerful and more obeyed by those of the new religion than I was ... with the result that once he had gained such power over my said subjects, I could no longer call myself absolute king, and could only command one part of my kingdom.'[16]

An absolute king, an uncontested sovereign who alone personified majesty – that was the regularly proclaimed ambition of Charles IX, who was so jealous of his power and so insistent on the respect that was owed to him. As the uncontrollable leader of a private army and member of a dissenting church, Coligny's authority rivalled the King's; that was without doubt the fundamental charge against him by the King, but which his desire not to destroy the peace had curbed until the Massacre. It was on the day after 22 August that the Protestants' attitude was viewed as a challenge to royal sovereignty, transforming the King's grudge into an open indictment. In the minds of Charles IX, the Queen Mother and their councillors, the sudden reappearance of such suspicion contributed to shaping fears of a sudden attack. And, as often happens in tense and uncertain situations, they anticipated the worst. The conviction that the monarchy was in serious danger from Huguenot subversion took on new life.

Of course, the Catholics also bestirred themselves on the day following the attack. The shops in Paris were closed; Protestant sources mention suspicious movements of armed men and indicate that the King sent his brother, the duc d'Anjou, and half-brother, the chevalier d'Angoulême, out into the streets to check on these disturbing signs.[17] But, as yet, Catholic nervousness presaged only a popular riot, perhaps no more serious than the one triggered by the relocation of the Gastines cross. For their part, by affirming that they would themselves administer justice even in the King's presence, the Protestants had crossed a symbolic Rubicon. They had, as we have seen, attacked the majesty of Charles IX and questioned his sovereignty. All of those who sought to strengthen that authority – Catherine de Medici, Gondi, Birague – would have seen, as the King did, that a line had been dangerously crossed.

But did they, for that reason, fear a long-premeditated 'conspiracy' by Coligny's friends to exterminate the royal family? This would be the pretext invoked by the King on 25 August to legitimate the measures taken against the Protestant leaders, once he had hastily dropped the first explanation given on 24th, which attributed responsibility for the murder of the Admiral to the Guises.[18] It is possible that – under the effect of fears generated by the meetings held on 23 August in Coligny's residence or, even more threateningly, in the rooms of the King of Navarre until late at night in the Louvre itself – the members of the royal council came to believe in a conspiracy prepared behind closed doors.[19] Giovanni Michiel claims that a Huguenot captain, Bouchavannes, betrayed his party and came to denounce to the King and his mother 'the order given to the Huguenots to assemble at Meaux on 5 September all of their infantry and cavalry in order to get what they wanted by force of arms'.[20] Cavriana reported rumours according to which an attack by Protestant forces was planned for 26 August, whose objective was a 'Sicilian vespers' of the leading Catholics, including Guise and Nevers; he added that it was probable that royal blood would not have been spared.[21] Gomicourt, the Duke of Alba's agent, even informed his master that the Admiral, believing himself mortally wounded in the attack of 22 August because he supposed that the assassin's bullet was poisoned, had Henri de Navarre brought to his bedside in order to confide that he was leaving him 'the kingdom of France as his inheritance'. The 'extremely sad and melancholic' Navarre foresaw disastrous consequences and told this story to his wife, who in turn recounted it to her mother and brother[22] … But these details are implausible. As far as we know, rumours of a plot had no substance, and the situation of the Protestants in Paris, far removed from their power bases, renders them scarcely credible. Yet rumours did circulate and reach the ears of the King, which meant they could provoke panic in him and his entourage. In such situations, facts matter less than the image of them that one has.

However, the thesis of a Huguenot conspiracy seems to have been presented primarily *ad usum populi*, and as best suited to the royal efforts at justification, both for the French people and for foreign courts. It is significant that such an argument had been useful for Charles IX following the surprise of Meaux. In a letter of 28 September 1567 to Fourquevaux, his ambassador in Spain, the King denounced the attack in terms that would be repeated virtually identically five years later: 'three days ago an incredible and unprecedented conspiracy against me and my state, against the life of my mother, my brothers and myself', was discovered.[23] In the immediate aftermath of 24 August 1572, the accusation was used essentially to convince observers of the long gestation of the Protestant danger and to stoke their indignation. Its value lay in its being an easy format in which to diffuse the certainty which the King and his entourage possessed – namely that the Huguenot leaders had offended the King's majesty and endangered the state. And that was, in fact, the fundamental crime attributed to them.[24]

EXTRAORDINARY JUSTICE

Faced with this situation, the council became convinced that the guilty should be punished. Precautions had been taken before 22 August to limit the potential danger that a gathering of a great number of Protestant nobles in the capital might represent. Charles IX had called up the royal guard – 'an unusual thing', as Ambassador Zuñiga noted. According to Capilupi and de Thou, the guards regiment entered the city on 19 August.[25] But it was clear that such measures were insufficient.

It is extremely difficult to know if there were several successive council meetings during the afternoon and evening and into the night of 23 August, or just one sitting throughout the day. The sources are simply too imprecise, but the point is a minor one. What is essential is that the sentencing to death of a certain number of Protestant leaders was, like all council decisions, resolved collectively, with the King sanctioning it with his authority. The legends propagated by the memoirs and other subsequent writings in order to exonerate certain individuals present at the council – such as that of Catherine de Medici terrorising her son and extracting his consent, or that of Charles IX ending by making the famous declaration, 'kill them all, and let not one of them live to accuse me of this' – are unreliable.[26] If certain pressures were brought to bear on the King, they coincided sufficiently with the resurgence of his own resentment for him to have little difficulty in agreeing; there is no proof that Charles IX needed to be steered in the right direction. The identity of those who participated in the decision can be hypothetically reconstituted. Alongside the King, his mother and his brother Henri d'Anjou, there were, without doubt, the duc de Nevers, the comte de Retz, René de Birague, keeper of the seals, and marshal Gaspard de Saulx-Tavannes.[27] Only Jean de Morvillier appears to have been reticent, and both Cavriana and Petrucci wrote that he wept as he accepted the council's decision.

But the significance of the decision has to properly measured. Everything suggests that, once it had been decided to punish the seditious, the key question facing the council was to determine what form it should take. The dilemma can perhaps be put in these terms: should they have recourse to the 'ordinary' justice of the King – bring the suspects to trial and judge them by the normal legal rules – or to his 'extraordinary' justice – execute them without a prior sentence? The first solution seemed impossible to implement: in a capital overheated with passions and in which many armed Protestant nobles still remained, the conduct of normal judicial procedures would certainly have been disrupted. These inconveniences of the 'ordinary' judicial forms were weighed up by the council. According to Pomponne de Bellièvre, 'there was not a single person who did not think that apprehending and punishing Coligny by the normal form of justice would be more dangerous for the King than for the Admiral; it was realised that there were at least 800 nobles in Paris, men accustomed to and formed by the civil wars, and who were well armed, under his command; and that there were at least 8,000 men in the city who belonged to the "religion" and were ready to do whatever he ordered'.[28]

It was, therefore, necessary to fall back on the King's 'extraordinary' justice, as he himself clearly outlined in his declaration of 26 August to the parlement of Paris, and which was preserved in the journal of a canon of Bordeaux, François de Syrueilh.[29] In it Charles IX explains that finding himself facing 'such a serious danger, if he had not dealt with it quickly by recourse to violent means, one would later seek in vain to do so by the ordinary remedies of justice'. For that purpose he had employed the 'sword that God had placed in his hands for the preservation of the good, the punishment and extermination of the evil ... without observing any form or solemnity of justice'. There was, therefore, nothing arbitrary in such violent action; exceptional situations demanded exceptional procedures. The King claimed that he had not previously done this; he was forced into it 'to his great regret and displeasure', and hoped not to have to do so again in the future. But he had acted properly and legitimately. In the letter already quoted of 13 September to Schomberg, Charles IX gives the same explanation: 'and I resolved to allow an extraordinary form of justice, one different to what I would have desired, to take its course'.

The 'I' word here is a collective one: it means 'the king in his council' and expresses the royal will as enlightened by his councillors. It would be pointless to seek to pin down individual responsibilities, which the sources do not allow us to establish with certainty. At the most, we can note that Catherine de Medici expressly declared, in a letter to Arnaud du Ferrier, the role that she played in counselling her son; refuting the accusations that she acted out of a desire for vengeance against Coligny, she declares that the action taken was legitimate, since the Admiral no longer saw himself as a subject and behaved as a rebel; that he had come to enjoy a power equal to that of the King over 'those of the religion'; and that he and his allies thus desired the 'overthrow of this state'. And she adds, by way of reaffirming the royal monopoly of justice: 'thanks be to God, everything is pacified, so that one now sees in this kingdom only one king and his justice, which is rendered to each and every one in line with obligation and equity'.[30] As for Henri d'Anjou, he said that he approved a decision that was necessary for the salvation of the state.[31]

The solution adopted was justified by the urgent danger of the situation with which the royal council believed it was confronted. But it did not exclude recourse to 'ordinary' justice; it merely preceded it. On this point, Jean de Morvillier's influence seems to have been decisive. According to his relative and biographer, Nicolas Le Fèvre, it was he who 'advised the king to authorise this action through the trials conducted of the dead body of the Admiral or on his effigy, as well as on the persons of Cavagne and Briquemault; this was done, after it had been communicated by royal order to the first president de Thou, who approved of it'.[32] In his *Histoire*, Jacques-Auguste de Thou confirms this fact and expounds its objective: 'thus, although the business was finished and one could only conduct a trial that was contrary to the natural order, nevertheless Morvillier persuaded the King and the Queen Mother to have recourse to the ordinary rules of justice, and to have the proofs of conspiracy collected with a view to securing a judgment against the guilty'.[33]

These trials actually took place. On 27 October 1572, François de Briquemault and Arnaud de Cavaignes, who had been arrested after the massacre – one in the English embassy, the other in the duchesse de Nemours' residence – were accused of being the leaders of the conspiracy and executed by hanging. The Admiral, judged *post mortem* and declared guilty of lèse-majesté, was hanged in effigy, which took the form of a model made out of hay and in whose mouth a toothpick had been placed as a reminder of one of his habits; his coat of arms was dragged through the streets of Paris and all his property was confiscated.[34] These trials have too often been neglected or derided as parodies of justice, but without realising that in the minds of the council members they were an essential complement to the decisions taken on 23 August. Immediate danger justified prior recourse to extraordinary measures, but did not disqualify ordinary ones. Taken together, the execution followed by the judgment were designed as an inseparable whole whose 'pedagogical' purpose was to demonstrate the King's two powers, that of simultaneously being an absolute king and a king of justice.

It may seem surprising that Charles IX waited two days before presenting this justification to the parlement. The first explanation – that of sedition sparked by the determination of the Guises to kill Coligny – was published, as we have seen, in the circular letters despatched to provincial governors on 24 August.[35] It had doubtless been prepared on the previous evening: it had the advantage of being plausible and, because framed in the context of private vengeance by the Guises against the Admiral, it exonerated the King in the eyes of his Protestant allies. The vendetta version had already been used by Charles IX in a letter written to his ambassador in London on 22 August after the attack on Coligny.[36] The credibility of such an interpretation probably encouraged the members of the council to propose it; in addition, by minimising the event and reducing it to a 'private quarrel' between rival families, it would allow the policy of concord and the maintenance of the edict of pacification to continue, since religion was viewed as playing no part in the disorder. But the scale of the killings that followed quickly changed all that. The Guises might accept being seen as the avengers of their honour, but it was difficult for them to assume responsibility for a generalised massacre.[37] By 25 August, it proved necessary to begin invoking the thesis of a Huguenot conspiracy and, on the following day, to make the case for the recourse to the King's sovereign justice against agitators who threatened the state.

This delay could lead one to suspect that the reasons offered on 26 August were invented *a posteriori*, under the pressure of events and with the aim of mollifying the Guises' discontent.[38] But such suspicion fails to do justice to the plausibility of the decision-making process outlined in the solemn declaration to the parlement, and to the fact that the King, the Queen Mother, and their councillors already disposed of well-worn concepts in making their judgement on the evening of 23 August. One can point here to the doctrines of Machiavelli on the extreme remedies available in cases of imminent danger; there were excellent connoisseurs of the Florentine thinker's works at court, such as Jacopo Corbinelli and Bartolomeo d'Elbene, who were influential in Valois circles. However, the decision of 23 August may well have been inspired by France's own monarchical tradition. Since the twelfth and thirteenth centuries, jurists admitted that the king could, through his 'certain knowledge' (*ex certa scientia*), dispense with the ordinary norms in cases of 'urgent necessity', in which he exercised his *potestas absoluta* and was responsible to nobody.[39] Absolute power was conceived as 'dispensational' par excellence, and emerged as the capacity to decide on what the exceptional was.[40] The royal motivation lying behind the Massacre should clearly be placed in the continuity of the arguments of medieval lawyers over *necessitas* and in the political tradition which, prefiguring the *Six Books of the Republic* (1576) of Jean Bodin, sought to define sovereignty. But these motives had an even greater scope than that. In a letter of 26 August to Claude de Mondoucet and the declaration of 27 August, Charles IX made it clear that he had had to *anticipate* the Huguenot conspiracy, forestalling its actions by striking first.[41] This argument in some ways prefigures the theories developed in the statist literature of the Richelieu ministry and which argued, if the state were in danger, for the need to inflict punishment even before a crime could be committed.[42] The sovereign power to set aside the ordinary laws, such as the King confirmed it on 26 August, had two features. It assumed the right to punish without a prior condemnation and to execute people on mere suspicion. It was indeed a logic of reason of state avant la lettre, activated by the sense of immediate danger.[43] However, this logic was not – or not yet – the product of an ideology or a doctrine; it was asserted during an emergency as a lesser evil designed to assist the return to 'ordinary' circumstances in the shortest time. There is no reason to question the 'great regret and displeasure' with which Charles IX declared that he had felt obliged to act.

The royal demonstration could appear acceptable to those of his subjects who shared the feeling of a threat to the state. A letter to the King of 7 October 1572 from Jacques de Lagebaston, first president of the Bordeaux parlement, attests to this. While claiming that the situation in Bordeaux did not require such an extreme remedy, he admitted that Paris needed exceptional measures:

> There is nothing here that resembles what happened in Paris, all the more so as Your Majesty, the queen your mother, and my lords your brothers were present there, and the conspiracy was about to erupt and was so urgent that it could not wait upon the ordinary course of justice. It was better to begin by action and prevent it rather than being caught napping – and, as you declared in your court of parlement in Paris, you did so for that reason only.[44]

Jacques-Auguste de Thou supplies another testimony. Writing a long time after the events, he was at pains to express the horror they aroused in him. But he also noted that 'people respectable for their piety, knowledge and integrity, holding major offices in the kingdom, and who were also enemies of every sort of trickery and artifice, such as Morvillier, de Thou [Christophe, his own father], Pibrac and Bellièvre', excused an act which in their hearts they condemned, because they were convinced 'that the circumstances in which they lived and the danger to the state obliged them to speak such language'.[45]

The explanation provided from 26 August onwards enabled the King to avow (in the sense of legitimating and giving his avowal to) the 'execution' of Coligny and his chief lieutenants. But his 'avowal' ended there; he took no responsibility for the generalised massacre that he attributed, in his letter to Mondoucet of 26 August, to a 'popular emotion'.[46] In his declaration of 27 August, he reiterated that his decision was not taken 'for any reason of religion', and repeated what he had said on 24th, namely that he intended to preserve the Edict of Pacification and ensure the protection of the Protestants. The religious and political spheres were clearly separated; the sole purpose of the resolution adopted was the salvation of the state.

Does that mean the decision was carefully thought through? By all accounts, it was not. The speed with which it was taken, the sense of urgency, the undoubtedly unreasoned fear of an imminent threat – all lead to the conclusion that its consequences could not be measured as they should have been. Jean de Monluc, bishop of Valence, who was entrusted with negotiating the election of Henri d'Anjou to the Polish throne and who was in despair at the disastrous effects of the killings on the Poles, made no bones about writing with brutal sincerity: 'since they wanted to gain this kingdom [of Poland], they could and should have deferred the execution'.[47]

But should we think that external pressures were decisive in the hasty manner in which the King's council had to make its decision? Such a hypothesis has been proposed – the double threat of a Catholic 'putsch' orchestrated by the Guises and a breakdown in relations with Spain, it is alleged, drove Charles IX to act as he did.[48] There is no proof to support the first element of this rather implausible conjecture; in particular, no document allows us to suspect the Guises of colluding with the radical Catholic preachers.[49] As to the second element, it is expressly contradicted by the sources, since the Spanish ambassador, Diego de Zuñiga, far from planning to leave the court on the evening of 23 August and breaking off relations with France, wrote that, if he did not go to the Louvre, it was because Catherine de Medici herself had asked him not to, because she preferred that he should not be seen entering the palace, no doubt to avoid increasing the anger of the Protestants. When Zuñiga informed her that in these circumstances he believed that she herself should write to Philip II, she replied that she did not wish to, for fear that her letters might be intercepted, but that she would soon talk to the ambassador.[50] And if, on 26 August, Zuñiga sent his envoy, Juan de Olaegui, to Madrid to report the details of what had happened, it was not, as has been suggested, in order to provide a secret oral account of events that would contradict the official story, but because he wanted to get rid of an agent who seemed to be colluding too much with the French court.[51] In his letter of 31 August to Alba, Zuñiga expressed his conviction that the decision to execute the Protestant nobles had been improvised; he had clearly been surprised by it.[52] There is no reason therefore to see in him 'the key figure of the situation' whose attitude determined that of the Guises.[53]

The only pressure endured by the members of the council was fear and resentment towards the Protestants, whose language suddenly revived the fear of a possible threat to the state; anticipating the worst, the council could see no way out other than having recourse to preventative justice.

'EXECUTION'

The elimination envisaged could not be confined to Coligny alone; it had to include all those nobles capable of taking up arms in his defence. A rumour spread that a list of the proscribed had been prepared.[54] If it existed, which is by no means proven, this list could have contained around fifty names. Three locations were necessarily targeted: Coligny's residence on the rue de Béthisy and the neighbouring houses in which his companions had been gathered; the Louvre, where a few Huguenot nobles were lodging; and finally the faubourg of Saint-Germain-des-Prés, where many other Huguenot captains were housed.

Conceived in this way, the application of royal extraordinary justice would develop on a terrible scale, one that was unprecedented and astonishingly risky. It is hard to imagine that the King and his mother could believe such an act to be compatible with maintaining concord. This enigma can be explained by the conviction, which was very common among the high-born, that the elimination of the leaders would suffice to crush the threat of Huguenot subversion. This same conviction is evident among individuals of lower status, for example Raymond de Cardaillac-Sarlabous, who was sent by the King to secure the city of Le Havre and who wrote on 25 August to his brother-in-law that the death of the Admiral and his accomplices would restore peace to the kingdom.[55] What was envisaged was a remedial surgical excision that would remove a gangrenous part from the body social, in order to preserve the health of the rest. In addition, the members of the royal council were ready to believe that the initial explanation – that of a private quarrel between two noble clans – would enable them to limit its consequences. According to the *Mémoires de l'Estat de France sous Charles IX*, it was agreed with the Guises that they would leave Paris immediately after the execution, and that would suffice, it was hoped, to satisfy the Protestants now bereft of their leaders.[56]

The sources enable us to chart the successive stages of the implementation of the King's plan with a reasonable degree of plausibility; only the precise time-scale is impossible to reconstruct.[57] According to the registers of the

Paris town hall, whose evidence is acceptable on this point, the prévôt des marchands, Jean Le Charron, was summoned to the Louvre on the evening of 23 August ('late in the evening'). The King, his mother, the duc d'Anjou and 'other princes and lords' ordered him to close all the gates of the capital and keep the keys; draw in all the boats on the right bank of the Seine and chain them up; arm the captains, lieutenants and bourgeois of the militia and 'keep them ready in the districts and squares of the said city'; and lastly, position the artillery both inside and in front of the town hall. The prévôt des marchands despatched the orders for this to those concerned 'very early in the morning' of 24 August.[58] The objective was without doubt to preserve order within the capital by preventing excesses on the part of both the Catholic radicals and the Protestants. De Thou's allegations that the King ordered the militia to engage in a generalised massacre are groundless.[59]

Once these precautions were taken, it was time to proceed to the executions that had been agreed upon. Priority had to be given to the area around the rue de Béthisy and the Louvre, but in which order? It is difficult to know, as the sources differ so much; the hypotheses presented by historians essentially mirror their reconstruction of events.[60] One thing is certain – the attacks in these two places occurred before dawn. To begin with the account of the Admiral's death is to follow the standard narrative.

In leading the soldiers sent to kill Coligny in his house, the duc de Guise was without doubt obeying an order given, according to Petrucci, by the King or, according to Étienne Pasquier, by Henri d'Anjou.[61] Sassetti indicates that they had to hastily obtain arms from the gunshops, which in his eyes was proof of the improvised character of the affair. According to the account of a captain involved in it, Joshua Studer von Winkelbach, the Swiss troops of the duc d'Anjou under his command and those of Alençon under the command of his brother, Joseph, took part of the expedition; the duc d'Aumale and the chevalier d'Angoulême accompanied Henri de Guise.[62]

There are several accounts of the Admiral's death. That of François Hotman can be adopted because the author affirmed that he obtained it from an eyewitness, while at the same time discounting its apologetic inspiration, which transforms the victim into an exemplary martyr. When the Guise force arrived, Cosseins, the commander of the musketeers stationed in front of the house on the rue de Béthisy on the King's orders, instead of resisting, broke open the doors with the help of the Swiss guards, routed the soldiers provided by Henri de Navarre, and killed all those in his way. Hearing the noise, Coligny ordered the Protestant minister Merlin to recite prayers and began to pray with him. Then, declaring himself ready to die, he exhorted his companions to flee. Many did so, 'finding a window out onto the roof', with only Nicolas de la Mouche (or Muss), his German interpreter, staying beside him. A 'man called Besme from the duchy of Wurttemberg' was the first to enter his room. The Admiral berated him, saying, 'young man, have respect for my grey hairs and my old age'. Disregarding this request, Besme struck him on the head with his sword, and Cosseins and his soldiers finished him off. His body was hurled through the window and hit the ground at the feet of Henri de Guise, who gave it a kick. After that, according to the indignant Hotman, 'he remained exposed to all sorts of ignominy, with some of his limbs cut off, dragged through the mud and finally, after three days, was strung up by the feet at Montfaucon, where he remained for several days as a trophy and a mark of the cruelty and rage which the people of Paris exacted on him, not just in life but also on his dead body'.[63]

The duc de Guise did not personally participate in the murder, but all of the sources agree that he stood at the entrance to Coligny's residence and, once the body had been defenestrated, guaranteed the identity of the corpse. Armed detachments pursued the fugitives and went about executing the Admiral's lieutenants in the nearby houses. François de la Rochefoucauld was killed in his house, near rue de Béthisy; Charles de Téligny, who managed to escape from his father-in-law's house, fled across the rooftops, only to be caught and killed shortly afterwards. The murderers then fanned out along other streets of Paris, since not all of their prey had lodgings near to Coligny.

In the Louvre, the Protestant nobles were woken up, disarmed and taken outside by a little door into the courtyard, where the Swiss and French guards killed them one after another with their pikes. In this killing spree, conducted in the heart of the royal palace, the personal responsibility of Charles IX is fully evident.[64] Those assassinated were his guests and, according to one account, they pleaded in vain with the King to postpone their expulsion until sunrise.[65] This clear violation of the laws of hospitality would be vehemently denounced by the Protestant chroniclers. Agrippa d'Aubigné presented it in a pathetic way: imagining the King himself, standing in a window, as a spectator at the sinister event, he has the baron de Piles declaim just before he was killed the painful words, 'Oh faithless king!' Aubigné adds that the baron then said to one of his assassins when giving him his overcoat, 'Sir, take this, Piles gives it to you, and always remember the death of a man killed so disgracefully'.[66]

In her memoirs, Marguerite de Valois gives some unverifiable details of the horrors of that night which have a ring of truth to them. Wounded, Gabriel de Lévis, seigneur de Léran, took refuge in her bedroom, throwing himself on her bed and then clinging to her on the floor in panic. Nançay, the captain of the guards who was chasing him, decided to spare him before escorting the Queen of Navarre to her sister the duchesse de Lorraine; on the way, the terrified Marguerite witnessed a nobleman being run through with a halberd before her very eyes.[67] Joachim de Ségur-Pardaillan, Louis Goulard de Beauvoir, François de Moneins, Charles de Beaumanoir, Marquis de Lavardin, the former chancellor of Navarre, Barbier de Francourt and many others perished wretchedly. As for Henri de Navarre and Henri de Condé, who were protected by their rank as princes of the blood, Charles IX brought them close to him so as to escape the massacre, and counted on forcing them to convert to Catholicism. According to a Protestant source, the King also pardoned the comte de Gramont, Bouchavannes, and four gentlemen of the King of Navarre, on the grounds that they had 'little or no religion'.[68]

At a moment difficult to determine, but perhaps simultaneous with the murder of Coligny, the tocsin of the church of Saint-Germain-l'Auxerrois begin to sound, and was soon followed by bells of the Palace of Justice. It was at that moment that the second St Bartholomew's Day Massacre, that of the people of Paris, began.

For the elimination of the 'war Huguenots' to be complete, those lodging in the faubourg of Saint-Germain-des-Prés had to be killed. The detachment of Guise soldiers tasked with killing Coligny undertook this operation once they had finished their first mission. But as they approached from the right bank of the Seine, they had to pass through the Île de la Cité (the Pont-Neuf did not yet exist); once on the left bank they had to pass through the Buci gate, which was locked, in order to get to the faubourg. Time was lost in fetching the key, as the one brought by the duc de Guise was not the right one. By the time these obstacles were cleared, it was daylight and the Huguenot captains who were targeted were already on the alert. Jacques-Nompar de Caumont, future duc de La Force, said later that his father, François, who was lodging along with him and his brother on the rue de Seine in the faubourg, was warned by a Huguenot horse-dealer who had swum across the river.[69] Hastily assembled on the river bank in an open space known as the Pré-aux-Clercs, the Protestant nobles saw soldiers who, having taken the boats from their moorings, were heading in their direction with decidedly hostile intentions; seeing that resistance was pointless, some of them had time to get on a horse and flee at full kilter. Among them were Jean de Ferrières, vidame de Chartres and Gabriel de Lorges, comte de Montgomery, the man who had mortally wounded Henri II on 30 June 1559 during a tournament organised on the occasion of the Peace of Cateau-Cambrésis and the marriages that had sealed it. Once he arrived with his cavalrymen, the duc de Guise unsuccessfully pursued the fugitives as far as Montfort-l'Amaury. According to Cavriana, a dozen nobles thus escaped death, while all the others were exterminated.[70]

Of all those targeted during the killings, the Caumonts' fate was singular. François, the father, would not leave the faubourg because his eldest son was ill. Arrested with his two sons by a captain Martin, he was brought into Paris and briefly reprieved, thanks to the promise of a ransom. Then, on two occasions, he refused to take advantage of offers to flee from the two Swiss guarding him: he told them that he would accept God's will.[71] Death came on the following Tuesday, when a detachment of soldiers led by the comte de Coconat came in search of him. He and his eldest son died of their wounds under the ramparts at the end of the rue des Petits-Champs. His youngest son, Jacques Nompar, terrorised but unharmed, collapsed between the bodies of his father and brother; covered with their blood, he seemed dead and kept silent, a helpless witness of their agony. Finally, he was saved by a tennis score-keeper who, taking pity on him, brought him to his house and then to that of his aunt, Jeanne de Gontaut, sister of marshal Biron and a Protestant; the marshal, himself a Catholic but of a tolerant disposition, hid him in the Arsenal.[72]

Geoffroy de Caumont, brother of François, managed to escape. The letters he wrote to Catherine de Medici, Charles IX and Henri d'Anjou on 14 September 1572, on arriving back home in Guyenne to his castle of Caselnau-des-Mirandes, are little-known evidence for the events in Saint-Germain. The longest and most interesting letter was sent to the Queen Mother.[73] The reason he gives for writing is a surprising one: he wished to justify his precipitate departure, on the morning of 24 August, without taking the time to request the permission and 'kiss very humbly the hands' of their Majesties; he feared that the King and his mother might hold this against him. So he went about explaining to them why he had to flee so quickly ...

On the fatal morning, alerted by a huge rumour triggered, in his opinion, by a 'popular emotion', and seeing a large number of armed men – the soldiers who crossed by boat –invading the faubourg in which he lived, he decided to mount his horse and leave, wondering what it was that could have provoked such a tumult. Four or five of his people joined him, wearing only their doublets and swords. Several extremely frightened nobles, some on foot, some on horseback, joined him in his flight. He looked to find his brother and his nephews, who were 'ill and very young', but, not seeing them, he decided to head back to find them. However, the faubourg was already surrounded and his brother's house was full of musketeers, making it impossible to approach it. Sick to death, 'saddened and greatly astonished', but also caught up in the panic which caused the headlong flight of the fugitives, he turned round, surviving an attack by horsemen (probably the duc de Guise's men) during which he lost some of his people. As his fellow fugitives chose a route that he did not know, he considered travelling via Chartres. But, he continued, 'hearing this commotion going on in Paris, I wondered that the same might not happen elsewhere, and that, given the state I was in, I would survive only with difficulty, which made me resolve to return home and immediately after I had done so, to inform your Majesties'.

What he feared most, as he declares in his three letters, and especially in that to Charles IX, was that if he was seen returning home in such a bad plight, people would believe that he had attracted the King's wrath and had fallen into disgrace.[74] Therefore he asked his royal correspondents to demonstrate clearly that he retained their favour and to 'make this known through good testimonies which could not be doubted'. He needed a sufficiently explicit sign that 'would be proof to all' because, he said, if he were to be deprived of their Majesties' favour, he would prefer to die. We can surmise that what was at stake here was his credit in his own province, on which depended the fidelity of his dependents and his 'friends', who might desert him if his intercession with the King lost its effectiveness.

These letters show how completely their author had failed to grasp the meaning of the tragedy; nothing indicates more clearly how far he and his co-religionists were from foreseeing the misfortune that befell them. By comparing Geoffroy de Caumont's account with the passages which his nephew later devoted to his flight in his memoirs, we can measure how far the latter embellished the facts *a posteriori*. Jacques-Nompar says there that Geoffroy had 100–120 horsemen with him and that when the Guise soldiers pursuing them sought to attack them 'they did not dare to do so, but backed off and allowed him to continue on his way, having seen the fine composure of Monsieur de Caumont and his companions'[75]...

How many nobles were killed during the elimination operations of the night and morning of 24 August? It is very difficult to know, given the widely varying estimates made by contemporaries. But what is surprising, if we are to believe contemporary accounts, is how few of the seasoned military captains defended themselves. Of course, most of them were surprised while asleep, while those in the Louvre were disarmed before being assassinated. Of the victims who died on the rue de Béthisy and in the nearby houses, according to Protestant sources, only François-Antoine de Guerchy tried to defend himself. Sword in hand and coat on his arm, he bravely battled to save his life before falling to greater numbers.[76] The nobles in the faubourg Saint-Germain did attempt, as we saw, to band together, possibly, as Jacques-Nompar de Caumont wrote, with a view to aiding the King, who, they briefly thought, was threatened by a 'popular emotion'. Quickly disabused and too few in number to resist the soldiers they faced, they could think only of fleeing, but they were, in most cases, unable to escape their fate.

THE ELIMINATION OF THE FRENCH IN MONS

However, the killing of the 'war Huguenots' was not quite finished on the morning of 24 August. There remained the Huguenot commanders besieged in Mons by the Duke of Alba's forces. To take the full measure of the first massacre, it is necessary to connect it to what happened shortly afterwards on the northern frontier. Charles IX dreaded most of all the return of the commanders who were still fighting in the Netherlands. So on 31 August he instructed his agent, Mondoucet, to transmit his wishes discreetly to Alba: he wanted him to retake Mons but, above all, that he should not agree to any 'composition', meaning that he should not negotiate with the French there or send them back safe and sound to France, because, as the King said, 'they are all factious people, full of ill will and badly affected, who would continue to oppose my intentions'. It would be better, he decided in another letter dated 31 August, that they should perish and be 'cut to pieces'. If Alba were to release them, the King added, Mondoucet was to alert the duc de Longueville, governor of Picardy, 'diligently and accurately as to how many of them they are, the company with which they leave [Mons], and the route that they will take to return to my kingdom'.[77]

It is easy to guess the King's objectives in seeking such information. The fate of the French besieged in Mons was sealed from that moment. But they tried to escape it. In a letter of 18 September, Mondoucet informed Charles that four of them asked to parley, and Alba had granted them an interview with one of his lieutenants, Noircarmes. The four nobles – La Noue, Soyecourt, Sénarpont and a Genlis lieutenant – pathetically made their case. They believed they had been serving the King in going to assist Mons; but now that recent events showed that they had been mistaken over Charles IX's intentions, they did not know what to do; they wished to throw themselves on the King's mercy, implore his forgiveness, and put their lives in his hands, as they could see no other way out.[78]

In reporting these details, Mondoucet stated that the Duke of Alba had promised to require of the besieged, should he agree terms (composition) with them, a solemn promise not to take up arms against their king. But Charles IX replied to his agent, on 21 or 22 September, that this was not acceptable because, he said, once freed, these rebels would, despite their promise, 'do their worst, as is their habit'. He could not trust them because they were 'the leaders and most involved in these rebellions', that is to say, those most capable of mobilising troops and accomplices for Huguenot subversion. Thus, one month after the Massacre, suspicion lived on. Charles IX remained convinced that the clemency exhibited towards the Protestant leaders after the Peace of Saint-Germain had been betrayed in an underhand way; the impulses that determined the decisions of 23 August still ruled his mind. Thus he recommended Mondoucet not to be fooled by 'the fine words of his subjects, which they have always used to colour their pernicious designs'. And he renewed his terrible instructions: 'the principal point, and I repeat it explicitly to you, is to be able clearly to warn my cousin the duc de Longueville of their departure, how many of them there are, the route they take, and the place where they will enter [France], so that without waiting upon the duc, we can decide how to deal with our affairs'.[79]

Mons capitulated on 19 September, and on 21st Alba allowed the besieged Frenchmen to leave under the terms of their composition. Some of them joined the ranks of the comte de Nassau; others, including François de La Noue, were, as a Spanish agent reported, 'escorted by two companies of gendarmes to the last frontier village near Guise'.[80] On 27 September Mondoucet wrote to the King that most of these soldiers had been killed on entering the kingdom.[81]

Philip II wanted to know how many of them there were, and Zuñiga replied
that he had initially estimated them at 600, but that, according to the comte
de Coconat, they in fact numbered more than 800; they were killed on the
King's orders by the duc de Longueville in and near Sedan, 'three or four days
before the feast of Saint Michael'.[82] In a letter of 29 September the ambassador
recounts that Catherine de Medici, whom he had pressed to reply to him about
the Mons survivors, laughed as she said to him: 'it is true, they are dead because
the duke of Alba did not wish to kill them, so that this time they could not go
to assist the prince of Orange against my son the king or against us'.[83] Distrust
was so dominant that all Huguenot leaders suspected of wishing to attack the
King's authority, whoever they were, were excluded, for the present at least,
from the royal dream of concord.

In his letter of 29 September, Zuñiga informed the King of Spain that La
Noue was still being searched for. He had not, in fact, escaped from his guards,
and a letter of 11 October 1572 from the duc de Longueville to Catherine de
Medici suggests that he and two of his companions were spared for particular
reasons. The duc declares to the Queen Mother that, on receiving orders from
their Majesties, he had La Noue and the two Sénarponts (Jean de Monchy
and his son) brought to him; he now wished to know what he should do with
them.[84] When the King asked to speak to La Noue, Longueville brought him to
Paris. The Protestant nobleman, known for his loyalty and held in high esteem
by his co-religionists, was to be employed by Charles IX in a delicate mission to
conciliate the Protestants in La Rochelle, who were by then in open resistance.[85]

The elimination of the Protestant leaders was thus complete. The King could
now believe he was done with the spectre of Huguenot subversion, henceforth
deprived of its leaders. But on the morning of 24 August he witnessed the emergence of another form of disorder, this time from the Catholics. The indignities
inflicted on Coligny's body, which was left on the street after his defenestration, were eloquent testimony of this new danger, whose gravity had not been
fully measured by the King's council. The Admiral's body was dragged around
Paris with a rope by children; castrated, decapitated, half-burned, dumped into
the Seine and pulled out again, it was strung up by the feet on the gibbet at
Montfaucon.[86] Such outbursts were not the violence of sovereign justice, but
of popular vengeance. The second massacre had already overtaken the first.

NOTES

1 As does Crouzet, *La Nuit de la Saint-Barthélemy*, pp. 515–516, who underlines the 'absolutely different' character of the second massacre.

2 Stegmann, *Edits des guerres de Religion*, p. 63. See the electronic edition of the full text by Bernard Barbiche at the website of the École des chartes, http://elec.enc. sorbonne.fr.

3 For examples of these Protestant texts, see *Défense civile et militaire des innocents et de l'Eglise du Christ*, published at Lyon during the first war, and regarded as so subversive that all copies were burned (its contents are known from the refutation by Charles Dumoulin); *Sentence redoutable et arrest rigoureux du jugement de Dieu à l'encontre de l'impiété des Tyrans*, also published at Lyon at the same time; *Question politique: s'il est licite aux subjects de capituler avec leur prince*, attributed to Jean de Coras and no doubt composed in 1568–69 at La Rochelle; and, finally, the *Discours par dialogues de l'Edict de revocation de la paix*, produced at La Rochelle around the same time.

4 Coligny to the King, 8 May 1571, quoted above, p. 31.

5 BnF, MS. Fr. 3193, fol. 68r–v, *Memoire des parolles dittes par feu Monsieur l'admiral au mois d'aoust au cabinet du roy Charles*. The date of 6 Aug. is also mentioned by Claude de Mondoucet, quoted by Champion, *Charles IX*, vol. 2, p. 83.

6 *Négociations diplomatiques avec la Toscane*, vol. 3, p. 785, Petrucci to Francesco de Medici, 24 June 1572.

7 Bellièvre, *Proposition faite aux Suisses*, fol. 210r–v.

8 *La Saint-Barthélemy devant le Sénat de Venise*, pp. 13–14.

9 *Négociations diplomatiques avec la Toscane*, vol. 3, p. 826, anonymous Italian letter to Francesco de Medici, Paris, 26 Aug. 1572.

10 In a letter to Schomberg subsequent to the Massacre and dated 13 Sept. 1572, Charles IX evokes his 'sustained patience' towards Coligny, despite his 'felony' (BnF, MS. Fr. 3951, fol. 51r, published but wrongly dated to 12 Sept in *Lettres de Catherine de Médicis*, vol. 4, p. 122, n. 1, from copy in BnF, MS Dupuy, 86, fol. 205r).

11 Sassetti, *Brieve Raccontamiento*, pp. 130–131.

12 *La Saint-Barthélemy devant le Sénat de Venise*, p. 22 (italics mine).

13 Bellièvre, *Proposition faite aux Suisses*, fol. 215v (italics mine).

14 *Négociations diplomatiques avec la Toscane*, vol. 3, p. 815, anonymous (Cavriana) to secretary Concini, Paris, 27 Aug. 1572; Charles Samaran, 'Un humaniste italien, Guido Lolgi, témoin de la Saint-Barthélemy', in *Studi in onore di Ricardo Filangeri* (Naples, 1959) vol. 2, p. 402, Guido Lolgi to Alessandro Farnese, Paris, 25 Aug. 1572 (italics mine).

15 Bellièvre, *Proposition faite aux Suisses*, fol. 210r–v.

16 BnF, MS. Fr. 3951, fol. 51r, Charles IX to Schomberg, 13 Sept. 1572 (see n.10).

17 *La Vie de messire Gaspar de Colligny*, p. 122; *Le Réveille-Matin des François*, (Edinbugh, 1574) vol. 1, p. 54.

18 The circular letters sent to provincial governors on 24 August explain that the Guises, having learned that the Huguenots would exact vengeance on them, 'took action this past night so that between them there occurred a great and regrettable sedition'. The letter to the duc de Longueville was published in Bourgeon, *Charles IX devant la Saint-Barthélemy*, pp. 44–45. But in his letter of 25 Aug. to ambassador

La Mothe Fénelon in England, the King refers to the Huguenot conspiracy against him, his mother and brothers (*ibid.*, p. 70), and in a memoir sent to Schomberg, he refers to the attack that they were planning (*Lettres de Catherine de Médicis*, vol. 4, p. 113, n. 2).

19 The testimony of Marguerite de Valois of an assembly of forty nobles in his chamber on the evening of 23 Aug. is credible, *Mémoires et autres* écrits, p. 98.

20 *La Saint-Barthélemy devant le Sénat de Venise*, p. 40.

21 *Négociations diplomatiques avec la Toscane*, vol. 3, p. 815, anonymous (Cavriana) to secretary Concini, Paris, 27 Aug. 1572.

22 Gomicourt's report is published in Erlanger, *Saint Bartholomew's Night*, pp. 248–50. What seems like a draft of this report is in AGS, Estado, K24, no. 78, *Relación de la muerte del Almirante y otros hereges de Francia*.

23 *Lettres de Charles IX à M. de Fourquevaux*, p. 119.

24 This interpretation partly coincides with that initially proposed by Denis Crouzet, *Les Guerriers de Dieu*, vol. 2, p. 28, where he shows that the first St Barthélemy was a 'defence of the state' by the King, whereas in his *La Nuit de la Saint-Barthélemy*, he insists more on the royal desire to safeguard the harmony of the kingdom. In his *Les Guerriers de Dieu*, the defence of the state appears 'sacral' in essence, and belonging to the religious sphere. In his *Le Haut Cœur de Catherine de Médicis*, p. 505, Crouzet downplays this motive, devaluing the political significance of the decision taken on the evening of 23 Aug.: 'the defence of the state was not an end in itself in this context. Reason is not an ideology but an instrument to be used on the occasion at hand'.

25 AGS, Estado, K1530, no. 20, Zuñiga to Philip II, 23 Aug. 1572; Bourgeon, *L'Assassinat de Coligny*, p. 35, n. 17. However, two days later, the governor of Paris, François de Montmorency, left the capital and retired to Chantilly.

26 The first of these legends comes from the *Mémoires de Gaspard de Saulx-Tavannes*, written by his son, Jean, and very hostile to the Queen Mother; the second comes from an apocryphal *Discours du Roy Henry troisiesme à un personnage d'honneur et de qualité, estant près de Sa Majesté, des causes et motifs de la Sainct Barthelemy*, published in 1623, but probably written in the Gondi entourage in order to exonerate the comte de Retz (the King supposedly said that he wished the Admiral to be killed, 'but also all the Huguenots of France, so that there would be none alive to accuse him of it later'). However, Sassetti's account (he says that Charles IX said '*Ammazzeteli tutti, accioche questa peste non ci molesti più*', *Brieve Raccontamiento*, p. 142) shows that these bloodthirsty words were already attributed to the King shortly after the massacre (unless of course the text was revised by a copyist in 1583).

27 Cavriana mentions the ducs de Montpensier and Guise, Sassetti the duc de Guise, and adds the name of the bâtard d'Angoulême.

28 Bellièvre, *Proposition faite aux Suisses*, fol. 218r.

29 Only the register of the *plaidoiries* of the parlement preserves a clear trace of this royal declaration. No minutes of the sessions between 16 and 26 August survive, which itself raises some questions. See Bourgeon, 'La Fronde parlementaire à la veille de la Saint-Barthélemy', p. 76, who suggests that it was on account of a strike by the magistrates, a hypothesis that becomes a certainty in his *L'Assassinat de Coligny*, p. 31, but without any supporting evidence. The *Journal* of François de Syrueilh is published in *Archives historiques du département de la Gironde*, 13 (1871–72), pp. 284–286, for the declaration of 26 Aug. There is a brief description of the session

of the parlement by a French priest in Augustin Theiner, *Annales ecclesiatici* [...] *ab anno MDLXXII*, 3 vols (Rome, 1856), vol. 1, p. 45, quoted in Bourgeon, *Charles IX devant la Saint-Barthélemy*, p. 83, n. 4.

30 *Lettres de Catherine de Médicis*, vol. 4, p. 130, letter to Arnaud du Ferrier, 1 Oct. 1572.

31 Henri d'Anjou to the French ambassador in Spain, 29 Aug. 1572, quoted by Nicolas Le Roux, *Un régicide au nom de Dieu. L'assassinat d'Henri III* (Paris, 2006), p. 63. Thierry Wanegffelen, *Catherine de Médicis*, pp. 357–358, attributes sole responsibility for the decision to Henri d'Anjou, who had joined with Henri de Guise, without the knowledge of Charles IX and Catherine de Medici – a thesis which is unverifiable, given the lack of supporting sources.

32 BnF, MS. Fr. 18288, Nicolas Le Fèvre, sieur de Lezeau, *La Vie de messire Jehan de Morvillier*; Gustave Baguenault de Puchesse, *Jean de Morvillier, évêque d'Orléans, garde des sceaux de France* (Paris, 1870), p. 291.

33 De Thou, *Histoire universelle*, vol. 6, p. 420.

34 Champion, *Charles IX*, pp. 131–134.

35 See above, n. 18.

36 See above, ch 3, n. 24.

37 This is the argument of the author of the *Relation du massacre de la Saint-Barthélemy*, p. 153, for whom the Guises, 'seeing the atrocity of what had happened, asked the king to avow all of it'.

38 Bourgeon, *Charles IX devant la Saint-Barthélemy*, p. 72, quotes a passage from de Thou's *Histoire* to support that suspicion, but the passage claims that the King wished 'to *confirm* via a *public* testimony' that what had happened was done on his orders (italics mine).

39 Jacques Krynen, *L'Empire du roi. Idées et croyances politiques en France, xiiie–xve siècle* (Paris, 1993), pp. 400–402. On the connections between medieval *necessitas* and reason of state, see the analysis of Michel Senellart, *Machiavélisme et raison d'Etat* (Paris, 1989), pp. 31–35.

40 'Sovereign power is nothing other than derogation from the civil laws', according to Bodin, *Six Livres de la République*, livre 1, ch. 8. See the conclusions of Vincent Houillon in David El Kenz, ed., *Le Massacre, objet d'histoire* (Paris, 2005), pp. 403–404.

41 Charles IX to Claude de Mondoucet, 26 Aug. 1572, and the royal declaration of 27 Aug., quoted by Bourgeon, *Charles IX devant la Saint-Barthélemy*, pp. 99–100, 104.

42 This was the thesis of Guez de Balzac, *Le Prince* (1631). See on this point Étienne Thuau, *Raison d'Etat et pensée politique à l'époque de Richelieu* (Athens, 1966), pp. 252ff.

43 Denis Crouzet, 'La nuit de la Saint-Barthélemy: confirmations et compléments', in Chantal Grell and Arnaud Ramière de Fortanier, eds, *Le Second Ordre: l'idéal nobiliaire. Hommage à Ellery Schalk* (Paris, 1999), pp. 56 and 80, identified 'themes of reason of state' in the decision of 23 Aug., but believes that, in the service of the 'Neo-platonic utopia' of Charles IX, it became a 'de-realisation of politics'. Similarly, when he insists, in *Le Haut Cœur de Catherine de Médicis*, pp. 398–399 and 536, on the role played by the notion of necessity in the political imaginary of the King and the Queen Mother, he sees it primarily as a historical dynamic which constrained the King to follow it, but to which the latter, having abandoned himself to God's will, somehow remained an 'outsider'.

44 BnF, MS. Fr. 15555, fols 124r–127r, Jacques de Lagebaston to Charles IX, Bordeaux, 7 Oct. 1572.

45 De Thou, *Histoire universelle*, vol. 6, pp. 457–458.

46 It is surprising to see that many historians write that the King had claimed paternity over the massacres as a whole, whereas he recognised only the execution of Coligny and his lieutenants; he attributed the killings to the fury of the 'people' while rejecting their insurrectional aspects (see especially the 'mémoire au vrai' in which he offers his version of events, quoted above, pp. 138, 163).

47 BnF, MS Cinq Cents Colbert 7, fol. 447r, Jean de Monluc to president Brûlart, 20 Nov. 1572, quoted by Venard, 'Arrêtez le massacre!', p. 659.

48 This thesis is defended by Jean-Louis Bourgeon.

49 Barbara Diefendorf, *Beneath the Cross*, p. 236, n. 11, clearly established this point. Crouzet, *La Nuit de la Saint-Barthélemy*, pp. 444–446, convincingly demonstrated the improbability of a Guisard 'putsch'.

50 AGS, Estado, K1530, no. 20, Zuñiga to Philip II, Paris, 23 Aug. 1572. Bourgeon's hypothesis, in *L'Assassinat de Coligny*, p. 91, of a Spanish threat to break off diplomatic relations is based on a single text from a passage in the *Mémoires des sages et royales œconomies d'Estat* by Sully written many years later. Sully seems to have confused Zuñiga with the previous ambassador, Francés de Álava.

51 AGS, Estado, K 530, no. 21, Zuñiga to Philip II, Paris, 23 Aug. 1572 ('*me paresce que tiene muchas rayzes en este Corte, y assi he procurado lo mejor que he podido descargarme del* [de el]'). Bourgeon's supposition on Olaegui is in his *L'Assassinat de Coligny*, p. 54, n. 27.

52 AGS, Estado, K1530, no. 29, Zuñiga to Alba, Paris, 31 Aug.1572 ('*no fue caso pensado sino repentino*'). Petrucci claims, in a letter of 16 Sept., that Philip II gave 6,000 écus to Besme, the presumed assassin of Coligny, but this is an isolated source; if it were true, it would indicate the King of Spain's satisfaction but would not make him responsible for Coligny's murder. See *Négociations diplomatiques avec la Toscane*, vol. 3, p. 838, Petrucci to Francesco de Medici, 16 Sept. 1572.

53 Bourgeon's entire interpretation of the Massacre is based on this unfounded hypothesis of an imminent breakdown of diplomatic relations, since he claims that, without Zuñiga, 'the Guises would never have embarked on their rebellion'. See his *Charles IX devant la Saint-Barthélemy*, p. 27.

54 Sassetti, *Brieve Raccontamiento*, p. 135.

55 The letter was published in Édouard Forestié, *Un capitaine gascon du xvie siècle: Corbeyran de Cardaillac-Sarlabous* (Paris, 1897), p. 162. On 25 Aug., Raymond de Cardaillac-Sarlabous attributes the execution of Coligny and his companions to the King as punishment for their conspiracy.

56 Crouzet, *La Nuit de la Saint-Barthélemy*, p. 454, for whom this interpretation enables us to understand how the King and his mother could hope to maintain concord. That supposes that the first explanation issued by the King on 24 Aug. was agreed with the Guises and not, according to another hypothesis mentioned in *ibid.*, p. 411, without their consent and taking advantage of their absence during their pursuit of Montgomery on 24–25 Aug..

57 On this point, see Anne-Marie Cocula, 'Regard sur les événements nocturnes des guerres de religion', in Dominique Bertrand, ed., *Penser la nuit, xve–xviie siècles* (Paris, 2003), pp. 464–485, who notes the disparities in the chronology presented by different historians.

58 *Registres des délibérations du Bureau de la Ville de Paris*, vol. 7, pp. 10–11. See the useful observations on their value as a source in Diefendorf, *Beneath the Cross*, p. 211, n. 22.

59 Diefendorf, *Beneath the Cross*, p. 97 notes that it is hard to see why the King would have placed the artillery in front of the town hall – a classic measure when riots were feared – if his intention was to have all the Protestants killed in their beds.

60 Crouzet, *La Nuit de la Saint-Barthélemy*, p. 402, gives chronological priority to the murder of Coligny, but Bourgeon, *L'assassinat de Coligny*, p. 111, to the killings in the Louvre.

61 *Négociations diplomatiques avec la Toscane*, vol. 3., p. 809, Petrucci to Francesco de Medici, 25 Aug. 1572; Étienne Pasquier, *Lettres historiques*, ed. Dorothy Thickett (Geneva, 1966), pp. 362 and 377, n. 6. In the memoir from the King to Schomberg of 25 Aug. 1572 quoted above (n. 18), Charles IX is said to have 'consented that members of the house of Guise could kill the Admiral and those of his faction on the twenty-fourth day of the said month of August'.

62 Sassetti, *Brieve Raccontamiento*, p. 141; the account by captain Joshua Studer quoted in Crouzet, *La Nuit de la Saint-Barthélemy*, p. 448. According to the anonymous account in *Dessein de ceulx qui soubz le nom et autorité de Sa Majesté ont faict le massacre*, the duc d'Anjou himself led his guards and participated in the operation: BnF, MS. Fr. 17309, fol. 60r.

63 *La Vie de messire Gaspar de Colligny*, pp. 127–130. According to the letter of 26 Aug. written by Father Joachim Opser, a native of Saint-Gall and then *sous-proviseur* in the college of Clermont, it was Martin Koch and Conrad Bürg, two Swiss soldiers belonging to the duc d'Anjou, who murdered Coligny: see 'Deux lettres de couvent à couvent écrites de Paris pendant le massacre de la Saint-Barthélemy', *BHSPF*, 8 (1859), p. 288. But after the event many people claimed the 'glory' of having killed the Admiral; they were so numerous, as Salviati wrote ironically on 22 Sept., that not even the piazza Navona in Rome would be big enough to hold them all! See *Correspondance en France du nonce Antonio Maria Salviati*, p. 249, letter of 22 Sept. 1572.

64 Bourgeon, *Charles IX devant la Saint-Barthélemy*, p. 36, attempts to exonerate Charles IX, but has to recognise here that the King had to 'consent and even facilitate' the massacre, although he adds that he was constrained and forced to do so.

65 'Relation de la journée de la Saint-Barthélemy; manuscrit trouvé dans les archives épiscopales de Wiener-Neustadt (Autriche)', *Bulletin des sciences historiques, antiquité, philologie*, 6 (1826), p. 228. This account was written by an Austrian ecclesiastic to the Bishop of Wiener-Neustadt.

66 Agrippa d'Aubigné, *Histoire universelle*, quoted by Garrisson, *La Saint-Barthélemy*, p. 105. Cavriana has Piles exclaim 'O sure peace, o complete faith': *Négociations diplomatiques avec la Toscane*, vol. 3, p. 820, letter to secretary Concini, Paris, 27 Aug. 1572.

67 Marguerite de Valois, *Mémoires et autres écrits*, p. 99.

68 *Négociations diplomatiques avec la Toscane*, vol. 3, p. 820, letter to secretary Concini, Paris, 27 Aug. 1572; *Mémoires de l'Estat de France sous Charles IX*, vol. 1, fol. 292v.

69 *Mémoires authentiques de Jacques-Nompar de Caumont, duc de La Force*, ed. Édouard Lelièvre, Marquis de Grange (Paris, 1843), vol. 1, pp. 1–37.

70 *Négociations diplomatiques avec la Toscane*, vol. 3, p. 818, Cavriana to secretary Concini, Paris, 27 Aug. 1572.

71 See Crouzet, *La Nuit de la Saint-Barthélemy*, pp. 59–63, on the Protestant imagi-
    nary which sustained the constancy of François de Caumont.

72 *Mémoires authentiques de Jacques-Nompar de Caumont*, vol. 1, pp. 1–37. The rue
    des Petits-Champs is now the rue Croix-des-Petits-Champs.

73 BnF, Ms. Fr. 15553, fol. 199r, Geoffroy de Caumont to Catherine de Medici, 14
    Sept. 1572. His letters were published in *Archives historiques du département de la
    Gironde*, 10 (1868), pp. 357–360.

74 BnF, MS. Fr. 15553, fol. 197r, Geoffroy de Caumont to the King, 14 Sept. 1572. The
    letter to the duc d'Anjou is at fol. 201r.

75 *Mémoires authentiques de Jacques-Nompar de Caumont*, vol. 1, p. 36.

76 *Mémoires de l'Estat de France sous Charles IX*, vol. 1, fol. 293v.

77 Gachard, *La Bibliothèque nationale à Paris*, vol. 2, p. 525, the King to Mondoucet,
    31 Aug. 1572; *ibid.*, p. 526, same to same, same date.

78 *Ibid.*, p. 533, Mondoucet to the King, 18 Sept. 1572.

79 *Ibid.*, p. 534, the King to Mondoucet, no date, but 21 or 22 Sept. 1572.

80 *Ibid.*, pp. 535–538, *Advis touchant le faict de Mons*, undated but Sept. 1572.

81 *Ibid.*, p. 540, Mondoucet to the King, 27 Sept. 1572.

82 AGS, Estado, K1530, no. 129, Zuñiga to Philip II, Paris, 15 Nov. 1572.

83 *Ibid.*, no. 71, same to same, Paris, 29 Sept. 1572 (*Dixome reyendose: es verdad que
    los han muerto, pues el duque d'Alba no los quiso hazer matar, por que esta vez no
    vayan a ayudar al Principe de Orange contra el Rey mi hijo ny contra nosotros*).

84 BnF, MS. Fr. 15555, fol. 143, Longueville to Catherine de Medici, 11 Oct. 1572.

85 Henri Hauser, *François de La Noue* (Paris, 1892), pp. 31–60.

86 See the analysis of these forms of violence in Crouzet, *Les Guerriers de Dieu*, vol.
    2, pp. 96–101. A few days later, François de Montmorency would recover the body,
    which was then transported in a lead coffin to Chantilly.

5

CATHOLIC FURIES

The scale of the generalised murders of Protestants unleashed in Paris early in the morning of 24 August and in several cities across France during the following days and weeks cannot but cause surprise. Their nature, and especially their motivation, raises questions. The characteristics of massacre were mixed with those of war. These two types of violence, it has been observed, belong to different categories: the first to the realm of the instinctual, while the second 'belongs to the world of rationality'.[1] The irrational was certainly at work in the carnage. Convinced that they were the armed hand of God, the ardent Catholics indulged in a murderous orgy of purification brought on by a 'collective hallucination of the presence of God' and of a 'trance of divine possession'.[2] However, because of its duration and its organised, systematic character, the extermination in the capital assumed the form of a war of defence against the Huguenots perceived not merely as heretics, but also and especially as dangerous agitators intent on every imaginable excess. If the Parisian Catholics fought for God, they also fought systematically to defend their lives and belongings, which they believed to be threatened by enemies positioned within the heart of their city. These two aspects are, of course, inextricable – so much did the horror of heresy fill the actions of the murderers with an irrational rage – but each feature can nevertheless be distinguished from the other. The exterminators of 24 August were determined to take their destiny into their own hands, in an indirect reproach to the King, who, in their eyes had failed in his double mission of guarantor of religious unity and protector of his subjects – a reproach that was soon transformed into open disobedience and even rebellion. It is this entanglement of the issues involved which makes the second Massacre, that of the Parisians, such a baffling – but also fascinating – subject for historians.

THE HUGUENOTS AS SUBVERSIVES?

If we are to understand the popular violence of 24 August, we need to recall that the image of the Huguenots in the mind of Catholics was often accompanied by fantasies which ascribed malicious intentions to them. Their origin probably lies somewhere in the memory of the conspiracy of Amboise in March 1560.

The conspirators, who were mostly Protestants, wished to drive the Guises (duc François and his brother Cardinal Lorraine) from power, but their attempt, which took the form of an armed attack on the château of Amboise, where the royal family resided, seemed to many contemporaries a subversive act directed against the King. It was at this point that the term 'Huguenot' became widely used to designate France's Protestants. The origins of this tag probably lie in the fusing of two terms, both of which had baleful connotations. The first is *Eidgenossen*, meaning conspirators or confederates, which was the name of a faction within Geneva involved in the city's struggle for its liberty.[3] In the French imagination, Geneva personified not just a hotbed of heresy, but also the spirit of independence and insubordination; beyond that, it conjured up the influence of the Swiss world and the republican structures of the cantons. According to Louis Régnier de La Planche, secretary of François de Montmorency, the Protestants were from then onwards accused of 'wanting to introduce their religion with their swords, to destroy the monarchy of France and reduce it to the condition of a republic and a canton ... and to pillage, loot and regard the best houses and the churches of the kingdom as their prey'.[4]

It was also after the events of March 1560 that a second etymology grafted itself onto the first. Since the Protestants, who until about 1555 were confined to clandestinity, conducted their religious services at night, they were identified with disturbing night-time ghosts – the 'drunken monk in Paris, Odet the mule in Orleans, the werewolf in Blois, and King Huguet in Tours'.[5] In a chapter of his *Recherches de la France*, Étienne Pasquier recounts that, eight or nine years before the Amboise affair, he heard friends from Tours speaking of the Huguenots as followers of 'King Hugon', another name for King Huguet.[6] The fear sparked by the furtive preparations of the conspirators around Amboise and Tours had the double consequence of establishing Hugon, the Touraine ghost, as the eponym of the Protestants and consolidating their image as dangerous conspirators.[7]

Thereafter, and despite the efforts of theologians like Calvin, Pierre Viret and Thédore de Bèze to counter this disastrous image, the Huguenots inspired fear.[8] The iconoclasm in which they engaged on the eve of and during the first civil war did not help; their religious motives and their zeal to purify places of worship were perceived by Catholics as a desire for systematic destruction. The dread that they inspired was not unconnected to the savagery of the massacres which they endured in 1562, especially at Sens and Tours, and which prefigured, on a lesser scale, that of St Bartholomew. In the year 1562, Ronsard did not hesitate to portray the Protestants as men wielding bloody knives, adjuring Théodore de Bèze as follows:

> Ne presche plus en France une Evangile armée
> Un Christ empistollé tout noirci de fumée
> Qui comme un Mehemet va portant en la main
> Un large coutelas rouge de sang humain

[Preach no more in France a gospel of war
Nor a pistol-brandishing Christ black with smoke
Who, like Mahomet, holds aloft
A cutlass red with the blood of men.][9]

In Paris, this threatening image prompted waves of irrepressible fear. In spring 1563, for example, during the first civil war, a farmer gave a captain of the city's bourgeois militia a letter of apparently innocent content written to a magistrate of the parlement who was suspected of Protestantism; but he said that when the paper was heated a very different message appeared: its author warned his correspondent to put his property in safe-keeping, because the Huguenots were preparing to attack Paris and reduce it to a field, i.e., to destroy it.[10] At the start of the second war, uncontrollable panic gripped the population of the capital even more markedly. After the surprise of Meaux, the Prince of Condé's army took Saint-Denis; during the night of 1 October 1567, it set fire to a dozen mills around the village. On seeing the fires lighting up the night sky, a terrifying rumour immediately circulated among the Parisians to the effect that the city's Huguenots were gathering firewood and powder in order to burn everything down. Some of the militia, which the King had allowed to carry arms again, targeted the houses of Protestants who had not yet managed to flee, with the aim of discovering the presumed conspirators; they went on to make arrests and even committed murders. An anonymous witness recounts that the authors of these excesses were convinced that they had the right to act as they did, and that anyone speaking in support of 'rebels' was threatened with death; he adds that, in a macabre omen, the skin of a man who had been flayed alive – the very punishment inflicted on St Bartholomew – was found in the street.[11] Étienne Pasquier, for his part, says that that night and the following days anyone who did not affix a white cross to his hat ran a real risk of being assassinated. It was this sign, the symbol of the crusade, which the killers of 24 August 1572 would wear.[12] In addition, these fears were fuelled by the fear of famine, since the Huguenots had attempted to blockade Paris and the city had recovered badly from the shortages that were rife during the years from 1564 to 1566.

During the third war, Parisian anxieties were again sharpened because, for the first time, the King had allowed the peaceful Huguenots to remain in the capital.[13] This explains the explosion of violence that followed the uncovering of clandestine Protestant worship in the Gastines family house, after which it was razed by court order.[14] The Peace of Saint-Germain in 1570 did not allay these fears. The parish priest Jehan de La Fosse noted in his diary that the edict which made it official contained 'articles that were sufficiently shocking to make all France tremble', since the Protestants, despite everything they had done, were still regarded as good servants of the King.[15] As for Simon Vigor, he warned Parisians in his sermons that the heretics would eventually kill them all, either by poison or by other means – a declaration that was bound to arouse the most irrational fears.[16]

The fears of the Parisian Catholics were all the more persistent, since they knew exactly where the Protestants resided. The latter were mostly their neighbours, since they were located relatively evenly throughout the capital. An analysis of 399 suspects imprisoned in the Conciergerie between 1564 and 1572 and whose place of residence is known reveals that they lived in each of the sixteen quarters of Paris; they were particularly numerous in those of Saint-Séverin and Sainte-Geneviève (left bank); in Sainte-Avoye, Saint-Martin, Saint-Eustache and Saint-Honoré (right bank); and, in the centre, the Notre-Dame quarter, to which we should add the faubourg of Saint-Germain-des-Prés, nicknamed 'little Geneva'.[17] During the riots generated by the removal of the Gastines cross, the Golden Hammer and Pearl houses on the Notre-Dame bridge were pillaged, as they would be again during the massacres of 24 August 1572, such was their reputation as Huguenot lairs. In an overpopulated city, with its cramped and poorly insulated dwellings, everyone knew about the activities of their district's inhabitants, which in turn enabled a network of collective surveillance to take shape, from which nobody would have been able to escape. As it has been accurately noted, 'a good number of the victims of the Massacre can be identified as having been implicated in previous quarrels or conflicts ... ordinary people who were victims of the massacres may seem anonymous at a distance of four hundred years, but they were not so for their killers. They were neighbours and acquaintances.'[18] To Parisians, the Huguenots appeared all the more dangerous, as they were spread throughout the city and ready to seize the first opportunity to attack them. It does not matter here that such apprehensions were clearly imaginary; fantasies do not make any less of an impression on people for having no foundation in fact.

The widespread nervousness in the capital fed on the difficulties that it faced. The price of cereals saw a notable hike between 1570–71 and 1571–72 (harvest years ran from the end of July to the beginning of August of the following year).[19] Disturbing rumours circulated; according to Jehan de la Fosse, people were saying that the King was about to tax everyone to the tune of one-tenth of their property.[20] Alarming omens, such as the huge brightness that appeared in the night sky on 15 January 1572, illuminating visions of combats and wars, seemed to presage an immediate catastrophe.[21] Parisians' obsessions were sufficiently powerful to conjure up the need to turn on the Huguenots as the scapegoats who would enable them to exorcise their fears and resentment.

It should be noted that another group also gave focus to such hatreds – namely, the Italians, who were relatively numerous in Paris and who were associated in the popular imagination with fiscal exactions, since the King turned to financiers of Italian extraction to levy extraordinary taxes. Genoese, Florentines, Milanese, Venetians and Romans – all belonged to communities which provoked mistrust. In June 1572, two months before the Massacre, several of them were either killed or wounded during a xenophobic riot; they were accused of killing children and taking their blood, according to an anonymous author, so as to enable the duc d'Anjou or the Queen Mother to recover from a secret illness.[22] According to the same author, they were called 'Marrabets', namely Marranos, converted Jews. The accusation of massacring children to take their blood belonged to those crimes habitually attributed to the Jews, to whom the Italians could be assimilated on account of their financial activities; but it could also be turned against the Protestants.[23] In this way the different figures of the Other, who did not belong to either the traditional faith or the nation, could be brought together in the same form of repulsion, an Other who could be more or less consciously held guilty for various misfortunes – the loss of religious unity, the difficulties of daily life, the omnipresence of anxiety-bearing signs. Italians were assassinated, admittedly in small numbers, alongside Protestants during the Massacre, but the fact is sufficiently noteworthy to suggest that the Parisians' attitude towards the Huguenots was not just that they were heretics, but also enemies who, like the hated Italians, had their eyes on their goods and their lives.[24]

On the eve of 24 August 1572, the feeling of insecurity was suddenly ramped up by the arrival in Paris of Henri of Navarre's companions for his marriage. The sight of these armed Protestant nobles openly moving around the city provoked apprehension. Anxiety reached its peak when, after the attack on Coligny, Catholics saw some of his friends regrouping around his residence in accordance with royal orders. Inflated in people's imaginations, these movements tipped Parisians into a state of trepidation, convincing them, as the parish priest Haton wrote, 'that the Huguenots were planning an upheaval in Paris'.[25]

It was in this context of obsessive fear, worsened by the perception of the threat from the behaviour of the Admiral's lieutenants, that the tocsin of Saint-Germain-l'Auxerrois rang out early on the morning of 24 August. The operation conducted that night against Coligny in the neighbouring rue de Béthisy had made some noise. For those Catholics who heard it – some had attended the office of matins early that morning – the noise was undoubtedly worrying.[26] Then the terrifying rumour must have begun to spread – the Huguenots are on the attack!

This misunderstanding, based on fear and uncertainty, provides the most plausible explanation for the ringing of the tocsin. It is unlikely that it was an agreed signal for a massacre planned in advance – a highly dubious plan, whether attributed to the Queen Mother (by the Protestant sources) or to Parisian Catholics. The instigators of the 22 August attack did not, of course, remain inactive after Maurevert's failure, and they must have busied themselves stirring up anti-Huguenot hatreds; but there is no proof that their action took the form of a planned and concerted killing, even though that was keenly hoped for. The only document that might lead one to think of an organised conspiracy, of which the tocsin was the prelude, consists of the evidence given later by a man questioned in a lawsuit brought by the prévôt des marchands against those who pillaged the house of one of the victims, Phillippe Le Doux. The witness, Guillaume La Faye, declared that he was ordered by a militia sergeant of his district to guard Le Doux's house and to ensure that nobody left it alive once the tocsin had sounded. But he added that the murders were committed by 'ordinary people'. This story is not confirmed by other evidence, and it was perhaps given in order to relieve its author of all personal responsibility.[27] More likely, it was the panic generated by the night-time tumult, itself attributed wrongly to the Protestants, which caused the alarm to be sounded, thereby offering the Catholic activists an opportunity that they hardly imagined would arise so soon.

Other church bells must have echoed that of Saint-Germain, although accounts vary on this point. The young Maximilien de Béthune, future duc de Sully, wrote years later that he had been woken, at around three o'clock in the morning, by a mixture of the sound of bells and shouts, a recollection sufficiently vivid to remain intact in his memory.[28] A polemical writer, Pierre Burin, alludes in his response to the royal justification written by Guy du Faur de Pibrac to 'the Paris matins which were well tolled and sounded.'[29] But the exact time at which this alert was sounded remains difficult to determine, as, once again, the accounts do not allow for certainty on this point. According to Simon Goulart, the Palace of Justice's clock was heard after the tocsin of Saint-Germain, accompanied by the announcement that 'the Huguenots had taken up arms and were preparing to kill the king', which strengthens the hypothesis of a sudden surge of panic among Parisians and also suggests that they believed Charles IX's life was under as much threat as their own.[30]

Very soon, however, popular fear mutated into joyful relief and the sense of the misunderstanding changed. Having checked that Coligny was really dead, the duc de Guise reportedly said out loud, according to Goulart: 'Be brave, soldiers, we have begun well, let's go for the others, since the king orders it ... it is the king's will, his express command.'[31] This assertion, which Guise evidently wished to confine to the execution of the Admiral's companions, was understood by those who heard it as the unexpected legitimation of their murderous intentions. Convinced that the King, illuminated by God's grace, had finally accepted the necessity to get rid of all heretics, and elated by the miraculous recovery of their union with their sovereign, Parisians immediately set about the task. It was this tragic misunderstanding which made generalised massacres possible. The concurrence of belief in an imminent Huguenot attack and the certainty of being authorised to act by both Charles IX and God provides the key to the launching of the mass killing which the King, in fact, had believed that he could avoid.

WAR AGAINST THE ENEMY WITHIN

The religious motivations for the carnage activated forms of behaviour mentioned in all of the records, so strongly did they strike the imagination. The murderers wore a cross of cloth or paper on their hats; they often had a simple band of white cloth wrapped around their arms, and sometimes a white cloak. The cross symbolised the crusade that they were determined to conduct against heresy, and the colour white indicated the purity that they wished to recover for their city. Their fury expressed their suffering in relation to what they considered to be an intolerable pollution of their universe, alongside a sharp feeling of guilt for having allowed such pollution to proliferate.[32] Confused readers of the Gospel, they rushed into tearing up what they saw as the chaff, thereby hoping to achieve the impossible Utopia of a field without weeds and a world without stain.[33] Their problem was how to identify the real chaff. To distinguish the 'good' from the 'bad', an external sign was needed so that the 'good' could recognise each other and unite against the 'bad'; and in such a situation, not having a sign stigmatised and laid people open to retribution from exterminators. On the other hand, the houses of the victims were perhaps marked out, possibly with a cross, which served as a simple sign to make the targets of purifying action visible. This detail seems credible, since Pierre de l'Estoile subsequently noted the reappearance of such marks on Protestant houses on 22 August 1579, something which made observers fear the imminence of a new massacre.[34]

On the morning of 24 August, the sudden flowering of a hawthorn in the Holy Innocents cemetery, which was said not to have done so for several years, sparked a redoubling of Catholic fervour. Parisians gathered in great numbers to witness the miracle, which they saw as an assurance that God approved of the extermination of the Huguenots. Father Joachim Opser, then sub-provisor of the college of Clermont, went there too and expressed his joy to a correspondent in Saint Gall:

> In recent days in the Holy Innocents cemetery, a hawthorn which for four years seemed withered, was covered with flowers, as I saw with my own eyes. It is a sure sign that religion will be restored, and everyone ardently accepts this omen. I piously held my rosary beads close to the hawthorn and touched them with it.[35]

For Catholics eager for omens and anxious for the future, the hawthorn miracle carried the promise of a 'restoration', a return to lost unity. They viewed it as a spectacular reply to the exile of the holy from this world preached by the Protestants; the miracle proved to them that some earthly realities, such as this humble shrub, could be mysteriously invested by the other world, and that everyday life still contained points of contact between the material and the spiritual that were doors to the supernatural. In this way, the permanence of 'enchantment' in a familiar universe was asserted, without which they would have felt themselves lost.[36]

Yet many clues indicate that mystical rapture alone does not explain every aspect of the killings. The preservation instinct born out of fear prompted forms of behaviour to which the defensive structures of the city's bourgeois militia, reactivated by the King, gave the appearance of war itself.

All of the sources show the existence of military control structures in the city. Witnesses referred to the presence of numerous groups of guards, controlling the movements of people. Maximilien de Béthune, then aged eleven and a half years, managed to leave his house wearing his schoolboy clothes and carrying a large Book of Hours, and made it to the college of Burgundy, whose principal took him in; but before he got there, he was stopped three times by suspicious guards, who nevertheless allowed him to continue.[37] The evidence of Charlotte Arbaleste, a devout Protestant and a young widow of twenty-two years, who would later marry Philippe Duplessis-Mornay, is similar. Having come to Paris with her three-and-a-half-year-old daughter to complete the probate of her father's and her husband's estates, she was woken up on the morning of 24 August by a frightened servant who said that 'they are killing everyone'. Having quickly dressed, she looked out the window of her lodgings on the rue Saint-Antoine and saw 'several groups of guards, each one with white crosses on their hats'. For eleven days, she moved from one refuge to another, as the relatives or friends who hid her were one after another obliged to turn her out, since the houses were systematically searched by the 'captains of Paris', the heads of the bourgeois militia; they were also searched, she says, by the 'domestics' of the duc de Guise, by which she means men belonging to his household. From the house of M. de Perreuse, a master of requests and her relative, she observed the duc de Guise himself and the duc de Nevers coming and going on the street. Finally, having entrusted her daughter to her maternal grandmother, 'a strong Roman Catholic', Charlotte decided to flee, dressed as an ordinary woman, by taking a boat on the Seine; but here, too, she encountered another group of guards, who halted the embarkation at the Tournelles. As she had no passport, the soldiers detained her, saying that she was a Huguenot and should be thrown into the water, before agreeing to let her go. But her encounters with the soldiery were not over. Disembarked at Ivry, where the boat stopped, she found a refuge a few miles further on, at Le Bouchet, with a winegrower who was a tenant of president Tambonneau, whose wife was a relative of hers, and where she observed the Swiss guards of Queen Elisabeth 'rummaging all over the village in order to find some poor Huguenot'. Fortunately, the house in which she lodged had a safe place and was not searched, but she heard her host deplore the fact that all of the neighbouring nobles had been massacred, which shows that the pursuit of Protestants extended far beyond the city itself.[38]

The account that she gave of the misadventures of her future husband conveys the image of a capital whose gates were closed or carefully guarded, its streets full of guards, with soldiers methodically searching its houses. Philippe Duplessis-Mornay, who converted to Protestantism while assiduously reading the New Testament, was in Paris when the attack on Coligny occurred; it was he who wrote for the Admiral the vehement appeal to the King to commit himself openly to the Dutch rebels against the King of Spain. His lodgings at the 'Golden Compass' on the rue Saint-Jacques were searched during the night of 24 August and he escaped only by slipping out across two rooftops. The following day, seeing that the next-door house had been pillaged, he took refuge with a bailiff on rue Troussevache who usually managed his affairs but who, after an inspection by the captain of the local militia, was unable to keep him. Duplessis then tried to flee the city, but had to abandon the idea of leaving by the Saint-Martin gate, which was closed, going instead to that of Saint-Denis, where his slippers, which in his haste he had forgotten to replace with his shoes, alerted the guards. Musketeers set out in pursuit, arrested and then freed him, on the favourable evidence which, at his request, the bailiff of the rue Troussevache provided about him. He still had to avoid the armed men who roamed the Vexin area in search of Protestants. Finally, with the help of his brother-in-law, the sieur d'Auberville, he managed to embark at Dieppe for England.[39]

How can the military supervision and the systematic searches which accompanied the massacres be explained? The tight control of the city resulted without question from royal orders. On the evening of 23 August, it will be remembered, Charles IX ordered that the captains, lieutenants and bourgeois of the militia be armed and kept ready 'in the cantons and the squares' of Paris. Officially, the objective was to maintain order, not to exterminate or pillage the Huguenots. Two incidents reported by Simon Goulart (who can be believed on this point, since they contradict the general convictions of this Protestant pastor, who interpreted both of them as ruses) suggest that the King's intention was indeed to ensure the protection of peaceful Protestants by this means. The first is the account of the ordeal of Pierre de La Place, president in the *cour des aides*. A visit from a captain who extorted a ransom of 1,000 écus from La Place was followed by one from the sieur de Sennecey, provost of the royal palace, who claimed to have a royal order to bring La Place to court and protect his house from pillage. When the president refused to move, he left him under the protection of one of his lieutenants and four archers. The prévôt des marchands, Jean Le Charron, then arrived and added four further archers to the guard who, along with the others, helped the master of the house to prepare his defence. Thus, notes Goulart, 'it seemed that these archers were placed in the house to preserve the said sieur de La Place and his family from the general calamity'. But things changed the following day. Sennecey returned with manifestly less peaceful intentions. This time he demanded that La Place go immediately to the King and proposed to have him accompanied by Captain Pezou, one the 'leading rebels'. Then, in response to La Place's protests, he offered to accompany him, but only for fifty paces, as his 'affaires', he said, required his presence elsewhere. Clearly, the ambush had been prepared, and murderers stationed on the rue de la Verrerie despatched La Place with their knives while he was being escorted by the archers, who did nothing to stop them. It is likely that Sennecey's change of mind was the result of pressure from the assassins, whose appetite was whetted by the prospect of serious loot; the president's house would be pillaged over five to six whole days.[40]

The second episode concerns Pierre Baillet, a merchant-dyer of the rue Saint-Denis. Hearing noise around midnight (a rather vague time-scale), he sent a servant to find out what was happening. Goulart recounts that 'his neighbours in arms ordered him to go back and tell his master to keep low; there had been an attack on Coligny, and they were under arms in order to prevent sedition'. In this case also, it was a band of murderers who, arriving somewhat later, changed Baillet's fate; on entering his house, they took him to the Saint-Magloire prison, where, failing to extort a rather large ransom from him, the murderers finished him off outside the prison gate.[41]

In these two accounts, the considerable difference between official instructions and violent actions by armed troops is clear. Should we think in terms of things 'getting out of control'?[42] The term fits as far as the 'royal soldiers of the royal guard' are concerned – namely, the guards of Charles IX and his brother Henri d'Anjou, whom the Italian humanist Guido Lolgi saw going from house to house, killing and pillaging. His testimony is corroborated by other sources, including the memoirs of Charlotte Arbaleste quoted above.[43] It is plausible that it was discontent caused by arrears in wage payments which drove these men to exceed royal orders and to ransack the houses they entered, rounding things off with generalised killings. In addition to such looting, numerous accounts mention the ransoms demanded of victims. Guido Lolgi claims that the booty collected in this way was incredibly high. With greater accuracy, Ambassador Petrucci estimated it at 600,000 écus (1.8 million *livres*), 120,000 of which were recovered, it was said, by a royal secretary acting on behalf of Charles IX.[44]

The case of the bourgeois militia is undoubtedly different in that the desire of some of its members to exterminate pre-dated the events themselves. Yet neither the incumbent prévôt des marchands, Jean Le Charron, nor his predecessor, Claude Marcel, can be suspected of drawing it into the massacre. If the Protestants and Jacques-Auguste de Thou in his *History* did accuse them of that, it was because this interpretation suited their view of the tragedy.[45] The turn towards acts of violence probably came from certain partisan captains, four of whom are named in the sources: the haberdasher Choquart, Jean du Perrier, a barrister in the parlement, Nicolas Pezou, and Thomas Crozier. The last three were widely known as ultra-Catholic, and we also know that in June

1569 Du Perrier was suspended from his duties as captain of the militia for excessive cruelty.[46]

It was no doubt these men and a few others who, disobeying their orders, committed the first murders, triggering a domino effect whose scale can be explained not just by the sheer will to exterminate all enemies of the faith, but also by the state of mind of the city's bourgeois militia. Its members, who comprised all of the 'bourgeois' of Paris (i.e. all of those resident for at least a year and with a profession held to be honourable) capable of bearing arms, were placed under military command (three captains for each 'territorial' unit); in it, 'notables' rubbed shoulders with shopkeepers and artisans. The role of the militia was, firstly, guarding the gates of the city at night and, secondly, the watch (defence and police) in each of the sixteen districts of the capital. These duties helped to give its members the sense of having a territory to defend that was inseparable from their common identity; the presence of a hostile group within this living space was regarded as an intolerable intrusion that endangered the community, whose integrity was thereby impaired.[47]

It was as dangerous intruders that the Huguenots came to be perceived by their neighbours: by setting themselves apart with their religious dissidence, they took on the appearance of suspects and traitors who were by their nature infused with evil intentions towards the community that they had renounced.

This ideological construction of the figure of the 'enemy within' was a process which could not but lead, at the slightest warning, to violent acts of rejection.[48] The scandalous character, in Catholic eyes, of the events experienced by Parisians before the Massacre and the paroxysm of fear and anguish of the night of 23–24 August gave this rejection the characteristics of a war for the methodical elimination of enemies who threatened their security. This feature can be compared with massacres committed in other times and places; it attests to the conviction of acting in legitimate defence, justified by the tacit argument that, since the enemy wishes to kill us, we need to kill him before he can put his evil plans into operation. Such an argument, it has been shrewdly observed, turns the individual preparing to act as executioner into a victim and his plans for destruction into an operation for survival.[49] This does not mean that all of the inhabitants of each district participated in the massacre; everything suggests that the assassinations were committed by an active minority operating together in armed bands, using the militia structures and acting without official orders. The rest of the population no doubt withdrew indoors, confining their participation to denunciations.[50]

Thus it was that a massive extermination could occur, one in which a mystical enthusiasm was inextricably coupled with the wish to defend one's life, property and family. Other, more sordid motives were involved, such as the taste for booty. A witness interrogated after the events during a lawsuit brought against the pillagers by the prévôt des marchands spoke artlessly of the 24 August as the 'day when the pillage of Huguenots in Paris was allowed'.[51] The sadistic pleasure of the killer is also visible, stimulated on this occasion by a more prosaic intoxication than that of religious zeal: we know, for example, from evidence given during a subsequent trial, that the especially cruel murderers of the jeweller Philippe Le Doux and his wife afterwards emptied their cellar of its wine bottles.[52] And some, of course, did not hesitate to take advantage of the situation to exact private vengeance. Was it not enough, as Ambassador Petrucci noted, to say of an enemy, 'here we have a Huguenot', for him to be butchered instantly?[53] This was how, if we believe Simon Goulart, the book-seller Oudin Petit was betrayed by his father-in-law, Jacques Kerver, over an inheritance dispute, or the celebrated Pierre Ramus, professor at the Collège royal, who was reportedly denounced by his rival, Jacques Charpentier, was then assassinated, defenestrated and disembowelled, and finally whipped 'by some schoolboys on the instigation of their teachers'.[54]

Having in vain given orders to 'all of the bourgeois, residents and inhabitants' of the city districts to put away their arms and to the royal troops to stop their pillaging, the powerless city authorities could only let things happen.[55] One factor, however, is surprising – the silence of the parlement throughout this bloody week. No record exists of its sessions from 16 to 26 August. Did it go on strike to show its resentment towards Charles IX, which would make it passively complicit in the massacre?[56] It is possible, but no source enables us to say so. It is also possible that the magistrates did not sit, since they had to move back from the convent of the Augustinians into the Palace of Justice, from which the celebrations of the marriage on 18 August had temporarily displaced them.[57] Most likely, the magistrates were so terrified by events that they went to ground, as did Christophe de Thou, who, having witnessed two friends being killed and dumped in the Seine, locked himself inside his house 'for fear of witnessing similar spectacles'.[58]

The social composition of the victims reflects, hardly surprisingly, the section of the population affected by the Reformation. In other words, there is no over-representation of the highest social groups, which might incline one to think that motives based on class hatreds were at work (such motives were extremely rare in the society of orders of that period). Although the sources are too thin, especially in Paris, to allow an exhaustive identification of the status of those killed, what indications they do contain allow us to form an approximate idea. Comparisons with the killings that occurred in other cities reveal similar characteristics, especially the predominance of merchants and artisans; in the capital, the relatively high number of nobles is explained by the royal 'execution'.[59]

The topography of the Parisian massacres maps onto that of the Protestants' habitat there. Many were killed on the Notre-Dame and the Meusniers bridges, which then had heavily populated houses on them, and from where it was easy to throw Protestants directly into the river. On the right bank, the streets most frequently mentioned are those around the Louvre and Saint-Germain-l'Auxerrois, near the cemeteries of the Holy Innocents and Saint-Jean, as well as the rue Saint-Denis; on the left bank, the University district and the faubourg Saint-Germain were the scene of many assassinations. As with the murder of Coligny's lieutenants, the absence of resistance by the Protestants surprised Catholic commentators (the Protestants saw in their resignation the sign of the martyrs offering their sufferings to God).[60] If we can judge from the *Mémoires de l'Estat de France sous Charles IX*, only a lieutenant of the marshalsy by the name of Taverny fought all day with his pistol and then his sword before dying; the remainder, caught unarmed in their own houses, were unable or unwilling to defend themselves.[61] Thus, according to an estimate that remains hypothetical, did 3,000 people go to their death in Paris.[62]

On the forms of the violence itself, the diplomatic sources provide few useful indications, apart from the fact that the massacre spared neither women, children nor the elderly. It is Protestant sources which offer most of the descriptions, amplifying the barbarity of the murders and the inhumanity of the killers with an obvious polemical intent. Their reliability cannot be entirely rejected, however, and certain events recorded by the most important of them, the *Mémoires de l'Estat de France* collected by Simon Goulart, are often indirectly supported by independent sources.[63] Without accepting every slip of information that these witnesses give on the atrocities committed, we can accept the most salient features of the carnage that they relate, not just because the details have a ring of truth about them, but also because they resemble the documented facts of the massacres committed before St Bartholomew's Day; in the 1572 massacre, which was the result of a violent explosion of hatred and anger hitherto bottled up, the difference was one of degree rather than of nature.

The first point to note is the ferocity towards women, especially pregnant women, who were sometimes victims of particularly savage treatment. Sexual associations were not absent from such cruelty, but the punishments inflicted on them also corresponded to a wish to destroy all chances of proliferation by the group that their murderers sought to eliminate. The castration of men was symbolically connected to the same obsession; it was also the reason why young children were also butchered. Of this massacre of the innocents, Protestant sources have transmitted some powerful images, no doubt enriched by their emotions. According to the Calvinist from Millau, the Seine was full of empty children's cradles, from which the assassins had torn the new-born in order to steal their swaddling-clothes before drowning them.[64] Simon Goulart offers another striking image: that of a child laughing as he played with the beard of his murderer, before being mercilessly thrown by the latter into the river.[65]

However, the desire among the killers to finally eradicate a rabble judged to be harmful was counteracted by the view that Protestants might be brought back to the true faith, since the pollution of heresy contaminated the soul and not the 'race'; in this respect, the massacre of the Protestants differs radically from a genocide.[66] Hence the conversions obtained under duress, which, by removing the 'pollution', sometimes saved *in extremis* the lives of the less determined Protestants. Thus the less courageous brothers of Charlotte Arbaleste escaped death by abjuring their faith; others, such as the son of president La Place, made people believe in their renunciation by fixing a white cross to their hats and were spared for doing so.

The nudity inflicted on the victims is another feature which emerges from the accounts of the killings. When the stripping of people preceded their execution, as happened with the richly dressed countess whose assassination was witnessed by the bourgeois of Strasbourg, the most obvious motive was to recover her clothes untorn by the blows. But other reasons no doubt played a part. By stripping the execrated adversary, their social identity was removed, and all of the bonds that linked them to the community were metaphorically ruptured; they were made anonymous, and the inhibitions arising from the memories of previous neighbourliness could disappear. But the disaggregation of the solidarity created by daily co-existence could also operate when the stripping of bodies followed an execution. In this case, should we blame the logic of the behaviour of crowds, in which the phenomenon of the 'de-individualisation' of the massacred and the loss of personal responsibility among the killers could both arise? If so, it would be necessary to establish how many people are required for such a 'crowd action'. And are blind acts of violence characteristic of big cities, whose large population allows for relative anonymity?[67] Doubt is permitted on this point, since, in Paris, it was the district, a relatively small unit in which everyone knew each other, which was the theatre of the outbreaks of ferocity and the process of dehumanising one's neighbours; the familiar dimensions of such a space rendered even more compelling the demand for cohesion, security and purity. The 'antagonistic polarisation' of 'we' and 'them', to quote the words of a recent analyst of the massacres perpetrated during human history, could work even more intensely here; people readily followed the logic which other forms of collective violence reveal, and according to which the destruction of 'them' is the proof of the existence of 'us'. 'To kill is not just to purify, it is also to purify oneself.'[68]

The mutilation of corpses (and sometimes of bodies still twitching) after the murders was intended to disfigure them and to destroy anything human in them in order to display their bestial and diabolical nature. In this sense, it can be said that these acts of violence had a didactic aim, that of showing that the dead were already prey to the demon; the outrages suffered by Coligny's body are a particularly significant illustration of this.[69] The dismemberment of bodies seems to have been characteristic of Catholic excesses during the Wars of Religion; Protestant crowds also showed their cruelty at certain times, especially when they tortured priests, but once their victims were dead they did not harass them any further.[70]

These pedagogical intentions were also expressed by parodies of the judicial executions of the Huguenots, where the desire to substitute popular justice for the failures of that of the King was clear. A remarkable example of this can be found in the account by Simon Goulart of the death of a poor bookbinder, burned to death before his house on a pyre consisting of his books. This was the punishment of heretics before heresy was decriminalised by royal legislation in 1560.[71] In reality, the books did not burn well, and the unfortunate victim had to be thrown into the Seine.

The river served as a sewer where rubbish was thrown away. Protestant corpses were treated as trash unworthy of burial, even though their numbers and rotting condition made it necessary to bury those which beached further up the river bank. All of the observers noted the sinister change in the colour of the river, which went red with blood. Here too, Protestant memory has left a poignant image, raising purity, viewed as the victim of barbarity, to the status of an icon. The long hair of the wife of a royal feather-dealer, tied to an arch on the Notre-Dame bridge, kept her body aloft for three days until her husband, arrested in the house of friends and slaughtered in turn, was thrown on top of her and dragged her down into the water; 'thus they were united in their burial' commented Goulart with restrained emotion. In his *Tragiques*, Agrippa d'Aubigné would expand on this story, in which he saw the incapacity of the men of blood to 'separate bodies which heaven had joined together.'[72]

However, not all Parisian Catholics approved of the massacres, and some of them, whose memory was preserved by the survivors, managed to save Protestants. Among them was the duc de Guise himself, which is surprising until one realises the partly bi-confessional composition of his clientele; his undoubted Catholic zeal did not prevent him from seeking to acquire the gratitude of survivors which might one day be useful to him.[73] He reportedly sheltered several Protestant nobles, and the anonymous Protestant author of the *Réveille-Matin des François* expressed his gratitude in the dedicatory letter that he addressed to him.[74] A young Protestant, Renée Burlamaqui, wrote that Henri de Guise had taken her into his Parisian residence along with her young children and several fugitives.[75] Other Catholics intervened on behalf of Protestants in flight, either through noble solidarity, lineal co-operation or simple compassion. The Catholic sieur de Lansac hid in his house the son of the comte de La Rochefoucauld, who had been assassinated, along with one of his nobles, Jean de Mergey.[76] The baron de Biron, from a family notoriously divided confessionally, hid Protestants in the Arsenal, which, as we saw, was how Jacques de Caumont was saved. Religious houses also served as refuges for the persecuted.[77] The Duke of Saxony's emissary, Hubert Languet, obtained the protection of Jean de Morvillier, and then of Pomponne de Bellièvre.[78]

Courage was required of Catholics who took Protestants under their protection or who even confined themselves to expressing their horror at the exactions; if their social status was not high enough to avert such danger, they risked their lives. In his enumeration of the victims, Simon Goulart mentions a 'papist solicitor' being killed for having expressed pity towards those who had been massacred.[79] Mostly, it was fear that dissuaded Parisians from helping the Huguenots; compassionate hosts who hid survivors turned them out as soon as the suspicions of the murderers got too close for comfort. The corn-merchant who took in Charlotte Arbaleste undoubtedly shared her anxiety while sheltering her in an upstairs room. She had orders not to light a candle or even walk around for fear that her presence might be revealed by a light or by unusual sounds. Moderate Catholics were indignant and disgusted by the massacres, as Protestant sources themselves reveal.[80] But most of them had, out of fear, to avoid expressing their disapproval, as did the chronicler Pierre de l'Estoile. He had in his house an antipapal pamphlet that revealed too much of his hostility towards Catholic extremism, so he hastened to burn it, 'fearing that it might burn him'.[81]

FROM WAR TO INSURRECTION

The violence of the Parisian reaction initially caught Charles IX unawares. As he himself acknowledged in the letters sent on 24 August to provincial governors (in which he referred to a 'sedition' caused by the murder of the Admiral by the Guises), he was obliged to remain inside his palace at the Louvre just as the massacres were beginning. To save face, he later presented the Catholics' fury as the effect of their anger on discovering that the Huguenots had tried to kill him. In a 'true memoir of how things happened during the recent emotions', which he despatched on 27 August to his ambassador in England, he laid out the interpretation of the facts to be presented to Queen Elizabeth: the people had been 'highly irritated to see that his said Majesty was obliged, along with the Queen Mother and my lords his brothers, to shut himself up in the Louvre, with his guards, and to keep the gates locked to defend himself against the force and violence that they were threatened with ... for which things the angry people of Paris exacted great violence on those of the new religion'.[82] A similar explanation of the popular intoxication figures in another memoir dated 27 August: 'the people were greatly moved to see the Huguenot conspiracy so widely known and so open'.[83] The Parisians' action expressed, according to the version which the King wished to impose, their love for him, while their excesses, of which he said he was 'truly saddened', were the consequence of the excess of passion with which they tried to protect him. For Charles IX, this was a way of excusing them and, thus, to escape the accusation of being powerless, while admitting that the Catholics had acted without his consent.

But he found it increasingly difficult to hide his inability to stop the carnage. Yet he had made his intentions clearly known. During the morning of 24 August (seven o'clock, according to Pibrac, nine, according to Salviati), the order was given to end the massacres.[84] According to the Venetian ambassador, Giovanni Michiel, the chevalier d'Angoulême and the duc de Nevers were despatched on horseback into the streets in order to end the killings. During the afternoon, those who had taken up arms were ordered to 'lay them down', an order immediately reiterated by the city authorities. Around five o'clock, a ban on the looting and killing of Huguenots was proclaimed 'to the sound of the trumpet and public cry at all of the squares and public places of the city'.[85] As the day of 24 August passed, it was impossible to believe, as it had been first thing that morning, that the King had authorised the killings.

Late in the evening, Charles IX's orders began to be carried out. A witness such as the Florentine Guido Lolgi wrote that the night of 24–25 August passed without any looting and that, on the morning of 25 August, when he was writing his account, few assassinations or acts of looting were being reported.[86] Simon Goulart's account also suggests a temporary reduction in disorder, at least during the night-time.[87] This relative lull shows that the Catholics' anger did not yet constitute an insurrection, which was in no way programmed in advance. On the contrary, the initial misunderstanding, which led the murderers to believe that God had enlightened the mind of the King by revealing to him the necessity of the massacre, had the effect of re-legitimating Charles IX by making him seem endowed with divine grace and, at last, worthy of the royal office. It was only gradually, under the impact of the disappointment and indignation experienced by the Catholic intransigents on realising their mistake, that the idea took shape in their minds that, faced with a weak king, it was for them to take up the cause of God and of the community. Disobedience gradually came to seem to be a duty, in the urgent necessity to obey a higher cause betrayed by the temporal authorities and which ordinary believers now had to assume.[88]

It was, therefore, from Monday 25 August onwards that the royal orders were knowingly diverted from their stated aim. On that day, Charles IX gave orders for a general search of Huguenots and 'to watch carefully over all those of the Religion, so that no harm or displeasure be done to them, on pain of death, but to guard them well and safely'. Then, on 27 or 28 August, he ordered that they be imprisoned.[89] The purpose was to place them in safety. This measure contradicted the declarations of 27 and 28 August sent to the provinces, the first of which invited the Huguenots to remain indoors and provisionally suspended the public exercise of their religion, while the second order released those in prison, those complicit in the presumed 'conspiracy' excepted.[90] This ambi-

guity perhaps explains why the murderers transformed the King's instructions
into an open hunt for Protestants; when they were taking them to prison, either
they massacred them along the way, though not before demanding a ransom,
or else they returned at night to assassinate them.

Thus, when the Guises returned from their wild pursuit of the comte de
Montgomery, they found a city in a state of open sedition. Perhaps they began
to think that they could turn the situation to their advantage. In particular,
they seem to have gained control of the passports needed to leave the capital,
no doubt exploiting the disorganisation revealed by Ambassador Zuñiga, who
wrote on 26 August to Phillip II that he was unable to despatch his letter earlier
as he had been unable to find a royal secretary capable of giving him the indispensable passport.[91] It was from the duc d'Aumale that the bourgeois of Strasbourg obtained his, while the one offered to Philippe Duplessis-Mornay was
signed by the duc de Guise.[92] Did the Guises go further than that? They were
certainly allied to the exclusivist Catholic faction, which had been reinvigorated
by these events; its most active members, like the ducs de Nevers and Montpensier, did not hide their hostility to the policy of reconciliation with the Protestants.[93] Henri de Guise and Louis de Gonzague-Nevers, whom an account like
Charlotte Arbaleste's shows going about the streets of Paris, could no doubt
have halted the carnage, given their reputation with the population of Paris.
In Nevers' case, we have clear proof of this in the misadventure of the English
Ambassador Walsingham, who had to hide in his house besieged by killers and
two of whose servants were assassinated. The duc de Nevers, happening to pass
by and seeing the danger, drove away the besiegers and placed a guard around
the house, which saved the ambassador's life and those of his household.[94] But it
is the only occasion on which we see Nevers stopping murderous activity. As for
the duc de Guise, he confined himself, as we have seen, to welcoming a number
of refugees. For the most militant Catholics at the court, the massacre seems
to have been a magnificent opportunity that they allowed to develop, without
having to take responsibility for it. At the very least, they played a passive role
in the non-implementation of the King's orders and thereby supported the
insurrectional dynamic of the movement, even though they did not deliberately
trigger it off. It is possible that they later tried secretly to keep it going: as late as
mid-October, if we can believe doctor Cavriana, Catherine de Medici suspected
the Guises of stoking discontent behind the scenes.[95]

In these circumstances, the measures taken by the King could only be
fruitless. On 24 August, according to the royal secretary Jules Gassot, he had
gibbets erected on street corners to intimidate trouble makers, and they were
still there in mid-September.[96] But effective forces were needed to render such
measures dissuasive. An episode recounted by Simon Goulart shows the King's
powerlessness. On 26 August, as Charles IX, escorted by the nobles of the
court and his guards, went to the parlement to announce that the death of

Coligny and his lieutenants had been on his orders, 'a noble among the troop was recognised as a Huguenot and immediately killed quite close to the King, who on turning around because of the noise and on hearing what it was about, said "Let's proceed, please God it will be the last"'.[97] If this anecdote is true – and it is quite plausible – we can measure the King's weakness: this murder committed so close to him was a crime of lèse-majesté, exactly the kind of affront which he would never have tolerated among the Admiral's companions, but which he had now to accept on the part of unknown killers. His attempt to restore the royal majesty was revealed here, on the steps of the parlement and in the middle of the capital, as a terrible fiasco.

One way of channelling the violence was to transform it into peaceful mani-festations of religious zeal. The solemn procession of actions of grace which occurred on 28 August was apparently a clerical rather than a royal initiative. But that of 4 September was ordered by Charles IX, bringing together around the reliquary of Sainte-Geneviève the entire court, the city authorities, the Parisian clergy and a large crowd. Medals were struck to celebrate the victory over heresy.[98]

However, much of the city of Paris remained beyond royal control. Walsing-ham's wife experienced it, as Zuñiga wrote in a letter of 12 September. Wishing to leave Paris, she went to one of the gates, but the guards recognised two clergymen among her escort; they took them aside and beat them with their sticks, despite the royal passports mentioning and authorising their presence. Alerted to this, Catherine de Medici had to send Jerome de Gondi in haste to escort the group out of the city.[99] Killings continued to occur in the prisons. For the month of September, the parish priest Jehan de La Fosse writes in his diary:

> During this month searches for Huguenots to make them prisoners did not stop, and the most obstinate of them were executed at night by the executioner. But those who wished to abjure and anathematise the heresies, and specifically the Lutheran and Huguenot ones, were received in mercy.[100]

Walsingham mentions the arrest and execution in mid-September of a canon of Notre-Dame and councillor in the parlement named Roulart, 'with no more recourse to justice than for the others [who were executed]'. His crime was that he said he disapproved of arbitrary executions.[101] Petrucci notes on 19, and then 25 September, that new prisoners were taken each day and were thrown into the river during the night.[102] The comte de Saint-Pol wrote similarly to the Duke of Savoy on 13 and again on 26 September.[103] In a radical inversion, it was now the people who exercised *their* extraordinary justice, replacing the King in the face of the urgent danger to the faith; at least they did so, after 31 August, during the night and clandestinely. But on 27 October, the Parisians showed their fury against the corpses of the Admiral's lieutenants, Briquemault and Cavaignes, who were hanged that day; in a macabre repetition of their ferocity towards Coligny's body, they tried to cut them in pieces; the bodies had to be hastily removed from the gibbet.[104]

Thus for over a month, Catholic gangs imposed a kind of reign of terror in the capital. The Huguenot Jacques Pape writes in his *Mémoires* that, imprisoned for fifteen weeks, he lived throughout that period in continual fear of execution.[105] By the end of October, royal authority seemed to be almost entirely restored, and the last letters patent forbidding murders and looting were issued on 28 October.[106] Court cases before the prévôt des marchands, involving looters rather than murderers, could then be started.[107] But in mid-November fear ratcheted up again and rumours spread that a new insurrection was being prepared in Paris; with the King absent hunting, a plan to kill all Protestants, converted or not, was reportedly hatched.[108] Charles IX was indignant, as he wrote to Pomponne de Bellièvre on 6 December: 'some villains, badly disposed towards to the good and repose of peace spread a rumour among the people as soon as I had left, that it was my wish that those of the new religion living in this city be exterminated and looted'.[109] In one of his letters, dated 1 December, Jacques Faye, a councillor in the parlement, provides some detail on this aborted sedition in which certain 'grands' were involved and which was quickly snuffed out by the energetic response of the prévôt des marchands and marshal Tavannes; Jehan de La Fosse also indicates its scale.[110] This episode says much about the frustration of those, at court and in the city, who were keen to finish off the Huguenots. Gripped by fear, three to four hundred recent converts left Paris.

The duration of the disorders reflects the gravity of the insurrection. Recent historians have rightly seen in it a prelude to the troubles of the Catholic League. The challenge to Charles IX's power; the substitution of the 'people's' justice – that of the community of the faithful – for the King's; the open assertion of the right of disobedience towards the temporal authorities when they betray the cause of God: all of this prefigures the regicide of Henri III on 1 August 1589.[111] The most determined opponents of the Huguenots also began to attack magistrates and Catholic nobles who were too lukewarm, as exemplified by some of Simon Vigor's virulent sermons which prefigure the leaguer diatribes against parlementaires and nobles as 'politiques' suspected of compromising with heresy.[112] The decision to eliminate Coligny and his lieutenants revealed certain latent tendencies which were already visible since at least the first Catholic leagues of 1561, and which gave the leagues an opportunity to express themselves with awesome violence.

THE AMBIGUITIES OF THE PROVINCIAL MASSACRES

During the days and weeks following 24 August, killings occurred in several cities of the kingdom. The main ones were at La Charité-sur-Loire (24 August), Orleans and Meaux (25–29 August), Bourges (26–27 August and 11 September), Saumur and Angers (28–29 August), Lyon (31 August–2 September), Troyes (4

September), Rouen (17–20 September), Romans (20–21 September), Bordeaux (3 October), Toulouse (4 October), Gaillac (5 October), Albi and Rabastens (probably the same date as for Gaillac).[113] Reports also mention violence in the South-East, at Valence and Orange; in the South-West, at Agen, Blaye, Moissac, Condom, Dax, Saint-Sever and Bazas; in the Loire valley there were looting and murders at Tours, Blois, Vendôme, Amboise and perhaps Beaugency and Jargeau; assassinations occurred in Picardy at Soissons and Montreuil; in Poitou at Poitiers and Parthenay.[114] The number of victims of these provincial massacres is hard to say; a minimal estimation would suggest about 3,000 persons, but the reality is probably twice that.[115] The most bloody cities were Lyon (from 500 to 3,000 dead, among them the great musician, Goudimel), Orleans (500 to 1500 dead) and Rouen (from 300 to 600).[116]

Yet many cities experienced no disturbances, either because of the vigilance of energetic governors, such as Matignon in Normandy or the comte de Tende in Provence; or, as in Limoges, because the municipal officials took effective measures in good time; or again because of the rapid reaction of the commissioners who were charged with implementing the clauses of the Edict of Saint-Germain – as at Montpellier, for example, with Jean de Bellièvre, president in the parlement of Grenoble and brother of Pomponne.[117] There were no massacres where the Huguenots were in a majority, as they were in La Rochelle, Montauban or Nîmes; or, at the other end of the scale, where they were too few to generate fears, as in Reims. Peace could also be the result of relatively good relations among the confessions, as in Rennes. The bloody excesses of the summer of 1572 should not lead us to forget that cordial relations sometimes existed between Catholics and Protestants, as is evidenced by those 'peace pacts' signed in order to avoid disorders which have recently been studied for certain towns of the Rhône valley and the Midi.[118]

How are we to explain the murderous contagion that took over the towns in which such carnage took place? Nowadays historians are certain that Charles IX never sent any order to the kingdom for the execution of the Protestants, even though the latter were convinced that he did. From 24 August onwards, the letters that he wrote to the governors ordered them to seek to maintain order and have the edict of pacification respected. On 27 and 28 August, the King reiterated these injunctions: the Protestants should be able 'to live and reside with their wives, families and children in their houses, under the protection of the said lord king'. However, they were forbidden to gather publicly to worship, though this measure was presented as provisional, 'in order to avoid disturbances, scandals, suspicions … until the said Lord, having provided for the tranquillity of his kingdom, orders otherwise'.[119] At the most, the letters despatched to the provinces where the Protestants were numerous stated that if they gave the impression of disobeying and did not remain indoors, they should be punished and 'cut to pieces'.[120]

One point raises some doubt, however. In several of his letters, such as those for Lyon and Bordeaux, the King asserts that he is revoking orders transmitted verbally by the bearers of his earlier letters, orders given, he claims, 'when he had good reason to worry and fear some fateful event, having discovered the conspiracy against him by the said Admiral'. What was the content of these oral orders? We can deduce it from the reply of the governor of Lyon, François de Mandelot, just before receiving the King's letter countermanding his oral instructions. He assured Charles IX that, acting in accordance with what his messenger, the sieur du Peyrat, had told him, he had seized 'the bodies and the property of those of the religion'.[121] There is thus every reason to believe that the unwritten orders, issued at a time when the King could fear a Huguenot revolt, provided only for the imprisonment of those Protestants most suspected and the confiscation of their possessions, in order to cope with every eventuality – but not for their extermination; the rapid revocation of this measure was itself clearly formulated. The decision to round up those who were 'notoriously factious' was, however, sometimes reiterated, as in the postscript to the instructions of 22 September 1572 for Jacques de Matignon, lieutenant-general of Normandy. As for the seizure of Protestants' property, it was officially ordered during the second half of September for those who had fled abroad, in theory to safeguard it from those coveting it.[122]

The King's determination to avoid killings within his kingdom is thus indisputable. But the revocation that he had to give of the verbal orders he had issued during the early hours of the Massacre reveals a certain initial hesitation as to what to do. Although short lived, this indecision could generate an element of perplexity among local authorities.[123] Above all, it was exploited by the Catholic faction at court to persuade people that Charles IX had expressly ordered the massacre of all French Protestants. At La Charité-sur-Loire, it was men from the duc de Nevers' company who committed the murders, probably on their commander's orders.[124] At Troyes, the incitement came initially from the governor of Angoulême, the sieur de Ruffec, who, on arriving from the capital, stopped off in the town and announced that the King desired the destruction of the Huguenots. Pierre Belin, one of the Guises' clients from Troyes, also returned from court and corroborated these statements, alleging that he bore a letter from the duc de Guise, who ordered their execution.[125] So the royal *bailli* had the Huguenots imprisoned, and they were assassinated on 4 September by a gang of armed men from the bourgeois militia, acting at the instigation of the militant Catholics in the town assembly. Before and after that date, slaughter was committed in the streets by an enraged crowd. At Nantes, the mayor, Jean Harouys, received a letter from the duc de Montpensier giving to believe that Charles IX wanted the elimination of the heretics. But in contrast to what happened at Troyes, Harouys put the letter in his pocket and only informed his colleagues after receiving the declarations of 27 and 28 August clearly indicating the King's will, with the result that public order was preserved there.[126] In Saumur and Angers, it was the emissary of the governor, Puygaillard, a lieutenant of Montpensier, who spread false rumours about the King's orders and activated the massacres.

The divergent examples of Troyes and Nantes show that, for external urgings to be effective, they had to encounter active local factions which used them to legitimate their action. But rumours and news from Paris could also provoke an explosion of Catholic crowds which the overstretched urban authorities were powerless to contain. This seems to have happened at Meaux, Bourges and Lyon, where the Huguenots were first thrown into prison and then killed, or at Orleans, where they were attacked in their own houses.

The later killings raise other problems, since their instigators must have known of the declarations of 27 and 28 August. It is possible, however, that the King felt himself too closely watched by the exclusivist Catholics at court to provide clear answers to the emissaries that some perplexed provincial governors sent to Paris. For example, he apparently gave an order to kill the Provençal Protestants to a first envoy from the comte de Carcès, lieuten-ant-general of Provence, before saying the opposite to a second envoy, whom he had taken the precaution of seeing alone in his chamber. This, at least, is what the sieur de Vauclause, the second envoy, himself said, and his message of peace was respected by Carcès.[127] In Toulouse, allegedly secret royal instruc-tions were brought by two merchants, Delpech father and son, and by Pierre Madron, a treasurer of France. These envoys took advantage of the hesitations of the municipal magistrates and the parlementaires to call for a massacre of the Huguenots then in prison, among whom were three eminent councillors of the parlement, Antoine Lacger, François de Ferrières and the famous Jean de Coras.[128] At Gaillac and Bordeaux, on the other hand, it was the civilian authorities who incited the carnage; at Gaillac, the military governor and the consuls claimed to have received directives authorising them to kill the impris-oned heretics; at Bordeaux, the governor, Charles de Montferrand, showed the town councillors, on the same day that they had proudly informed Charles IX that their city was quiet, a list of names of the Huguenots whose execution, he said, the King had ordered, and which sparked off massacres and looting.[129] In Rouen, the factor which prompted the killings remains a mystery; the town council tried to impose order, but was clearly overtaken by the activities of the crowds.[130] The same powerlessness of the magistrates was revealed, it seems, in Albi and Rabastens.

It is difficult to know if the bearers of alleged royal orders were themselves sincere or not. It is possible that, misled by contradictory rumours, they believed that they were in line with the King's wishes; but they could also use such a pretext to give their actions a cloak of legitimacy and, in doing so, satisfy their hatred of the heretics or, quite simply, get rid of political adversaries. Whatever the case, their initiatives provided the occasion for a fundamental rethinking of the nature and limits of the obedience owed to superiors. As he informed the King on 7 October of how Montferrand had used royal orders to have the Huguenots massacred, the president of the Bordeaux parlement, Jacques de Lagebaston, accused the city's governor of having acted too hastily. The use of 'reason' should have moved him to delay taking action until he had further information. Lagebaston dared even to write to his royal correspondent: 'even when the executions such as those commenced and continued in this city were of your express command, reason would demand, Sire, that those who are in situ and who see what the situation is like at close quarters inform you once, twice and three times before undertaking its implementation.'[131] This maxim of temporising when dealing with an order judged to be contrary to justice was also suggested by Pierre Jeannin, who in 1572 was a young barrister in the Dijon parlement. In a *Discours apologétique* (written, it is true, long afterwards in 1622), Jeannin relates how he was asked to give his opinion at a council urgently convened by the lieutenant-general of Burgundy, Léonor Chabot, comte de Charny, after the arrival of two nobles bearing supposedly secret instructions from the King. Jeannin referred to the 'law of Emperor Theodosus', who, having in a moment of anger ordered the extermination of a large number of Christians, and then repented of his decision, forbade provincial governors 'in the future to implement such extraordinary commands which were against the order and forms of justice without waiting for thirty days, during which they would approach the Emperor to obtain a new command in good and proper form.'[132] The comte de Charny took the point and decided to suspend action, before receiving royal letters commanding him to keep the peace and not to take any action against the Protestants.[133]

Whatever the falsity of the rumours attributing murderous intentions to the King, for the most conscientious provincial magistrates – who could well believe them in the absence of other information – they raised the terrible issue of the legitimacy of obeying a command that was held to be unjust. This was a question to which the Massacre would add particularly acute relevance, not just in the writings of the Protestants, but in those of Catholics too.

The cities in which massacres took place had similar characteristics. Firstly, there was a powerful Catholic movement to regain souls, as is evident in the impact of the sermons of the Jesuit Edmond Auger in Bordeaux; secondly, there was an obsessive fear of the Huguenots, owed either to the memory of the iconoclastic violence experienced during the previous wars, or to a 'psychosis of encirclement', especially in those provinces where the Protestants were strongly entrenched.[134] As in Paris, the killings represented an aspect of both religious cleansing and war against the internal enemy; to which was added in some cases, especially in the southern cities, the desire to eliminate a rival political clan. The urge to protect the urban space was particularly clear in Toulouse, where the memory of the Protestants' attempt to seize the city in 1562 had bred a kind of siege mentality, such that the Toulousain killers of 4 October 1572 saw in the murder of the Huguenots not just the accomplishment of a duty towards God, but also the legitimate defence of their living space against dangerous rebels. Their aggression was also directed, as it would be later during the troubles of the League, against the moderate Catholics – those 'marshalists' who were supporters of the governor of Languedoc, marshal Henri de Montmorency-Damville – whom they suspected of betraying their cause and surreptitiously facilitating Protestant infiltration.[135]

Another remarkable example of the connection between religious passion and defensive zeal is visible in the events at Orleans, where the killings gave rise to some astonishing festivities. An eyewitness, Johann Wilhelm von Botzeim, left a long account of the events, written six months afterwards. This German student was brought under guard, along with other German fellow-students, to a house by the river Loire, where they remained prisoners for some time. They had to share the house with the executioners, whom they had to entertain and regale out of their own pockets, while being in an ideal position to see the horrific character of the murders being committed.

> And so they killed without a shadow of pity and with the utmost barbarity. This is how it was generally done. You were first pierced by a pistol shot, after which all of those present were free to strike you with their blood-stained swords and massacre as they pleased; when this was done they threw you into the river ... not only did we have to eat and drink with these ruffians and ensure that their table was well provided, but we had to entertain them with music by playing the guitar and the lute, and divert them with dancing. Women also came in the middle of the night when our people were in bed (not all of them, as some had to sleep on the ground), and began to sing obscene songs. This life of debauchery was unending. They were inhabited by an unrestrained joy after their victory over the Huguenots; everyone congratulated each other, rejoicing in having adorned their houses with the property of the Huguenots and having killed practically all of them.[136]

These methodical and happy killers of Orleans claimed to 'represent' the King and to be his secular arm, but it was a king that they had invented, since they had nothing but contempt for the real King, who, in their view, had shown himself too complacent towards heretics and did 'many things without adequate examination'.[137] Their behaviour also reflects the long-suppressed anger at having to submit to incomprehensible orders – for example, having to tolerate, after the Peace of Saint-Germain, that soldiers protected the movement of the Huguenots on Sundays as they left for the suburbs to attend the communion service. That earlier fury now exploded in fierce sarcasms:

> And as the hour approached when the Huguenots normally went to hear the sermon and the guards were stationed at the gates to protect them, they [the

Catholics] all shouted: 'where are these Huguenots? Oh, poor Huguenots! They are off to the sermon now, but there are no guards to protect them! Good God, let them go to hell', and similar things were said.[138]

Several noteworthy features of this evidence enable us to surmise particular aspects of the killers' psychology: the feeling of impunity which enabled them to see themselves as enjoying a form of legitimacy that was both religious and political, and which they defined as they pleased; the desire to accomplish a kind of fraternity in blood, one in which each person was invited to strike an adversary who was already dead; the fascination of murder itself, transformed in this case into a spectacle which outsiders were invited to observe; and, finally, the pleasure, or even the enjoyment, derived from the act of killing, spiced with other more commonplace sensations.

The Orleans killing spree ended in a disturbing turn for the local notables. Over four hundred peasants invaded the town to loot the Protestants, 'so that it was to be feared that having devastated the Protestants' houses, they would do the same to the Catholics', as Botzeim notes; the royal prosecutor was obliged to chase after them and expel them. In this episode we can see the emergence of antagonisms that were no longer religious – here it was that pitting town against country. Disorder descended into anarchy: as the German student wrote, 'brigandage and murders were everywhere, in the countryside as in the town'.[139]

The same drift to anarchy was visible in other places, with armed gangs appearing to take advantage of the situation in order to commit exactions. Nicholas Pithou encountered them as he was leaving Troyes to take refuge in Germany.[140] In Bordeaux, the procurator-general, Mulet, informed the King on 8 October of 'the devastation, murders and looting happening to all of your subjects in the countryside' close to the city.[141] In Normandy, it was the unpaid reiters who were threatening to sack towns and the countryside.[142] Beginning with his declaration of 28 August, the King was obliged to forbid people 'from hunting and seizing in the fields, farms and holdings any cattle, goods, crops or corn or anything else, or mistreating or insulting the farmers' – an injunction that was repeated in all of the letters patent until 28 October.[143]

The fear sparked by these disorders among the urban notables and the provincial authorities was not unrelated to the efforts that both parties made to support the royal measures for restoring order, not least because Charles IX clearly manifested his discontent at the massacres. For that reason, he bitterly scolded the Rouen town councillors for not preventing the murders; he wrote to their Bordeaux counterparts to say that the 'disaster' that had occurred in their city showed that they had failed in all of their duties; to marshal Cossé in Touraine he spoke of his exasperation at seeing his orders scorned, and reaffirmed his determination to punish the guilty.[144] And these are just a few examples. By the end of October, if we exclude the Parisian alarm of November, the return to order was almost complete, at least among the Catholics, because other anxieties were beginning to appear. Contrary to what the King expected, the decapitation of the Protestant party failed to prevent it from turning to open resistance, based in La Rochelle and the south of the kingdom. News of the massacres spread among them with incredible speed, thanks to messengers galloping flat out. For example, when, on 31 August, the news reached Le Vigan in the Cevennes from the consuls of Nîmes, it had already led to the taking up of arms at Ganges and small towns like Sumène and Saint-Jean-de-Buèges.[145] This new Huguenot uprising was the signal for the fourth civil war.

Thus, the relative calm that followed the killings was brief. The decision to eliminate Coligny and his companions released impulses on both sides that were difficult to control. Worse still, it had given new relevance to challenges to royal power and raised questions about the legitimacy of obedience. The Saint Bartholomew's crisis, which arose from a determination to restore royal authority, actually delivered it a terrible shock, the consequences of which it would take a long time to erase.

NOTES

1 Hervé Guineret, 'La Science de la guerre comme antidote au massacre', in El Kenz, ed., *Le Massacre, objet d'histoire*, p. 231. The word 'massacre' was used mainly by Protestant sources, in order to underline the savagery of the killings; Catholic sources prefer the vocabulary of war, referring to heretics as being 'cut to pieces'.

2 These expressions are taken from Crouzet, *La Nuit de la Saint-Barthélemy*, pp. 515 and 530, who has magisterially analysed the religious motives of the generalised massacre.

3 Sutherland, *The Huguenot struggle for recognition*, pp. 101–102. In this sense, the word appears quite early, as we find the term *anguenotz* used by Jean de Gachy in 1535, as quoted by Francis Higman, *La Diffusion de la Réforme en France, 1520–1565* (Geneva, 1992), p. 225.

4 Louis Régnier de La Planche (attributed), *Histoire de l'Estat de France, tant de la république que de la religion, sous le règne de François II* (1576), ed. Jean-Alexandre Buchon (Paris, 1836), p. 247. The author attributed the diffusion of such accusations to the influence of the Guises.

5 *Ibid.*, p. 262.

6 Étienne Pasquier, *Les Recherches de la France*, ed. Marie-Madeleine Fragonard and François Roudaut (Paris, 1996), vol. 3, p. 1675 (livre VIII, ch. 55).

7 In the same chapter, Pasquier also refers to the Swiss term *eidgenossen*, which he transcribes as '*Hens quenaux*, which in that country means seditious people', noting that 'the first time that this word [huguenot] began to be known throughout France was after the faction of Amboise'.

8 Wylie Sypher, '"Faisant ce qu'il leur vient à plaisir": the image of Protestantism in French Catholic polemic on the eve of the religious wars', *SCJ*, 11 (1980), pp. 59–84.

9 Pierre de Ronsard, *Continuation du Discours des misères de ce temps*, in *Œuvres*

complètes, ed. Jean Céard, Daniel Ménager et Michel Simonin (Paris, Gallimard, la Pléiade, 1994), vol. II, p. 998.

10 R. Decimon, 'Paris on the eve of Saint-Bartholomew', p. 69, based on BnF, MS. Fr. 11733, fol. 45, 6 March 1563. Descimon suggests that these Parisian fears could have been fuelled by the still active memory of the sack of Rome by the Lutheran soldiers of Charles V in 1527.

11 Diefendorf, *Beneath the Cross*, pp. 80–81.

12 Pasquier, *Lettres*, in *Œuvres*, vol. 2, livre V, cols 117–118.

13 Diefendorf, *Beneath the Cross*, p. 166.

14 See above, ch. 1, p. 36.

15 La Fosse, *Les 'Mémoires' d'un curé de Paris*, p. 95.

16 Diefendorf, *Beneath the Cross*, p. 156.

17 *Ibid.*, pp. 111–113.

18 *Ibid.*, pp. 86.

19 Garrisson, *La Saint-Barthélemy*, p. 51.

20 La Fosse, *Les 'Mémoires' d'un curé de Paris*, p. 98.

21 Crouzet, *La Nuit de la Saint-Barthélemy*, p. 512.

22 *Tocsain contre les massacreurs*, p. 27.

23 Henry Heller, *Anti-Italianism in sixteenth century France* (Toronto, 2002), ch. 4, 'The Italians and the Saint Bartholomew's Day Massacre', pp. 80ff.

24 Simon Goulart includes in the list of victims 'a Venetian called Maphé, Simon of Lucca, Lazare Romain, from Piedmont', in *Mémoires de l'Estat de France sous Charles IX*, vol. 1, fols 309r–311v. During the summer of 1573 there were rumours of a future 'Saint Batholomew's Massacre of Italians'. See Nicolas Le Roux, 'La Saint-Barthélemy des Italiens n'aura pas lieu: un discours envoyé à Catherine de Médicis en 1573', in Bernard Barbiche, Jean-Pierre Poussou and Alain Tallon, eds, *Pouvoirs, contestations et comportements dans l'Europe moderne. Mélanges en l'honneur du professeur Yves-Marie Bercé* (Paris, 2005), pp. 165–183. There would be another anti-Italian riot in 1575.

25 Haton, *Mémoires*, vol. 2, p. 456.

26 According to the *Relation du massacre de la Saint-Barthélemy*, p. 118, a fight broke out before the Coligny murder, between the Louvre guards and Protestant nobles, which might have increased anxiety in the city.

27 For the text of this document, see Diefendorf, *Beneath the Cross*, p. 102, who underlines its ambiguity.

28 Sully, *Œconomies royales*, eds David Buisseret and Bernard Barbiche, vol. 1, *1572–1594* (Paris, 1970), p. 12.

29 Pierre Burin, *Response a une epistre commenceant Seigneur Elvide*, in Goulart, *Mémoires de l'Estat de France sous Charles IX*, vol. 1, fol. 630v.

30 *Mémoires de l'Estat de France sous Charles IX*, vol. 1, fol. 290r.

31 *Ibid.*

32 This pain and guilt are analysed in Crouzet, *Les Guerriers de Dieu*, vol. 2, pp. 82–93.

33 In the Gospels, the master of the harvest asks his servants not to tear out the chaff. The comparison of heresy with chaff can be found in François de Bellefor-est, *Discours sur les rébellions* (Paris, 1572), p. 49, but he attributes the initiative to remove it to Charles IX.

34 L'Estoile, *Registre-Journal du règne de Henri III*, vol. 3, p. 46, 'Saint Bartholomew's Day – on Saturday 22 [August 1579] several Protestant dwellings were marked with

a cross, which alarmed many people, because the feast of St Bartholomew was approaching'. Garrisson, *La Saint-Barthélemy*, p. 96, sees a legend at work in these markings.

35 'Deux lettres de couvent à couvent', p. 293.

36 Marcel Gauchet, *Le Désenchantement du monde: une histoire politique de la religion*, Paris, 1985.

37 Sully, *Œconomies royales*, vol. 1, pp. 12–15.

38 *Mémoires de Madame de Mornay*, ed. Madame de Witt (Paris, 1868), vol. 1, pp. 58–71.

39 *Ibid.*, pp. 9–46.

40 *Mémoires de l'Estat de France sous Charles IX*, vol. 1, fols 300r–303r.

41 *Ibid.*, fol. 308v.

42 Crouzet, *La Nuit de la Saint-Barthélemy*, p. 451.

43 Samaran, 'Un humaniste italien, Guido Lolgi, témoin de la Saint-Barthélemy', pp. 397–404.

44 *Négociations diplomatiques avec la Toscane, vol.* 3, p. 830, Petrucci to Francesco de Medici, Paris, 31 Aug. 1572.

45 Diefendorf, *Beneath the Cross,* pp. 168–171, for a well-documented account. For the limited confidence to be given to de Thou's *History*, see Jean-Louis Bourgeon, 'Une source sur la Saint-Barthélemy: l'*Histoire de Monsieur de Thou* relue et décryptée', *BSHPF*, 134 (1988), pp. 499–537.

46 Diefendorf, *Beneath the Cross,* pp. 168–169.

47 Robert Descimon, 'Solidarité communautaire et sociabilité armée: les compagnies de la milice bourgeoise à Paris (xviᵉ–xviiᵉ siècles)', in Françoise Thélamon, ed., *Sociabilité, pouvoirs et société* (Rouen, 1987), pp. 599–610. Descimon uses the term *defensible space* developed by Oscar Newman (New York, 1973).

48 Jacques Sémelin, *Purifier et détruire. Usages politiques des massacres et génocides* (Paris, 2005), pp. 49–53.

49 Sémelin, 'Analyser le massacre', p. 12.

50 This is the convincing suggestion of Diefendorf, *Beneath the Cross*, p. 105.

51 *Ibid.*, p. 104.

52 *Ibid.*, p. 102.

53 *Négociations diplomatiques avec la Toscane*, vol. 3, p. 830, Petrucci to Francesco de Medici, Paris, 31 Aug. 1572.

54 *Mémoires de l'Estat de France sous Charles IX*, vol. 1, fols 303r–303v and 306r–v.

55 *Registres des délibérations du Bureau de la Ville de Paris*, vol. 7, pp. 13–14.

56 This hypothesis of Bourgeon, 'La Fronde parlementaire', p. 76, becomes a certainty without proof in his *Assassinat de Coligny*, p. 31. See the criticisms of Nancy Lyman Roelker, *One King, one faith. The parlement of Paris and the religious reformations of the sixteenth century* (Berkeley, 1996), p. 319, and of Sylvie Daubresse, *Le Parlement de Paris ou la voix de la raison (1559–1589)* (Geneva, 2005), p. 195.

57 Diefendorf, 'La Saint-Barthélemy et la bourgeoisie parisienne', p. 346.

58 *Mémoires de Jacques-Auguste de Thou, depuis 1553 jusqu'en 1601*, ed. Claude-Bernard Petitot (Paris, 1823), p. 232.

59 See the Appendix for the table of the socio-professional distribution of the victims of the 1572 massacres throughout the kingdom, based on the lists provided by Protestant sources, and compiled from Crespin's *Histoire des martyrs*, with additional material for Lyon from the *Première liste des chrétiens mis à mort et égorgés*

à Lyon par les catholiques romains à l'époque de la S. Barthélemi en août 1572, ed. P. M. Gonon (Lyon, 1847) by Natalie Zemon Davis, *Society and culture in early modern France*, p. 177.

60 Both Étienne Pasquier and Tomasso Sassetti noted this passivity. See Pasquier, *Lettres historiques pour les années 1556–1594*, pp. 205–213; T. Sassetti, *Brieve Raccontamiento, op. cit.*, p. 41.

61 *Mémoires de l'Estat de France sous Charles IX*, vol. 1, fols 305v–306r. But the bourgeois of Strasbourg's account cites the heroic defence mounted by three nobles and a woman who took refuge in a chapel; see R. Reuss, 'Un nouveau récit', p. 379.

62 See above, pp. 2–3.

63 This is true of the accounts of the deaths of Mathurin Lussaut and Philippe Le Doux (*Mémoires de l'Estat de France sous Charles IX*, pp. 306v and 307v). Both were rich merchants, which in the case of Lussaut is confirmed by his post-mortem inventory, and in the case of Le Doux, by the verdict rendered before the prévôt des marchands against those who looted his house. These documents were discovered in the Archives nationales by Barbara Diefendorf, *Beneath the Cross*, pp. 100–102.

64 *Mémoires d'un calviniste de Millau*, p. 236.

65 *Mémoires de l'Estat de France sous Charles IX*, fol. 313v.

66 André Chamson, in an address to the Assemblée du Désert in Sept. 1972, spoke of a 'partial genocide'. On the difference between a massacre and genocide, see the introduction by Mark Levene in Mark Levene and Penny Roberts, eds, *The Massacre in history* (New York, 1999), pp. 1–37.

67 This hypothesis is advanced by Mark Konnert, 'La tolérance religieuse en Europe aux xviᵉ et xviiᵉ siècles. Une approche issue de la psychologie sociale et de la sociologie', in Thierry Wanegffelen, ed., *De Michel de L'Hospital à l'édit de Nantes. Politique et religion face aux Églises* (Clermont-Ferrand, 2002), pp. 97–113.

68 Sémelin, 'Analyser le massacre', p. 11.

69 See the analysis in Crouzet, *La Nuit de la Saint-Barthélemy*, pp. 515ff.

70 As observed by Natalie Zemon Davis, *Society and culture in early modern France*, p. 179.

71 *Mémoires de l'Estat de France sous Charles IX*, fol. 312 r. On these aspects, see Davis, *Society and culture in early modern France*, pp. 161–162, and Diefendorf, *Beneath the Cross*, p. 103.

72 *Mémoires de l'Estat de France sous Charles IX*, fol. 308r; Agrippa d'Aubigné, *Les Tragiques*, in *Œuvres*, ed. Henri Weber (Paris, 1969), *Fers*, p. 172, verses 919–920. See the commentary in Huchard, *D'Encre et de sang*, pp. 377–378. D'Aubigné's indignation against Charles IX makes him depict the King standing in one of the windows of the Louvre and amusing himself by firing at the bodies in the Seine which were 'too slow in drowning'. This is obviously a legend.

73 For Protestants within the Guise clientele, see Carroll, *Noble power during the Wars of Religion*, p. 140.

74 *Mémoires de l'Estat de France sous Charles IX*, fol. 315r; *Le Réveille-Matin des François* (Edinburgh, 1574), dedicatory letter to the duc de Guise.

75 *Mémoires de Demoiselle Renée, fille de Michel Burlamaqui*, published by Gilles-Denijs and Jacob Schotel, *Jean Diodati* (The Hague, 1844), p. 88, quoted in Diefendorf, *Beneath the Cross*, p. 104.

76 *Mémoires de Jean de Mergey*, ed. Michaud and Poujoulat, *Mémoires pour servir à l'histoire de France*, vol. 9 (Paris, 1838), p. 577.

77 Crouzet, *La Nuit de la Saint-Barthélemy*, p. 52.

78 Nicollier, *Hubert Languet*, p. 279.

79 *Mémoires de l'Estat de France sous Charles IX*, fol. 310v.

80 Thus Simon Goulart alludes to the 'confusion' of Catholics at the sight of Philippe Le Doux's wife, who was about to give birth to her twenty-first child and who was left dead in the street with her baby partly protruding from her womb: *ibid.*, fol. 307v.

81 This is mentioned under the date of 27 June 1607 in the catalogue edited by Florence Greffe and José Lothe, *La vie, les livres et les lectures de Pierre de L'Estoile* (Paris, 2004), p. 599, item 992.

82 *Supplément à la correspondance diplomatique de Bertrand de Salignac de La Mothe-Fénelon, ambassadeur de France en Angleterre de 1568 à 1575. Lettres adressées de la Cour à l'ambassadeur*, vol. 7 (Paris-London, 1840), p. 331, instruction to La Mothe-Fénelon *(mémoire justificatif de la Saint-Barthélemy)*. The despatch of this memoir was announced on 26 Aug, by the King in a letter of that day to the ambassador, but it was not sent until the 27th, as the bearer of the letter, Lespinasse, was delayed.

83 BnF, 500 Colbert 7, fol. 425r, *Mémoire donné au s[ieu]r de Changy allant trouver le sieur de Villiers*, 27 Aug. 1572.

84 Bourgeon, *Charles IX devant la Saint-Barthélemy*, p. 41.

85 *Registres des délibérations du Bureau de la Ville de Paris*, vol. 7, pp. 13–14; Bourgeon, *Charles IX devant la Saint-Barthélemy*, p. 41; Crouzet, *La Nuit de la Saint-Barthélemy*, pp. 410–413.

86 Samaran, 'Un humaniste italien, Guido Lolgi, témoin de la Saint-Barthélemy', p. 402.

87 *Mémoires de l'Estat de France sous Charles IX*, fol. 300r: after the royal proclamation, made around five o'clock in the afternoon, 'several people, having heard it, believed that the affair was dying down, but the next day and the day after it began to stir again'.

88 On their conception of obedience, see Denis Crouzet, 'Le devoir d'obéissance à Dieu: imaginaire du pouvoir royal', *Nouvelle Revue du XVIᵉ Siècle*, 21 (2004), pp. 19–47 (special number on *Métaphysique et politique de l'obéissance dans la France du xviᵉ siècle).

89 Documents quoted by Bourgeon, *Charles IX devant la Saint-Barthélemy*, p. 41, n. 4.

90 *Ibid.*, pp. 104, 106.

91 AGS, Estado, K1530, no. 21, Zuñiga to Phillip II, 23 [26] Aug.1572.

92 Reuss, 'Un nouveau récit de la Saint-Barthélemy par un bourgeois de Strasbourg', p. 378; *Mémoires de Madame de Mornay*, p. 40–42. Duplessis-Mornay refused this passport, unwilling to admit owing his life to Henri de Guise.

93 Ariane Boltanski, *Les Ducs de Nevers et l'Etat royal. Genèse d'un compromis (vers 1550–vers 1620)* (Geneva, 2006), pp. 345–358. Nevers seems to have believed in a Protestant conspiracy against the King's life.

94 AGS, Estado, K1530, no. 29, Zuñiga to Phillip II, 31 Aug. 1572.

95 *Négociations diplomatiques avec la Toscane*, vol. 3, p. 848, anonymous (Cavriana), 19 Oct. 1572.

96 Gassot, *Sommaire Mémorial*, p. 107; Champion, *Charles IX*, vol. 2, p. 155, based on AGS, Estado, K1530, 18 Sept. 1572.

97 *Mémoires de l'Estat de France sous Charles IX*, fol. 319r.

98 Josèphe Jacquiot, 'Médailles et jetons commémorant la Saint-Barthélemy', *Revue d'histoire littéraire de la France*, (Sept.–Oct. 1973), pp. 784–793.

99 AGS, Estado, K1530, no. 39, Zuñiga to Alba, 12 Sept. 1572.

100 La Fosse, *Les Mémoires d'un curé de Paris*, p. 115.

101 *Mémoires et instructions pour les ambassadeurs, ou lettres et négociations de Walsingham*, p. 289, quoted in Bourgeon, *Charles IX devant la Saint-Barthélemy*, p. 135.

102 *Négociations diplomatiques avec la Toscane*, vol. 3, p. 841, Petrucci to Francesco de Medici, Paris, 19 Sept. 1572.

103 Letters quoted by La Ferrière, *Le xviᵉ siècle et les Valois*, p. 323.

104 Champion, *Charles IX*, p. 132.

105 *Mémoires de Jacques Pape*, p. 497.

106 Bourgeon, *Charles IX devant la Saint-Barthélemy*, p. 173.

107 Diefendorf, *Beneath the Cross*, p. 104, notes this in relation to the trial of the looters of the house of the Huguenot Jean Lat.

108 *Négociations diplomatiques avec la Toscane*, vol. 3, p. 860, Vincenzo Alamanni to Francesco de Medici, Paris, 19 Nov. 1572.

109 Charles IX to Bellièvre, 6 Dec. 1572, in *Lettres de Catherine de Médicis*, vol. 4, p. 145, n. 1.

110 Jacques Faye to (probably) Bellièvre, quoted in Bourgeon, *Charles IX devant la Saint-Barthélemy*, p. 177; La Fosse, *Les Mémoires d'un curé de Paris*, p. 118.

111 Denis Crouzet regards the regicide of Aug. 1589 as 'virtually included in the massacre of 24 August 1572': *La Nuit de la Saint-Barthélemy*, p. 545. Jean-Louis Bourgeon has done much to demonstrate the insurrectional character of the massacres; according to him, 'the League begins on Saint Bartholomew's Day': *Charles IX devant la Saint-Barthélemy*, p. 200.

112 Diefendorf, *Beneath the Cross*, p.157.

113 This list, based on the *Mémoires de l'Estat de France sous Charles IX* and other contemporary accounts is taken from Garrisson, *La Saint-Barthélemy*, p. 139; Crouzet, *Les Guerriers de Dieu*, vol. 2, p. 106, and Philip Benedict, 'The Saint Bartholomew's Massacres in the provinces', *The Historical Journal*, 21 (1978), pp. 205–225.

114 Brunet, '*De l'Espagnol dedans le ventre!*', pp. 524–535; Crouzet, *Les Guerriers de Dieu*, vol. 2, p. 107.

115 The figure of 3,000 is that proposed by Benedict, 'The Saint Bartholomew's massacres in the provinces', p. 207.

116 Estimates proposed by Crouzet, *Les Guerriers de Dieu*, vol. 2, pp. 107–111.

117 Cassan, *Le Temps des guerres de Religion*, pp. 240–243; BnF, MS. Fr. 15555, fol. 67r, Jean de Bellièvre to the King, 10 Sept. 1572.

118 Olivier Christin, *La Paix de religion. L'autonomisation de la raison politique au xviᵉ siècle* (Paris, 1997), pp. 122–132; idem, 'Amis, frères et concitoyens. Ceux qui refusèrent la Saint-Barthélemy (1572)', *Cahiers de la Villa Gillet*, no. 11 (2000), pp. 71–94.

119 Bourgeon, *Charles IX devant la Saint-Barthélemy*, pp. 104, 106, for these documents.

120 Letters of 28 Aug. to Jean de La Valette, governor of Armagnac, and Charles de Montferrand, mayor and governor of Bordeaux, published in *ibid.*, pp. 109–110. See also the letter of 30 Aug. to the comte de Charny, lieutenant-general in Burgundy, in *Mémoires de l'Estat de France sous Charles IX*, fol. 374r–v.

121 Paris, *Correspondance du roi Charles IX et du sieur de Mandelot*, p. 42.

122 Postscript to Charles IX's letter to Matignon, published in Bourgeon, *Charles IX devant la Saint-Barthélemy*, p. 167; BnF, MS 500 Colbert 7, fol. 435r, the King to royal procurator, Dijon, 20 Sept. 1572.

123 Benedict, 'The Saint Bartholomew's massacres in the provinces', p. 213.

124 Boltanski, *Les Ducs de Nevers*, p. 359–366.

125 Benedict, 'The Saint Bartholomew's massacres in the provinces', pp. 215–216. It is hard to know if this letter from the duc de Guise was actually written or forged by Pierre Belin. See Penny Roberts, *A city in conflict. Troyes during the French Wars of Religion* (Manchester, 1996), p. 146. Guise could well have let his followers believe that the King wanted the extermination of the Huguenots; Simon Goulart, who is usually reliable in reproducing the texts that he collected (many are corroborated by the originals when they survive in the archives), published a letter from Henri de Guise to his mother, the duchesse de Nemours, and dated 27 Oct. 1572, in which he affirms that Charles IX had decided to 'totally exterminate and erase this seditious vermin': *Mémoires de l'Estat de France sous Charles IX*, fols 575v–576r.

126 Benedict, 'The Saint Bartholomew's massacres in the provinces', p. 217.

127 *Ibid.*, pp. 211–212 and Bourgeon, *Charles IX devant la Saint-Barthélemy*, pp. 148–150. Vaucluse's account also suggests some curious words by the King of a 'killing' that he was envisaging: was this a subterfuge by a king who did not feel he was a free agent, as Bourgeon suggests?

128 Garrisson-Estèbe, 'Les Saint-Barthélemy des villes du Midi', in *L'Amiral de Coligny et son temps*, pp. 717–729. The perplexity of the authorities is reflected in the letters of the first president of the parlement, Jean Daffis, who on 8 Sept. wrote to the King that the court had had the Huguenots imprisoned, 'believing that that could be your intention', and on 12 Sept. he informed him of his and his colleagues' efforts at pacification, 'which we believe to be your intention': BnF, MS. Fr. 15555, fols 62r and 75r.

129 Letter from the mayor and councillors (*jurats*) of Bordeaux to the King, 3 Oct. 1572, in *Archives historiques du département de la Gironde*, vol. 3 (1861–1862), p. 204. A long letter to the King from president Jacques de Lagebaston relates the events in Bordeaux: BnF, MS. Fr. 15555, fols 124r–127r, 7 Oct. 1572.

130 Philip Benedict, *Rouen during the Wars of Religion* (Cambridge, 1981), pp. 125–134.

131 Lagebaston to Charles IX (as in n. 129).

132 Pierre Jeannin, *Discours apologétique* (1622), in *Les Négociations* (Paris, 1656), pp. 745–746, as quoted by Bourgeon, *Charles IX devant la Saint-Barthélemy*, pp. 73–74.

133 On this council convened by the governor of Burgundy and the role that Pierre Jeannin claims to have played in it, see David El Kenz, 'La Saint-Barthélemy à Dijon: un non-événement?', *Annales de Bourgogne*, 74 (2002), pp. 139–157.

134 Henri Hauser, 'Le père Edmond Auger et le massacre de Bordeaux, 1572', BSHPF, 60 (1911), pp. 289–306; Garrisson, *La Saint-Barthélemy*, pp. 136–137.

135 Souriac, *Une Guerre civile; Briefve instruction de tout ce qui a passé en la ville de Thoulouze depuis l'emprisonnement faict de ceulx de la nouvelle pretendue religion* (Nov. 1572), in Dom Devic et Dom Vaissète, *Histoire générale de Languedoc* (reprint Paris and Toulouse, 2004–2006), vol. 12, col. 1028, *preuve 316*.

136 Charles Read, 'La Saint-Barthélemy à Orléans racontée par Johann Wilhelm de Botzeim, étudiant allemand, témoin oculaire', BSHPF, 21 (1872), p. 383. The text was translated by Charles Read.

137 *Ibid.*, pp. 360 and 391.

138 *Ibid.*, p. 386.

139 *Ibid.*, pp. 365–366.

140 Pithou, *Chronique de Troyes et de la Champagne*, pp. 698–699.

141 Letter from the procurator-general to the King, 8 Oct. 1572, *Archives historiques du département de la Gironde*, 10 (1868), p. 361.

142 Bourgeon, *Charles IX devant la Saint-Barthélemy*, p. 172.

143 *Ibid.*, pp. 106 and 173.

144 Benedict, 'The Saint Bartholomew's massacres in the provinces', p. 210; Charles IX to the mayor and *jurats* of Bordeaux, 21 Oct. 1572, in *Archives historiques du département de la Gironde*, 15 (1874), p. 573; Bourgeon, *Charles IX devant la Saint-Barthélemy*, p. 170.

145 Archives municipales de Millau, CC 42, letter dated 31 Aug. 1572, Le Vigan, signed by C. de Gasques (probably a consul of the town), to the Protestants of Meyrueis. My thanks to Jacques Frayssenge for sending me this document.

6

THE KING'S TRUTH,
REASON OF THE STATE

As soon as news of the Huguenot massacres spread across Europe, they caused a considerable stir, varying from jubilation among Catholics to indignation in Protestant countries. But these contrasting responses had a common feature – all evinced alarm as to the reasons for such blood-letting, alarm which was all the greater because of the rapid spread of rumours and unverifiable accusations which were fuelled, in particular, by Huguenot propaganda. Charles IX and his entourage soon grasped that urgent action was needed, firstly to convince the European courts of the legitimacy of the execution of Coligny and his followers and, secondly and corelatively, to deflect responsibility for the ensuing urban bloodbaths onto the 'people'. The task was a difficult one. Legitimacy comes from conforming to an unwritten rule of equity and justice, distinct from positive law; it involves inner conviction and adherence to collectively internalised values. But the notion of extraordinary justice, especially when it has such bloody consequences, flouted the usually accepted norms. The King was thus required to explain, argue and demonstrate – in short, to orchestrate a campaign to persuade neighbouring princes by 'shedding light on the truth', as Catherine de Medici put it. In this case the 'truth' was, as the Queen Mother added, 'that which the king believes'; or the 'sincere and real truth', as Charles IX himself would insist.[1]

The winning over of international opinion was an inescapable element of the task of restoring monarchical authority launched on St Bartholomew's Day, since it involved the King's and France's credibility in Europe. For the purpose in hand, Charles IX had a remarkable team of committed diplomats and publicists, all of whom, aware of the importance of what was at stake, united behind him. Their task was especially difficult in Protestant countries, where, regardless of their own views, they developed an argument based on reason of the state, which was presented as distinct from confessional considerations.

Such an undertaking might well have succeeded, had the King conducted it without flinching. But under powerful pressure from Catholics both inside and outside of France, Charles IX faltered. Little by little, he was forced to abandon the idea of preserving the edict of pacification of Saint-Germain, which would

have served as the only real proof in Protestant eyes of the 'political' character
of the execution of 24 August. However, that does not change the fact that the
arguments deployed to legitimate the first massacre, the King's, are of major
interest for the history of ideas about royal power.

PERPLEXITY AND SUSPICION IN EUROPE

As we have seen, Charles IX claimed in his justificatory declarations as early as
27 August that religion played no part in his decision.[2] The first reactions from
neighbouring princes, both Catholic and Protestant, show that they did not
believe a word of this, or that if they did, they questioned its validity.

At first, the Catholics engaged in ostentatious actions of grace for what
seemed like a victory over heresy. In Rome, the Pope had a *Te Deum* sung and
a commemorative medal struck; he commissioned Vasari to paint three frescoes celebrating the Massacre; on 11 September 1572, he promulgated a jubilee
preceded by three days of prayers and processions inaugurated by a solemn
mass in Saint-Louis-des-Français, on whose façade the Cardinal of Lorraine
had an inscription added to the glory of Charles IX and his advisors.[3] But this
euphoria gradually became tinged with a certain unease as the scale of the
atrocities perpetrated became known. The Curia quickly distanced itself from
the defence of Charles IX's 'stratagem' as outlined in Camillo Capilupi's book
published in Rome at the instigation, perhaps, of Cardinal Lorraine, since it
glorified the blood-letting. In Paris, nuncio Salviati confided to Zuñiga, the
Spanish ambassador, the fear which the pontifical jubilations inspired in him;
he bitterly reproached himself for having taken too long – being deceived by
appearances – in informing Gregory XIII that the Parisian murders were not
designed to serve religion, but only to enable the King of France to get rid of
his enemies.[4]

In Madrid there was the same delight, but it was soon followed by similar
questions about the exact nature of the events in France. Philip II publicly
displayed his satisfaction and went to the monastery of Saint Jerome to thank
God; then, receiving the French ambassador, Saint-Gouard, he began to laugh
'in a show of extreme pleasure' and declared that Charles IX deserved his title
of 'Most Christian King'.[5] But when he came to re-read the draft of the instruction (probably prepared by secretary Zayas) to be given to the emissary that
he was about to send to France, the Marquess of Ayamonte, Philip II revealed
his perplexity. In this first draft, Zayas presented the most widely accepted
version of events: the attack on Coligny was long planned by Catherine de
Medici; Maurevert's failure convinced the Queen Mother, the King and the
duc d'Anjou, with the complicity of the comte de Retz, to give orders to the
ducs de Guise and Aumale for the Admiral's execution. In the margin of this
paragraph, Philip noted: 'we cannot know this with certainty, nor learn more

from the reports of the ambassador, who I suspect knows scarcely more than we do about what really lies behind all this'. He concluded that it was better to remain vague, in a preamble designed to prepare the Marquess of Ayamonte's mission.[6] Expressed in a note written for internal use, this embarrassment seems sincere.

Other Catholic sovereigns accepted the French thesis of a Huguenot conspiracy and of the danger that Coligny represented. The Duke of Savoy regarded Charles IX's action as 'a resolution and an execution that was truly royal and generous', one which freed him from 'a subjection and a yoke that were too great'. But, as the French agent of the King, Pierre Forget de Fresnes, wrote, he immediately gave a religious and providential meaning to the massacre: the Duke saw in the miraculous flowering of the hawthorn in the Holy Innocents cemetery on 24 August the proof that God wished 'more than ever to see the faith, the prince and the kingdom that had suffered so much to sustain it, flourish'.[7]

The correspondents of Florence and Venice also accredited the theory of a Protestant threat. In his report, the Florentine doctor, Cavriana, supplies details of the attack on the Louvre that the Admiral's friends had reportedly planned in order to avenge his injury, which was what triggered the royal condemnation.[8] The Venetian ambassador, Giovanni Michiel, for his part, thought that Coligny 'had a sort of state separate from, and independent of the king within the kingdom', and that 'since the peace, things had got to the point that whenever the king issued an edict on any subject, the Protestants went to the admiral to ask him if they should obey and accept it or not'.[9]

Yet even those foreign Catholics who accepted the thesis of a political punishment could not but express their disapproval of the methods used. Giovanni Michiel, for example, felt that the King showed 'dispositions towards becoming a bad egg', and added: 'this latest action begins to show the proof of that'.[10] The damage done by the Massacre to the reputation of the royal family throughout Europe was expressed crudely to Catherine de Medici by the French ambassador at Venice, Arnaud du Ferrier: the murder not just of the Admiral and his lieutenants but also of 'so many poor innocent people' scandalised even those best disposed towards France in the neighbouring countries, Catholics included; they accused the Queen Mother and the duc d'Anjou, and did not refrain from saying that, in order to overcome the Huguenot leaders accused of sedition, 'there were other means just as effective and which would not have offended foreigners as much or given posterity so much to talk about'.[11] As for the Emperor Maximilian of Habsburg, du Ferrier wrote in the same letter, he used the occasion to discredit the candidature of Henri d'Anjou for the throne of Poland in order to advance that of his son with the Polish electors, while recalling the protection that he himself granted to the Protestant subjects of his states. Unlike the Pope and Phillip II, he saw nothing in the massacres that deserved approval.[12]

Quite naturally, it was in the Protestant camp that horror and indignation were the strongest. For years, they had been obsessed by the myth of an international Catholic conspiracy that was determined to snuff out the true religion in Europe.[13] Events in France seemed to provide a resounding confirmation of the gravity of the threat. The German Protestant princes accused Charles IX of having treacherously failed to keep his promises to his subjects; there was a widespread clamour of execration in the Swiss cantons.[14] The anger was fuelled by the arrival of thousands of terrified refugees who had escaped the bloodletting. Most of them did no more than retell their own depressing experiences, but some nourished dreams of revenge; some set about raising funds to finance a war against France, while the nobles drew up plans of attack; others again began to publish retaliatory pamphlets against the royal family, some of which were illustrated by suggestive images which showed, for example, as Bishop Jean de Monluc wrote, the King carrying the head of the Admiral on the tip of a lance or taking pleasure, along with his brother Henri d'Anjou, in watching a pregnant woman being eviscerated.[15]

The opinion that counted for most in Protestant Europe was that of England, since it was tied by a treaty of alliance to France, signed on 19 April 1572. Would Queen Elizabeth renounce it? Along with the Polish election, it was the major question mark for a time in Europe's courts. For Charles IX it was of critical importance: if he persuaded his English neighbour to remain his ally, French credibility among European Protestants could be restored and relations with them could be sustained.

Initially, the problem seemed insurmountable, so violent was the repulsion aroused in England by the Massacre. Emotions ran all the higher as some English people had witnessed the murders, especially at Rouen, and added their own accounts of them to those of the Huguenots. According to Ambassador La Mothe-Fénelon, the news which they disseminated provoked 'a marvellous [stupefying] hatred of the French'. Elizabeth's advisors vehemently denounced 'the worst crime since Jesus Christ came into this world ... an act of such excessive bloodshed, where most people were innocent; an act of such fraudulence which violated the safeguard of a great king and troubled the peace of the royal marriage of his sister, one that was unbearable to the ears of princes and abominable to all kinds of subjects, an act against every kind of divine and human law, and without any comparison to another act undertaken in the presence of a prince'.[16] The thesis of a Huguenot conspiracy was rejected as improbable, because, as the ambassador's interlocutors believed, so many unhappy victims, among them women, the elderly and children, 'could in no way be conspirators'.[17] This argument showed the difficulty that the English had in conceiving that urban massacres could be distinguished from the 'execution' of Coligny and his lieutenants.

The English condemnation was stirred by the rapid diffusion of the premeditation thesis, as the ambassador also states. According to him, everyone was convinced that the wedding of Marguerite de Valois and Henri de Navarre was a trap that had been decided upon for a long time between the Pope and the King of Spain; it was believed that the French of Mons had been eliminated in order to 'please' the Spaniards.[18] The breaking of the 'faith' towards his Protestant subjects by Charles IX seemed the most disturbing feature – would not the King behave with the same duplicity in the alliance concluded with Queen Elizabeth? Was not the marriage envisaged between the Queen and Francois d'Alençon just as monstrous a trap as that prepared for the King of Navarre and a prelude to a cowardly attack upon England with the object of overturning Elizabeth in favour of Mary Stuart? Such questions recurred endlessly in conversations with the ambassador.[19]

However, by dint of repeating that the King was in urgent danger and that he had 'to allow an arm to be cut off to save the rest of the body', La Mothe-Fénelon succeeded in persuading the Queen and her councillors to examine and discuss the French interpretation of a political 'execution', in which religion played no part and which was separate from the generalised massacres that had followed it. But here he encountered a formidable argument which was much more developed in England than elsewhere. The controversy was over the central question posed by the first massacre: how far does the King's power of life and death over his subjects, even in a case of extreme necessity, extend? This suggests something of the value of the closely argued exchanges conducted by Elizabeth and Charles IX through their respective ambassadors.

Essentially, the Queen of England reproached the King of France for not following the 'order of justice' – for acting before any legal judgment was given. In vain did La Mothe-Fénelon reply that this was impossible, since Charles IX had only a few hours to make his decision, but Elizabeth stuck to her principled objection. The right of kings to condemn people to death, she said, was limited by clear rules: 'it is only licit for kings to kill or have people killed in two situations – one, during a legitimate war, and two, when imposing justice for the punishment of crimes'. In the second case, the power to punish should follow the laws. It was possible to imagine that such laws did not exist in France, since the King, in a strange move, had to seek, *a posteriori*, the approval of the parlement of Paris. By deciding alone, and without a trial, the elimination of the Admiral and his followers, Charles IX risked 'God's wrath'; his method of governing gave the impression that he wished to defy the Ten Commandments and that homicide was not considered a sin in his kingdom.[20] He had thus broken both the divine and the human laws.

It was thus Charles IX's 'way of governing' that was on trial, as he seemed to deny the union of the spiritual and the temporal orders. The idea of a derogation from the normal laws in cases of necessity was not widely accepted in England, and the shock produced by the extraordinary way in which the King had exercised his prerogative as judge was all the more notable for that.[21] Of course, the Queen of England did not hesitate to exercise her own power on occasion without too many moral scruples, but the act of publicly *justifying*, in the name of the higher interests of the state separated from that of religion, a sentence of death against rebels without a prior verdict seemed to her an innovation with serious political consequences. In this respect, by repeating quite simply to La Mothe-Fénelon the arguments that she had put to Ambassador Walsingham and which she believed sufficient to convince the English Queen, Catherine de Medici was singularly mistaken about the attitudes reigning in London; she believed that she could demonstrate that Elizabeth's attitude was not fundamentally different to hers or her son's, which she expressed as follows:

> and even if we had killed all of our subjects whom we thought willing to do us harm and attack our state and person, nobody should change position or break friendship with us on account of that – anymore than we ourselves made difficulties when the said queen executed those who had wished to trouble and attack her; nor had we changed our position because of what she [as she was entitled to] had to do in her kingdom when there were people desiring to trouble her, just as these people [Huguenots] did, and still wish to do to us. And even if it was against all of the [English] Catholics that she [Elizabeth] took harsh measures, that would not indispose us nor alter in any way the friendship between her and us.[22]

In this defence of the absolute right of life and death of kings over their subjects during a moment of urgent peril for the state, Catherine de Medici was advocating a disturbing extension of royal power. She probably envisaged this transformation as only a provisional remedy to deal with the tragic alteration of the old order, a remedy imposed by circumstances and ultimately designed to restore the harmony that had momentarily been lost; it remains true, however, that the categorical twist of her opinions could indeed have shocked her English counterparts, at the risk of seeming to establish them as general principles. Elizabeth's reactions to Charles IX's and his mother's defence reflected the opinions of her councillors; they evidently express the feeling that such a legitimation of exceptional forms of justice, coming from the mouths of those enjoying absolute authority and not from lesser theoreticians, set a precedent which could trigger a profound shift in the universally accepted ideas on good government. Thus the Queen of England vehemently exhorted her neighbour to present to 'the princes and potentates of Christendom' an explanation of his behaviour that was sufficiently convincing for them to accept it without causing a scandal.[23] In this she repeated the demand insistently made by the King's own ambassadors, witnesses to the anger sparked in Protestant countries by the Massacre. But for Elizabeth, it was her international position that mattered: she could not, without losing face, remain allied to a prince branded with reprobation within his own camp. And if the Anglo-French treaty was abandoned, the entire diplomatic structure so patiently put together by France would collapse. Aware of the urgency of this, Charles IX orchestrated a vast European campaign of self-justification.

CHARLES IX AND THE CONTROL OF INFORMATION

The task was all the more difficult in that the 'truth' which the King wished to circulate was initially twofold. He thus had to supersede the initial explanation presented on 24 August, that of a quarrel between the Guises and the Châtillons, with a second one, which he proposed from 25–26 August onwards. This contradiction produced disastrous effects abroad, as the French ambassadors in England and the Swiss cantons attested.[24] In Bern and Zurich, a version of the first interpretation of events was circulated by the treasurer of the Swiss Leagues, Jean Grangier. On 3 and 8 September, Grangier addressed 'the magnificent lords' of these cities and attributed exclusive responsibility for the events of 24 August to the perpetrators of the attack on Coligny (their names were not mentioned, though that of the Guises was clearly suggested).[25]

Charles IX was, however, determined to erase the initial incoherence and to provide the neighbouring countries, and especially the Protestant ones, with a 'truth' that conformed to his declaration of 26 August to the parlement of Paris. On 26 August, he despatched to England a 'true memoir of how things really happened in the recent commotion', in which he explained how the 'Admiral's faction' had conspired against him and the punishment he had received for it.[26] But as this 'true memoir' and the instructions to the ambassador did not seem sufficient, he recommended the latter also to circulate the work of a former professor at the Geneva academy, Pierre Charpentier, and dated 15 September at Strasbourg, in which the subversive plans of the most seditious Huguenots were denounced; but, the King added, nobody should know the origin of this initiative, which would surely destroy its effectiveness:

> Monsieur La Mothe, I am sending you a dozen copies of a letter written by Charpentier, which I wish to see clandestinely published and circulated from hand to hand, but without anyone knowing that it comes from you or me; let people say and believe that it was printed in Germany. I shall shortly send you copies of it in French, and which you will deal with in the same way.[27]

It was also indispensable to secure the favour of the Polish electors to whom Henri d'Anjou was to present his candidacy. It was no doubt on the King's orders that the advocate-general of the Paris parlement, Guy du Faur de Pibrac, composed a long 'letter', dated 1 November 1572, supposedly to a fictitious Polish lord, Stanislas Elvide, and which attempted to justify the King's and his brother's behaviour. It appeared anonymously in France in 1573, in both Latin and French, from two publishers, one in Paris, the other in Lyon; copies were distributed in Poland and probably in some German states through diplomatic channels.[28] Charpentier's text, which exists in both Latin and French, was widely circulated in Poland. Jean de Monluc received it on 22 January 1573 and had it printed immediately; it was also disseminated in several parts of Germany.[29] Monluc himself had a *Vera et brevis descriptio tumultus postremi Gallici Lutetiani*, which he probably wrote himself, published in Cracow. He reprised its themes in his *Defense* of the duc d'Anjou, published in Latin in France and Germany, and then translated into French and later into Polish. In these two texts, Monluc justified, as he had in his speech to the electors on 10 April 1573, the execution of the Admiral and his friends, exonerating the King's brother from any role in the massacres.[30]

Moreover, Charles IX relied heavily on the eloquence of his ambassadors to turn around opinion at the European courts to his favour. In Basel, it was Pomponne de Bellièvre who, in a clever speech, attempted to persuade his listeners of the rightness of the crown's action. In her letter of 3 December to him, Catherine de Medici congratulated him for having had his speech translated and published in German 'so that it be circulated within Germany.'[31] Experienced diplomats such as Gaspard de Schomberg and Jean-Galéas Frégoso were also sent to German Protestant princes in order to calm their anxiety and anger; other agents, such as Jean de Vulcob and M. de Montmorin, were sent to Vienna to sweeten the Emperor.[32] Even the Sultan was included in this intense pro-French propaganda campaign.[33]

Charles IX's objective was to be the sole source of information, so as to be able to control its content. This is clearly expressed in his recommendation of 23 March 1573 to Christophe de Thou, first president of the parlement, not to publish his personal account of the events of the Massacre:

> Monsieur le president, in order that what you have written on the events of Saint Bartholomew's Day should not be published among the people or even among foreigners, since there are always people who are inclined to write and who might seize the opportunity to reply to you, I beg you that none of it be printed, either in French or in Latin, and if you have kept some of it, that you retain it in your own possession, as I did with what you sent me and which I had copied by hand only, so as to have it in just one place.[34]

With this injunction, Charles IX openly showed his acute awareness of the extraordinary power of print. He did not require president de Thou to destroy his memoir, nor even that it should correspond to the sense of the official discourse; he only desired that de Thou should not have it printed, so as not to place in the public space opinions which were doubtless useful and respectable – the King himself acknowledged that he would use them if necessary, albeit in manuscript form – but which could inconsiderately stoke the fires of a polemic that was still burning strongly. Prudence was all the more necessary, as the election of the duc d'Anjou was not yet certain when the King was writing and pamphlets were being circulated attempting to blacken his reputation in the eyes of the Polish electors.

Subsequent historians have been disturbed by the docility – and even the zeal – of the ambassadors and publicists serving the cause of royal justification. It is quite obvious that those who spoke or wrote on royal orders set about their task with utter application. However, they sometimes showed, or allowed their personal views to surface. Jean de Monluc made no bones about saying that the council's decision to kill Coligny and his lieutenants was rushed and unconsidered.[35] Bertrand de La Mothe-Fénelon was no doubt filling an inner need by reporting at such length the English objections to the killings. As to Guy du Faur de Pibrac, he probably expressed a deep conviction in the two famous verses of his quatrains:

Je hay ces mots de puissance absolüe,
De plain pouvoir, de propre mouvement
[How I hate those words – power absolute,
full authority, and of our own volition.][36]

If these men suppressed their possible personal objections while acting on the King's behalf, it was doubtless because they were aware of the need for a united front against the storm of anger with which they were confronted. They were perfectly placed to judge how far the image of France had been defiled in Europe, its credibility on the international scene shaken. La Mothe-Fénelon, for example, heard it said that the atrocity of the killings could be explained by 'the condition of the French nation, which was murderous, seditious and very inhuman'.[37] In a despatch of 20 October 1572, the Venetian envoys, Cavalli and Michiel, observed that the 'French nation' was odious everywhere, while Schomberg could vouch for the violence of the insults and the gibes heaped on Charles IX in Germany.[38] It was of urgent necessity to remedy this state of affairs. Ambassadors and royal agents, most of them champions of balance and the happy mean, realised that if the royal campaign failed, France would have to turn towards Spain; she would lose all her support in the Protestant camp and would be heavily dependent on the Catholic camp, while within the kingdom itself the factions most hostile to peaceful confessional co-existence would impose their rule. This was the argument, for example, that La Mothe-Fénelon presented to Catherine de Medici.[39] Success was indispensable if these dangers were to be avoided.

The task was all the more ticklish, as it involved simultaneously reassuring Catholic princes of Charles IX's desire to restore religious unity in his kingdom and convincing the Protestants that he had only acted against rebellion by some of the Huguenot leaders. The need to adjust the arguments for different audiences produced variations which historians have sometimes interpreted as contradictions.[40] Yet, despite these modulations, the official justifications of the first Massacre, especially those presented to the Protestants, are not without coherence.

The objective of most of the discourses or speeches orchestrated by the King was to establish a clear distinction between, firstly, the 'execution' of Coligny and his lieutenants and, secondly, the generalised urban massacres which ensued. The documents attribute these killings to the fury of the Catholics, this 'unthinking populace' whose anger was compared by Pibrac to the violence of an unstoppable storm.[41] According to these authors, the King was irritated by their excesses and condemned them. For Bellièvre, the killings were motivated by the 'spirit of vengence' and the 'cupidity' of the populace. Pibrac is rather more indulgent: the anger of the murderers was evidence, in his opinion, of their love for their sovereign, since they believed him to be endangered. In his speech of 10 April 1573 to the Polish electors, Monluc sought above all to exonerate Henri d'Anjou, clearly suggesting that the Parisian outbursts added an unforeseen turn to the punishment of the Admiral and his lieutenants.[42] All of them insist on the efforts immediately made by the King to stop the assassinations.

The execution of the Huguenot conspirators before being brought to trial was justified by the urgent danger. On the nature of the danger itself, opinions differed slightly, but the aim of the arguments was the same – to underscore the urgency of the situation which had to be faced. For Bellièvre, the life of the entire royal family was threatened by the desire of Coligny's friends for revenge after the attack on him, and their determination to kill the Guises, even at the King's side. But Pibrac, Charpentier, La Mothe-Fénelon and Monluc adopted the official view of a long-planned conspiracy that was suddenly revealed on 23 August. The Admiral is mostly mentioned as the conspirators' leader, but Charpentier stands out by incriminating Théodore de Bèze, who is not named in person but under the biblical figure of Sheba, whose name, the author adds, is an anagram for 'the evil enemy of the kingdom and public order' who preaches sedition from Geneva.[43] François Portes, professor of Greek at the Genevan academy, to whom Charpentier's 'epistle' is addressed, was summoned by his former colleague to abandon the 'ministry of Satan' and leave the city in which he was rampant.

For the interpretation being constructed to be credible, it was necessary to underline that only the rebellious, and not the Protestants of France as a whole, were targeted for royal punishment. It is Pierre Charpentier who goes furthest in differentiating the 'religion' of most of the Protestants from the objective pursued by the dissident Huguenots, an objective he calls 'the Cause'. He writes that religious men aspire only to live peacefully and obey their ruler; but the conspirators of the Cause, on the other hand, wanted war in order to impose their yoke on France and 'to establish a new kingdom under the king's nose', as he put it.[44] By their peaceful and law-abiding behaviour, religious people showed that it was entirely possible to be *both* a Protestant and an obedient subject. Before 24 August, the author continues, Charles IX relied on these moderates to show that good government was possible in a kingdom where two confessions lived together; desiring to preserve a 'balance', the King could say: 'I do not force people into a religion.'[45] In Charpentier's writing, the idea of civil tolerance reveals its innovative content: it presupposes that belonging to a different faith from the Prince's does not to alter the respect due to him and that it is necessary to dissociate, as belonging to two different registers, religious commitment and political obedience to the King. This argument places the crown as the supreme arbiter between the confessions, thereby tacitly proposing public order rather than the defence of the one and only religious truth as the essential objective of government. Charpentier regrets that the pernicious initiatives of the supporters of the Cause caused the failure of this ideal of peace which had begun to take shape, in his view, since the Edict of Saint-Germain; following the tragic events of the Massacre, royal anger was such that it viewed without distinction the peaceful and the rebellious.

As we saw in the reactions of Elizabeth of England, the most difficult point for the royal apologists to justify was the absence of any judgment delivered before the killing of Coligny and his companions. To explain this, they invoked the defence of the state. On this point, their arguments are of the greatest interest, not because of their rigour – which is faulty – but because they give a glimpse of a still-timid but nevertheless crucial stage in the genesis of the notions of the state and, corelatively, of reason of state. The understanding of the word 'state' varies in these writings. Pibrac, in arguing that the conspirators wanted to 'change the state and transfer the crown elsewhere', and Charpentier, in affirming that their objective was 'to abolish the name of Valois and overturn the state of France', both suggest the risk of a change of form of rule.[46] Some uses of the term 'state' indicate an abstract entity symbolising the general interest. Thus Jean de Monluc refers to the 'public estate', while Pibrac uses as a synonym the word 'republic', meaning *res publica*, the public thing.[47] The final sentence of Pibrac's letter refers to the hope of restoring 'the prosperity of this state', i.e. the kingdom. In each of these versions, the 'state', whether it be the form of rule or the good of the community or country, is a common patrimony which is the king's responsibility.

It is Pibrac who analyses this royal responsibility with the greatest incisiveness. Using examples taken from Roman history and law, he claims that the prince does not need to employ 'the common and usual manner of criminal trials for those in whose prompt punishment the republic has an interest'. When the danger is imminent, he argues, that is not the time for recourse to the laws and the 'subtleties of the law'; one must only consider what is 'the most expedient', i.e. to punish before judging.[48] Such recourse to the value of utility could suggest the influence of Machiavelli, who was familiar to Pibrac.[49] However, the King's advocate differs from the Florentine thinker on an essential point

– he champions the divine right of kings. Indeed, he insists on 'that which is divine in the estate of kings and their persons'; they are 'established and constituted by God to govern us'. When they punish, he adds, it is 'with the sword that God gave them'; the punishments they inflict prefigure those of the afterlife.[50] The power which Pibrac grants kings consists in the possibility of freeing themselves from the positive laws with a view to ensuring the purely temporal survival of the state. The justification of that possibility through divine right gives a religious basis to the argument; but that basis is in the service of political power, and not the opposite. This is the sense in which Pibrac legitimates, without using the term, a form of reason of state, of which the sole judge is the sovereign; it is a reason of state sacralised by the sacrality of the person who sets it in motion and who, because of that, is beyond any criticism by his subjects.

Pibrac's demonstration does, however, contain a surprising paradox: the king, in his system, does not have the monopoly of the discretionary power to be used in cases of serious danger. Lower magistrates can also 'during a dangerous riot and a bloody disturbance, or any other just cause which brooks neither delay nor suspension ... punish in order to avoid the danger, and then write to the prince'.[51] This concession was no doubt explained by the length of time necessary to obtain a royal order, taking account of the means of communication in the kingdom then; when faced with a serious threat, speed was essential. It remains, however, that in granting such powers to lower magistrates, Pibrac is suggesting that they share in the authority of the divine-right kings; he presents the preventative punishment that they can inflict as legitimate in itself, with the sovereign only informed *a posteriori* – which of course could present risks for him.

Finally, all of Charles IX's apologists insist – and this is an essential element of their efforts – that his actions do not point to a bloodthirsty personality. He was upset, they said, at having to use an 'extreme remedy', but in such instances, clemency would have been cruel. 'Such leniency towards evil and dissolute men is cruelty towards good people', wrote Charpentier.[52] Discussing the debates in the royal council of the evening of 23 August, Pibrac puts in the mouths of the wisest councillors this warning to the King to help overcome his scruples: 'by wishing too much to spare your clear and sworn enemies, you will only be – against your will and intention – cruel towards the country'.[53] The punishment of the guilty was so necessary and so urgent that Charles IX could neither pardon them nor bow to 'the order of justice', but he did intend returning as quickly as possible to the 'ordinary' laws of the kingdom.

The French campaign of justification did not go without a riposte, and writings were published in reply to Pibrac, Monluc and Bellièvre.[54] But their arguments did not prevent the efforts of the agents and ambassadors in the King's service from bearing fruit.

The Anglo-French alliance officially remained in force, but its real significance was reduced to virtually nothing; it did not prevent England from negotiating with Spain and signing a treaty with it on 13 March 1573. Elizabeth
allowed Montgomery to gather a fleet of ships to help the rebel Huguenots in
La Rochelle; however, she officially disavowed the English seamen and nobles
who assisted them. The Queen agreed to become the godmother of Charles
IX's daughter, born on 27 October 1573; the negotiations for her marriage
with the duc d'Alençon would be suspended – and then temporarily – only in
September 1573.[55] As for Henri d'Anjou's candidacy for the Polish throne, it was
successful in the end, and on 11 May 1573 he was proclaimed king. But Jean de
Monluc had to promise that the new sovereign would undertake to tolerate the
plurality of confessions in his kingdom and that he would agree to his power
being limited by that of the Diet.

French diplomacy proved less skilful in the German lands. The Protestant
princes greeted Charles IX's advances coldly, and the elector of Saxony went
as far as to break off all communication with him. However, the Palatinate
remained in touch with France. For their part, the Swiss cantons did not accept
the King's request that they expel the Huguenot refugees or hinder the raising
of money or the publishing of pamphlets supporting their cause; but neither
did they oppose the recruitment of Swiss mercenaries by the King.[56]

As for relations with Spain, they were hardly changed at all. Three days
after the Massacre, however, Catherine de Medici expressed her anxiety: she
thought that henceforward the French were 'on the same ship of fortune' as
the Spaniards, who, should they cease fearing that Charles IX would help the
Dutch rebels, would no longer need to bother retaining their friendship with
France.[57] This fear, it should be noted here, shows that for the Queen Mother
the question of French assistance in the Low Countries was a factor favouring
rapprochement rather than a break with Phillip II. In any event, it proved to
be in vain. William of Orange's resistance was shaken but not annihilated by
the murder of Coligny; many French refugees joined his forces, while the 'Sea
Beggars', allied to the La Rochelle pirates, continued to attack Spanish ships;
and covert French support for the Dutch rebels would soon resume.[58] The
Massacre did not lead to France's becoming dependent on Spain, and Ambassador Zuñiga's influence at the French court was somewhat less after 24 August
than previously.[59] Relations between the two countries remained as before – a
mixture of suspicion and a refusal of open conflict.

Thus France succeeded in limiting the negative effects that the massacres
had on its international position. Should this result be attributed exclusively to
arguments of the campaign of royal justification? Probably not. It was obtained
primarily by the intense diplomatic activity of France's envoys abroad. The
arguments made in the writings and speeches in the King's service could only
be fully convincing if they were corroborated by concrete acts. Their central

thesis, particularly that of the absence of a religious motive for the execution of Coligny and his lieutenants, was only acceptable if the edict of pacification of 1570 was still observed. The maintenance of that edict and the limited freedom of worship that it granted the Protestants thus became, for the Protestant princes, the critical test of Charles IX's sincerity, but also of his ability to ensure concord among his subjects. He himself was fully aware of this, as is clear from the insistence with which he proclaimed, in his letters of 24 August and his declarations of 27 and 28 August, his determination to keep the edict. But achieving this objective became increasingly difficult.

THE IRRESISTIBLE NOSTALGIA FOR LOST UNITY

As early as 27 August, fear of the disturbances that the Huguenots might provoke led the King, in the letters that he sent to the governors, to ban Protestant worship in public; this measure, as we have seen, was presented as provisional until 'otherwise ordained'. The English government was alarmed by this, however, and on 22 September, Charles IX ordered his ambassador, La Mothe-Fénelon, to reassure it by confirming that the suspension of public worship was temporary.[60] However, by that date, the King's claim was no more than a desperate tactic designed to forestall Queen Elizabeth's suspicions. Exposed to strong pressure from intransigent Catholics in his own council, and also from the Pope and Phillip II, but perhaps also moved by the secret hope of recovering religious unity more quickly than he had expected, the King found himself gradually forced to abandon the idea of a full reinstatement of the edict of pacification of Saint-Germain.

It was probably in mid-September that this shift took shape. On 13 September Catherine de Medici, cornered by insistent questioning from Ambassador Walsingham, finally admitted that her son 'had resolved no longer to allow [the Protestants] their sermons and assemblies; that he did not wish that anyone be constrained in their religion (as is being done), but that everyone should live in peace under his obedience as, thank God, we see that all subjects are disposed to do, since large numbers of them had returned to our Catholic religion and all of the cities are at peace'.[61] On 24 September, Charles IX himself clearly indicated to the provincial governors that while he was preserving the edict of pacification, he was revoking the authorisation to hold 'sermons and assemblies'.[62] Liberty of conscience was preserved, but not of worship; the heart of the edict was now torn out.

On 22 September, a new step was taken towards a draconian restriction of the concessions given to the Protestants in 1570. Letters patent sent to the governors banned Protestant royal officials from exercising their functions until further notice, even if they had converted to Catholicism; the letters did say, however, that they would still be paid.[63] This decision triggered a considerable reaction among the magistrates who had abjured after the Massacre; some of them, who had perhaps renounced their faith only in the hope of keeping their offices, complained bitterly.[64]

On 3 November, new instructions sent by the King to the governors left no doubt as to his intentions; each recipient was to return to his government, assemble the Protestant nobility, and 'admonish them in friendly fashion not to persevere any longer in the error of the new opinions and to return to the Catholic religion, reconcile themselves to the Catholic, Apostolic and Roman church, in the doctrine of, and obedience to which the king and his predecessors and their subjects had always lived in a holy manner, and in which the kingdom by its actions had been well preserved'.[65] The fact that this 'friendly' admonition was addressed to the nobility is revealing about the King's hopes: he judged that once they were brought back to Catholicism, the commoner Protestants could only follow their example. The royal instruction suggested the kinds of arguments that the governors should use to convince the nobles. Their central theme was the necessity of mutual trust between sovereign and nobility: how could the King trust nobles of a different confession to his own and give them important offices? Those who would not return to the Catholic church would be reduced to 'an unfortunate and miserable condition', since they would lose the King's favour; thus if they wished 'to be employed by him in his service, they should henceforth profess and live in same religion as him'. The dilemma facing the recalcitrants was clear: they were free not to abjure their faith on condition of remaining peacefully at home, but would lose all hope of obtaining honourable employment.

Charles IX accepted the possibility of obedient Protestants keeping their liberty of conscience without fear of being troubled, but a sentence in his instructions shows that he remained as suspicious as ever that they desired 'in their heart only to change king and state'; hence his reluctance to give them public duties. He went as far as to say he was convinced of the impossibility of 'preserving in the same kingdom this repugnance of religion that would lead to him losing the goodwill and obedience of his subjects'. Mistrust had regained possession of Charles IX, and the Edict of Saint-Germain was well and truly dead and buried.

But does that mean that the ideal of concord was forgotten? Not entirely. The expected conversions were not meant to be obtained by force, but by persuasion, with the intention that the lost sheep would return of their own accord to Catholicism. Alongside that, the royal instructions stated that an effort at reforming the church would be made in order to make that return more inviting. Prelates would reside in their dioceses and parish priests in their parishes; all would preach and proclaim the word of God; and the ways in which those holding abbeys, priories, parishes and other benefices administered them would be supervised. This moralisation of the clergy would be accompanied by a reform of the judicial system. Those in charge of the bail-liage and *sénéchaussée* courts should be nobles, and those who were not would resign their offices – a measure which exceeded the often-expressed wishes of the nobility and which was certainly capable of winning over those nobles targeted by the instructions to the governors. And finally, judicial officials would be required to reside where their courts were located.

Two extremely interesting examples of the application of these instructions, in Metz and Champagne, have survived. In late November 1572, the governor of Metz reported to the King on what he had done. He began by visiting the villages around Metz where the Protestants were not numerous; according to him, they 'willingly listened and observed, entirely and devoutly committing themselves to the Catholic faith'. He had more problems with the Protestants of Metz. In his first letter, of 25 November, he informed Charles IX that he had met 'a great number of the leading bourgeois', who had agreed to confer with him; 'the common people', he asserted, 'would be easy to settle, and would follow the example of the others'. Three days later, on 28 November, he recounts how he communicated the King's wishes to them and challenged them to convert. The task proved far harder than imagined. As he wrote to the King, 'in truth, I should tell your Majesty that I found them extremely obdurate ... so that on this first occasion I did not dare go any further than enjoin them very explicitly to take [religious] instruction'.[66]

The governor of Champagne, Henri de Guise, apparently had fewer difficul-ties. Once the instructions of 3 November had arrived, he instructed the baillis, *présidial* court judges and the provosts of his governorship to convene the nobles of the 'new opinion' in the major towns. Journeying from Paris to Reims, he stopped off in Meaux, where he found no Protestant nobles, since they had all left; but he had the King's instructions read out in the presence of the royal officials, town councillors and Catholic nobles, so that they could inform those absent on their return. Arriving in the provincial capital [Reims], where the Protestant nobility of the bailliage of Vermandois had been summoned, he found five persons, whose names are listed in his report and who, having listened to the royal exhortations, 'all promised and swore to live henceforth as Catholics, and to accept all and each of the points of the instruction'. The same ceremony was held at Châlons, where he obtained the conversion of eleven nobles of the town and the bailliage of Vitry. Guise then went to Joinville (where six converts gave a written and signed promise of obedience) and then to Troyes (two converts only), Sens (six) and Provins (seven).[67]

During his progress, the governor of Champagne dispensed justice over the looting suffered by the Protestants, in accordance with the King's promises to take under his protection those who would live in peace at home and submit to the laws. But Guise also reminded them of the need to have all of the refugees return to the kingdom. On 8 October, the King had ordered the fugitives to return, otherwise their goods would be confiscated.[68] Yet many of them, now in Geneva, the Swiss cantons, Germany or England, refused to obey. The distribution of their confiscated possessions and those of the victims of the massacres whetted many appetites.

The conversion campaigns conducted by the governors of Metz and Champagne are interesting examples of how Charles IX hoped to achieve in 'friendly fashion' the unity of faith; after the storm of the massacres, this is the sole trace of his desire for conciliation. However, most of the abjurations that followed the massacres happened under pressures that were anything but 'friendly'. They were especially numerous in the cities of northern France; south of the Loire, the more numerous and better-organised Protestant communities resisted more effectively. In Rouen, for example, over 3,000 Protestants made their profession of Catholicism and allowed their children to be rebaptised, thus sealing the virtual disappearance of the city's Protestant community.[69] Such abjurations were mostly the result of discouragement among the faithful, no longer capable of living in perpetual fear of persecution. For their part, the Catholic authorities incited them to abjure by widely circulating the *Confession* of a famous convert, the minister Hugues Sureau du Rosier, in which he exhorts his former co-religionists to return to the Catholic church.[70]

The princes of the blood also ended up doing the same. Henri de Condé did so first: on 18 September, he publicly renounced his Protestant faith in the church of Saint-Germain-des-Prés, as had his wife and two of his brothers in the church of the Grands-Augustins on 14 September; on 6 December, his marriage was celebrated a second time, this time according to the Catholic rite.[71] Henri de Navarre also abjured, but in private, on 26 September, while on 27 October his marriage to Marguerite de Navarre was validated by the absolutions for the bishops who had attended it and for the degrees of consanguinity, which Gregory XIII had finally granted. Then, on 16 October, the young King had to sign an edict restoring Catholic worship in Béarn, an additional sign of the provisional failure of peaceful co-existence between the confessions.[72]

Charles IX's attempt to occupy the passion-free position of reason of the state – of which, under God's watch, he would be the sole guardian and judge – did not last long. Undertaken in a moment of improvisation and panic, supported by the subtle arguments of publicists entrusted with justifying it on the European stage, it could only have been convincing if the pacification of Saint-Germain had been fully preserved. But the new vigour that the Catholic intransigents derived from the Massacre put such an objective beyond reach. More than that, the instructions of 3 November made it clear that relations between the King and the nobility who served him were still seen in affective terms, in which mutual confidence was essential. The Prince required personal allegiance involving their whole being – body, heart and soul – in return for which he would reward them with offices and honours; in these relations based on reciprocity, suspicion could only have devastating consequences. It was exceptionally difficult to prevent confessional differences from engendering distrust between the King and those servants who were not of the same faith.

Does that mean that the French propaganda campaign was no more than a smoke-and-mirrors exercise mounted to impress the rest of Europe? Probably not, because it corresponded to the 'truth' that the King wished to diffuse from 26 August onwards, namely that by executing Coligny and his lieutenants he had chastised only their presumed rebellion, and not their religion. But this 'truth' was too hard for the most committed Catholics to accept; nor could it, at this point, successfully lead to dissociation between the spiritual and the temporal orders, of which it was implicitly the harbinger. For that reason, the fact that Charles IX and his committed publicists temporarily managed to mount such a case is even more remarkable. In presenting the sovereign as the only judge of what the interest of the state was and of the means to be used in its defence, their arguments contained the seeds of developments that would be of major importance for the future of royal power.

NOTES

1 *Lettres de Catherine de Médicis*, vol. 4, p. 141, letter to M. de La Fontaine, 13 Nov. 1572; p. 130, to the Duchess of Ferrara; pp. 142–144, n. 1 (letter of Charles IX, 18 Nov. 1572).

2 See above, ch. 4, p. 108.

3 *Correspondance du nonce Antonio Maria Salviati*, pp. 195–196, Tolomeo Galli, Cardinal of Como, secretary of state to Gregory XIII, to Salviati, 8 Sept. 1572; Erlanger, *Saint Bartholomew's Night*, p. 199. For reactions in Rome, see Edgar Boutaric, 'La Saint-Barthélemy d'après les archives du Vatican', *BEC*, 5th series, 23 (1862), pp. 1–27.

4 Simonin, *Charles IX*, p. 358; AGS, Estado, K1530, no. 61, Zuñiga to Philip II, 22 Sept. 1572.

5 BnF, MS. Fr. 16105, fol. 179r, Saint-Gouard to Charles IX, 12 Sept. 1572, quoted by Vásquez de Prada, *Felipe II y Francia*, p. 220.

6 AGS, Estado, K1530, no. 90, undated chancery minute, quoted by Vásquez de Prada, *Felipe II y Francia*, p. 222.

7 BPU, Geneva MS. Fr. 90, fol. 163v, Pierre Forget de Fresnes to Catherine de Medici, 10 Sept. 1572; fol. 162v, same to Charles IX, same date.

8 *Négociations diplomatiques avec la Toscane*, vol. 3, p. 815, anonymous (Cavriana) to secretary Concini, Paris, 27 Aug. 1572, quoted above ch. 4, p. 103.

9 *La Saint-Barthélemy devant le Sénat de Venise*, p. 50. For a brief panorama of the reactions in the Italian courts, see Anne Denis, 'La Saint-Barthélemy vue et jugée par les Italiens', in Danielle Boillet and Corinne Lucas-Fiorato, eds, *L'Actualité et sa mise en écriture dans l'Italie de la Renaissance.* (Paris, 2005), pp. 202–225.

10 *La Saint-Barthélemy devant le Sénat de Venise*, p. 53.

11 La Ferrière, *Le xvie siècle et les Valois*, p. 327, Arnaud du Ferrier to Catherine de Medici, Venice, 16 Sept. 1572.

12 Amedeo Molnar, 'Réactions à la Saint-Barthélemy en Bohême', in *L'Amiral de Coligny et son temps*, p. 370.

13 Nicollier, *Hubert Languet*, p. 283.

14 Vogler, 'Huguenots et protestants allemands vers 1572', in *L'Amiral de Coligny et son temps*, p. 184; Pierre de Grantrie, French Ambassador to the Swiss cantons, to Catherine de Medici, 19 Sept. 1572, in *Lettres de Catherine de Médicis*, vol. 4, p. 143, n. 1.

15 Kingdon, *Myths about the St. Bartholomew's Day Massacres*, p. 109; Crouzet, *La Nuit de la Saint-Barthélemy*, p. 596, nn. 3–4.

16 *Correspondance diplomatique de Bertrand de Salignac*, vol. 6, pp. 121 and 128, letters to the King, 14 Sept. 1572.

17 *Ibid.*, p. 142, letter to the King, 29 Sept. 1572.

18 *Ibid.*, p. 116, La Mothe-Fénelon to the King, 2 Sept. 1572 ; p. 182, Walsingham to Smith, 8 Oct. 1572.

19 *Ibid.*, p. 127, to the King, 14 Sept. 1572, and pp. 246–247, to same, 2 Feb. 1573.

20 *Ibid.*, pp. 125, 129, letter of 14 Sept., and p. 186, 2 Nov. 1572, for the repetition of these arguments.

21 On the singularity of English 'constitutional' thought, see the classic work of Ernst Kantorowicz, *The King's two bodies* (Princeton, 1957), pp. 322–325.

22 *Lettres de Catherine de Médicis*, vol. 4, p. 123, letter to La Mothe-Fénelon, 13 Sept. 1572. The Queen Mother alludes here no doubt to the execution of the Duke of Norfolk, who was at the heart of the rising of the Catholic lords of the North. La Mothe-Fénelon had informed her of this execution, and even added that it had been preceded by a trial.

23 *Correspondance diplomatique de Bertrand de Salignac*, vol. 6, p. 126, opinions reported in the Ambassador's letter to the King, 14 Sept. 1572.

24 *Ibid.*, p. 167, letter to the King, 13 Oct.; *Lettres de Catherine de Médicis*, vol. 4, p. 143, n. 1, Grantrie to Catherine de Medici, 19 Sept. 1572.

25 Jean Grangier to the Swiss Leagues, 27 Aug. 1572, announcing the content of the speeches that he was preparing to make to them and which is published in the *Mémoires de l'Estat de France*, vol. 1, fols 319v–321v; his letter stating that he had made the speeches is quoted by Bourgeon, *Charles IX devant la Saint-Barthélemy*, p. 49.

26 *Supplément à la correspondance diplomatique de Bertrand de Salignac*, vol. 7, pp. 328–333, for the memoir quoted above, ch. 5, p. 138. The same 'memoir of the truth' was given to Jean-Galéas Frégoso so that he could inform William of Orange of it: see Crouzet, *La Nuit de la Saint-Barthélemy*, p. 453.

27 *Supplément à la correspondance diplomatique de Bertrand de Salignac*, vol. 7, p. 402, postscript by Charles IX to his letter of 3 Dec. 1572.

28 Frédéric Morel produced three editions of the Latin original and one of the French translation in Paris; Benoît Rigaud published the Latin text in Lyon: Kingdon, *Myths about the St. Bartholomew's Day massacres*, p. 92.

29 *Ibid.*, p. 112; Crouzet, *La Nuit de la Saint-Barthélemy*, p. 375.

30 Marc Venard, 'La présentation de la Saint-Barthélemy aux Polonais en vue de l'élection d'Henri de Valois', in *Les Contacts religieux franco-polonais du Moyen-Âge à nos jours* (Paris, 1985), pp. 116–127; Kingdon, *Myths about the St. Bartholomew's Day massacres*, pp. 95–99. The texts written by Charpentier and Pibrac, as well as the French translation of the *Défense* by Monluc and his speech of 10 April 1573,

were published by Goulart, *Mémoires de l'Estat de France, op. cit.*, vol. 1, fols 450r–474r, 600r–621r, and vol. 2, fols 61v–70r, 197r–214r.

31 Bellièvre, *Proposition faite aux Suisses; Lettres de Catherine de Medici*, vol. 4, pp. 146–147, letter to Bellièvre, 3 Dec. 1572.

32 P. Champion, *Charles IX*, pp. 148–152; Molnar, 'Réactions à la Saint-Barthélemy en Bohême', p. 370.

33 AGS, Estado, K1530, no. 39, Zuñiga to Alba, 12 Sept. 1572, *'tambien embian al Turco a justificar lo del Almirante'.*

34 BnF, MS. Dupuy 428, fol. 80, 23 March 1573, quoted by Daubresse, *Le Parlement de Paris ou la voix de la raison*, p. 199.

35 Letter quoted above, p. 108.

36 Guy du Faur de Pibrac, *Les Quatrains*, ed. Loris Petris (Geneva, 2004), quatrain no. 93, p. 179.

37 *Correspondance diplomatique de Bertrand de Salignac*, vol. 6, p. 149, letter to Catherine de Medici, 19 Sept. 1572.

38 The Venetian ambassadors' despatch and Schomberg's report are quoted by Champion, *Charles IX*, p. 149, n. 2.

39 *Correspondance diplomatique de Bertrand de Salignac*, vol. 6, p. 131, letter to Catherine de Medici, 14 Sept. 1572.

40 See, for example, Marie-Madeleine Fragonard, 'L'établissement de la raison d'état et la Saint-Barthélemy', in *Miroirs de la Raison d'État. Cahiers du Centre de recherches historiques*, 20 (1998), p. 55.

41 *Traduction d'une Epistre latine d'un excellent personnage de ce Royaume*, [Guy du Faur de Pibrac] (Paris, 1573) p. 7.

42 Jean de Monluc, *Harangue faicte et prononcée de la part du Roy treschrestien le 10ème jour du mois d'avril 1573* (Paris, 1573), p. 43.

43 *Lettre de Pierre Charpentier jurisconsulte addressée à François Portes Candiois* (n.p., n.d.), fols 15r–24v and 36r. Sheba was a rebel against King David (Second book of Samuel, ch. 20).

44 *Ibid.*, fols 3v–4v and 19r.

45 *Ibid.*, fol. 7v.

46 *Traduction d'une Epistre latine*, p. 18; *Lettre de Pierre Charpentier*, fol. 15r.

47 Jean de Monluc, *Défense*, fol. 62r; *Traduction d'une Epistre latine*, p. 38.

48 *Traduction d'une Epistre latine*, pp. 38–39. This thesis is also clearly stated in a work attributed to the historian Bernard de Girard, seigneur du Haillan: 'because on the question of intelligence concerning the life of princes, once one is fully informed, one must proceed to execution and punishments before dealing with the investigation, trial and judgment later': *Discours sur les causes de l'execution faicte és personnes de ceux qui avoient conjuré contre le Roy et son Estat* (Paris, 1572), quoted in Crouzet, *Le Haut Cœur de Catherine de Médicis*, p. 405.

49 Salvo Mastellone, *Machiavellismo et antimachiavelismo nel Cinquecento* (Florence, 1969), pp. 74–75.

50 *Traduction d'une Epistre latine, op. cit.*, pp. 9–10.

51 *Ibid.*, pp. 38–39.

52 *Lettre de Pierre Charpentier*, fol. 31v.

53 *Traduction d'une Epistre latine, op. cit.*, p. 24.

54 Against Charpentier: *Response de François Portus Candiot aux lettres diffamatoires de Pierre Charpentier advocat* [1573], French translation (n.p., 1574), and Pierre

Fabre, *Response au cruel et pernicieux conseil de Pierre Charpentier, chiquaneur* [...], *translated from Latin* (n.p., n.d., [1575]); against Pibrac: *Response de Stanislaus Elvidius* [Joachim Camerarius ?] *a l'epistre d'un certain excellent personnage touchant les affaires de France*, 1573, and Pierre Burin, *Response à une epistre commencant Seigneur Elvide, où est tracté des massacres faits en France en l'an 1572* (Basel, 1574); against Monluc: *Response de Zacharie Furnesterus, soustenant l'innocence et justice de tant de milliers de personnes massacrées au royaume de France*, French translation of the Latin original published in 1573; against Bellièvre: *Response de Wolfgang Prisbachius polonois* [pseudonym of Théodore de Bèze, or François Hotman?] *à une harangue soustenant les massacres et brigandages commis en France*, French translation of the Latin original published in La Rochelle in 1573. These replies are in Simon Goulart, *Mémoires de l'Estat de France*, vol. 1, fols 474r–512r, 621r–655r, and vol. 2, fols 28r–47r, 70v–95r.

55 *Correspondance diplomatique de Bertrand de Salignac*, vol. 6, pp. 230–233 and 234–237, *mémoires* on the replies to the Queen Mother transmitted to the King by La Mothe-Fénelon in his letters of 2 and 9 Jan. 1573.

56 Vogler, 'Huguenots et protestants allemands vers 1572', pp. 184–186; Henri Fazy, 'La Saint-Barthélemy et Genève', *Mémoires de l'Institut national genevois*, 14 (1879), pp. 12–13, 53.

57 *Lettres de Catherine de Médicis*, vol. 4, p. 114, Catherine to Saint-Gouard, 29 Aug. 1572.

58 Vásquez de Prada, *Felipe II y Francia*, pp. 224–229.

59 *Ibid.*, p. 226, 233.

60 *Supplément à la correspondance diplomatique de Bertrand de Salignac*, vol. 7, p. 358, letter from Charles IX, 22 Sept. 1572.

61 *Lettres de Catherine de Médicis*, vol. 4, p. 123, Catherine to La Mothe-Fénelon, 13 Sept. 1572.

62 Paris, *Correspondance du roi Charles IX et du sieur de Mandelot*, p. 91, the King to Mandelot, governor of Lyon, 24 Sept. 1572. Bourgeon found similar letters to Matignon, lieutenant-general in Normandy and to marshal Cossé, governor of Touraine: see his *Charles IX devant la Saint-Barthélemy*, p. 161, n. 12.

63 Letters published in Simon Goulart, *Mémoires de l'Estat de France*, vol. 1, fols 419r–421v, under the title of *Memoires envoyez par le Roy à tous les gouverneurs et lieutenans de ses provinces pour destituer et démettre de leurs estats et charges tous ceux de la Religion, encore qu'ils la voulussent abjurer*.

64 See, for example, the complaints forwarded to the King by the 'persons who make up the court of the parlement of the Daulphiné', 22 Oct. 1572, BnF, MS. Fr. 15555, fol. 153r.

65 A copy of the instructions to the governor of Normandy was attached to the King's letter of the same date, 3 Nov., to ambassador La Mothe-Fénelon (*Supplément à la correspondance diplomatique de Bertrand de Salignac*, vol. 7, pp. 388–391). There is therefore no need to doubt their provenance or paternity, as does Bourgeon, *Charles IX devant la Saint-Barthélemy*, pp. 174–175. The text can also be found in the *Mémoires d'Estat* of Morvillier in BnF, MS. Fr. 5172, fols 6r–7r. The copy sent to the duc de Guise was published by Simon Goulart in the *Mémoires de l'Estat de France*, vol. 1, fol. 580v–583r, and that for Champagne by Nicolas Pithou, *Chronique de Troyes et de la Champagne*, p. 755.

66 BnF, 500 Colbert, 7, fols 449r and 453r, letters from the governor of Metz to the King, 25 and 28 Nov. 1572.

67 *Ibid.*, fols 461r–469r, *Memoire pour faire entendre au Roy le succès du voyage que Monsieur le duc de Guyse* [...] *en ses pays de Champagne et Brye*, 15 Dec. 1572.

68 Declaration published in *Mémoires de l'Estat de France*, vol. 1, fols 549r–550r.

69 Benedict, *Rouen during the Wars of Religion*, pp. 129–130.

70 Hugues Sureau, dit des Rosiers, *Confession et recognoissance de Hugues Sureau dit du Rosier touchant sa cheute en la Papauté et les horribles scandales par luy commis* (Heidelberg, 1573). Sureau returned to Calvinism, however, as soon as he left France.

71 *Correspondance du nonce Salviati*, p. 231, Salviati to Tolomeo Galli, 15 Sept. 1572, and p. 236, same to same, 19 Sept.; *Négociations diplomatiques avec la Toscane*, vol. 3, p. 863, Vincenzo Alamanni to Francesco de Medici, Paris, 7 Dec. 1572.

72 Babelon, *Henri IV*, pp. 190–193.

PART III

CLARIFICATIONS AND RESPONSES

7

PROTESTANT MISFORTUNE
IN BIBLICAL PERSPECTIVE

The years immediately after 1572 were haunted by the memory of the atrocities. The Massacre was a major trauma for all French people, Protestant and Catholic. The enormity of the event confronted them with the difficulty of finding a meaning for actions that went beyond the normal, and of *thinking* their savagery. We shall now examine their efforts to decipher what they had just lived through and to determine their behaviour in relation to it – efforts which were not without their effects on the evolution of the monarchy. The revival of civil war, the passions and the intellectual debates which obsessed people, as well as the political strategies of the rulers: all were marked by the desire to exorcise, by one means or another, the sinister shadow of the killings.

The most widespread reading of the events was essentially a religious one. Most people believed they saw God's will in what had happened, shrouding the tragedy in an aura of holy terror. The savage and unexpected eradication of thousands of Protestants seemed too prodigious in their eyes to be the result of human action alone; they saw in it the work of God's anger.

But those who took such a view still had to penetrate the causes which had unleashed the cataclysm. It was in the Bible that all parties looked for the precedents capable of accounting for the misfortune that had struck the Protestants so suddenly. This approach to explaining matters was, paradoxically, common to both camps, but they obviously drew different conclusions from it. Decoding God's design seemed easy to Catholics, even if the jubilation felt by the most fervent of them was at times accompanied by a muted disappointment that 'heresy' had not been completely eradicated. For the Protestants, on the other hand, elucidation proved more taxing. The thesis of royal premeditation only gave them a plausible explanation of the course of events: it was a key that revealed only the appearances. The basic question – why had God permitted the ordeal which had struck them? – still remained. Had he abandoned them? The answers worked out at the prompting of this painful questioning were to have an enduring influence of the future of the French Reformation.

GOD'S JUSTICE

People of this period were convinced that God intervened in their history. They felt that he did so especially when their sins became too monstrous; his anger cut loose at that point and punished sinners. The Christian mind-set was haunted by the memory of the great Biblical chastisements such as the Deluge, the destruction of Sodom and Gomorrah, the fall of Jerusalem, and the Babylonian exile.

For the intransigent Catholics, divine wrath was bound to fall upon heretics who had broken the unity of the body of believers, contaminated the purity of the faith and uttered their blasphemies in public. The duration of the scandal was beyond explanation, but punishment, when it did arrive, was felt to restore the meaning and intelligibility of the events in question. The intensity of the anxiety and the incomprehension triggered by the long wait for God's judgment among the most impatient resulted, once the blow had been struck, in an explosion of intoxicating joy expressed in a flood of pamphlets, poems and explicitly titled handbills.[1] The defeat of their enemies was put into song, adapting new words to well-known airs. 'Tremble, tremble Huguenots' went a popular song called *Noble ville de Paris, le Coeur de toute la France* (Noble city of Paris, heart of all France).[2] Sonnets posted on the walls of the capital on 28 August indulged in crude irony over the 'stinking carcasses' of those massacred, floating on the river and already being used as fishing bait.[3] In his poem *Allegresse chrétienne*, Jean Touchard, a friend of Jacques Amyot, noted that, for all its delay, God's vengeance was no less effective:

> Mais Dieu qui lentement prent du peché justice,
> Et pour l'attente, rend au double le suplice
> Des cieux a entendu et exaucé la voix
> [But God, who exacts slow punishment for sin
> and doubles the penalty for such delay
> has heard and satisfied the heavens' wish.][4]

Many 'coarse-grained Catholics', as Pierre de l'Estoile amusingly calls them, found in the carnage an opportunity to wield the pen.[5] Poems, speeches and even a tragedy – by François de Chantelouve, a Bordeaux noble who was a knight of Malta – constantly trumpeted the victory of Catholicism.[6] The cosmic dimension that these overheated texts ascribed to the Massacre was, in their eyes, proof of its supernatural character. The anonymous author of a *Discours sur la mort de Gaspart de Coligny* showed that neither earth, water nor fire wished to receive his body; the poet Jean Dorat imagined the ocean throwing back onto its shores the corpses brought by the rivers so that their infamy would not pollute its waves; on the other hand, the priest Artus Désiré attributed a homicidal fury against the Huguenots to the elements themselves:

L'air demande à les étouffer,
La terre à les reduire en cendre
Le feu à les ardre [brûler] en enfer.
[The air demands that they be smothered
Earth that they be turned to ash
Fire that they burn in hell.][7]

What is surprising is the similarity between the borrowings from the Bible made by the authors of these diatribes and those which are characteristic of normal Protestant rhetoric: quotations from the Psalms; comparisons of the enemy church to the 'great prostitute' of the Apocalypse or to the 'house of Babylon'; and evocations of the history of the Jews. The Deluge theme fuelled the exultation of Catholic pamphleteers, as in the *Déluge des Huguenotz, avec leur tumbeau*. This theme is common in Huguenot lamentations, but with an opposite meaning. Religious polemic, regardless of which camp it belongs to, takes its interpretative framework from the same sacred texts.[8]

It was the most radical Catholics who were the loudest, while the moderates remained mostly silent. Some, like Christophe de Thou, deliberately set out to forget: his son, Jacques-Auguste, said that he discovered a marginal note in Latin verse in his hand, in which, on the subject of an episode from Roman history, he implicitly expressed the wish to erase the memory of the Massacre of 24 August.

Des crimes de ce jour périsse la mémoire
Que les siècles futurs refusent de les croire
De nostre nation taisons ces noirs forfaits
Et qu'une épaisse nuit les couvre pour jamais.
[May the memory of this day's crimes perish
May future ages refuse to believe they happened
Of our nation's crimes let us be silent
And let night's darkness envelop them forever.][9]

Others, such as Montaigne, observed silence, possibly because they thought language was incapable of translating the cruelty of the massacre. There is no mention of the Massacre in his *Essays*, in which bloody images of the civil wars are quite numerous. Was it, as it has been suggested, a means of making the 'blank' of such an absence even more intense?[10]

If the exclusivist Catholics were so keen to proclaim their jubilation, it was because they were driven by the urge to see in the killings the implementation of God's design. Faced with the horror of the Massacre, they found in such a conviction a way of exculpating themselves: they considered themselves the agents of a will which was far above them, and the docile enforcers of God's terrible justice. But the biblical reading of the event still raised a disturbing question for them: why had God not finished his work and completely wiped out the heretics? This question would later become an obsession for the *ligueur*

Louis Dorléans, for whom the Massacre was a failure. In his *Advertissement des catholiques anglois aux François catholiques* (1586), he deplored Charles IX's retreat from the ultimate completion of his mission: because of 'the cruel clemency and inhuman mercy of Saint-Bartholomew's Day', the 'blood-letting' was incomplete; 'a residue of bad blood remained, which soiled and corrupted the rest of the blood'.[11] Faced with the resistance of heresy, the joy experienced by the militants of religious unity would give way to profound disappointment, to be followed by the resurgence of a feeling of guilt. If God had prematurely lifted the scourge of his vengeance, was it not because the faithful had shown themselves too lukewarm, insufficiently eager for his glory, and too attached to their material interests? This self-scrutiny by Catholics – conducted not in regret over the fury of the Parisian massacres but in order to assume the blame for the abortion of the 'great purification' – would result, among the *ligueurs* after 1576 and especially after 1585, in a vast penitential movement of collective expiation for their sins; they now turned their violence on themselves rather than on the heretic, especially in the flagellations of the hooded penitents during the processions in the towns, which were driven by a touching desire to effect a reconciliation with God.[12]

The Protestants, for their part, had experienced the anxiety of guilt far earlier than the Catholics. Many of them were inhabited by a powerful sense of chastisement. One question preyed on their minds: had they deserved being punished with such unprecedented severity? Some refused to accept such a position, putting the blame purely on human agency – that of the King and his council – and seeking above all to avenge themselves by human means, like taking up arms, seeking military and financial support or circulating vindictive pamphlets throughout Europe.[13] But those whom the enormity of the massacres had imbued with a kind of mystical terror came to believe that it was God who had punished them.

The question then was – what meaning should be attributed to the terrible blow they had received? Some people, overwhelmed by events, began to doubt the justice of their cause and to believe that God had shown his rejection of them. This was the main argument used by the former pastor Hugues Sureau du Rosier to justify his conversion, while such discouragement lay behind many of the abjurations that followed the Massacre.[14] Others, reviewing their past behaviour, accused themselves of attracting misfortune through their sins. The Huguenot Jacques Gaches notes in his memoirs that before the tragedy his co-religionists were 'as in the days of Noah, thinking only of pleasures and self-indulgence, with no one caring to serve God, but rather their own foolish inclinations. God, wishing to avenge this, sent a flood of evils, murders and massacres throughout France, beginning with his house and striking his churches with a great scourge.'[15] For Simon Goulart, it was the co-existence prompted by pacification which exposed the Huguenots to insidious temptations. He too referred to the time of Noah, and argued that as soon as negotiations for the marriage of Marguerite de Valois with Henri de Navarre began, the far-sighted sensed that a 'horrible deluge of God's anger' was brewing; 'those of the religion' got too close to the vices of the courtiers and let themselves be contaminated by 'infection'; nearly everywhere in the realm, vanity and pride had taken possession of people, so that the only visible difference between Catholics and Protestants was that 'the first went to mass, the second to the sermon', but all resembled each other through their sinful behaviour.[16]

Put in another way, it was rapprochement with and the habit of frequenting and mixing with the Roman Catholics, thanks to the peace, which made the Protestants lose their awareness of their specificity, leading them to believe that ultimately there was no essential difference between them and Catholics; for that reason, they had become easy prey to worldly corruption. Odet de la Noue offered the same diagnosis: the Huguenots, persecuted like the Jews as slaves among the Egyptians, had 'given their hand to Egypt' instead of leaving it.[17] The extremists reached the bitter conclusion that it was folly to believe in peaceful co-existence with Catholics. That was the lesson of the Massacre for Agrippa d'Aubigné, one which Coligny himself taught from heaven to the survivors:

Venez voir comme Dieu chastia son Église
Quand sur nous, non sur luy, sa force fut assise,
Quand, devenus prudens, la paix et nostre foy
Eurent pour fondement la promesse du Roy. [...]
Nous voulions contraster [rivaliser de ruse avec] du peuple les finesses
Nous, enfans du Royaume, et Dieu mit nos sagesses
Comme folie au vent [...].
[Come and see how God chastised his church
When he chose to embody his power in us
And when we, grown too wordly-wise,
Based our peace and faith on the king's promise. [...]
And when we, the children of the kingdom,
tried to match the cunning of the people,
God blew our reasonableness to the wind [...].][18]

Thus was 'a theological acceptability of the massacre' constructed for the Protestants.[19] However, it did not drive those accepting it to despair, since persecution had cleansed sinners of their faults and restored their lost purity. But should an unconscious desire for punishment, predating the Massacre, as the only way to expiate their sinfulness be attributed to those most eager for such purity?[20] Whatever the case, it was possible for them to discover, after the event, a comprehensible religious meaning for what they had experienced.

The teaching of Jean Calvin helped them in this regard. In his *Institution de la Religion chrestienne*, he distinguishes between two types of divine justice. The first is revenge justice, which strikes the wicked in order to eliminate them; the second is corrective justice, which chastises the elect in order to reform them.[21] Thanks to this doctrine, the Protestants convinced themselves that, far from being proof of disinterest or abandonment, the terrible lesson administered by God was a sign of the care that he took to rescue them from the slavery of sin. It is no surprise that one of the biblical episodes most frequently invoked to understand the great ordeal was the crossing of the Red Sea, which had enabled the Jews to escape from slavery in Egypt – a crossing which, for the victims of the Massacre, had been a bloody one.[22] Agrippa d'Aubigné develops this theme in his pulsating verses which outline for the escapees the hard road they have to take:

> Qui voudra se sauver de l'Egypte infidèle,
> Conquérir Canaan et habiter en elle,
> O tribus d'Israël, il faut marcher de rang
> Dedans le golfe rouge et dans la mer de sang
> Et puis à reins troussés passer, grimper habiles
> Les déserts sans humeur [sans eau] et les rocs difficiles.
> [You who would flee unbelieving Egypt
> Conquer and settle in Canaan,
> O tribes of Israel, you must march in line
> In the red gulf and the sea of blood
> And then, with backs upright
> Climb the arid deserts and the arduous rocks.][23]

From this viewpoint, the Protestants saw themselves being punished for their blindness and their compromises, but their chastisement also amounted to a form of deliverance, a path from death to life. The judgment had fallen mainly on the world and its vanities, in whose mirages they had allowed themselves to be trapped. Human justice, with its terrible sword, was only apparently victorious; the eyes of the faithful, opened by God's hand, should learn to discern that, in reality, it was human justice which was condemned. And the massacred martyrs themselves were witnesses to that condemnation.

THE MARTYRS' WITNESS

In 1554, the publisher-printer Jean Crespin published in Geneva his catalogue of all those who had died for the Protestant cause. This *Book of Martyrs* was so successful that the author frequently republished it, adding new sketches each time; from 1564 onwards, it was divided into 'books' and its contents arranged in chronological order. As he died on 12 April 1572, Crespin was unable to add the victims of the Massacre to his list; but Simon Goulart, who assumed the task of continuing his work, entered their names in the revised edition of 1582, using both the *Mémoires de l'Estat de la France*, which he himself had compiled, and the *Histoire ecclésiastique des églises réformées* of Théodore de Bèze, published in 1580.[24]

Based on the teaching of Saint Augustine and Calvin, Crespin set out strict criteria for granting people the label of 'martyr'. The two most important ones were that they had died defending their faith, and that a court sentence had certified that as the reason for their condemnation.[25] The definition was tight: those who died in the summer and autumn of 1572 had not been subject to legal judgment. Should they be excluded from the martyrology on such grounds? The question was asked by Goulart in the 'advertisement' to the reader placed at the beginning of the tenth book of his edition covering the years 1563 to 1572. Those massacred in 1572, he noted, were brutally killed, with private persons acting as their executioners and filling the role of 'parties, witnesses, judges, decrees and executioners in the strangest cruelties ever inflicted upon the church'.[26] According to Crespin's rules, these unfortunates could claim only to be 'persecuted believers'. Goulart thought such rigour unjust, so he included them among the suffering members of the church martyred for their faith, and whose death was thereby exemplary. Other problems could hide the value of their witness: most of them were anonymous and the precise conditions of their deaths often remained obscure. By this 'strange ruse of the devil', which the publishers of the martyrology deplored, the memory and meaning of their sacrifice risked being obscured. It was a necessity to restore their identity.

However, not everyone agreed that removing the anonymity of the victims was necessary. There were those who, alongside the moderate Catholics, believed that it was preferable not to rekindle the memory of the horrors and to practise voluntary amnesia, as the royal edicts prescribed. For example, François de La Noue wrote of the Massacre: 'it was a horrible deed, which deserves to be buried'.[27] Others, too, and for different reasons, judged it pointless to seek to remove the anonymity of the martyrs. What would it achieve? The pastor Jean de Serres thought that 'it is enough that their names are written in heaven'.[28] What mattered was that they were known to God, the supreme judge of the secret of men's hearts.

Such silence did not seem acceptable to Simon Goulart. He conducted a dogged enquiry, questioned the survivors and – in the first edition of the *Mémoires de l'Estat de France* – launched an appeal for witnesses. It seemed essential to him to be able to name the faithful who had been massacred, give them a face, and see how they had been executed. There were several reasons for this. Firstly, there was a duty of piety and memory not just on the part of the Protestant community, but of future centuries. It was necessary to show to what degree of barbarity men had sunk; if unpunished in their own time, the murderers would, by this means, be charged before the tribunal of posterity.[29] An even more serious reason justified the urgent obligation to preserve the memory of the martyrs: they helped to reveal the meaning of history. They were witnesses to the final defeat of appearances and the confusion of the wicked, thus rendering the invisible visible to the eyes of the believers.

All of the victims of the Massacre who died for their faith had this revelatory power, but some, more exemplary than others, possessed it *par excellence*. The chroniclers and poets fixed their gaze on a number of individuals, not in order to make them into some kind of Protestant saints – which would have been nonsense for people who had fought so fiercely against aspects of Catholic worship that they judged idolatrous – but to identify them as guides in the task of understanding the world, capable of teaching the comprehension of God's design in human history.

THE MARTYROLOGY OF THE ST BARTHOLOMEW'S MASSACRE

The first name proposed for edification was, obviously, that of Coligny, to whom an evangelical patience and gentleness in the face of death were attributed. In his biography, François Hotman first recalls the courage with which he endured the operation on his arm after the attack on 22 August. Hotman relates that, on seeing those around him lamenting, the victim criticised them for crying, believing himself happy 'to have received these wounds in the name of God', and thanked the Lord for having judged him worthy of such an honour.[30] Then, Hotman adds, the Admiral implored God's mercy in a long, fervent prayer asking that, if the hour of his death was approaching, he might be received into a 'heavenly and happy peace'. The minister, Merlin, reminded him of the example of the ancient martyrs, and Coligny replied 'that he was mightily fortified by these words and found a singular consolation and relief from his pain in the story told to him about the piety of the Fathers and Martyrs'. In such a manifestly hagiographic passage, François Hotman clearly locates the Admiral in the line of succession from the first Christians, who suffered under pagan persecution. He then depicts his constancy in facing death: when Coligny heard his murderers forcibly entering his house at dawn on 24 August, he began to pray, waiting serenely for the final blows. Another hagiographer, François Portes, professor of Greek at Geneva, noted that the Admiral asked Merlin to add a prayer for the King's and the kingdom's salvation, thereby practising the forgiveness of offences.[31]

Numerous Protestant poems also celebrated the Christian firmness and resignation of their heroes. All of them placed Coligny as an emblematic figure of faith persecuted and dignity in adversity.[32] In Genevan Protestant calendars, in which the leading names of the Protestant reformation had replaced the Roman Catholic saints, the Admiral was placed after Luther, Martin Bucer, Edward VI and Calvin.[33]

Simon Goulart also goes into great detail about the Admiral's death, but he offers other models of death to the memory of the Protestants. In his *Mémoires de l'Estat de France*, the list of those massacred begins symbolically with a long account of the ordeal suffered by president La Place, who was selected as the archetype of the victim who peacefully accepts his fate. At the first sign of danger, Goulart writes, the president's wife was overcome by despair, but he, 'fortified by the Spirit of God, with an incredible constancy, corrected her sharply, reminding her how such afflictions should be received meekly and as coming from the hand of God'. He assembled his servants and, as he did every Sunday, began praying with them, and then read them a chapter of the Book of Job and Calvin's commentary on it. This choice is revealing, as it is the Old Testament book which the mostly unsparingly confronts the faithful with the enigma of evil. With the help of Calvin's teaching, La Place showed his household that afflictions could be salutary for Christians and that Satan's attacks on them were in vain. Fear was thus pointless, and the power of the enemy could only affect men's bodies.[34]

This episode shows the direction in which the narrative is moving; by including his hero's message of hope, Goulart is thinking of his own readers who are still saddled with the terrible doubts sown by the tragedy. He then describes La Place's preparations for dealing with the inevitable. Seeing the paper cross that his eldest son had placed in his hat in the hope of escaping the massacre, the president reprimanded him, saying that the only cross to be borne was the God-sent tribulations which were as a down-payment for future happiness. Finally, hassled by the troop of murderers who were to assassinate him, he took his overcoat, embraced his wife and urged her to retain the honour and fear of God, 'and then went out with a light heart'. He was slaughtered 'like a poor lamb'. Virtually all of the other deaths reported by Goulart conform to this design in which serene acceptance accompanies a refusal to abjure; most of the victims he mentions allowed themselves to be sacrificed without a struggle. The lamb to which he compares La Place implicitly alludes to the paschal lamb. Agrippa d'Aubigné went as far as comparing the 'slaughtered lambs' of the Massacre to a 'procession of sacrificial victims'.[35]

Certain towns, such as La Rochelle, Sancerre and Sommières, also collectively achieved the status of martyrs for their determined resistance, with the terrible sufferings it entailed, to the royal armies sent to reduce them to obedience. The siege of Sancerre was the subject of a book by its pastor, Jean de Léry.[36] In it he recounts how the arrival of survivors of the killings at La Charité and Orleans stimulated the intransigence of the inhabitants of Sancerre. Refusing any form of negotiation, the besieged soon experienced the pangs of hunger; with no meat available, they ate the skin of dogs, cats and rats, and even chewed boiled leather and parchment. According to Léry, parents were driven to eating the corpse of their three-year-old daughter, an excess which he compared to the cannibalism of the Indians of Brazil, but which he includes the better to show the seriousness of the temptations which assailed the unfortunate residents. In this account, it was the children, all of whom under the age of twelve perished, who were the most exemplary, and Léry quotes the last words of some of them as perfect models of Christian resignation. The heroic resistance of Sancerre lasted until 19 August 1573, although the Edict of Boulogne had ended the war in July; the city benefited by being added to the list of three towns entitled to conduct Protestant worship in private only, and not in public. Sancerre remained in the memory of the Protestants as a symbol of the collective fight for the faith which, though lost in human terms, was won in a spiritual sense.

All of these edifying accounts were designed to make violence intelligible, even acceptable: it belonged to God's plan, and was a sign of election. The Massacre thus contributed to reinforcing 'the Protestant martyr culture' that began with the first persecutions.[37] It was a culture exclusively focused on the memory of those who 'from Jean Hus to the present time had signed with their blood the truth of the Gospel'.[38]

From this point of view, the Protestants were ahead of the Catholics. It was not that the latter did not denounce the brutalities they suffered from their enemies, especially the assassination of priests; they worked on stoking up indignation by circulating accounts and prints illustrating the atrocities committed by the Protestants during the conflicts.[39] But they were slow to build a martyrology devoted specifically to the victims of the Wars of Religion. It was only in the 1580s that Catholic authors began to write hagiographical works hailing the assassinated martyrs for their fight against heresy, especially the faithful persecuted by Queen Elizabeth. In 1581 an anonymous work appeared in Paris in Latin, and which was translated into French the next year, relating the death of Edmund Campion, who had gone to England to try to regain souls for Catholicism.[40] Two years later, Richard Verstegan published in Paris a Latin edition of his *Théâtre des cruautés des hérétiques de notre temps*, which would be republished several times with additions before finally being translated into French in 1587.[41] It was thus rather slowly that a kind of 'competition of memories' arose, in which each side flaunted its moving and didactic narratives.

In the aftermath of the Massacre, it was not yet critical for the Protestants to indulge in a memory contest with the Catholics; it was more important to show that the faithful who had been massacred were not really losers, but victors. The ignominy of their death was really that of those who governed France. The martyrs thus offered an image of the world turned upside down, in which defeat was victory and vice versa. An 'Address to the church of Our Lord' placed at the beginning of the *Histoire des Martyrs* alerted readers to what they should seek in the book: they would find in it unprecedented triumphs, which would not be about glorious chariots or laurel crowns rewarding victorious generals, but 'a new way of conquering while being condemned'.[42]

The writings devoted to the memory of the exterminated called for a spiritual reading of events and adjusting people's vision to the supernatural reality lying hidden behind appearances. Believers should *learn to see*, decode the events before their eyes and recognise the truth hidden in them. Agrippa d'Aubigné was one of those who persevered the most in educating people how to see in this way. He was not himself an eyewitness to the Massacre, since three days previously he had had to flee Paris and the King's justice for having acted as a 'second' to a duelling friend and for having struck a sergeant who tried to arrest him. But this absence did not prevent him from feeling solidarity with the victims of 24 August. Seriously wounded some time afterwards in an ambush, he took refuge in the château of Talcy with his beloved Diane Salviati and set about symbolically reinterpreting his sufferings as a form of communion with those of his co-religionists.[43] In order to make the duality of the events in question more intelligible, he invented a striking fiction. In Book 2 of the *Tragiques*, he tells how, as he lay unconscious in his room at Talcy, he saw a feminine figure representing Virtue who led his spirit into Heaven. There he met Coligny, who, far from being sad-looking, was laughing *at the very moment* when, on earth, the crowd 'played bowls with his trussed-up body'.[44] In Book 5, he imagines the Lord's angels painting on the heavenly ceilings representations of the misfortunes of the elect, which the Admiral himself explained to those spectators allowed to contemplate them:

D'un visage riant nostre Caton tendoit
Nos yeux avec les siens, et le bout de son doigt
A se voir transpercé ; puis il nous monstra comme
On le coupe en morceaux : sa teste court à Rome
Son corps sert de jouët aux badauds ameutés
Donnant le bransle au cours des autres nouveautés.
[With a cheerful countenance our Cato aligned our eyes with his
And pointed with his finger to his pierced body
And showed us how it was cut in pieces;
His head gone to Rome, his body a toy for gaping onlookers,
Setting in motion other novelties.][45]

According to d'Aubigné, the travails of the victims were situated on three levels. While the good angels composed their allegorical works in Heaven, the black angels of Satan painted other pictures ... in the Vatican – an allusion to the frescoes commissioned from Vasari by the Pope to commemorate the Massacre.[46] For the poet, there were three ways of reading reality: the superficial one, which brought disappointment and discouragement; the angelic one, that of the elect, which brought salvation; and the satanic vision, that of the murderers, which brought damnation. The conversion of the Protestants to a mystical perception of events took nothing away from the monstrosity of the barbarism or the scandal of the cruelty involved. In describing the sufferings of the victims, the author of the *Tragiques* does nothing to devalue their unbearable gravity. He wishes to bear witness to that aspect of events, and not to minimise the tension between the horrors people experienced and their metaphysical meaning.[47] At least, seen from God's perspective, the killings lost something of their atrociousness, and thus ceased to generate despair.

By providing an image of the world turned upside down, the story of the punishments was subversive of the established hierarchies and powers, since it demonstrated their impotence.[48] The subversion caused by the martyr is not without resemblance to that of the rebel: the first creates a symbolic desta-bilisation, while the second tries to undermine the material foundations of a temporal power deemed to be tyrannical. François Hotman, for example, exalts the supernatural victory of Coligny in the account that he gives of his death, but in his *Francogallia* he appeals implicitly to his readers to rebel; in both cases, the defeat of worldly iniquity and the triumph of the righteous are announced; they may be slow to appear in this world, but are at least assured in the afterlife.

Thus the Protestants succeeded in finding spiritual and affective strategies that would stem the huge wave of discouragement that followed the massacres, and they undeniably facilitated the survival of their churches during the storm.

A HISTORY FULL OF EXTRAORDINARY SIGNS

Yet the martyr's wreaths only supplied part of the meaning of the tragedy. For it to be entirely intelligible, it was necessary that the other manifestation of God's justice – the punishment that blasts the wicked – be equally apparent. But reality cruelly denied that demand. The more time passed, the more the Protestants identified themselves with the cry of the souls of the persecuted whom the author of the Apocalypse (6:9) shows hidden beneath an altar – 'Lord, until when?'[49]

In addressing the anxiety of that question, the authors who reflected on the place of the Massacre in the development of the faith constructed a prophetic reading of human history. They tried to identify, beyond events themselves, not just the simultaneities which linked the natural to the supernatural, but also the cyclical analogies which connected events from the history of Israel both to those of the present and to those of the Last Judgment.[50]

This vision of history, far from being new, had already been much used during the earlier persecutions suffered by the Protestants. But the scale of the massacres of the summer and the autumn of 1572 now made it both more present and systematic. The first step was to identify resemblances between episodes in the Old Testament and contemporary situations; the latter then appeared as repetitions of the former, revealing the same divine intervention. Thus, history is seen as the eternal return of events bearing the same meaning. This reading was no longer the typological approach of the kind employed by the Fathers of the Church, but a pure and simple identification of two series of events. An example of this is the account in the *Tragiques* of the miraculous deliverance of pastor Merlin. Escaping from the murderers chasing him and hiding in a loft full of hay, Merlin found enough to eat for several days, with hens' eggs, just as the prophet Elias, fleeing the vengeance of King Ahab, had been fed by the birds of the sky. The poet literally superposes the two events: the salvific bird lays its egg in Elias's hands, just as it was Ahab's anger that pursued Merlin.[51]

Another feature of the prophetic reading is the addition of an eschatological perspective to the connections among different historical developments: the situations experienced by the Protestants were thought of not just as repetitions of those of Israel, but also as prefigurations of what they would experience at the Last Judgment. Three 'times' – and no longer two – are thereby linked by mysterious similarities; and historical time itself retracts metaphorically into a unique instant which manifests the triumph of the Truth. Thus, in the *Tragiques* the drift of the bodies in the bloody waters of the Rhône at Lyon, Tournon, Valence and Viviers, repeats the Red Sea crossing by the Jews, but it also anticipates a particular moment at the end of the world announced in the Apocalypse, when an angel will pour into the world's rivers the third of the seven bowls of God's anger in an apocalyptic gesture which, in the poet's eyes, has already happened.

> Icy l'Ange troisiesme espandit à son rang
> Au Rhosne sa fiole et ce fleuve fut sang.
> [Here the third angel in its turn
> spread God's fury into the Rhône
> and the river turned to blood.][52]

This eschatological interpretation reveals the intensity of the waiting for the end of time so common in the sixteenth century, in which the Protestants equalled the Catholics. If they denounced the Roman papacy as the Antichrist predicted by the Apocalypse, it was because they believed the end of human history was near. 'The world is near its end. For that reason it resembles a man inching towards death as best he can', was the view of Pierre Viret, one of the most influential pastors.[53] The scale of the upheavals brought on by the Wars of Religion, and especially the horror of the Massacre, appeared to many as signs announcing the cataclysms which would precede the destruction of the temporal universe. In this perspective, the future was not viewed as a long, indefinite stretch of time, but rather as a short spell. This made the urgency of deciphering the present signs all the greater; the hope of seeing the wicked quickly punished was also reinforced. Some people hoped to see the punishment of the persecutors in this life, as a foretaste of the damnation that the Last Judgment would deliver.

These expectations concerned Catherine de Medici in particular. The most vindictive Protestants, forgetting that earlier, at the outset of the conflicts, they had compared her to Esther – the mediator who intervened with her husband,

Assuerus, in favour of the Jews – now identified her with Jezabel, who persecuted the prophet Elias and his people. According to the Old Testament, the
corpse of this queen was devoured by dogs; in evoking this death, the Protestant pamphleteers did not conceal their hope of seeing the Queen Mother
meet the same fate and perhaps also – who knows? – in the near future. This
is what the anonymous author of the *Tocsain contre les massacreurs* of 1577
suggests: 'we expect the same judgment in France against she who imitated
such an impiety'.[54] More cruelly, verses collected by Pierre de l'Estoile hinted
that such a punishment would be too soft:

> Enfin le jugement fut tel
> Les chiens mangeront Jezabel
> Par une vengeance divine.
> La charogne de Catherine
> Sera differente en ce point
> Les chiens mesmes n'en voudront point.
> [At last it was decreed
> That the dogs should eat Jezabel
> As God's revenge
> Catherine's rotting remains
> Will suffer a different fate
> Even the dogs will not want any of them.][55]

The deaths of others considered to be butchers of the Massacre were also
seen as precursor signs of the final judgment. The Troyes chronicler, Nicolas
Pithou, writes that 'two weeks after the horrible massacre in Troyes, God in
his goodness visited the beginnings of his fury and just vengeance on several
of its executors'. He then recounts how one of the murderers, Laurent Hillot,
was killed by an accomplice who coveted a ring stolen from a poor painter who
had been assassinated; how another, Nicolas Régnier, was struck by a severe
fever and a despair so massive that he had publicly to confess his crimes; and
how a third, called Perronet, a soldier in the royal army, died pitifully, burned
alive under the walls of the besieged city of La Rochelle.[56] It is no surprise to
see how keenly the death of Charles IX was anticipated by many people, who
were ready to see it as God's judgment.[57]

Schooled in this type of narrative, the Protestants gradually became accustomed to seeing important events as the signs of a supernatural history. In that
they were less different from the Catholics than used to be thought; the world
they inhabited was only slightly less 'enchanted'. A week after the Massacre, if
we are to believe Agrippa d'Aubigné, 'a great flock of ravens was seen, some of
them clinging to, and others croaking over the grand pavilion of the Louvre' –
a sinister invasion which terrified the King and the courtiers. That night was
heard, according to the same chronicler, 'a huge noise and a mass of voices
shouting, groaning and shrieking, along with other voices that were furious,

threatening and blaspheming – the whole thing resembling what had been heard on the night of the massacres'.[58] These extraordinary happenings symbolised the remorse of Charles IX and prefigured his punishment.

A little later, on 11 November 1572 (or the 8th, according to de Thou), a comet was seen in the sky, which the Protestants immediately identified with that of Bethlehem announcing the defeat of Herod – actually, of Charles IX. Théodore de Bèze composed a poem on it which finished with these lines:

> O Chrestiens fugitifs, o prisonniers, qu'on oye
> Vostre chant de victoire et vos esclats de joye :
> Mais, Herodes sanglants, c'est a vous de trembler.
> [Oh fleeing Christians, oh prisoners, let us hear
> Your song of victory and your shouts of joy
> as for you, bloody Herods, it's your time to quake.][59]

God showed himself through prodigies that were viewed as announcing the proximity of the Last Judgment. The Protestants were called upon to decode its meaning and to await more patiently an end of the world that was seen as imminent, but which nevertheless was strangely slow to materialise.

Thus did the Massacre contribute to shaping Protestant identity. Early during the Reformation, the French Protestants had hoped to convert the entire kingdom to their faith and thereby melt into the mass of the faithful who had been brought back to the truth; but the persecutions and the ferocity of the wars gradually forced them to recognise the vanity of such hopes. Under the shock of Catholic rejection and the acts of violence towards them, they gradually realised their own religious singularity, which was characterised by the tension between their apparent defeat and their supernatural victory. The scale of the massacres of the summer and autumn of 1572 could not but strengthen this conception of their history. Resorting to the biblical image of 'the little remnant of Israel' as a persecuted minority, but one which mysteriously held the ultimate meaning of human history, they saw in the massacres the sign of their election and in their martyrs the precursors who announced God's purpose. Historical time thus became the time of witness; in their eyes the role of historians was not to impartially report events, but to teach their readers to identify in them the manifestations of God's will.[60]

This identification with Israel would be corroborated, but in a disparaging register, by the vision of the Protestants which the Catholics would later adopt. In 1585, a pamphlet by Richard Verstegan denounced the 'heretical synagogue' as an assembly of Jewish doctors wearing fur robes and long beards; anti-Protestantism and anti-Judaism would end up feeding off each other.[61] In this way, the two antithetical readings of the Massacre, paradoxically, converged, as both drew on a common biblical culture, even though the Protestants were more profoundly steeped in the Scriptures.

NOTES

1 For an inventory of them, see Nicole Cazauran 'Échos d'un massacre', in Marguerite Soulié and Robert Aulotte, eds, *La Littérature de la Renaissance. Mélanges d'histoire et de critique littéraire offerts à Henri Weber* (Geneva, 1984), pp. 239–261.

2 *Ibid.*, p. 243 for the quotation.

3 *Advertissement du peuple de Paris aux passants*, as quoted in *ibid.*, pp. 246, 256. Pierre de L'Estoile attributed it to Étienne Jodelle.

4 Jean Touchard, *Allegresse chrestienne de l'heureux succès des guerres de ce Royaume* [...] (Paris, 1572), quoted by Cazauran, 'Échos d'un massacre', p. 249.

5 L'Estoile, *Mémoires pour servir à l'histoire de France depuis 1515 jusqu'en 1574*, p. 475.

6 François de Chantelouve, *Tragédie de feu Gaspar de Colligni*, composed in 1574 and published the followed year (see edition by Keith Cameron, Exeter, 1971); François de Belleforest, *Discours sur l'heur des presages advenuz de nostre temps, signifiantz la felicité du regne de nostre Roy Charles IX* (Paris, 1572); Jean Dorat, *Œuvres poétiques*, ed. Charles Marty-Laveaux (Paris, 1875, new ed. Geneva, 1974), p. 31; Jean-Antoine de Baïf, *Oeuvres en rime*, ed. Charles Marty-Laveaux (Paris, 1881–91, new ed. Geneva, 1966), vol. 4, p. 219.

7 *Discours sur la mort de Gaspart de Coligny*, by I. S. P. (Paris, Martin, 1572) et Artus Désiré, *La Singerie des Huguenots marmots et guenons de la nouvelle derrision theodobeszienne* (Paris, 1574), quoted in Cazauran, 'Échos d'un massacre', pp. 252–253 ; Jean Dorat, *In alios Haereticos cum ipso interfectos*, poem published in the collection *Tombeaux des Brise-Croix* (Lyon, 1573), quoted by Marguerite Soulié, *L'Inspiration biblique dans la poésie religieuse d'Agrippa d'Aubigné* (Paris, 1977), p. 365, n. 136.

8 Cazauran, 'Échos d'un massacre', p. 252.

9 French translation quoted by Crouzet, *La Nuit de la Saint-Barthélemy*, p. 377. The episode in question, the mother of Crispinus's attempt to poison one of her sons.

10 Géralde Nakam, *Les Essais de Montaigne, miroir et procès de leur temps. Témoignage historique et création littéraire*, new ed. (Paris, 2001), p. 320.

11 Louis Dorléans, *Advertissement des catholiques anglois aux François catholiques* (1586), p. 22, quoted in Crouzet, *Le Haut Cœur*, pp. 480–482.

12 As shown by Crouzet, *La Nuit de la Saint-Barthélemy*, pp. 537–538.

13 See ch. 8.

14 Thierry Wanegffelen, *Ni Rome ni Genève. Des fidèles entre deux chaires en France au xvie siècle* (Paris, 1997), pp. 364–366; Robert Kingdon, 'Problems of religious choice for sixteenth century Frenchmen', in Robert Kingdon, *Church and society in Reformation Europe* (London, 1985), p. 108.

15 Jacques Gaches, *Mémoires sur les guerres de religion à Castres et dans le Languedoc, 1555–1610*, ed. Charles Pradel (Paris, 1879), new ed. (Geneva, 1970), p. 110.

16 *Mémoires de l'Estat de France*, vol. 1, fols 215v–216r.

17 The sonnet was entitled *Sur les misères des Églises françoises, l'an 1572*, published in *L'Uranie, ou nouveau recueil de chansons spirituelles et chrestiennes* (Geneva, 1591), quoted by Jacques Pineaux, *La Poésie des protestants de langue française (1559–1598)* (Paris, 1971), p. 211.

18 Agrippa d'Aubigné, *Les Tragiques*, Book V, *Les Fers*, verses 705–715.

19 For this formula, see Huchard, *D'Encre et de sang*, p. 304.

20 Crouzet, *La Nuit de la Saint-Barthélemy*, pp. 177–178, for this hypothesis.

21 Jean Calvin, *Institution de la religion chrestienne*, ed. Jean-Daniel Benoît (Paris, 1961), ch. 3, pp. 132–133. On the two forms of justice, see Elliott Forsyth, *La Justice de Dieu. Les Tragiques d'Agrippa d'Aubigné et la Réforme protestante en France au xvi⁰ siècle* (Paris, 2005), pp. 65–72.

22 Soulié, *L'inspiration biblique*, p. 46.

23 Agrippa d'Aubigné, *Les Tragiques*, Book V, *Les Fers*, verses 521–526.

24 Théodore de Bèze, *Histoire ecclésiastique des Églises réformées de France* (Geneva, 1580). Alain Dufour has shown the pertinence of the attribution to de Bèze: *Théodore de Bèze, poète et théologien*, (Geneva, 2006).

25 Frank Lestringant, *La Cause des martyrs dans les Tragiques d'Agrippa d'Aubigné* (Mont-de-Marsan, 1991), pp. 69–92; David El Kenz, *Les Bûchers du roi. La culture protestante des martyrs (1523–1572)* (Seyssel, 1997), p. 128.

26 Quoted by El Kenz, *ibid.*, p. 129.

27 La Noue, *Discours politiques et militaires*, p. 784.

28 Quoted in 'Les victimes de la Saint-Barthélemy à Paris. Essai d'une topographie et d'une nomenclature des massacres d'après les documents contemporains', *BSHPF*, 9 (1860), p. 44, but without giving the source.

29 See Huchard, *D'Encre et de sang*, for a fine analysis of Goulart's struggle.

30 *La Vie de messire Gaspar de Colligny*, p. 108.

31 Quoted in Kingdon, *Myths about the St. Bartholomew's Day massacres*, p. 117.

32 Marguerite Soulié, 'La poésie inspirée par la mort de Coligny. Exécration et glorification du héros', in *L'Amiral de Coligny et son temps*, pp. 389–405.

33 Max Engammare, *L'Ordre du temps. L'invention de la ponctualité au XVI⁰ siècle*, (Geneva, 2004), p. 129.

34 *Mémoires de l'Estat de France*, vol. 1, fol. 301r–v.

35 Agrippa d'Aubigné, *Les Tragiques*, Book V, *Les Fers*, verses 889–890.

36 Géralde Nakam, *Au lendemain de la Saint-Barthélemy. Jean de Léry, Histoire memorable du siège de Sancerre* (Paris, 1975). The work was published in 1574.

37 This is the subtitle of El Kenz's book, *Les Bûchers du roi*.

38 This expression figures in the title of the last edition of Crespin's book during his lifetime (1570).

39 David El Kenz, 'La victime catholique au temps des guerres de religion. La sacralisation du prêtre', in Benoît Garnot, ed., *Les Victimes, des oubliées de l'histoire?* (Rennes, 2000), pp. 192–199.

40 *L'Histoire de la mort que le R. P. Edmond Campion, prestre de la compagnie du nom de Jesus, et autres ont souffert en Angleterre pour la foy Catholique et Romaine*, (Paris, 1582).

41 Richard Verstegan, *Théâtre des cruautés des hérétiques de notre temps* (1583), ed. Frank Lestringant (Paris, 1995).

42 Quoted by Frank Lestringant, *Lumière des martyrs. Essai sur le martyre au siècle des Réformes* (Paris, 2004), p. 39, who conducts a long analysis of the *topos* of the world turned upside down in Protestant apologetics.

43 Frank Lestringant, *Agrippa d'Aubigné. Les Tragiques* (Paris, 1986), pp. 39–42.

44 Agrippa d'Aubigné, *Les Tragiques*, Book II, *Princes*, verses 1431–1432.

45 *Ibid.*, Book V, *Les Fers*, verses 831–836. See the commentary by Géralde Nakam, 'Le rire de Coligny', in Nakam, ed., *Chemins de la Renaissance* (Paris, 2005), pp. 193–212.

46 Agrippa d'Aubigné, *Les Tragiques*, Book V, *Les Fers*, verses 255–258.

47 André Tournon, 'La poétique du témoignage dans *Les Tragiques* d'Agrippa d'Aubigné', in Olivier Pot, ed., *Poétiques d'Aubigné* (Geneva, 1999), pp. 135–146.

48 David El Kenz, 'Les usages subversifs du martyre dans la France des troubles de religion: de la parole au geste', *Revue des sciences humaines*, 269 (2003), special issue on *Martyrs et martyrologes*, eds Frank Lestringant and Pierre-François Moreau, pp. 33–51.

49 The image of the souls hidden under the altar is to be found in verses 13–14 of Book I (*Misères*) and 53–54 of Book IV (*Les Feux*) of Agrippa d'Aubigné's *Tragiques*.

50 The two aspects of the prophetic reading are clearly analysed by Marie-Madeleine Fragonard, *La Pensée religieuse d'Agrippa d'Aubigné et son expression* (1981, new ed., Paris, 2004), pp. 611–662.

51 Agrippa d'Aubigné, *Les Tragiques*, Book V, *Les Fers*, verses 1175–1178.

52 *Ibid*, verses 1087–1092

53 Pierre Viret, *Le Monde à l'empire et le monde démoniacle*, Genève, 1550, p. 203, quoted by Jean Delumeau, 'Les Réformateurs et la superstition', in *L'Amiral de Coligny et son temps*, p. 466.

54 *Tocsain contre les massacreurs*, quoted by Forsyth, *La Justice de Dieu*, p. 362.

55 L'Estoile, *Mémoires pour servir à l'histoire de France depuis 1515 jusqu'en 1574*, p. 479.

56 Pithou, *Chronique de Troyes*, vol. 2, pp. 722–724 and 769.

57 See ch. 9.

58 Agrippa d'Aubigné, *Histoire Universelle*, ed. André Thierry, vol. 3 (Geneva, 1985), pp. 367–358. Verses describing the event are in *Les Tragiques*, Book V, *Les Fers*: 'Il [Charles IX] tremble, il fait trembler par dix ou douze nuicts / Les cœurs des assistans, quels qu'ils fussent, et puis / Le jour effraye l'œil quand l'insensé descouvre / Les corbeaux noircissans le pavillon du Louvre.' (verses 1015–1019). [Charles IX trembles and renders fearful during ten to twelve nights, the hearts of those present, regardless of who they were; and then daylight scares his insane gaze, on discovering the crows darkening the pavilion of the Louvre.]

59 Quoted by Jean-Raymond Fanlo in his edition of *Tragiques* of Agrippa d'Aubigné (Paris, 2003), in a note to verses 1297–1300 of Book V, *Les Fers*, pp. 645–648.

60 Lestringant, *Lumières des martyrs*, pp. 121–123. The Protestant historian La Popelinière, for example, was condemned by the synod of La Rochelle in July 1581 for trying to remain impartial and for having spoken badly of 'the sacred things of religion'.

61 Lestringant, *Lumières des martyrs*, p. 198–199.

8

POLITICAL READINGS
OF THE FRENCH TRAGEDY

The meaning of the divine will was not the only interrogation sparked by the Massacre. Beyond the ordeal endured by the Protestants, many saw in it a symptom of the malaise afflicting France as a whole, introducing an unheard-of break in the course of the kingdom's history. Was it not the paroxysm of civil war which pitted the best people from each camp against each other? How could the fratricidal fury which led the French to kill each other be explained? Those most profoundly obsessed by such questions were not confined to examining the Bible in order to understand the hidden designs of God – they offered a political response to the enigma. If such a disaster had occurred, they argued, it was because France's institutions had suffered a catastrophic malfunction.

Such an explanation is not in contradiction with the religious one seen in the previous chapter: reference to God remains central to this approach. But it leads to a much more active engagement in the *polis*, the communal city, in order to restore the structures of monarchy which seemed to be sliding towards tyranny. It is this second interpretation of the Massacre and its consequences that will be explored here.

ABSOLUTE POWER IN THE DOCK

The Protestants were the first to speak in such terms. One of the most startling works of the period immediately after the Massacre, the jurist François Hotman's *Francogallia*, was published in Geneva in 1573. In a remarkable preface dated 21 August 1573, he explained the motives for writing it. Exiled in Geneva, having fled from Bourges just before the killings, he expressed his suffering at seeing his 'poor unfortunate country ... continually sapped and racked by civil wars'. He then proposes a daring diagnosis which overturns the usual perspectives. Everyone believes that the 'internal partialities and divisions' are the cause of France's misfortune. This is an error – they are its consequence. Its origin needs to be sought higher up – in the weakening of the 'good laws and statutes of our ancestors'. Previously, France's political regime was so balanced that it resembled a fine musical composition. It was therefore necessary to rediscover the secret of this lost harmony and to understand why the 'fine old balance of the time of our fathers' had been disturbed.[1]

In order to do this, Hotman says that he began reading those French and German historians who wrote about French history. He was convinced by them that the first Gaulish kings were elected and did not possess absolute power; on the contrary, their power was limited by the laws, 'so that they were as much under the power and authority of the people as the latter were under theirs.'[2] When the Franks invaded the country, they united with the Gauls, and in the resulting France-Gaul kings did not have any more power than before, as they were controlled by assemblies representing the interests of the people, and which prefigured the Estates General. Government then was the one that Plato, Aristotle and Polybius judged to be the best: 'namely that which is composed and tempered by the three types of government: Monarchy, in which a single King commands with sovereign power; Aristocracy, which is that state of the nobility, and where a small number of the best people holds authority; and finally the state in which the people are sovereign.'[3] In the ideal mixed monarchy, the aristocratic element is represented by the council and the democratic one by the Estates General.

The kingdom of France had had such a well-tempered regime for about a thousand years. Things had begun to go wrong with Louis XI, who wished to free of all constraint and, in so doing, pushed the monarchy onto the path of tyranny. Hotman defends the principle that royal power should be curbed, for if 'a regal authority is left unfettered, it can attain such great power over all things that it stands, as it were, upon slippery ground, and very easily falls into tyranny.'[4] Those who skirt along precipices end up falling into them; monarchs end up usurping 'an infinite power over their citizens' and 'mistreat their citizens as if they were slaves or cattle.'[5] This usurpation, argues Hotman, was encouraged by precepts of Italian provenance – those of Roman law, which provided an arsenal of maxims to reinforce royal authority; those of Machiavelli, which elevate treason and lying into an art of governing.

Driven by an appetite for power, France's kings came to believe that they could do whatever pleased them, and allowed favourites to govern according to their whims. Their subjects were exposed to arbitrary action, which made disasters like the Massacre possible. Paradoxically, neither Charles IX nor the massacres of 24 August 1572 are mentioned in the *Francogallia*. Hotman had been careful on this, for in order to obtain permission from the Geneva city council to print it, all polemical allusions had to be removed, since the Genevans were determined to remain on good terms with France. When he wished openly to denounce the French atrocities – in the *De furoribus gallicis* – he did so under the pseudonym of Ernestus Varamundus and without official approval.[6] But every reader of the *Francogallia* could easily apply its historical examples to the contemporary situation. How could they not recognise, for example, Catherine de Medici in the misdeeds of the evil queens who were depicted in the book, such as Clotilde, the Italian mother of kings Childebert and Clothaire; Fredegonde, who caused a civil war; and Brunehilde, who was in love with an Italian?[7] How could they not see, in the history of the rejection of Roman domination by the united Gauls and Franks, an invitation to reject everything Italian? The lively controversy sparked by the book shows that nobody misconstrued its political content. All 'good Frenchmen', according to Pierre de l'Estoile, approved it, and only 'a few corrupt Machiavellists and Italianised Frenchmen' criticised it.[8]

Other Protestant treatises denounced tyranny, while framing their arguments more emphatically in the contemporary context. Théodore de Bèze, who was then moderator of the Genevan company of pastors, published anonymously in 1574 in Geneva and Heidelberg a book entitled *Du droit des magistrats sur leurs subjets*, which was written during June–July 1573. In it he answered the anxious questions of the persecuted Huguenots and examined the legitimacy of armed resistance.[9] Bèze had played a decisive role since at least 1559 in the elaboration and diffusion of Protestant publications; after the Massacre he probably co-ordinated a campaign orchestrated from Geneva, thanks to its links with Europe's Protestants and printers sympathetic to the cause in Strasbourg, Heidelberg, London, La Rochelle, Frankfurt, Basel, Dordrecht and Edinburgh.[10] Like Hotman, he was one of those who combined eschatological hope and the certitude that immediate, even armed action, was possible.

A third significant treatise, comprised of two dialogues, appeared in 1574 with the picturesque title of *Réveille-Matin des François et de leurs voisins*, under the striking pseudonym of Eusèbe Philadelphe Cosmopolite, with a dedication to the Queen of England.[11] The fourth of the works that were most representative of this current of thought was published in Basel in 1579 (although written in 1574–75) with the title *Vindiciae contre tyrannos*, also under a pseudonym – Stephanus Junius Brutus – and probably written by Philippe Duplessis-Mornay.[12] A French translation appeared in 1581 with the title *De la puissance légitime du prince sur le peuple et du peuple sur le prince*.[13] Lastly, alongside the major works, we find treatises of lesser impact yet of great interest. Simon Goulart republished some of them in his *Mémoires de l'Estat de France sous Charles neufiesme*.[14]

The authors of these works have been called 'monarchomachs' – those who fight against the power of one person – a name which derives from the polemical label that one of their critics ascribed to them.[15] All share the same diagnosis of a disorder in France's institutions. The solutions they propose have considerable similarities, when allowance is made for the diversity of the conditions in which they wrote. According to them, subjects' obedience could only be conditional. They believe that prince and people are bound by a contract based on an original pact which obliges the prince to guarantee their liberties; the coronation oath is meant to re-actualise its contents at each succession. If the monarch fails to respect his commitments, the people are freed of their duty of obedience. This justifies disobedience towards an unjust command. The institution charged with overseeing the implementation of royal promises is the assembly of the Estates General, made up of representatives of the kingdom. It should be regularly convened and have the power to dethrone the king in the case of serious faults. According to the monarchomachs – who interpreted French history here as they wished it to be – the Estates had the task of proposing laws for the public good; it should be impossible without its consent to abrogate laws that had been established by this means, and which were invested with quasi-constitutional status.[16] This was the remedy for the extraordinary instability of the laws, and for the incoherent succession of measures of tolerance and intolerance that France had experienced for over ten years.

In this demand for oversight we see a remarkably clear intuition: religious division could only increase the crown's power, since it enabled kings to confirm their power to change the edicts of pacification for reasons of which they were the sole judges. The role assigned to the Estates General by the monarchomachs would allow such a disturbing tendency to be checkmated, as 'all the people', Protestants as well as Catholics, would be, theoretically, represented there.[17] Subjects, without distinction of their religion, would have a role to play in the preparation of laws via their deputies; that would serve to guarantee civic concord, channel royal power and restore the nation's indispensable coherence. In the preface to the *Francogallia*, Hotman emotionally mentions this attachment to the motherland as a factor of unity which should urge all French people, whatever their divisions, to pull together to reburnish the lost splendour of the kingdom. While the other authors insist more on the specific preoccupations of the Protestant minority in their treatises, they still argue that the most urgent problem is that of tyranny – 'power exercised in defiance of the laws', as Bèze put it – against which everyone, regardless of religious confession, should fight.[18]

These arguments supplied the ferment for a serious destabilisation of royal authority.[19] However, the monarchomachs took every possible precaution to prevent their arguments from becoming a pretext for uncontrollable rebellion; they insisted that only duly established magistrates or the Estates General could take the responsibility for disobedience upon themselves. The responses envisaged in cases of royal breaches of trust ran from admonishment to deposition of the guilty king, including the recourse to arms as a legitimate form of defence. It was also possible to appeal to neighbouring princes for help: the author of the *Vindiciae contra tyrannos* explicitly theorised what nowadays is called the right of intervention.[20] Arguments like these legitimated Huguenot resistance during the fourth civil war triggered by the Massacre, and especially the heroic defence of the three martyr-cities, La Rochelle, Sancerre and Sommières.

THE END OF LOVE'S REIGN?

Hostility among France's Protestants to absolute power did not begin in 1572; it had already been expressed in 1560 in the justifications of the conspiracy of Amboise, to which François Hotman and Théodore de Bèze had contributed. Besides, it is known that the writing of the *Francogallia* began around 1567– 68.[21] Moreover, a clear precursor of monarchomach theories can be found in the treatise entitled *Question politique: s'il est licite aux subjects de capituler avec leur prince*, the work of a Toulouse parlementaire, Jean de Coras, and probably written during the winter of 1568–69.[22] It was not the Massacre that hatched the ideas that the Protestants publicised during the years immediately afterwards. As a result, the question arises as to the exact influence of the massacres on the diffusion of such ideas. It is clear that the shock of the event led to their being expressed in a more coherent and systematic form; and it created the conditions for their reception within a broad public.[23] However, these observations do not of themselves suffice to measure the scale of the ideological shock triggered by the 1572 upheaval, nor to evaluate the new resonances of monarchomach ideas after 1572.

A passage from the first dialogue of the *Réveille-Matin des François* may help to grasp this. A mysterious ruling, dating from the autumn of 1572 or early 1573, was published in it, presented as a 'decree' promulgated by the prophet Daniel. It contained forty articles for the political organisation of the Protestants in the cities they held.[24] The preamble announces the following decision: 'that the day of the massacre, 24 August, shall be forever named the Day of Treason, and the King (like several of his predecessors who had been called "debonnaire", "father of the people", etc.), be called Charles the Traitor, and have as his coat of arms, in an anagram of his name, Disloyal Hunter.'[25] It is this sentence which inspired the surprising date of the 'epistle to the reader' at the beginning of the French version of the first dialogue – 'Basel, the seventh day of the fifth month after the day of Treason'; the same date was used in the Latin version published at the same time '*die 7 mensis quinti ab infesto et funesti die proditionis*'.[26] The last page of the French version includes the following: 'printing completed on the twelfth day of the sixth month after the day of Treason.'

This new system of dating, beginning with 24 August 1572 rather than the birth of Christ, suggests that the Massacre had ushered the kingdom into a radically new era. The one which had closed was that of 'public faith', a concept that the author of the *Réveille-Matin* defined as the 'unbreakable link sustaining human society.'[27] Public faith was primarily the trust between rulers and the ruled, and was often illustrated by metaphors from the world of nature, such as the familiar relations between children and fathers or sheep and shepherds. It was also the unwritten guarantee of one's promised word, central to relations between both vassals and lords and people and princes. All of these were ultimately based on the faith of the believer in God, so that the community of men ideally belonged to the kingdom of love.

In a state of this kind, there is no need for a written constitution to guarantee people's liberties, since the king is expected to voluntarily obey the natural and divine laws, as well as a small number of 'laws of the kingdom', which were still poorly defined; his subjects trust his goodwill.[28] In 1519, in his work, *L'Institution du prince*, Guillaume Budé summarised perfectly the nature of the trust granted to sovereigns: 'it is to be assumed that they are so perfect in prudence, nobility and equity that they do not need a rule or written form to compel them by fear or necessity as is the case for others'.[29] The written gives way to the spoken word, which is accepted and respected by a king who is exemplary. This kind of political and social structure, depending essentially on 'faith', characterised states that preceded constitutional regimes, which are determined, according to one historian, by the mechanisms for institutionalising trust, credibility and oversight.[30] But were not efforts to institutionalise trust an insult to love?

Until the Massacre, the Protestants believed that faith was not entirely dead and that it was still possible to avoid a detailed codification of relations between sovereign and subjects. In accepting the invitation from Charles IX to come to Paris, Coligny trusted him, deliberately ignoring the bad auguries which pointed to a trap. The author of the *Réveille-Matin* reveals the indignation with which he rejected the idea that the whole court could have been perverted by the doctrine of Machiavelli.[31] The bait that was presented was attractive, as Aubigné wrote:

> La flûte qui joua fut la publique foy,
> On pipa de la paix et d'amour de son Roy
> [The flute that played was public trust,
> A music of peace and the love of one's king.][32]

The Protestants' insistence on Coligny's candour was their way of dramatising the difference between two worlds – that of treason and that of faith. The collision had such terrible consequences that they were obliged to think the unthinkable, namely the end of the realm of love.

It was this loss that the Massacre presaged, from the Protestants' viewpoint. The cynicism of the ambush laid for them made them foresee that the situation it created was likely to be irreversible and that a simple restoration of ancient customs would not be enough. The monarchomachs had dreamt in vain of a return to 'the good old accord' celebrated by Hotman, but they realised the necessity of attaching more importance henceforth to guarantees for subjects. The powers of the prince needed to be more strictly regulated in the future, so that potential royal perfidy would be considered less as a sin against honesty (against which only moral indignation could be mobilised) than as a 'constitutional' transgression subject to penal retribution.

The idea of contract expresses perfectly this abandonment of the ideal of natural trust and obedience. By their very existence, legal forms of oversight would express the fear, henceforth permanent, of possible royal slip-ups. A sovereign who could be dethroned, and subjects represented by Estates General who were co-authors of the laws and protectors of their public liberties – this was, in fact, the institutionalisation of mistrust. France would enter a new era, which was symbolised by the calendar change suggested by the *Réveille-Matin*. The paternal monarchy would be succeeded by a contractual one, in which the seeds of a constitutional monarchy were visible.

Does this mean that the monarchomachs cheerfully envisaged such a change? Probably not, as one of the texts which contains an undeniable echo of their thinking suggests – a petition presented to Charles IX by the deputies of the Protestant churches assembled at Montauban, and bearing the highly symbolic date of 24 August 1573. The signatories asked the King to 'contract a union and alliance of a new promise, enduring union and friendship' with the Protestant princes, on the one hand, and with his subjects of the two confessions, on the other, with the first contract guaranteeing the second. An edict of pacification could then be promulgated and solemnly accepted by both Catholics and Protestants, who would sign a third contract between themselves, taking an oath before the royal officials 'on mutual condition and promise henceforth not to commit massacres against each other'.[33] This audacious programme was instantly and contemptuously rejected by Charles IX and Catherine de Medici.[34] Yet this document bears the traces of an irrepressible nostalgia for the old paternal monarchy, 'because we would have preferred', wrote its authors to the King, 'that all such measures were proposed to us by your paternal good-will and favour, and of your own initiative'.

The lack of concrete details from the monarchomachs on key points – such as the desired frequency of the Estates General – no doubt reveals their secret reticence. The chilling notion of a sovereign bound by precise rules facing subjects constantly on their guard was, in their view, the result of a tragic deterioration of the traditional political order; in reality, it was too far removed from their deepest aspirations for them not to be willing to abandon it if a favourable set of circumstances permitted. When, after 1584, the prospect of the accession to the throne of their leader, Henri de Navarre, became sufficiently credible, the hope of a possible renaissance of the kingdom of love would make a return; Henri IV would again personify the figure of a king as father of his people, who expects filial piety and not distrust from his subjects.[35]

But in the aftermath of the tragedy of 24 August 1572, such a perspective had little credibility; the horizon seemed wholly sealed off. Driven by despair, the monarchomachs imagined, behind the appearance of a return to mythical origins, a political system that was full of novel potential which, although it remained in embryonic form, contained promising seeds of later developments.

'DEFENDING THE PUBLIC GOOD'

Some Catholics joined with Protestants in challenging absolute power and in wishing to prevent any repeat of the circumstances that had made the Massacre possible. They were essentially nobles and their networks of dependents, followers and clients, mobilised behind duc François d'Alençon, Henri de Navarre, Henri Prince of Condé and Henri de Montmorency-Damville, governor of Languedoc. 'They call themselves the Malcontents', wrote an English ambassador about their recourse to arms in early 1574.[36]

The term 'Malcontents' has to do with the peculiar relations between king and nobility. The latter see their obedience to the king as a gift, a freely offered allegiance; in return, they expect love and protection from their sovereign, which take the form of honours, offices and pensions. This reciprocity is guaranteed by the good faith of the parties. When one of them avoids his obligations, the other publicly declares itself 'malcontent'. It could be the king, but it is mostly the nobles, quick to feel badly rewarded for their services. When they attribute their 'malcontentment' to a defect in the role of the king as arbiter, who is accused of exercising it tyrannically, their attitude extends beyond individual cases and assumes a general political significance, especially when they involve their clienteles with them.

The Massacre was an occasion for these Malcontents to express their aspirations. A quite specific reading of the massacres quickly spread among part of the nobility – that the killings ordered by the King on the pretext of eliminating the Huguenot leaders were in reality directed indifferently at the most prestigious noble houses, whether they were Catholic or Protestant. The roots of this interpretation are visible as early as the summer of 1568, the date of the alliance between Louis de Condé, Gaspard de Coligny, William of Orange and Louis of Nassau. Scandalised by the execution of the Counts of Egmont and Horn, the allies affirmed that their respective sovereigns, manipulated by their evil counsellors, sought to exterminate not just the 'true religion', but also the higher nobility, 'hoping that this would enable them to establish their tyrannies and extend their domination'.[37] Four years later, the Massacre would be seen in France as the monstrous realisation of the project attributed to the kings. Montmorency-Damville clearly expresses this conviction in the declaration of 13 November 1574, in which he made his union with the Protestants official: according to him, what happened on 24 August 1572 was the 'cruel, treacherous and inhuman massacre of most of the nobility of France in the city of Paris'.[38] In fact, Catholic nobles, among them marshals Montmorency and Cossé and the baron de Biron, were thought to have been included alongside the Protestants on the list of the proscribed supposedly drawn up before the killings.[39]

Declarations and tracts broadcast this interpretation and supported it by affirming that the nobility were the guardian of the ancient laws of the kingdom; by virtue of existing, they reminded kings that they were not free to rid themselves of the laws and prevented them from governing according to their whims. There was thus a radical incompatibility between the great nobility and absolute power, which was what drove kings and their perverted counsellors to get rid of such a nuisance. The thesis appears in the documents justifying the armed revolts of February and April 1574, especially in the declaration by François d'Alençon of 15 September 1575 and the *Brieve Remonstrance à la noblesse de France*, which was a commentary on it attributed to the jurist Innocent Gentillet.[40] It was also present in anonymous treatises written probably by authors close to the Malcontents, and which defended the legitimacy of resistance by inferiors against superiors, denounced the baseness of Catherine de Medici, and compared the tyranny dominating France to that practised in Turkey.[41] Echoes of them are to be found also in the *Mémoires de l'Estat de France* compiled by Simon Goulart.

According to these works, kings had several ways of getting rid of dependency on the great nobility. One consisted in making the nobles reliant on their favour and turning them into clients. Simon Goulart sees this as the objective of Catherine de Medici and her favourite, the comte de Retz: both 'had for a long time planned and resolved that, in order to strengthen their authority and exercise it at will and without oversight throughout the kingdom, it was first of all necessary that there should be no lord in France who was not a client of the Queen and elevated by her liberality'. Only those nobles who became their dependents would be tolerated.[42] But the Montmorencys, the Châtillons and the Guises were not made of such submissive stuff. The solution was to get rid of them. The murder of the Admiral, cleverly attributed to the Guises, was contrived, according to this interpretation of events, in order to have the first two (related) families and the third wipe each other out. The Massacre was, therefore, a diabolical method of eliminating the great nobility, who, owing to the antiquity of their lineage and the status they derived from it, were the best placed to oppose arbitrary rule.

The demonic character of the subterfuges at work identified, in the minds of those who denounced them, their foreign origins. Only Italians, it was said, could have imagined them, such was their jealousy of the grandeur of France. Those accused included the Florentine Catherine de Medici, her compatriot Albert de Gondi, comte de Retz and marshal of France, the Milanese René de Birague, chancellor since 1573, and the Mantuan Louis de Gonzague, duc de Nevers by marriage. These foreigners were suspected of having deliberately provoked civil war by stoking up religious hatred; according to words attributed to chevalier Poncet, a dependant of Retz, it was the surest way of getting rid of the great nobles: 'it is very necessary to take advantage of the religious disturbances, because it is the best method that one could wish for to kill and have people killed on every side'.[43]

One event certainly contributed to diffusing these ideas among the nobility – the siege of La Rochelle from late 1572 to early July 1573, which was particularly murderous for the nobles involved in it. A list composed by an anonymous observer estimated that out of 155 leading officers of the royal army, sixty-six (42.6%) died and forty-seven (30.3%) were wounded.[44] Such carnage could well have prompted among them an awareness of the devastating character of the civil wars for a nobility that was losing its best members. Another factor almost certainly played a part in this: the bi-confessional character of the besieging troops. Under the command of Henri d'Anjou, they included nobles of differing religious convictions – among them were Navarre and Condé, who brought some of their clients with them, along with François d'Alençon, Henri de Guise, the ducs d'Aumale and Nevers. This strange medley elicited the indignation of the Spanish ambassador, Zuñiga, who grumbled, in a manner worsened by bad humour, that there were more Huguenots in the royal camp than within La Rochelle.[45] The nobility, which included many families divided by religion, could more readily grasp from this experience the need to devote their energies not to killing each other, but to uniting in order to restore civil concord.

A leader existed for such a cause – François d'Alençon. The King's young brother had openly shown his disapproval of the Massacre. Unhappy at being kept out of military decision-making under the walls of La Rochelle, he welcomed approaches from nobles, whatever their religious affiliation, anxious for a change of policy.[46] His role as a junior royal prince was difficult to shoulder: taking on the role of heir to the throne on his brother Henri's election as King of Poland, he aspired to play an important role which the suspicious King denied him. The rallying around him of all discontented nobles would bring him the authority of which he dreamt.

This was how, during 1573 and early 1574, the rapprochement between the moderates of both confessions took shape. So soon after the Massacre, it was a surprising alliance; it would lead to a joint rebellion and make the fifth war something quite different from a 'war of religion', as Catholics and Protestants would fight together against the royal forces under the banner of the King's own brother. It took a powerful impetus to generate such an association throughout the kingdom and to impel its members to overcome their dissensions. Until then, inter-confessional union had only occurred locally, in towns where the notables signed pacts to stave off disorder.[47] The unifying effect of the cause they defended was sufficiently strong this time to overcome religious hatreds to a considerable extent.

The Malcontents' opponents tried to denigrate their motives as the simple frustration of embittered ambition. The accusation was partly true, as almost all of the members of the coalition had reasons for feeling more or less wronged. Henri de Navarre and Henri de Condé, who had both nominally converted to Catholicism, were kept under a humiliating surveillance. François d'Alençon aspired to being lieutenant-general of the kingdom, a position which was left vacant by the departure of his brother Henri d'Anjou. Among the Montmorencys, François, the eldest, felt the effects of the return to power in the Council of the faction hostile to heresy; his brother, Henri, complained of being exposed to the King's suspicion; and their younger brothers, Thoré and Méru, as well as their cousin Artus de Cossé, marshal of France, shared their discontent. The Montmorency brothers had remained Catholic, but their nephew, the vicomte de Turenne, who was also one of the Malcontents, would soon change to the Protestant religion. Behind these leader figures were nobles of lesser standing who mostly belonged to their clienteles.[48]

However, to disparage their commitment as a simple desire to restore a role that was threatened or compromised would be to underestimate the emotional power of the watchword they had adopted – the defence of the 'public good'. This term refers to the collective legacy of their ancestors, a collection of customs, laws and privileges intended to guarantee the liberties of subjects and to prevent arbitrary royal rule. It was this common good that the Malcontents vaguely sensed to be endangered by the evolution of the monarchy; they suspected that the political future of the realm was as much at stake as was its religious future. It was for that reason indispensable to reinvigorate the institutions entrusted with preventing any trend towards tyranny – the council, in which the major noble families should be represented, and the Estates General, which should be held regularly, all of which would establish the ideal of mixed monarchy and which would be at once royal, aristocratic and 'democratic'. It was of the greatest urgency to escape from confessional passions, which prevented people from seeing the facts. Eyes had to be opened. The appeal to clear-sightedness was launched in the form of images – as by the author of the *Réveille-Matin*, who wished to wake his readers from their sleep, or the pamphlet which asked people to put on 'glasses of rock crystal' the better to see how France was in danger of being reduced 'to the same servitude as Turkey'.[49]

An elementary form of civic awareness, sustained by the feeling of belonging to the same country, is evident in these writings. Of course, each of the Malcontents conceived the public good in terms of his own aspirations; the great nobility, for their part, saw in it an opportunity to demand a major role in government. Nevertheless, beyond the diversity of motives there was clearly a common disquiet about the country's political identity which had been marred by dangerous innovations, an identity whose defence demanded union among all those of goodwill. It was at this point that the expression *bons Français* ('good Frenchmen') spread. Pierre de l'Estoile uses it mainly to describe those who were favourable to Hotman's *Francogallia*, whose purpose was to catalogue France's ancestral traditions.[50] It was the *bons Français* that François d'Alençon wished to unite around him.[51] As for Henri de Montmorency-Damville, he deplored in his declaration of 13 November 1574 the misfortune of his compatriots who were deprived, through either exile or massacre, of 'learned men from the universities', from whom they could have obtained information about 'the ancient laws of the establishment of this kingdom'.[52]

The cause of the public good had been defended during earlier movements; in 1567, a pamphlet had compared the rebellion of Louis de Condé to the 'war of the public good' waged in 1464–65 by the dukes in revolt against the 'tyranny' of Louis XI.[53] What was new about the period after the Massacre was that the watchword now mobilised Catholics alongside the Protestants. It brought about a rapprochement between Malcontents and monarchomachs, despite the differences which separated them – the former were primarily concerned with the role and make-up of the council, which they wished to dominate; while the latter focused on the Estates General and the notion of a contract for rule. Common ground existed with the 'Politiques', who, as we saw, had begun to be seen from 1568 onwards as clearly identifiable kindred spirits.[54] Indeed, some observers confused Malcontents and 'Politiques', even though the latter were more conscious of the need to spare royal authority.[55]

Thus the electric shock of the Massacre was remarkably successful in uniting the elites of the two confessions around a common objective perceived as more immediately urgent than doctrinal reconciliation – that of the political reform of the monarchy. That this project was proposed as a restoration only reflects the ideological conventions of the age; in reality, it involved a refoundation designed to protect subjects against arbitrary rule. The fact that the King's brother led the movement shows the attractiveness that the trauma of 24 August gave to the cause; the adherence of numerous nobles would inject a formidable visibility and effectiveness into the hope of regenerating the kingdom and thereby of building, through the regular assembly of the Estates General, indestructible barriers against abuses of power.

The mobilising power of the theme of the common good was clear to see in the muted agitation which exercised the kingdom during the autumn of 1573. It worried the King, who, informed of the action of the Malcontents, sent a circular letter to the governors on 13 December 1573, warning them against movements which he explained in detail: in several provinces, he wrote, people 'went from house to house, urging nobles and other subjects to rebellion and disobedience under the pretext of the common good'. These troublemakers, having evoked the scale of the evils from which the kingdom suffered, dared to say that Charles IX, far from wishing to find remedies for them, only 'intended to sustain division among his said subjects and especially among the highest of them, in order to be able with less opposition to continue, and even increase, all kinds of exactions and taxes'.[56] We see here, in the King's denunciation, the thesis of the stratagem of which he was accused in his desire to get rid of the oversight of his rule by the great nobility. In his instructions sent on 9 January 1574 to Jean Ébrard de Saint-Sulpice, Charles IX made it clear that the activities he was condemning originated in Poitou and Saintonge, where, he said, emissaries visited the houses of nobles, both Catholic and Protestant, 'working on them to band them together under the pretext of the common good'; and in La Rochelle, where a conspiracy had just been thwarted.[57] In Poitou, the nobles gathered around François de La Noue were known as the 'publicans', the defenders of the public good.[58] These secret goings-on confirm that, for a section of the nobility, political motives were now more effective mobilising agents than religious ones. Circumstances would soon cement a real alliance between the moderates of both camps, uniting to prevent what they judged to be a harmful turn by the monarchy.

UNITED AGAINST TYRANNY

However, the situation at the end of the fourth war was more reassuring for the apostles of the 'public good'. They could even believe that, through a strange shift in circumstances, they were back in the time when peaceful co-existence between the confessions was the main concern. The negotiation of the Treaty of Boulogne (so-called because it was signed in the palace of Madrid in the bois de Boulogne), which made peace official in July 1573, and the need to reassure the Poles on the occasion of Henri d'Anjou's election as King of Poland had reduced the influence of the exclusivist Catholics in the royal council; the champions of civil concord gradually returned to power. The eldest of the Montmorency clan, duc François, marshal of France, was seen as their leader and was known as 'L'Hospital with a sword'. It was to his château of Chantilly that the King and his entourage went to celebrate at Christmas.[59] On 10 January 1574, François de Montmorency agreed to come to court at Saint-Germain. He stayed there for six weeks, during which Charles IX made numerous efforts to reduce dissensions. Attempts at reconciling the Montmorencys and the Guises were made, and to marry Guillaume de Montmorency, seigneur de Thoré, to a daughter of the recently deceased duc d'Aumale.[60] On the marshal's insistence, Charles IX promised the duc d'Alençon the lieutenancy-general of the kingdom, vacant since the new King of Poland's departure; then, on 29 January, hesitating to take a step that might have proved dangerous, he simply made him instead chief of the council, keeper of the privy seal and commander of the royal forces.[61] Alençon was embittered by this volte-face, but the powers that he had received were considerable. Everything seemed to presage an enduring decline of the hard-line Catholic faction and a reversal of the policy of intransigence. Were the consequences of the Massacre about to be erased?

To round off the analogy with the situation before the massacres, the Dutch question became central to French political discussion. Charles IX had received, in late June 1573, an emissary from William of Orange who brought tasty offers if France were to assist him. Alerted to this, the Spanish Ambas-

sador Zuñiga experienced the same anxieties as before 24 August 1572: would
the King 'keep the mask' or opt to support the Dutch rebels secretly? Or would
he commit himself openly? The Council, he informed Alba, had met several
times to discuss it; some members believed that they should take advantage
of the offer, while others expressed their distrust towards people who rebelled
against their sovereign, recalling the Mons affair. For his part, the ambassador
believed that French support would remain indirect.[62] It was indeed covert
assistance to the Prince of Orange that Charles IX decided to renew. From
November 1573 onwards, he promised him financial support. At the end of
the same month, Catherine de Medici, who accompanied her son Henri to the
frontier on his journey to Poland, met Louis of Nassau and Count Christopher,
son of the elector of the Palatinate, and paid the first instalment of the promised monies to Nassau.[63]

But the discontent of the Huguenots continued to worry Charles IX. They
were unhappy with the clauses of the Edict of Boulogne, which were far
more restrictive than that of Saint-Germain in 1570. Liberty of conscience
was granted to them, but liberty of worship was limited to three towns – La
Rochelle, Nîmes and Montauban – to which Sancerre was added after its
capitulation. Lords enjoying the rights of 'high' justice were entitled to have
marriage and baptism services (but not communion) in their houses with a
congregation limited to ten persons in addition to their family. The Protestants
from northern France agreed to these terms, but those of the South judged
the edict scandalous and remained under arms, keeping a limited war going.
More importantly, they held numerous political assemblies, modelled on the
Estates General, though without the clergy. The ruling adopted at Millau in
December 1573 provided for a confederal structure, a union of provinces, with
its own institutions and which, without constituting the secession that it has
often been seen as, declared the Huguenots' determination to call for a 'reformation of the state'.[64]

To reduce the ill-feeling of the Protestants, Charles IX relied on the mediation
of François de Montmorency. The marshal was held in some esteem by them
since his repression of the Catholic riots in Rouen in March 1571 and in Paris in
December of that year, but also for having taken on the task of burying Coligny's
body. Montauban Protestants even wrote to him in autumn 1572, asking him
to become their protector, with emoluments similar to those enjoyed by the
assassinated Admiral.[65] His younger brother, Henri de Montmorency-Damville,
negotiated at Pézenas with the southern Huguenots on the orders of the King,
who had instructed him to refuse their most radical demands.[66] Moreover, the
elder Montmorency was close to François d'Alençon.[67] He thus seemed to have
the qualities necessary to negotiate with opponents from all sides.

The King's wish to restore concord was accompanied by a desire to prepare
a programme of reforms for the kingdom that were capable of achieving a

wide consensus. In the circular letter, already quoted, to provincial governors of December 1573, Charles IX declared his wish to assemble at Compiègne 'many notable gentlemen and other men of law from all the provinces' in order to deal with abuses. The assembly was held at Saint-Germain-en-Laye in early February 1574, and was attended by members of the Paris parlement and fifteen provincial deputies, who were given the task of examining ways of improving the judicial system.[68] These royal initiatives were such as to defuse the criticisms of those who accused the monarchy of veering towards tyranny.

But then, in a dramatic turn of events with which the Valois court was familiar, the situation changed completely, and as a result of a minor issue. On 16 February, on a staircase at the château of Saint-Germain, the duc de Guise struck with his sword, without killing him, a gentleman of the house of the duc d'Alençon called Scipion de Ventabren, whom he accused of having been suborned by Montmorency in order to kill him. The incident ratcheted up tensions; François de Montmorency defended himself against the accusation, but, feeling himself no longer safe, left court at the end of February, which had the effect of reviving the Guises' favour. A sign of their new status was the granting of the lieutenancy-general of the kingdom to their cousin Charles, duc de Lorraine.

This episode might have had only minor consequences had it not aroused the anger of the impatient younger figures on the militant wing of the Malcontent movement. As long as duc François de Montmorency was in power, he could exercise a moderating influence on his brothers Thoré and Méru, as well as on their cousin Turenne, or even on François d'Alençon. After his departure, the champions of energetic action, deprived of the support on which they counted close to the King, saw the hopes that they had generated being suddenly closed off; with this, they yielded to the temptation of violent action, which in turn forced Charles IX into an authoritarian policy.

The decision to resort to arms materialised in two conspiracies, the first in February, the second in April 1574. In both cases, the objective was to 'liberate' Navarre and Alençon and to organise their flight to the Netherlands. No doubt it was also a matter of driving out the Guises and reorienting royal policy towards greater civil tolerance, in the secret hope that François d'Alençon would soon succeed Charles IX, despite the latter's express designation of his brother Henri as his successor.[69] Marshal Montmorency seems to have been informed of, but was not involved directly in the organisation of, these conspiracies, which included both Catholics and Protestants.

The first conspiracy gave rise to an episode not dissimilar to the surprise of Meaux in 1567 – namely the 'fright of Saint-Germain'. During the night of 27–28 February 1574 part of the court fled precipitately to Paris, panicked by the presence around the château of forces commanded by one of the conspirators, the sieur de Chaumont-Guitry; Charles IX, escorted by soldiers, left on the morning of the 28th. The Spanish ambassador wrote of his pity – coloured with sarcasm – for 'a king like him, so thin from illness, riding on a miserable old nag' and poorly guarded by soldiers in disarray.[70] A few days earlier, during the night of 23–24 February, the Protestants had seized the towns of Fontenay and Lusignan, a coup known as the 'Shrove Tuesday surprise'. In Languedoc, Dauphiné and Guyenne, open military hostilities resumed.

Paradoxically, this first alert did not immediately turn the King away from his dreams of reconciliation. Removing himself to Vincennes and already seriously ill, he made an effort to bring Montmorency back. Was it to trap him? It is possible, given the events that followed it, yet not likely, if we follow the opinion that Zuñiga expressed on 13 March – that is, before the outcome was known: 'the objective and intention of the kings [Charles IX and his mother] is to make peace with their rebels, which they know they cannot do without Montmorency'.[71] The marshal responded to their invitation in early April and returned to court.

However, his return did not dissuade the conspirators from trying again. During the days before Easter Sunday (11 April), a new plot was discovered. This time, Charles IX's reaction was severe. François de Montmorency was suspected of conniving at it, and was placed under surveillance as tight as for the princes; on 13 April, these men were given a tough interrogation; the King of Navarre, in a defence not lacking in panache, referred to the threats to his life and that of the King's brother.[72] Two close companions of Alençon, La Molle and Coconat, were imprisoned, and around fifty people were arrested. Turenne fled just in time; Thoré and Méru joined Condé, who had reverted to Protestantism, in Strasbourg. The interrogation of La Molle and Coconat raised suspicions of complicity in Germany and England, but in the present state of knowledge, the precise scale of the enterprise remains difficult to establish.[73]

At that point, on 14 April, a decisive event occurred which increased the authoritarian inflexion of royal policy. At the battle of Mook Heide in the Netherlands, Spanish forces destroyed the troops of Louis of Nassau and his ally, Count Christopher, both of whom were killed. The defeat may be compared to that of Genlis at Saint-Ghislain on 17 July 1572, and their consequences were similar: Spain's international position was strengthened, while the intransigent Catholic faction's influence in the council and the effectiveness of its pressure on the King were increased. Charles IX feared a massive arrival in France of Dutch exiles. This conjuncture drove him to take very harsh measures: on 30 April, La Molle and Coconat were tried by the Paris parlement and executed the same day. On 4 May, François de Montmorency and his cousin, Artus de Cossé, were accused of having participated in the conspiracy and were consigned to the Bastille, where they would be imprisoned for a year and a half.

The arrest of two officers of the crown – both were marshals of France – had a political significance that should not be underestimated. According to the arguments of both the monarchomachs and the Malcontents, the officers of the crown served, by virtue of their offices, an entity higher than the King himself. Thus the arrest of two of them, attributed to the influence of the Guises, and especially that of the old Cardinal Lorraine, was considered as a crime against the crown, perpetrated by people who wished to relieve the royal power of an inhibiting oversight. As a result, the accusation of tyranny regained its topicality; Montmorency and Cossé, like Coligny before them, were regarded as victims of arbitrary rule. There are striking analogies in the *Mémoires de l'Estat de France* between the account of the incarceration of Montmorency and the murder of the Admiral: the same warnings to the victim, the same contrast between the cordial welcome first given him by the King and the ruthless measure that was to follow, the same Christian resignation in the face of injustice.[74] The coup of 24 August 1572 seemed to be repeating itself, and was this time clearly directed against the natural leaders of the nobility.

But for Charles IX, this decision was a new manifestation of his sovereignty – one that was necessitated, according to the arguments that he used to justify it, by a conspiracy against his person and his 'state'.[75] The implications of his action can be compared to the elimination of the Huguenot leaders ordered on the night of the Massacre, though with the critical difference that a proper trial was envisaged in order to judge the two prisoners. The King's feelings towards François de Montmorency appear to have been as ambiguous as they were towards Coligny. On the one hand, he saw in him, as in the Admiral, a man capable of making connections with the moderate Protestants; and on the other, and even more so than in the case of the late Huguenot chief, an 'overmighty' subject, capable of assembling potentially dangerous forces. Marshal, admiral, owner of vast domains, patron of numerous clienteles and linked to the Protestants, the elder Montmorency enjoyed considerable credit; at the same time, his brother, Damville, the very active governor of Languedoc, was beginning to envisage an alliance with the southern Protestants, which made him a danger.

The death of Charles IX on 30 May 1574 did not alter royal distrust of this powerful dynasty. In a letter to Phillip II, Zuñiga made a shrewd observation: the King and his mother think that if 'Montmorency is freed and if Damville retains his governorship, the two brothers will be greater than themselves in the kingdom'.[76] It was the same fear of over-influential subjects, who were feared for their potential ties with Huguenot rebels. On 18 June 1574 Catherine de Medici stripped Damville of his powers as lieutenant-general in Languedoc, which emptied his title of governor – which he theoretically retained – of its substance; but the Queen Mother was not powerful enough to implement her decision.[77] On his return to France, Henri III kept François de Montmorency and his cousin in prison. Damville would accuse Charles IX of trying to have him assassinated and Henri III of wanting to execute François in his cell. That is possible, but difficult to prove.

These events triggered the union of the Catholics and the Protestants. The civil war which started – the fifth in the standard chronology – was profoundly different from those that had preceded it; the struggle against the excesses of absolute power, whatever the diversity of personal objectives held by the individuals involved, gave the ensuing conflict a more political character. The Prince of Condé went off to raise troops in Germany and seek support from Elizabeth of England. Manifestoes were published in the name of the Protestants and the 'united Catholics'. Condé, and then Damville after the confirmation of his alliance with the Languedoc Huguenots, and finally Alençon after his flight from court on 15 September 1575, published declarations justifying their actions.[78] The wish to diffuse widely the idea that the enterprise was politically justified conformed to the desire to rally adherents from both confessions, all of whom could become '*bons Français*'.

The Massacre thus became, paradoxically, a unifying factor which could incite indignation and mobilise the energies of both Catholics and Protestants. Méru, the younger brother of duc François de Montmorency, refers to it in his vibrant defence addressed in December 1574 or January 1575 to the Queen of England. Having recalled the efforts of the Guises to subvert the state with the assistance of the Italians in the royal council, he underlined the common interests of the 'Protestants who profess the Gospel' and 'those who for some time now have joined with the Protestants for the public good and the service of the king and the crown'. He then showed how the nobility had been, without distinction, the victims of the August 1572 massacres:

> There is no need to recite what has happened since then, how often faith was sworn and then broken, how much more innocent blood was spilt in peace than in war, until the awful day when the flower of the valiant men of France died so pitifully and cruelly in a betrayal that had been planned for a long time.[79]

Given such 'treason', the taking up of arms was not a rebellion, it was an act of legitimate defence.

A letter by François Hotman, written just after the discovery of the April 1574 conspiracy, gives an idea of the high expectations sparked by the revolt, which the author of the *Francogallia* for his part attributed indifferently to the 'Politiques': 'in Paris itself more than a thousand people, nobles, men of the robe, merchants, were thrown into prison. They took the name of Politiques, and with the support of the king's brother demanded the restoration of the ancient constitution of France and the convocation of the Estates General.'[80]

No doubt not all of the monarchomachs made such an enthusiastic judgement on the nature of the movement. Philippe Duplessis-Mornay, for example, was party to the Shrove Tuesday conspiracy, in liaison with François de La Noue and along with his younger brother, Pierre, seigneur de Buhy, who had remained Catholic; yet, despite the proximity of his ideas to those of the Malcontents, he experienced a certain reluctance to fight alongside them.[81] As for Théodore de Bèze, if he placed some hope in François d'Alençon and in Montmorency-Damville, he was also suspicious of the alliance with the Catholics, in whom his intransigence continued to make him see people who despised the Scriptures.[82]

But for many of those who, in the spring of 1574, took part in the action sanctioned by Alençon, Condé, Navarre and Damville, the fifth civil war carried a message of hope. They hoped it would arrest the drift towards tyranny; they set as its objective the elimination of the 'foreigners' from the council so as to restore the princes of the blood and the encouragement of more frequent meetings of the Estates General. A restored monarchy would be established, which would guarantee the liberty of subjects, whatever their religion might be, and which would make any return to the St Bartholomew's Massacre impossible.

NOTES

1 François Hotman, *Francogallia*, eds Ralph Giesey and John Salmon (Cambridge, 1972), Preface, pp. 137–145. François Hotman, *Franco-Gallia* (facsimile edition of the French trans. of 1574), ed. Antoine Leca (Aix-Marseille, 1991), unpaginated preface. There were three editions of *Francogallia* in 1573, a French translation (probably by Simon Goulart) in 1574 entitled *La Gaule françoise*, two expanded editions in 1576 and 1586, and a posthumous one in 1600.

2 *Ibid.*, p. 155.

3 *Ibid.*, pp. 293, 297.

4 *Ibid.*, p. 155.

5 *Ibid.*, p. 305 (104). Hotman tends to replace the term 'subjects' with that of 'citizens'; in two instances he even speaks of 'citizens of France' (*Francigenae cives* in the Latin original).

6 *De furoribus gallicis, horrenda et indigna amiralii Castillionei, nobilium atque illustrium virorum caede, scelerata ac inaudita piorum strage passim edita per conplures civitates [...] Ernesto Varamundo Frisio auctore* (Edinburgh, 1573).

7 Hotman, *Francogallia*, pp. 485–487 (185–186).

8 L'Estoile, *Registre-Journal du règne de Henri III*, vol. 1, p. 226.

9 Théodore de Bèze, *Du Droit des magistrats sur leur subjets*, ed. Robert M. Kingdon (Geneva, 1971).

10 Kingdon, *Myths about the St. Bartholomew's Day massacres*, p. 11; Scott M. Manesch, *Theodore Beza and the Quest for Peace in France, 1572–1598* (Leiden, 2000), p. 56. Bèze's commitment is also evident in the fact that he probably wrote the reply to Pomponne de Bellièvre's speech to the Swiss (*Response de Wolfgang Prisbachius polonois*) under the pseudonym of Wolfgang Prisbach.

11 *Le Réveille-Matin des François et de leurs voisins, composé par Eusèbe Philadelphe Cosmopolite* (Edinburgh, 1574; facsimile reprint, Paris, 1977). The two Dialogues both had separate editions, the first of them in 1573 (in Latin and then French); the second in 1574 (in Latin). Their author may be Nicolas Barnaud, a doctor from the Dauphiné, or the lawyer Hugues Doneau.

12 Daussy, *Les Huguenots et le roi*, pp. 241–254, shows that this was probably the case.

13 Stephanus Junius Brutus, *Vindiciae contra tyrannos*, ed. George Garnett (Cambridge 1994).

14 Two of them, the *Discours politiques des diverses puissances establies de Dieu au monde* and *Le Politique: Dialogue traitant de la puissance, autorité et du devoir des Princes*, are especially audacious.

15 William Barclay, *De regno et regali potestate adversus Buchanan, Brutum, Boucherium et reliquos monarchomaquos libri sex* (Paris, 1600).

16 Arlette Jouanna, '"Capituler avec son prince": la question de la contractualisation de la loi au xvi⁰ siècle', in Paul-Alexis Mellet, ed., *'Et de sa bouche sortait un glaive'. Les monarchomaques au xvi⁰ siècle* (Geneva, 2006), pp. 131–143.

17 By modern standards, subjects were imperfectly represented. The deputies to the Estates General, elected through complex procedures, resembled procurators charged with communicating to the king the grievances of their electors. The monarchomachs conferred far greater powers on them.

18 Bèze, *Du Droit des magistrats sur leur subjets*, p. 27.

19 See the analysis in Emmanuel Le Roy Ladurie, *The Royal French state 1460–1610* (Oxford, 1994), p. 189.

20 See *Vindiciae contra tyrannos*, p. 173, especially the 'fourth question', which is formulated as follows: 'whether neighbouring princes may by right, or ought, to render assistance to subjects of other princes who are being persecutes on account of pure religion or oppressed by manifest tyranny?'

21 *Francogallia*, eds Giesey and Salmon, p. 7.

22 Paul-Alexis Mellet, *Les Traités monarchomaques. Confusion des temps, résistance armée et monarchie parfaite (1560–1600)* (Geneva, 2007), pp. 76, 117, who discovered an edition of 1569, published in Poitiers; it was republished in 1570 in the *Histoire de nostre temps, contenant un recueil de choses memorables passées et publiées pour le faict de la religion et estat de la France depuis l'Edict de pacification du 23⁰ jour de mars 1568* (n.p.). Robert M. Kingdon produced a critical edition (Geneva, 1989).

23 Mellet, *Les Traités monarchomaques*, p. 193.

24 On this text, see Janine Garrisson, *Protestants du Midi, 1559–1598* (Toulouse, 1980), pp. 179–182.

25 *Le Réveille-Matin des François*, p. 138.

26 *Dialogus quo multa exponuntur quae Lutheranis et Hugonotis gallis acciderunt* (Oragnae [Heidelberg ?], 1573).

27 *Le Réveille-Matin des François*, p. 94.

28 Among the laws of the kingdom, which Théodore de Bèze was apparently the first to label as 'fundamental laws' (*Du Droit des Magistrats*, p. 61), the Salic law (that of the transmission of the crown through the eldest male heir) was the only one which enjoyed a long-standing unanimity. That of the royal majority at the age of thirteen was only finally codified in 1563, that of the inalienability of the royal domain in 1566. The Catholicity of the king would still be debated in 1593.

29 Guillaume Budé, *L'Institution du Prince*, ed. Claude Bontemps, in Claude Bontemps et al., *Le Prince dans la France des xvi⁰ et xvii⁰ siècles* (Paris, 1966), p. 80.

30 Hilton Root, *La Construction de l'état moderne en Europe. La France et l'Angleterre* (Paris, 1994), p. 311.

31 *Le Réveille-Matin des François*, pp. 37–40.

32 Agrippa d'Aubigné, *Les Tragiques*, Book V, *Les Fers*, verses 760–761.

33 *Articles et requestes de ceux de la religion prétendue réformée de Languedoc assem-blés à Montauban,* BnF., MS Nouvelles acquisitions françaises, 7178, fols 36r–47r; published by dom de Vic and dom Vaissète, *Histoire générale de Languedoc* (Paris-Toulouse, 2002–6), vol. 12, cols 1046–1060. Garrisson, *Protestants du Midi,* p. 184, quotes the slightly different version published in Basel by Pierre de Ray, n.d.

34 Another slate of Huguenot demands would, however, be accepted by Henri III at the end of the fifth civil war and included in the edict of May 1576, notably the rehabil-itation of Coligny, Briquemault and Cavaignes.

35 The *ligueurs,* when faced with adversity, would take up monarchomach themes, but gave them a quite different meaning.

36 *CSPF,* vol. 4, p. 474, no. 1336, Dr Dale to Lord Burghley, Paris, 8 March 1574.

37 Groen van Prinsterer, *Archives ou Correspondance inédite de la maison d'Or-ange-Nassau,* 1st series, vol. 3, pp. 282–286; see above, ch. 2, p. 51.

38 *Déclaration et Protestation de Monseigneur de Dampville, maréchal de France,* 13 Nov. 1574, published in Strasbourg in 1575, reprinted in Vic and Vaisette, *Histoire générale de Languedoc,* vol. 12, *preuve* 336.

39 This conviction is reflected in the *Discours merveilleux de la vie, actions et déporte-ments de Catherine de Médicis,* first published in 1575, and republished the follow-ing year with additions by perhaps another hand. See the critical edition by Nicole Cazauran (Geneva, 1995), pp. 206–209.

40 *Déclaration de Monseigneur François, fils et frère de Roy, duc d'Alençon* (n.p., 1575); *Briève Remonstrance à la noblesse de France sur le faict de la Déclaration de Monsei-gneur le duc d'Alençon* (attrib. to Innocent Gentillet), (n.p., 1576), esp. pp. 62–63.

41 *Résolution claire et facile sur la question tant de fois faicte de la prise des armes par les inférieurs* (Bâle, J. Oporin, 1575), p. 92. This treatise was reprinted in Reims in 1577. *Discours merveilleux de la vie, actions et déportements de Catherine de Médicis,* p. 220; *La France-Turquie, c'est-à-dire conseils et moyens tenus par les ennemis de la Couronne de France pour réduire le royaume en tel estat que la tyran-nie turquesque* (Orléans, 1576), especially the last tract in this collection entitled *Lunettes de christal de roche par lesquels on veoyt clairement le chemin tenu pour subjuguer la France à mesme obeissance que la Turquie.*

42 *Mémoires de l'Estat de France,* vol. 1, fol. 266r–v.

43 *La France-Turquie,* p. 10.

44 List quoted by James B. Wood, 'The Royal army during the Wars of Religion, 1559–1576', in Mack P. Holt, ed, *Society and institutions in early modern France* (Athens, Ga., 1991), p. 26.

45 AGS, K1532, no. 17, Zuñiga to Alba, 2 July 1573.

46 Mack P. Holt, *The Duke of Anjou and the politique struggle during the Wars of Reli-gion* (Cambridge, 1986), pp. 28–30.

47 O. Christin, *La Paix de religion.*

48 Among the most active was a veteran of the conspiracy of Amboise, Jean de Ferrières, vidame of Chartres. Others include the brothers Jean and Jacques de La Fin, the first of whom, seigneur of Beauvoir La Nocle, was brother-in-law of Ferrières. Paul Choart, seigneur de Grandchamp, was unhappy at having been recalled from his embassy at Constantinople and replaced by François de Noailles, bishop of Dax. Town gover-nors also offered their support, for example, Jean de Chaumont-Guitry of Auxerre and Jean de Thévalle, governor of Metz and brother-in-law of marshal François de Scépeaux, seigneur de Vieilleville. In Poitou, the nobles coalesced around François

de La Noue who accused the King of trying to regain La Rochelle despite his promise to the contrary. See Arlette Jouanna, *Le Devoir de révolte. La noblesse française et la gestation de l'État moderne, 1559–1661* (Paris, Fayard, 1989), pp. 154–179.

49 *Les Lunettes de cristal de roche par lesquelles on veoit clairement le chemin tenu pour subjuguer la France à mesme obeissance que la Turquie.* This is one of the tracts in the collection entitled *La France-Turquie.*

50 Arlette Jouanna, 'Être *bon français* au temps des guerres de Religion: du citoyen au sujet', in Ouzi Elyda et Jacques Le Brun, eds, *Conflits politiques, controverses religieuses. Essais d'histoire européennes aux xvie–xviiie siècles* (Paris, 2002), pp. 19–32.

51 Gentillet, *Brieve Remonstrance*, pp. 8, 11, 40.

52 *Déclaration et protestation par monsieur le mareschal Dampville.*

53 *Mémoires des occasions de la guerre, appellée Le Bien-Public, rapportez à l'estat de la guerre présente* (n.p., 1567).

54 See above, ch. 1, p. 24.

55 As was François Hotman, in his letter of 27 April 1574 quoted in the conclusion to the present chapter. The author of the *Lunettes de christal de roche*, p. 42, does the same. Later historians would attribute the 1574 movements to the Politiques: see, for example, Francis Decrue, *Le parti des Politiques au lendemain de la Saint-Barthélemy* (Paris, 1892).

56 BnF, MS. Fr. 15558, fol. 195r.

57 *Instructions du roi pour Jean de Saint-Sulpice*, published in Edmond Cabié, *Guerres de Religion dans le Sud-Ouest de la France et principalement dans le Quercy d'après les papiers des seigneurs de Saint-Sulpice, de 1561 à 1590* (Paris-Toulouse, 1906), col. 240.

58 *Ibid.*, col. 272.

59 *Négociations diplomatiques avec la Toscane*, vol. 3, p. 894, Vincenzo Alamanni to Francesco de Medici, 23 Dec. 1573.

60 *Ibid.*, p. 896, same to same, 16 Jan. 1574.

61 Decrue, *Le parti des Politiques*, p. 131.

62 AGS, Estado, K1532, no. 17b, Zuñiga to Alba, 2 July 1573.

63 Holt, *The Duke of Anjou*, p. 35.

64 On this structure and the meaning of the misleading term 'the United Provinces of the Midi' proposed by Jean Delumeau and Janine Garrisson to describe it, see Arlette Jouanna et al., *Histoire et dictionnaire des guerres de Religion* (Paris, 1998), pp. 223–228.

65 Champion, *Charles IX*, p. 177. This letter was intercepted by royal agents, and Montmorency prudently claimed that it was a forgery.

66 Joan M. Davies, 'Languedoc and its gouverneur. Henri de Montmorency-Damville, 1563–1589' (unpublished dissertation, University of London, 1974), pp. 135–139.

67 *Négociations diplomatiques avec la Toscane*, vol. 3, p. 861, Vincenzo Alamanni to Francesco de Medici, Paris, 20 Nov. 1572.

68 *Ibid.*, p. 899, same to same, 9 Feb. 1574; *Correspondance en France du nonce Antonio Maria Salviati*, pp. 195–196, letter of 9 Feb. 1574.

69 Hector de La Ferrière, 'Les dernières conspirations du règne de Charles IX', *Revue des questions historiques*, 48 (1890), pp. 421–470; Holt, *The Duke of Anjou*, pp. 38–39; *Correspondance du nonce en France Antonio Maria Salviati*, p. 793, letter of 13 March 1574. A first aborted attempt to flee by Navarre and Alençon had occurred in Dec. 1573.

70 AGS, Estado, K1533, no. 40, Zuñiga to Phillip II, 2 July 1573, quoted by Vásquez de Prada, *Felipe II y Francia*, p. 228, n. 127.

71 AGS, Estado, K1533, no. 9, same to same, 13 March 1574.

72 Éliane Viennot published this document, written by Marguerite de Valois for her husband, in her edition of Marguerite's *Mémoires, op. cit.*, pp. 239–350.

73 Holt, *The Duke of Anjou*, p. 43, 'it seems highly unlikely that the full story of what happened at court in March and April 1574 will ever emerge from the evidence'.

74 *Mémoires de l'Estat de France*, vol. 3, fols 296–299.

75 Royal letter quoted by Decrue, *Le parti des Politiques*, p. 213.

76 AGS, Estado, K1537, no. 5, Zuñiga to Phillip II, 23 Jan. 1575, quoted by Vásquez de Prada, *Felipe II y Francia*, p. 231, n. 146 (*paresciéndoles que, suelto Montmorency y quedando el de Danvile en su gobierno , serán los dos hermanos más parte en este reyno que ellos*).

77 Mark Greengrass, 'War, politics and religion in Languedoc during the government of Henri de Montmorency-Damville (1574–1610)' (unpublished D.Phil dissertation, University of Oxford, 1979), p. 161.

78 The declarations by Alençon et de Damville have already been mentioned above, p. 206; Condé's was published in La Rochelle in 1574 with the title *Déclaration de Henri de Bourbon aujourd'huy troisiesme Prince du sang de France, prince de Condé, accompaigné de plusieurs gentilshommes de l'une et l'autre Religion*.

79 Memorandum from the seigneur de Méru to the Queen of England, published by Joseph Kervyn de Lettenhove, *Documents inédits relatifs à l'histoire du xviᵉ siècle* (Brussels, 1883), pp. 194–209.

80 Letter from François Hotman to his friend Gwalter, quoted and translated from Latin by Rodolphe Dareste, 'François Hotman. Sa vie et sa correspondance', *RH*, 2 (1876), pp. 374–375.

81 Daussy, *Les Huguenots et le roi*, pp. 96–108.

82 De Bèze, *Correspondance*, vol. 13 (1573), letter to a great lord [François de La Noue?], 16 Aug. 1573, pp. 173–178; and vol. 14 (1574), letter to Zanchin, 15 March 1574, pp. 54–55; Manetsch, *Theodore Beza*, pp. 74–91.

9

THE KING'S DEATH, OR THE MEANING OF A MASSACRE REVEALED

In the spring of 1574 the political debate seemed to have settled at least in part on desacralised ground. It was the preservation of the state that, in the King's eyes, justified the arrest of François de Montmorency, as it had previously the 'execution' of Gaspard de Coligny. Likewise, in demanding 'contractualised' guarantees for subjects, Malcontents and monarchomachs situated the 'public good' above confessional divergence. If all invoked God's support and if the ultimate destiny of mankind still bounded their thinking, they nevertheless employed, each in his own sphere, secular principles regarding the exercise of power or the temporal ordering of the earthly city. It is possible to detect, in the conflicting concepts of the time, the beginnings of a tentative 'autonomisation of political reason' which was distinct from an exclusively religious interpretation of history.[1]

However, through the passions that it aroused, the final agony of Charles IX reinvigorated the spiritual reading of events. Anxious finally to see the real meaning of the violence inflicted on the Protestants revealed, victims as well as defenders of the Massacre tried hard to find the signs that would support their version of the massacres. The feverish pens of those who wrote about the King's last moments devised poetical 'monuments' or composed funeral orations that turned his death into the judgment of God. An ideological context solidified in this way, favouring the extremes and reducing the chances of a rapid victory for the coalition of the moderates.

A BLOODY DEATH, THE DEATH OF A MARTYR

Charles IX (born on 27 June 1550) was not yet twenty-four when he died on Whit Sunday, 30 May 1574, worn out by the tuberculosis that had killed his brother François in December 1560. Contemporaries were startled by the spectacular haemorrhages which he experienced before his death. Throughout his life he suffered from frequent nosebleeds; later, under the pressure of his illness, he began to spit blood, sometimes abundantly. At the end of April he nearly suffocated when vomiting blood.[2]

For people of that time, the manner of one's death revealed the quality of a life. It was the final proof that did not deceive.[3] The most militant Protestants and Catholics both tried to provide the evidence that the death of the King showed the signs that would prove, on the one hand, the divine reprobation which hung over him or, on the contrary, his divine election. The event thus became a major focus of polemic.

The 'red death' of Charles IX, as Agrippa d'Aubigné called it, offered the Protestants a choice theme.[4] On 23 June 1574 Théodore de Bèze wrote to one of his correspondents: 'we must marvel at God's judgement: the tyrant is dead, with blood pouring from every orifice of his body'.[5] In Agrippa d'Aubigné's writings, these orifices (*cava*) become 'all the pores' of the King, which transforms the blood-lettings into bloody sweats, a terrible punishment and an evident sign of divine malediction; on two occasions Aubigné writes that he saw Charles IX in such a state, 'with God's anger blazing all over his face'.[6] Simon Goulart mentions another squalid detail borrowed from the Protestant historian Jean de Serres: having fainted, the King collapsed into the basin into which he had bled, and 'wallowed in it'.[7] For the Protestants, the entire reign was placed under the sign of blood: Charles IX's passion for hunting gave him a taste for it, because, as Goulart or La Popelinière wrote, he delighted in disembowelling the captured animals and tearing out their entrails with his bare hands.[8]

Not all Protestant authors deduced from the King's death the proof of his damnation; some found in it evidence of his repentance. The difference between the two editions of the *Mémoires de l'Estat de France* is suggestive in this regard: in the first edition, Simon Goulart presents the King's demise as a terrible punishment of a guilty man, while in the second he indicates that the King had resolved to punish the advisers who had urged the massacres on him, but that he had not the time to do so.[9] For his part, Sully recounts that Charles IX, 'seeing himself covered in his own blood in bed, confessed to having no greater regret than having spilt the blood of the innocent on 24 August 1572'; and that he had confided to his surgeon, Ambroise Paré, soon after the Massacre, that he was haunted by visions of 'hideous and bloody faces' and wished the 'weak and the innocent' had been spared.[10] The King's remorse is also attested by an anonymous document relating the 'notable thoughts' which he supposedly confided to his nurse before dying. She was a Protestant, but the King 'loved her greatly'. She was sitting on a chest and had begun to slumber when she heard the dying man 'complaining, groaning and sighing'. Opening the blinds, she heard these words, interrupted by sobbing: 'Ah, nurse, my friend, nurse – so much blood, so many murders. What a terrible Council I had. God, pardon me my sins and give me mercy, if it please you; I do not know where I am, they perplex and agitate me so badly. What will come of all this? What can I do? I am lost, I see it clearly'.[11] The anonymous author who provided this anecdote commented on it as follows: 'this is how the judgment of God arraigns the consciences of kings and the great, as it does those of the modest and the little people'.

Thus, for some Protestants the death of Charles IX revealed the diabolical character of the massacres rather than of the King, and blame was diverted onto those who had inspired his crime.[12] Nevertheless the insistence, in all of the Protestant accounts, on the King's haemorrhages is highly symbolic. For his contemporaries, blood was not merely the crucial liquid which circulates in the body's veins; it was held to contain the physical and moral characteristics which shape the personality of a family, such that terms like 'race', 'blood' and 'lineage' were often used as synonyms. The blood of the ruling dynasty was reputed to be superior to that of others; it had a pre-eminent sacrality, conferred by God's grace. Thus, in emphasising Charles IX's blood losses the Protestant writings aimed to generate a sense of repulsion: they were engaged in a real de-sacralisation of the royal blood and, beyond that, a de-legitimation of the Valois. It is detectable in the invectives of Agrippa d'Aubigné against François d'Alençon, who reportedly died like his brother, in a bloody sweat:

> Le sang l'a suffocqué dont il eut tant d'envie
> Avant l'aage et trop tard son ame il a vomie
> Eschantillon pourry du gros sang des Vallois
> [The blood he so craved so young
> Suffocated him, while he,
> putrid specimen of the coarse blood of the Valois,
> Vomited up his soul too late.][13]

Aware of the danger that the accounts peddled by the Protestants could represent for the image of the royal family, the Catholics took very rapid counteraction. The first to do so was Arnaud Sorbin, the King's confessor, who had the task of delivering the funeral orations, the first on 12 July at Notre-Dame in Paris and the second on the following day at Saint-Denis. He then quickly published a *History* of Charles IX, with a preface also dated 12 July 1574.[14] Catherine de Medici commissioned another funeral sermon from Jean-Baptise Bellaud, the French translation (from Latin) of which was also published in 1574.[15] Two works, one by Joachim Desportes, the other anonymous (but possibly by Sorbin) contained the last words of Charles IX.[16] Court poets like Ronsard and Jean Dorat composed 'monuments' in the late sovereign's memory, alongside which there appeared 'deplorations' and 'lamentations' expressing the sorrow of those close to the King and of France as a whole.[17]

The aim of all these publications was identical – an edifying version of Charles IX's death. The first point they made was that the King behaved like a perfect Christian. He confessed and took communion, piously listened to his confessor's exhortations and expressed his hope of being numbered among the elect; if he did not receive extreme unction, although he requested it, it was because death took him before this sacrament could be administered to him.[18]

Another aim was to show that the sovereign died serenely, with none of the torments described by the Protestants. Arnaud Sorbin, especially, tried to show this:

> And shortly afterwards, a quiet sleep came on and his soul left its earthly taber-nacle, a departure expressed by two or three small sighs, without the good Prince seeming to endure any kind of passion ... because, once dead, his face was more beautiful than it used to be before death, unlike those of men of bad faith and a worse conscience, whose faces remain frightful, hideous and disfigured after death.[19]

According to Joachim Desportes, the King's face expressed the joy of the dying man at the idea of soon entering Paradise, where he would share in the glory of Christ and the beatitude of the just. He died peacefully, 'at which point, without tormenting himself unduly, although he was in his prime, he gave up his spirit to God on the day and feast of Pentecost, the thirtieth of May, at three o'clock in the afternoon, in the château of Vincennes'.[20]

The author of the *Vray discours des derniers propos memorables* distances himself somewhat from the texts just quoted, in that he does not hesitate to refer to the sufferings of the dying King – but without mentioning his haem-orrhages. In this version, the King, wanting to drink, was overcome by a 'great vomiting of sticky, yellowish and very black stuff, then began to shiver greatly, which gave him such torment and pain that nobody could have failed to have great compassion at seeing his Prince suffer so much'.[21] But this detail is only provided the better to exalt the 'constancy' of the sick man who endures his pains 'without anyone noticing in him a single flicker of fear or apprehension of death'. When the final moment came, everything was serene: 'and the said lord gave up his spirit with such sweetness and tranquillity that after his soul had left his body, one would have thought on seeing him that he lay in the rest-fulness of natural sleep rather than of death'.[22]

The authors of these accounts went still further. The better to counter the sinister image that the massacres of 24 August might affix to the memory of Charles IX, they did not hesitate to make him ... a martyr of the faith. According to them, his entire reign had been a fight against heresy, of which the Massacre was the apogee. The young King had consumed his energy in an endless struggle to cleanse the kingdom of that infamous stain; the never-ending perversity of the rebels had shortened his life. Arnaud Sorbin thundered from the pulpit of Notre-Dame: 'It is you, heretics, it is you who have crowned him with the crown of martyrs; you, believing that you can benefit from his death, you have added the blood of your innocent Prince to that of so many of his poor subjects, inhumanly murdered almost everywhere in the realm.'[23] Here the blood unjustly spilt is that of Catholics persecuted by Protestants; and it mystically mingles with that of the King to form the sacred flow that will redeem all believers. For his part, Jean-Baptise Bellaud resorts to mythological themes to express the same idea: Charles IX had to engage in works more difficult than had Hercules. The hydra of heresy had far more heads than the monster of Lerna; the fight against the three Châtillon brothers was far harder than against the three bodies of King Geryon; purifying France was more difficult than cleansing the Augean stables – so much so that the hardships endured and the sorrow of seeing the kingdom torn apart ended up causing the King's death.[24] Ronsard also refers to Hercules and the revolt of the Titans before concluding that Charles IX 'died in his prime, a martyr for Jesus Christ'.[25]

Thus, in the Catholic accounts, Charles IX appears as a sacrificial king who gave his life for his subjects.[26] According to the *Vray Discours*, his last thoughts were for 'his poor people, who he knew had been greatly afflicted by the troubles, civil wars, and divisions that occurred in the kingdom', which he entrusted to his mother until the return of his brother Henri.[27] In his funeral oration, Arnaud Sorbin did not hesitate to draw a parallel between Christ and the King, comparing the latter to 'the Lamb' massacred by the wolves.[28] A Christ-like king, Charles IX died as a martyr, in perfect communion with his subjects persecuted by heretics. This edifying image, and its hagiographical embellishment, were a calculated response to the outbreaks of hatred prompted by the massacre of 24 August.

THE SUPER-SACRALISATION OF THE KING

This polemic over the King's last moments is hugely important in the history of representations of royal power. All of the writings, both Protestant and Catholic, describe the death of Charles IX as the crucial moment in which he found himself confronted by the Massacre, the event in which the authors include indifferently the execution of the Huguenot leaders and the generalised killings. On account of the enormity of the event and the personal involvement in it that the King assumed, it implicitly raises the question of the nature of royal responsibility in the monarchical system.

Faced with such a question and its subversive potential, the Catholic militants' response was to locate the King's actions in the sphere of the sacred, the better to place them beyond critical examination by his subjects. According to them, Charles IX possessed a double sacrality. Firstly, that of his 'race', on which Jean-Baptiste Bellaud strongly insisted in his funeral sermon: the extraordinary 'prudence' which the young King showed in governing the state proves that he belonged to a lineage blessed by God, that of Hugues Capet, the successor of the 'noble and illustrious families of Merovius and Charlemagne'; so that, 'for five hundred and eighty years we can follow the true branch and source of the race of the most Christian king, Charles IX, who since his childhood clearly bore the imprint of the virtue and generosity of his ancestors, valiantly enduring and suffering thousands of trials'.[29]

More decisively, the Catholic authors proclaimed the sacrality not just of the lineage, but of the King in person. During previous centuries, it was the royal dignity rather than the man who personified it that was sacralised. This way of seeing things began to change during the Renaissance, when theoreticians and publicists under Francis I did much to exalt the person of the sovereign.[30] The shock arising from the Massacre would give a decisive spur to the personal sacralisation of the King.

Thus, the *Histoire* written by Arnaud Sorbin and the *Vray Discours* of the King's last words endeavour to show that Charles IX was a 'miraculous king', in that he benefited from an extraordinary intensification of God's intervention in the course of human history. Having related the King's life, enumerated his virtues and recounted his pious death, Sorbin went on to compile a 'short extract of the rare and memorable things with which God had blessed his reign, during which everything seemed rare and remarkable'.[31] Among these signs of divine election, he notes the manner in which Charles IX and the royal family survived so many conspiracies hatched by the heretics, from the surprise of Meaux to those of La Molle and Coconat, via the Coligny conspiracy; he then recalls the miracles bestowed on fervent communities (such as those of Toulouse saved from a Huguenot attack in 1562) or people possessed by demons (such as Nicole Aubry in 1566 at Laon); he also mentions supernatural visions granted to devout individuals; and lastly, the comet of 1573, which the Huguenots saw as a prediction of the King's death, whereas it heralded their own defeat.[32] The conclusion, said Sorbin, was clear: the reign of Charles IX can 'rightly be said to be the reign of wonders'.[33] In this respect, the King and his age were in perfect accord: 'since he was a miraculous king in his virtue, goodness, piety, modesty and other qualities of a great king, nearly everything in his reign was miraculous'.[34]

The author of the *Vray Discours des derniers propos mémorables* saw prodigious signs in the very date of the King's death. It was Whit Sunday and 'the gate of heaven, having been opened by the Ascension of Jesus Christ, which had been celebrated ten days earlier, remained open ... in order to bring and receive into this place of rest on this solemn and illustrious day, the soul of a king so good-natured, endowed with so many virtues and so many gifts, and perfected by so many good deeds'.[35] It was also the day, the author adds, that the jubilee ordained by Pope Gregory XIII was celebrated; finally he demonstrated – after a complicated calculation of the number of weeks and years that had passed since Christ's Resurrection – 'the perfection of the number seven'. It followed that 'the perfection of the works of our good king was pre-ordained on that day by God'.[36] Such factors indicated the sacred character of Charles IX. The same theme is illustrated by the poetical monuments which depict the children of Henri II and Catherine de Medici as quasi-divine beings.[37]

It is obviously necessary to discount the rhetorical exaggeration of funeral orations or monuments. But we can also see in them the absolute necessity for the royal panegyrists to convince as many people as possible of their conception of the royal sacrality, which the Huguenots had so strongly challenged. The controversy between the two *Réveille-Matin* – that, already seen, of the monarchomach movement, and that which Arnaud Sorbin wrote to refute it – is especially interesting from this point of view. The second, entitled *Le Vray Resveille-Matin des calvinistes et publicains François*, was dedicated to the 'eternal memory and immortality of the soul of the most high and very Christian king of France, the late Charles IX, defender of the Catholic faith'. It opens with two hymns, one in praise of the 'Holy Night' of the Massacre, a 'night of rest for France', 'brighter than the day', which had occurred miraculously in that 'beautiful month of August'; the other hymn was dedicated to the Apostle Saint Bartholomew.[38]

Sorbin noted the indignation produced by the massacres; it had led the Huguenots to publish subversive works such as the *Réveille-Matin* which he attacked, as well as the *Discours de la servitude volontaire*, the *Fureurs gauloises* and the *Francogallia*, and persuaded the 'Malcontents, Publicans or the Mixed' to ally with them. Then, with some audacity, he shifted the debate to the most controversial terrain – that of royal responsibility. Having defined the bases of royal authority, Sorbin raises, in Book 3 of his work, the key question: is he who holds legitimate authority permitted to 'employ tricks, finesses, ruses, traps and other such methods against those disturbing the state'?[39] In other words, does urgent danger justify recourse to exceptional measures that ordinary morality condemns? The reply is positive, and supported by biblical examples. Sorbin disparages the proposal of the author of the *Réveille-Matin des François* to baptise the 24 August 1572 as the 'day of Treason'; there was no treason involved, but rather, obedience to God's design.[40] The confessor even managed to praise the capacity to dissimulate that Charles IX showed in the preparation of the Massacre. To a courtier who expressed surprise at not foreseeing anything, the King replied 'even my hat knew nothing of it'.[41] Reason of state was subsumed here into God's reason, and that was nobody's business but the King's.

Sorbin, it is clear, did not hesitate to adopt the thesis of a cleverly organised trap, but he did so in order to insist that royal actions are immune to ordinary judgements and are subject to heavenly justice alone. In the event, Charles IX acted in accordance with God's will: 'he only undertook and carried out what he could by the express commandment of God'.[42] Here Arnaud Sorbin diametrically opposes the monarchomach theses on the King's individual responsibility before his subjects represented in an assembly and, in case of a felony, a high court of justice. For all that, the confessor does not conclude by exonerating the monarch completely, any more than he idealises his person: 'neither God, nor Angel, nor a sin-less man', he says of his master.[43] Book 4 of his *Réveille-Matin* contains a long litany of the virtues which a king is bound to practise and the vices he must avoid. The individual sacrality which envelops a man, who is as subject to sin as everyone else, does not confer divinity or sanctity on him; its function, wished by God, is 'operational' – namely, to place the sovereign beyond the reach of criticism by his subjects; the king renders accounts to his Creator alone, and that divine choice removes him from the normal human condition and locates him far above those over whom he reigns.[44]

Thus the controversy over Charles IX's death and the consequences of the Massacre for his salvation contributed to the slow process which would gradually lead to the super-sacralisation of the royal person as the only means of removing him from the censures of the governed.

THE EPHEMERAL VICTORY OF THE MALCONTENTS

However, the affirmation of the King's personal sacrality did not mean the end of the other process that characterises the ancien régime monarchy – namely, the gradual autonomisation of the political. The two movements, whose parallel progression can be traced during the events following the bloody massacres of 1572, would, paradoxically, come together by the end of the Wars of Religion in a surprising association sanctioned by the Edict of Nantes in 1598.

The fifth civil war would end with victory for the Malcontents, due to the superiority of the forces that they mobilised against the royal army. Peace was proclaimed at Étigny and Sens, on 6 May 1576; it was seen as a victory for François d'Alençon, hence its nickname of the 'peace of Monsieur'. Étienne Pasquier saw in it, not without some bitterness, 'a new form of capitulation which subjects have adopted with their king since the little peace of 1568'.[45] The edict of pacification of Beaulieu that followed was extraordinary in many ways. Scarcely four years after the Massacre, it granted more concessions to the Protestants than they had previously obtained; their worship was henceforth authorised nearly everywhere, except inside and two leagues outside of Paris, as well as in towns where the court might reside; they obtained eight places of security and 'mixed-party' tribunals (composed of magistrates from both confessions) in each parlement; Coligny and his lieutenants Briquemault and Cavaignes were publicly rehabilitated; and finally, the new King, Henri III, promised to convene the Estates General within six months. The Malcontents and monarchomachs could thus hope to see the 'reformation of state', which they had been calling for, materialise.[46] Individual royal letters-patent rewarded the Malcontent leaders. François d'Alençon had his apanage increased with Anjou, Touraine and Berry, and took the title of duc d'Anjou; Condé was confirmed as governor of Picardy and Henri de Navarre as governor of Guyenne – to which was added Poitou and the Angoumois; and Montmorency-Damville as that of Languedoc.

It was the very scale of their success that would boomerang against the victors. The concessions to the Protestants appeared intolerable to the zealous

Catholics. Henri III had to force the parlement of Paris to register the edict; more seriously, when he wished to have a *Te Deum* sung at Notre-Dame to celebrate the peace, 'the people and clergy', according to Pierre de l'Estoile, prevented him from entering the cathedral.[47] Those most hostile to compromise, who had begun to band together in defensive leagues before the war had ended, now openly associated in Paris, Picardy, Normandy, Brittany, Poitou and Champagne; the Picardy league launched a ringing manifesto under the invocation of the 'Holy Trinity' for the defence of the 'Holy, Catholic, Apostolic and Roman church'.[48] All of these associations were probably in touch with each other, and the confederate structure that the texts evoke shows that the formula of 'union' already used by the southern Huguenots was now adopted by the *ligueurs*. The influence of the Guises was also evident through the activity of their clients.

The effectiveness of this Catholic mobilisation explains why the elections to the Estates General, summoned to meet at Blois on 6 December 1576, did not produce the results expected by the moderate Catholics and the Huguenots. The *ligueurs* brought pressure to bear to have deputies favourable to them elected. Théodore de Bèze was indignant at their manoeuvres; unable to obtain their objectives by arms, he wrote on 11 September 1576, they now do everything to win the electoral battle.[49] The assembly that met at Blois had only one, or possibly two, Protestants deputies among the nobility, and only a handful among the third estate.[50] The Catholic deputies favourable to the maintenance of the edict of pacification were a small minority, which led Henri de Condé and Henri de Navarre to protest, solemnly and pre-emptively, against whatever decisions the Estates might take.

However, the 1576 assembly did not hesitate to raise clearly the question of sovereignty, to which the St Bartholomew's tragedy had given an unprecedented prominence, and which the monarchomachs and Malcontents regarded as central to their concerns. A commission of thirty-six deputies, twelve from each order, was established. On 12 December 1576 it presented to Henri III a petition which, had he accepted it, would have instituted a real division of power between the sovereign and the Estates General.[51] The King was not alone in finding the propositions of the commission too audacious; they produced heated discussions, whose tenor the journal of Guillaume de Taix, dean of Troyes cathedral, recorded. Many deputies pointed out that the application of the propositions by the thirty-six commissioners was dangerous: 'the king would be no more than the servant of the Estates, or at least would be neither king nor chief, which debases his sovereignty too much'.[52] Was such a serious diminution of royal authority really acceptable in a time of religious division and civil war? This awareness of the seriousness of the stakes involved no doubt explains why the supporters of reform did not show the vigour in imposing their ideas that one might have expected of them. It is true, nevertheless, that the

Estates of 1576 were a remarkable public forum during which the consequences of the political choices on offer for the monarchy's future were clearly examined.

In the end, and after heated debates among the nobility and the third estate, the three estates voted for a return to religious unity and the revocation of the edict of pacification.[53] This wiped out the hopes of the Huguenots and the Catholic moderates; they realised that the Estates General could be infiltrated by the supporters of intransigence, and was vulnerable, like all assemblies, to manipulations more dangerous than those to which the King was exposed by his evil counsellors. This bitter conclusion would be borne out several years later by the second Estates of Blois, in 1588, and even more so by that of Paris in 1593, both of which were dominated by the Catholic Holy League.

From this point on, only a few people would continue to believe in the effectiveness of the Estates General in reforming the state, with the exception of much later and more fleeting occasions, such as 1614, the Fronde and, in a very different context, 1789. The 1576 Estates sounded the knell of the high hopes which had energised the different protagonists – Catholics as well as Protestants – who participated in the fifth civil war.

RESIGNATION AND TOLERATION

Subsequent events underlined the simplicity of the alternatives facing the French – shared sovereignty or absolute power – while at the same time reinforcing the position of those wishing to see royal authority removed from every kind of institutional oversight. A quick sketch of the main lines of this development is necessary, insofar as its dénouement, in 1598, resolved for good the crisis that had been so spectacularly exacerbated by the 1572 tragedy.

After the abrogation of the 1576 edict, civil war – the sixth in the usual chronology – resumed. It ended in September 1577 with the Edict of Poitiers, which seriously limited the liberty of worship granted to the Protestants. As its predecessors, the new edict represented another step towards the autonomisation of the state, since it implied a difference between believers and citizens and recognised the possibility of being a good servant of the king without sharing his religion. Concrete measures were put in place to render the co-existence of the confessions viable in daily life. Public order and social concord were thus implicitly proposed as the objectives of temporal power, and carried their own intrinsic value; the postulate of relative independence for the political sphere was returning, even if the hope of a future reunion of the Protestants to the Catholic church still persisted.

The respite which this afforded lasted, more or less, for seven years; the seventh war, from November 1579 to November 1580, did not involve the majority of the Huguenots. A new twist changed everything: the death of François d'Anjou on 10 June 1584 made Henri de Navarre, in the absence of a male heir by Henri

III, the presumptive heir to the throne. Terrified by the prospect of the accession of a Protestant sovereign, the zealous Catholics united in a Holy League, which this time was powerfully structured. The eighth war, which began in 1585, was the longest – nearly fourteen years – and the most devastating of all. The assassination of Henri III by a fanatical monk, Jacques Clément, on 1 August 1589 revealed the seriousness of the crisis and the excesses to which de-sacralisation of the king, arising from the theories of the monarchomachs – which the Catholic extremists had now taken up – could lead.[54] His successor, Henri IV, had to abjure his Protestant faith and it took him many years to overcome resistance from the *ligueur* towns and princes.

These events clearly raised the question of authority and obedience. One lesson emerged from them: on the one hand, the friendship pacts agreed between Protestants and Catholics were unable to provide a model that was valid for the entire kingdom; on the other, the resort to arms which united the belligerents on both sides proved incapable of reforming the monarchy. Henceforth, it seemed that if tolerance were to endure, it could not be the result of initiatives, warlike or peaceful, by subjects, but should be imposed from on high by an effective authority; in addition, this authority should be able to claim a transcendence that would enable it to impose itself on everyone else.

But what kind of transcendence? Not everyone accepted the super-sacralisation of the king's person to which the controversy over the death of Charles IX had given such a strong thrust. Some major thinkers tried to publicise the idea of an impersonal transcendence that was linked more to the value of public order than to the person holding that power. Jean Bodin was one of them. In the *Six Livres de la République*, published in 1576, the jurist makes sovereignty into an absolute which suffices unto itself, legitimated by the hierarchical principle that governs the whole universe.[55] Another, Montaigne, went perhaps further still in this direction. Examining in his *Essays* the function of the laws, he insists they remain in force 'not because they are just, but because they are laws. That is the mystic foundation of their authority ... whoever obeys them because they are just does not obey for the reason he should.'[56] Their hold on people has no other justification than that which is attached to the established order. Yet Montaigne recognises that this 'mystical foundation' will not of itself ensure the docility of subjects; he believes that it is also useful for those who govern to resort to 'some admixture either of empty ceremony or of untruthful opinion to serve as a curb to keep people in their duty. This is why most of them [laws] have their fabulous origins and beginnings enriched with supernatural mysteries.'[57] But this was a feeble pretence, one which the author of the *Essays* himself implicitly ridiculed. There is no better way of saying that the transcendence of the law alone will not infallibly generate obedience and silence all disputes.

Ultimately, the only effective way to impose royal authority on subjects who were religiously divided was indeed the one which the Catholic accounts of the death of Charles IX had resurrected, namely the sacralisation of the king. But thanks to the genius of Henri IV and the talents of the publicists in his service, the sacrality of the monarchy would be brilliantly detached from the Catholic exclusivism where the panegyrists of Charles IX had confined it; it would be mobilised in the service of civil tolerance.

The edict which ended the wars of religion was signed at Nantes, probably on 30 April 1598. In a sense, it was the culmination of the process of the relative autonomisation of the political sphere already at work in the previous edicts. Its clauses reproduced, clarified and extended those of 1577, while the peaceful co-existence that it instituted between the confessions would last nearly a century.[58] But it concomitantly enshrined the process of sacralising the person of the King. In the gleeful preface which precedes the edict, Henri IV congratulates himself on the graces that God has given him – 'virtue', 'strength', 'toil', constancy in adversity, physical courage – personal qualities which are here elevated to the rank of providential instruments of God's will. The speech that he made to the parlementaires, summoned to the Louvre on 7 January 1599 to oblige them to register the edict, also strongly expressed the certainty of having been 'chosen' by God.[59]

This conviction was abundantly disseminated by the King's eager publicists.[60] The Peace of Vervins, signed on 2 May 1598 with Spain (on which war had been declared in January 1595), offered an occasion for the King's eulogists to ratchet up the hyperbole even further. Poets and writers vied in celebrating the virtuous King, showered with divine blessings and bearer of quasi-messianic hopes.[61] Men as sober as Pierre de l'Estoile, Jacques-Auguste de Thou and Étienne Pasquier were happy to see in Henri IV a miraculous king. L'Estoile regarded as 'the miracle of miracles' the encounter between him and Henri III at Plessis-lès-Tours on 30 April 1589, which opened the way to the throne for him; de Thou thought that God had 'miraculously' led him to power; as for Pasquier, he enumerates the miracles which permitted the royal triumph with even more gusto.[62] The same themes that had served to exalt Charles IX were reworked here. In the eyes of French people, tired of conflict, the king's person personified henceforth the temporal salvation of the state, the 'public good', and the pre-eminent sacrality of God's elected one.[63]

The celebration in 1598 of the king's person may thus be considered as, on the one hand, the final obstacle against the shockwaves, amplified by the Massacre, which so powerfully troubled the monarchy; and, on the other hand, as the completion of the defensive measures taken by Catholic panegyrists, when Charles IX died, in order to arrest the de-sacralisation of royal authority. Henri IV's talent was to succeed in filling the need for order felt by the French, while making them forget the demand for an oversight of government which the monarchomachs and the Malcontents had expressed with such force. The demand had not disappeared, but it was repressed. It would reappear only in periods of monarchical weakness, especially during the minorities of Louis XIII and Louis XIV, but without ever really obscuring the sacral character of the king's person.[64] In the seventeenth century, the king's power would benefit from a hitherto unknown theological dimension which would doubtless not have been as widely accepted without the terrible shock of the Wars of Religion, of which the massacres of 24 August 1572 were the most tragic event.

NOTES

1 This 'autonomisation' began in the edicts of pacification and in the 'friendship pacts' between Catholics and Protestants: see Christin, *La Paix de religion. L'autonomisation de la raison politique*.

2 Champion, *Charles IX*, vol. 2, p. 385, based on the Venetian Ambassador Cavalli's letter of 2 May 1574. The autopsy report of the surgeon, Jacques Guillemeau, Ambroise Paré's assistant, can be found in *Les Œuvres de chirurgie de Jacques Guillemeau* (Rouen, 1649), p. 856.

3 Hélène Germa-Romann, *Du 'bel mourir' au 'bien mourir'. Le sentiment de la mort chez les gentilshommes français (1515–1643)* (Geneva, 2001) especially ch. 4, pp. 87ff, 'la mort comme preuve'.

4 Agrippa d'Aubigné, *Les Tragiques*, Book VI, *Vengeances*, verse 809.

5 De Bèze, *Correspondance*, vol. 15 (1574), p. 112.

6 Agrippa d'Aubigné, *Lettre au Roy* [Henri IV], quoted by J.-R. Fanlo in his edition (*op. cit.*) of the *Tragiques*, note to verses 803–812 of Book VI, *Vengeances*, p. 846 ; *Histoire universelle*, vol. 4, p. 220.

7 *Mémoires de l'Estat de France*, vol. 3, fol. 371v. Goulart's account is based on Jean de Serres, *Commentarii de statu religionis et reipublicae in regno Galliae*, published in 1571 (n.p.), to which a fourth part, extending the account to the death of Charles IX, was added in 1575.

8 Henri Lancelot Voisin de La Popelinière, *L'Histoire de France* (n. p., 1581), vol. 2, p. 219; *Recueil des choses memorables avenues en France sous le regne de Henri II, François II, Charles IX, Henri III et Henri IV*, 2nd ed. (1st ed., 1595) (n.p., 1598), p. 506. This work is sometimes attributed to Jean de Serres, but was certainly written by Simon Goulart.

9 Huchard, *D'Encre et de sang*, p. 559.

10 Sully, *Œconomies royales*, vol. 1, p. 31, and vol. 2, p. 16.

11 BnF, MS. Fr. 10304, *Propos notables dudit Roy, estant au lict de la mort, et de sa nourrice*, 1574, in *Recueil divers de ce temps*, fols 366r–368r, published by M. Lazard and G. Schrenk at the end of L'Estoile, *Registre-Journal du règne de Henri III*, vol. 1, appendix 1, pp. 251–253. The Huguenot nurse, called Philippe Richard, really did exist: see Champion, *Charles IX*, vol. 2, p. 405.

12 See Bourgeon, *Charles IX devant la Saint-Barthélemy*, pp. 50–51, for his comments in this sense on the anonymous Protestant text *Response des Gentilshommes, Capitaines, Bourgeois et aultres estants en la ville de La Rochelle aux commandemens qui leur ont esté faits soubs le nom du Roy*.

13 Agrippa d'Aubigné, *Sonnets* épigrammatiques, *n° XVI*, in *Œuvres complètes*, eds,

Eugène Réaume and De Caussade (Paris, 1873–1892, reprint Geneva, 1967), vol. 4, p. 337.

14 Arnaud Sorbin, *Oraison funebre du tres hault, puissant et tres chrestien Roy de France, Charles IX, piteux et debonnaire, propugnateur de la Foy Catholique et amateur des bons esprits, prononcée en l'Eglise Nostre-Dame en Paris, le XII de juillet M.D.LXXIIII* (Paris, 1574); *Histoire contenant un abrégé de la vie, mœurs, et vertus du Roy Tres-chrestien et debonnaire Charles IX, vrayement piteux, propugnateur de la Foy Catholique et amateur des bons esprits* (Paris, 1574).

15 Jean-Baptiste Bellaud, *Oraison funebre du trespas du Roy treschrestien Charles Neufiesme* (Paris, 1574).

16 Joachim Desportes, *Discours sommaire du règne de Charles neufiesme Roy de France Tres-Chrestien, ensemble de sa mort, et d'aucuns de ses derniers propos* (Paris, 1574); *Le Vray Discours des derniers propos memorables et trespas du feu Roy de tres bonne memoire Charles neufiesme* (Paris, 1574).

17 Pierre de Ronsard, *Le Tombeau du feu Roy Tres-Chrestien Charles IX, prince tres-debonnaire, tres-vertueux et tres-eloquent* (Paris, n. d. [1574]); Jean Dorat et al., *Le tombeau du feu Roy* (Lyon, 1574); *Les Regretz et lamentations de tresillustre et vertueuse princesse Elisabeth d'Autriche sur la mort et trespas du Roy Charles neufiesme son espoux, n'agueres decedé. Par A. de la T. D* (Paris, 1574); Antoine Du Part, *Déploration de la France sur le trespas du Tres Chrestien Roy Charles IX* (Paris, 1574), which is in verse, and followed by the *Complainte de la ville de Paris.*

18 Sorbin, *Histoire*, fol. 24r–v.

19 *Ibid.*, fols 26v–27r.

20 Desportes, *Discours sommaire*, unpaginated.

21 *Le Vray Discours des derniers propos memorables*, fol. 11v.

22 *Ibid.*, fols 19v–20r.

23 A. Sorbin, *Oraison funebre*, fol. 25r.

24 Bellaud, *Oraison funebre*, pp. 8–11 and 15.

25 Ronsard, *Le Tombeau du feu Roy Tres-Chrestien Charles Neufieme*, verse 57.

26 See the commentary on this aspect in Crouzet, *La Nuit de la Saint-Barthélemy*, p. 609. See also the analyses in Jean-Marie Le Gall, Le *Mythe de saint Denis entre Renaissance et Révolution* (Seyssel, 2007), p. 406.

27 *Le Vray Discours des derniers propos memorables*, fol. 12v.

28 Sorbin, *Oraison funebre*, fol. 25v.

29 Bellaud, *Oraison funebre*, p. 7.

30 Anne-Marie Lecoq, *François 1er imaginaire* (Paris, 1987).

31 Sorbin, *Histoire*, fol. 45v.

32 *Ibid.*, fols 46r–67v.

33 *Ibid.*, fol. 63v.

34 *Ibid.*, fol. 65v.

35 *Le Vray Discours des derniers propos memorables.*, fol. 6r–v.

36 *Ibid.*, fol. 7v.

37 See, for example, the epitaph and sonnets of Amadis Jamyn published after Ronsard's *Tombeau.*

38 Arnaud Sorbin, *Le Vray Resveille-Matin des calvinistes et publicains François: où est amplement discouru de l'auctorité des Princes, et du devoir des sujets envers eux* (Paris, 1576), dedication (dated All Souls 1574) and preliminary page.

39 *Ibid.*, fol. 68r.

40 *Ibid.*, fols 71r and 88r.

41 Sorbin, *Histoire, op. cit.*, fols 37v–38r.

42 Sorbin, *Le Vray Resveille-Matin des calvinistes et publicains François*, fol. 72v.

43 Sorbin, *Histoire*, fol. 38v.

44 In 1575, Claude d'Albon would call kings 'demi-gods': *De la majesté royale, institu- tion et preeminence, et faveurs divines particulières envers icelle* (Lyon, 1575), fol. 5, quoted by Fanny Cosandey and Robert Descimon, *L'Absolutisme en France* (Paris, 2002), pp. 90–91.

45 Pasquier, *Les Œuvres*, vol. 2, Book VI, col. 139, letter to M. de Sainte-Marthe.

46 Mark Greengrass, 'Pluralism and equality: the peace of Monsieur, May 1576', in Keith Cameron, Mark Greengrass and Penny Roberts, eds, *The Adventure of reli- gious pluralism in early modern France* (Berne, 2000), pp. 45–63.

47 L'Estoile, *Registre-Journal du règne de Henri III*, vol. 2, p. 31.

48 Text published by Agrippa d'Aubigné, *Histoire universelle*, vol. 5, pp. 103–106. A different text was published in 1576 by the League's adversaries with the pejorative title of *Conspiration faite en Picardie, sous fausses et mechantes calomnies, contre l'édit de pacification*.

49 Be Bèze, *Correspondance*, vol. 17 (1576), p. 157.

50 Mack P. Holt, 'Attitudes of the French nobility at the Estates-General of 1576', *SCJ*, 18, (1987), p. 492; *idem, The French wars of religion, 1562–1629* (Cambridge, 1995), p. 106.

51 Enumerated in the diary of a noble deputy from the Nivernais, Pierre de Blanche- fort, they contained three central points: the unanimous decisions of the Estates would become inviolable laws, which the king would authorise by these words 'by us and our Estates'; those which did not attract unanimity would be arbitrated by a commission composed of princes of the blood and peers, advised by deputies to the Estates; and finally, if members of the Council were part of this commission, the list should be presented to the Estates so that they could remove those whom they did not trust: BnF, MS. Fr. 16250, fol. 188r, Pierre de Blanchefort, *Compte de mes actions et recœuil depuis la proclamation des Estats tenus à Blois nottez par mois et jours*.

52 *Journal de Guillaume de Taix*, in MM. Lalourcé and Duval, eds, *Recueil des pièces originales et authentiques concernant la tenue des* États *généraux* (Paris, 1789), vol. 2, pp. 269–271.

53 Georges Picot, *Histoire des* États *généraux*, 2nd ed. (Paris, 1888) vol. 3, pp. 27–31.

54 See Le Roux, *Un Régicide au nom de Dieu*.

55 Jean Bodin, *Les Six Livres de la République* (Paris, Fayard, 1986), Book 1, ch. 6, p. 192. This edition is a reprint of that of 1593.

56 Michel de Montaigne, *The Complete works*, Everyman Library edition (London, 2003), p. 1000.

57 *Ibid.*, p. 580.

58 Janine Garrisson, ed., *L'édit de Nantes* (Biarritz, 1997).

59 The text of the speech is in Roland Mousnier, *L'Assassinat d'Henri IV*, Paris, Galli- mard, 1964, pp. 334–337 [English trans, *The Assassination of Henry IV* (London, 1973), pp. 364–367]. For the issues at stake in the neo-sacralisation of the king's person, see Marie-France Renoux-Zagamé, 'Du juge-prêtre au roi-idole. Droit divin et constitution de l'État dans la pensée juridique française à l'aube des temps modernes', in Jean-Louis Thireau, ed., *Le Droit entre laïcisation et néo-sacralisation* (Paris, 1997), pp. 143–186.

60 Corrado Vivanti, *Guerre civile et paix religieuse dans la France d'Henri IV* [1963], French trans. (Paris, 2006), pp. 65–68; Alexandre Y. Haran, *Le Lys et le globe: messianisme dynastique et rêve impérial en France aux XVIᵉ et XVIIᵉ siècles* (Seyssel, 2000), pp. 223–225.

61 Roger Baury, 'Célébration de la paix de Vervins et propagande royale', in Jean-François Labourdette, Jean-Pierre Poussou and Marie-Catherine Vignal, eds, *Le Traité de Vervins* (Paris, 2000), pp. 347–372.

62 L'Estoile, *Registre-Journal du règne de Henri III*, vol. 6, p. 174; Jacques-Auguste de Thou, letter of autumn 1592, quoted by Vivanti, *Guerre civile et paix religieuse*, p. 11; Étienne Pasquier, *Congratulation sur la Paix, adressée à M. de Sainte-Marthe*, in *Les Œuvres*, vol. 2, Book XVI, cols 465–480.

63 James B. Collins, 'La guerre de la ligue et le bien public', in *Le Traité de Vervins*, pp. 81–95.

64 The components of the seventeenth-century sacral image are analysed by Joël Cornette, *Le Roi de guerre. Essai sur la souveraineté dans la France du Grand Siècle* (Paris, 1993), especially in Part 3, entitled *Les outils symboliques de la puissance*.

CONCLUSION

Was 24 August 1572 a decisive day in French history? Yes, without doubt. The Massacre signalled, once and for all, the end of the Protestants' hope of converting the kingdom to their faith. France would not now be Protestant. Before the tragedy this had not been clear. In the early 1560s, especially, the country's religious future could rightly seem uncertain, and the force of the new ideas was considerable. According to Blaise de Monluc, who was himself tempted, 'there was no son of a good mother who did not want to try them out'.[1] Many, driven by a spiritual thirst or simple curiosity, went to hear the sermons of the itinerant ministers. It was a time when the Protestants could see in Charles IX a new Josias, the King of Judea who restored the true worship of God, and when their slogan – an anagram of Charles de Valois – was 'Va chasser l'idole' ('get rid of the idol') – meaning the Roman church, of course.[2]

The decline of these hopes began as early as the first civil war of 1562–63. Rejection by the vast majority of Catholics, the end of the illusion of a quick conversion of the royal family, growing insecurity, periods of persecution alternating with brief periods of respite – all these factors contributed to the progressive erosion of the Protestant communities, at least in those provinces where they were isolated and small in number. The Protestant notables, in particular, found it difficult to conduct their activities normally; they were often obliged, when conflicts erupted, to abandon house and work; they risked being arrested; and on the return of peace, they faced so many obstacles in regaining their property and offices that they were tempted to revert to the dominant faith.

But none of the ordeals endured before 1572 had results as devastating for the Huguenots as did the Massacre. In the towns where the killings occurred, their churches were decimated and many survivors lost courage. We find an example of it in the letter written by the Parisian merchant-draper Jean Rouillé to two colleagues in Albi on 22 September 1572. 'It is over', he wrote, 'the King has given a clear sign that he only wants one faith, one law, one God and one King'. This was no longer the time 'to play around in the vain hope that it might turn out differently'. Hence the disabused advice that he gave them: everyone who wished to preserve his life, protect his property and escape poverty should profess the Catholic religion. He concluded thus: 'if you do not accept my counsel, you will be lost, ruined, destroyed, you and your house, from top to bottom, believe me.'[3]

The numerous abjurations that followed the massacres, as well as the exile in countries of 'refuge' of those not resigned to conversion, led to a collapse in the number of Protestants in France. They numbered nearly two million in the early 1560s, but by the end of the Wars of Religion they had fallen to around one million.[4] This contraction mainly affected the northern provinces; in the southern areas, where their communities were well entrenched, they held up better and showed real dynamism, both spiritually and politically. But henceforth they were no more than a minority – 'a little leftover' – fervent and faithful to the memory of the misfortunes they had endured.

The Massacre also had a considerable effect on the evolution of the French monarchy. It is often believed that the religious wars were just a bloody interlude in a linear development whose beginnings are visible by the end of the fifteenth century and which led necessarily to the absolutism of Louis XIV. This bespeaks a teleological conception of history, driven by an improbable determinism. It overlooks the fact that the tragedy of 24 August clearly highlighted the key question raised by the religious division. In order to prevent such horrors in future, should the monarchy become either absolute or one moderated by institutions exercising some checks; or, as the monarchomach thinkers advocated, one that was contractualised and defined by a set of laws agreed by the Estates General, and opening the door to a kind of constitutionalism?

The answer to such a question was not self-evident; it is not because we now know the outcome which later developments fashioned that we should minimise the gravity of the dilemma and the uncertainty as to its outcome for those who were preoccupied by it. The Massacre certainly helped to clarify what was at stake. It produced an extreme dramatisation of a debate which, until then, had been limited mainly to Huguenot circles. The paroxysm of the passions ignited by the event ensured a huge reverberation for the clash of arguments involved in it. At the same time, however, it infused it with fear. The scale of the troubles and of the disorders that followed the carnage contributed to the sense of the need for a strong monarchy. Most thinking people realised that a contractualised monarchy, with an Estates General meeting regularly and acting as co-legislators, entailed too many risks in a time of confessional division. The quality of the debates, during the Blois Estates of 1576, about how to construct laws shows that the deputies had clearly understood the consequences of their choices – just as did the counsellors of Henri III and the King himself. The excesses of the Catholic League would finally tilt the balance towards absolute power, one freed from all institutional checks and moderated only by the King's own desire to obey God's law and the few fundamental laws.

Likewise, the Massacre raised the question of the nature and significance of royal responsibility, since the monarch had personally assumed it for the execution of the Admiral and his lieutenants, which was decided on by virtue of his right of extraordinary justice. But does imminent danger to the state justify exceptional measures contrary to morality and the ordinary laws? The Huguenots saw in the crime of 24 August 1572 a manifestation of tyranny, which deserved both divine and human reprobation; they thought that subjects had a duty to ask whether or not the commands of their ruler were in conformity with equity; if they judged them evil, they were bound in conscience to refuse to obey them. That constituted a risk for the effective exercise of authority, even if this duty was confined to those who represented the governed. Catholic responses, especially at the time of Charles IX's death, prefigured the way in which the monarchy would go about avoiding that danger – namely, by the sacralisation of the sovereign's own person, metaphorically situated in a super-human space, where he was beyond the judgements of the people, 'in between angels and men', to repeat the words of a spokesman for the Politiques in the *Satyre Ménippée*, a work which expressed their ideals at the end of the civil wars.[5] In a country riven by conflict, this was the only outcome that could justify, for everyone, a reverential obedience to royal authority. But the sacred character assigned to the royal person – and no longer just to his office – ended up leaving the king in complete solitude vis-à-vis God, the only judge of his actions. Of course, he did have a council, whose members helped to shape his decisions, but he was expected to decide on his own, enlightened by divine grace, and to take sole responsibility for his resolutions. This was a terrible burden on his shoulders, and its excessiveness would one day discredit the doctrine of divine right.[6]

The super-sacralisation of the king did not eliminate the other political orientations that emerged from the need to resolve the crisis. The solutions attempted during the civil wars opened up the possibility of dissociating the political and religious spheres from each other; they enhanced the notion of the citizen as distinct from the believer; they laid the basis for a secularisation of the state, traces of which are visible in the Edict of Nantes, where, paradox-ically, they co-exist with the processes which strengthened the king's sacrality. Reflection on the Massacre of August 1572 thus contributed to the difficult learning process of religious tolerance and, in the longer term, reinforced the legitimacy of the right of the governed to protection against arbitrary power and to check the acts of those who govern; it also illuminated the fundamental debate over the conditions of legitimate obedience and its relation to the demands of the individual conscience.

However, this positive aspect of the consequences of 24 August 1572 has rarely been part of the collective memory. The Massacre has an important place

– and this is a third feature which enables us to claim that it contributed to 'the making of France' – in the memory that the French have of their past. But its place within it is mostly negative.[7] In 1639, Gabriel Naudé celebrated it as a model of a successful coup d'état, but by the Enlightenment it gradually came to symbolise intolerance. Voltaire wrote that 'the greatest example of fanaticism was that of the bourgeois of Paris who on Saint Bartholomew's night set about assassinating, killing, throwing from windows, and butchering their fellow-citizens who did not go to mass'.[8] Suspected of obscurantism, the Catholic church and Catholicism generally were put in the dock. In this sense, Voltairian France – anticlerical and laïcist – is an heir to the Massacre.

In the nineteenth century, the Catholics tried to counteract the diffusion of too unfavourable an image of the church. For example, they countered the Massacre with the *Michelade*, a massacre of Catholics in Nîmes by their Protestant compatriots on Saint Michael's day in 1567. The novelist Alexandre de Lamothe had this to say in 1864: 'the Michelade perpetrated by the Protestants was an aborted Saint Bartholomew's massacre, more atrocious than that of 1572, because the latter was no more than a bloody and sudden reprisal, which can to some extent still be partly excused by fear, whereas the Michelade, coldly calculated and prepared well in advance in a situation where the Protestants had no need to fear, had no alibi either in trouble caused by fear or in a previous Catholic massacre'.[9] Even during the quatercentenary of the 24 August 1572, there were cases, in the southern areas with a strong Protestant presence, where Catholics and Protestants eyed each other accusingly – albeit in a somewhat disguised fashion – the former over the Michelade, the latter over the St Bartholomew's Massacre.

These efforts to find attenuating circumstances for the Catholic authors of the 1572 killings have not changed the image inherited from the Enlightenment which is etched into the collective mind. The church itself, influenced by the turn to 'repentance' of the end of the twentieth century, felt it should admit a form of guilt by confessing its fault and celebrating, on 24 August 1997, during the World Youth Day in Paris, an anniversary mass dedicated to the victims.

More generally, the Massacre tends nowadays to figure among a series of dark episodes in France's history which are offered as objects of the edifying 'duty of remembering'. This evolution is significant. Until recently, the dominant view was that such barbarous deeds belonged to the savagery of a bygone age and that their return in more civilised times was unthinkable. The current resurgence of inter-communal tensions raises doubts about the dampers that 'civilisation' could put on the eruptions of violence. In its second phase, that of the generalised killings, the Massacre was a dramatic instance of the fear of the Other, a fear that made people see difference as a threat and, in particular, made them confuse religious otherness and subversion. 'Before it becomes an atrocious physical act, massacre emerges from a mental process and an imaginary way of "seeing" an Other who has to be destroyed."[10] Are not such fears and anxieties, such distortions of the human gaze, always ready to resurface? This is the question that the tragedy of 24 August 1572 still raises in our time.

NOTES

1 Monluc, *Commentaires*, p. 481.

2 Pineaux, *La Poésie des protestants de langue française*, pp. 134–135

3 Letter published by Pradel, 'Un marchand de Paris au xvie siècle (1560–1588)', pp. 421–423. See the commentary by Denis Richet, 'Aspects socioculturels des conflits religieux à Paris dans la seconde moitié du xvie siècle', *De la Réforme à la Révolution. Études sur la France moderne* (Paris, 1991), pp. 34–35.

4 Philip Benedict, *The Huguenot population of France, 1600–1685* (Philadelphia, 1991), p. 76.

5 *La Satyre Ménippée*, ed. Charles Read (Paris, 1892), p. 224.

6 Ran Halévi, 'Le Testament de la royauté. L'éducation politique de Louis XVI', in Ran Halévi, ed., *Le Savoir du Prince* (Paris, 2002), pp. 311–361.

7 Philippe Joutard, Janine Estèbe [Garrisson], Élisabeth Labrousse and Jean Lecuir, *La Saint-Barthélemy ou les résonances d'un massacre* (Neuchâtel, 1976).

8 Voltaire, *Dictionnaire Philosophique*, article entitled *Fanatisme*.

9 *Histoire d'une pipe*, quoted by Bernard Peschot, 'Alexandre de Bessot de Lamothe (1823–1897) et les protestants du Midi', in Joël Fouilleron and Henri Michel, eds, *Mélanges Michel Péronnet*, vol. 2, *La Réforme* (Montpellier, 2003), p. 323.

10 Sémelin, 'Analyser le massacre', p. 12.

APPENDIX:

SOCIO-PROFESSIONAL DISTRIBUTION OF THE MASSACRE VICTIMS ACCORDING TO LISTS IN PROTESTANT SOURCES

Town	A	B	C	D	E	F	G	Total
Bourges	–	7	6	–	8	–	9	23
Meaux	–	5	13	–	15	1	–	29
Troyes	–	1	11	–	22	2	–	36
Orleans	2	15	50	2	47	11	15	142
Rouen	3	9	18	3	119	3	31	186
Lyon	–	6	34	3	88	5	5	141
Paris	36	14	13	5	40	2	11	121

Note: A = nobles and 'sieurs'; B = men of law, royal officials; C = merchants; D = teachers, pastors; E = artisans; F = servants and 'of no condition'; G = unknown profession.

Source: Natalie Zemon Davis, *Society and Culture in Early Modern France* (Stanford, Calif., 1975), p. 177, based on Jean Crespin, *Histoire des martyrs* and, for Lyon, P. M. Gonon, ed., *Première liste des chrétiens mis à mort et égorgés à Lyon par les catholiques romains à l'époque de la S. Barthélemi en août 1572* (Lyon, 1847).

SOURCES AND BIBLIOGRAPHY

MANUSCRIPTS

Bibliothèque nationale de France

Correspondence from reign of Charles IX

MS Fr. 15553, year 1571, especially fols 197ff, letters of Geoffroy de Caumont on his flight from the faubourg Saint-Germain, 24 Aug. 1572.

MS Fr. 15554, Jan.–June 1572, especially fols 124r–127r, letter from president Lagebaston to Charles IX, 7 Oct. 1572.

MS Fr. 15555, July–Dec. 1572.

MS Fr. 15556, Jan.–Feb. 1573.

MS Fr. 15557, March–May 1573.

MS Fr. 15558, June–Dec. 1573.

MS Fr. 15559, 1574.

Correspondence and other original documents on wars of religion

MS Fr. 3193, especially fols 68–69: 'memorandum on the words spoken by Admiral Coligny in the King's study in August 1572'.

MS Fr. 3209, especially fols 66 and 79: letters from duc de Longueville, governor of Picardy, to M. d'Humières, 28 Aug. 1572 and 16 Oct. 1572.

MS Fr. 3256, especially fol. 59, royal circular, 2 Sept. 1572.

MS Fr. 3951, especially fol. 5, letter of Charles IX to Schomberg, 13 Sept. 1572, and fol. 142, Charles IX to Cardinal Lorraine, 31 July 1572.

MS Fr. 16104, especially fol. 45, circular letter from Charles IX to provincial governors, 4 May 1572.

MS 500 Colbert, MS. 7, especially fol. 425, mémoire for sieur de Changy on mission to the sieur de Villiers, 27 Aug. 1572; fols 449 and 461, records of campaigns to convert Protestant nobles of Metz and Champagne.

MS 500 Colbert, MS. 24, especially fol. 415, Coligny's letter to Charles IX, La Rochelle, 8 May 1571.

Narrative accounts

MS Fr. 17309, fols 56ff, *Dessein de ceulx qui soubz le nom et autorité de Sa Majesté ont faict le massacre* (probably written in Autumn 1573 or early 1574 by a Protestant or a Catholic close to the duc d'Alençon).

MS Fr. 17529, fols 1ff, *Discours particulier où est amplement descrit et blasmé le massacre de la St-Barthélemy*, and fols 176ff, *Discours du Roy Henry troisiesme a un personnage d'honneur* [...] *des causes et motifs de la Sainct Barthelemy* (an apocryphal account, probably emanating from the Gondi family entourage, and published in 1623 with a view to exonerating the comte de Retz).

Embassies and diplomatic papers

MS Fr. 16040, Roman embassy of M. de Ferrals, 1572–73.

MS Fr. 18895, fols 205ff, Pomponne de Bellièvre, *Proposition faite aux Suisses* [...] *sur la mort de Monsieur l'admiral de Colligny et journee de St Barthelemy.*

MS Fr. 16104, Spanish embassy of M. de Saint-Gouard, Jan.–Dec. 1572.

MS Fr. 5172, Jean de Morvillier's *Memoires d'Estat*, especially fol. 2r, 'Charles IX's proposals to princes and lords assembled in his presence in 1571'; and fol. 6ff, 'instruction sent to provincial governors', 3 Nov. 1572.

Other documents

MS Fr. 16250, Pierre de Blanchefort, *Compte de mes actions et recœuil depuis la proclamation des Estats tenus à Blois nottez par mois et jours.*

MS Fr. 18288, *Vie de messire Jehan de Morvillier*, by Nicolas Le Fèvre, sieur de Lezeau.

MS. Nouvelles acquisitions françaises, 7178, fols 36r–47r, articles and petitions from the 'so-called reformed religion' of Languedoc assembled at Montauban.

Archivio General de Simancas

(Microfilm in Archives Nationales, Paris)

K1524–K1536: correspondence between ambassador Diego de Zuñiga, Duke of Alba and Philip II, 1572–74, especially K1524, no. 78, relation of the death of the Admiral and other heretics in France, and no. 79, what Juan de Olaegui, secretary of the ambassador don Diego de Zuñiga ... reported on matters in the French court; and K1530, nos 19, 20, 21 and 29: Zuñiga's letters of 20, 23 (erroneously dated 22), 26 (erroneously dated 23) and 31 Aug. 1572.

Bibliothèque publique universitaire de Genève

MS Fr. 90: correspondence of Pierre Forget de Fresnes, France's envoy to the Duke of Savoy.

PRINTED SOURCES

Arbaleste, Charlotte, *Mémoires de Madame de Mornay*, ed. Madame de Witt, 2 vols, Paris, 1868.

Archives ou Correspondance inédite de la maison d'Orange-Nassau, ed. Guillaume Groen Van Prinsterer, 1st series, 8 vols, Leiden, 1835–96.

Archivo Documental Español. Negociaciones con Francia, 1557–1568, 11 vols, Madrid, 1950–60.

Aubigné, Agrippa d', *Histoire Universelle*, ed. André Thierry, Geneva, 11 vols, 1981–2000.

—, *Les Tragiques*, ed. Jean-Raymond Fanlo, 2 vols, Paris, 2003.

Baif, Jean-Antoine de, *Œuvres en rime*, ed. Charles Marty-Laveaux, 5 vols, Paris, 1881–90, reprint Geneva, 1966.

Barbiche, Bernard, ed., *L'Édit de Nantes et ses antécedents*, electronic edition of the edicts of pacification of the wars of religion: http://elec.enc.sorbonne.fr.

Barclay, William, *De regno et regali potestate adversus Buchanan, Brutum, Boucherium et reliquos monarchomaquos libri sex*, Paris, 1600.

Bellaud, Jean-Baptiste, *Oraison funebre du trespas du Roy treschrestien Charles Neufiesme*, Paris, 1574.

Belleforest, François de, *Discours sur l'heur des presages advenuz de nostre temps, signifiantz la felicité de nostre Roy Charles neufiesme tres chrestien*, Paris, 1572.

—, *Discours sur les rebellions auquel est contenu quelle est la misere qui accompagne les trahistres seditieux et rebelles et les recompenses qui les suivent selon leurs rebellions, avec un arraisonnement fort proffitable sur l'infelicité qui suit ordinairemenet les grans*, Paris, 1572.

Benoist, René, *Advertissement du moyen par lequel aisément tous troubles et differens tant touchant la Croix, de laquelle y a si grande et si dangereuse altercation en ceste ville de Paris, que autres concernans la Religion*, Paris, 1571 (reprinted in Simon Goulart, ed., *Memoires de l'Estat de France sous Charles IX*, 2nd ed., Middleburg, 1578, vol. 1, fols 88r–95r).

Bèze, Théodore de, *Correspondance*, ed. Alain Dufour and Béatrice Nicollier, vol. 13 (1572), Geneva, 1988; vol. 14 (1573), and vol. 15 (1575).

—, *Du Droit des magistrats sur leur subjets*, ed. Robert M. Kingdon, Geneva, 1971.

[Bèze, Théodore de], *Histoire ecclésiastique des Églises réformées de France*, Geneva, 1580, ed. Jean-Guillaume Baum and Edouard Cunitz, 3 vols, Paris, 1883–89.

Bodin, Jean, *Les Six Livres de la République*, Paris, Fayard, 1986 (reprint of 1593 edition).

Botzheim, Johann Wilhelm von, 'La Saint-Barthélemy à Orléans racontée par Johann Wilhelm de Botzeim, étudiant allemand, témoin oculaire' [trans. from Latin by Charles Read], in *BSHPF*, 21 (1872), pp. 345–392.

Bouquet, Simon, *Brief et sommaire recueil de ce qui a esté faict et de l'ordre tenuë a la joyeuse et triumphante Entrée de Charles IX de ce nom en sa bonne ville et cité de Paris*, Paris, 1572.

Bourdeille, Pierre de, seigneur de Brantôme, *Œuvres complètes*, ed. Ludovic Lalanne, 11 vols, Paris, 1864–82.

Boutaric, Edgar, 'La Saint-Barthélemy d'après les archives du Vatican', *Bibliothèque de l'École des Chartes*, 23 (1862), pp. 1–27.

Briefve instruction de tout ce qui a passé en la ville de Thoulouze depuis l'emprisonnement faict de ceulx de la nouvelle pretendue religion (Nov. 1572), in Dom Devic and Dom Vaissète, *Histoire générale de Languedoc* (Paris-Toulouse, 2004–6), vol. 12, col. 1028, preuve 316.

Budé, Guillaume, *L'Institution du Prince*, ed. Claude Bontemps, in Claude Bontemps et alii, *Le Prince dans la France des xvie et xviie siècles* (Paris, 1966), pp. 77–139.

Burin, Pierre, *Response à une epistre commencant Seigneur Elvide, où est tracté des massacres faits en France en l'an 1572*, Bâle, 1574.

Cabié, Edmond, *Guerres de Religion dans le Sud-Ouest de la France et principale-*

ment dans le Quercy d'après les papiers des seigneurs de Saint-Sulpice, de 1561 à 1590, 2 vols, Paris-Toulouse, 1906.

Calendar of State Papers, Foreign Series, Reign of Elizabeth, 1566–1577, vol. 3 (1572–1574), London, 1876.

Calendar of State Papers relating to English Affairs, preserved essentially at Rome, in the Vatican Archives and Library, vol. 2, *Elizabeth, 1572–1578*, ed. James M. Rigg, London, 1926.

Calvin, Jean, *Institution de la religion chrestienne*, ed. Jean-Daniel Benoît, 4 vols, Paris, 1961.

Capilupi, Camillo, *Lo Stratagema di Carlo IX, re di Francia, contro gli Ugonotti, rebelli di Dio et suoi*, Roma, 1572; anonymous French trans., *Le Stratagème de Charles IX, Roy de France, contre les Huguenots rebelles à Dieu et luy*, reprinted in Louis Cimber and Charles Danjou, eds, *Archives curieuses de l'Histoire de France*, 1st series, vol. 7 (Paris, 1835), pp. 401–471.

Caumont, Jacques-Nompar de, *Mémoires authentiques de Jacques-Nompar de Caumont, duc de La Force*, ed. Edouard Lelièvre, Marquis de La Grange, 4 vols, Paris, 1843.

Chantelouve, François, *La tragedie de feu Gaspar de Colligni, jadis amiral de France: contenant ce qui advint à Paris le 24 aoust 1572*, [n.p., n.d., 1575], ed. Keith Cameron, Exeter, 1971.

Charpentier, Pierre, *Lettre de Pierre Charpentier jurisconsulte addressée à François Portes Candiois, par laquelle il monstre que les persécutions des Églises de France sont advenues non par la faulte de ceux qui faisoient profession de la religion, mais de ceux qui nourrissoient les factions et conspirations qu'on appelle la Cause*, n.p., n.d. [n.p., n.d., 1572].

Coras, Jean de, *Question politique: s'il est licite aux subjects de capituler avec leur prince*, ed. Robert M. Kingdon, Geneva, 1989.

Correspondance de Philippe II sur les affaires des Pays-Bas, publiée d'après les originaux conservés dans les archives royales de Simancas, ed. Louis Gachard, 5 vols, Brussels, 1848–79.

Correspondance diplomatique de Bertrand de Salignac de La Mothe-Fénelon, ed. Charles Purton Cooper, 7 vols, Paris-London, 1838–40 (vol. 7 is a supplement, subtitled *Lettres adressées de la Cour à l'ambassadeur*).

Correspondance du nonce en France Antonio Maria Salviati (1572–1578), ed. Pierre Hurtubise and Robert Toupin, 2 vols, Rome, École française de Rome, 1975.

Correspondance du roi Charles IX et du sieur de Mandelot, gouverneur de Lyon, pendant l'année 1572, ed. Paulin Paris, Paris, 1830.

Déclaration de Henri de Bourbon aujourd'huy troisiesme Prince du sang de France, prince de Condé, accompaigné de plusieurs gentilshommes de l'une et l'autre Religion, La Rochelle, 1574.

Déclaration de Monseigneur François, fils et frère de Roy, duc d'Alençon, n. p., 1575.

Déclaration et protestation de Monseigneur de Dampville, maréchal de France, [13 Nov. 1574] in Dom Devic and Dom Vaissète, *Histoire générale de Languedoc*, Paris-Toulouse (2004–6), vol. 12, cols 1105–1111, preuve 336.

Désiré, Artus, *La Singerie des Huguenots marmots et guenons de la nouvelle derrision theodobeszienne*, Paris, 1574.

Desportes, Joachim, *Discours sommaire du règne de Charles neufiesme Roy de France Tres-Chrestien, ensemble de sa mort, et d'aucuns de ses derniers propos*, Paris, s.d. [1574].

'Deux lettres de couvent à couvent écrites de Paris pendant le massacre de la Saint-Barthélemy (25 et 26 août) par Joachim Opser de Wyl, jésuite sous-proviseur du collège de Clermont à Paris', *BHSPF*, 8 (1859), pp. 284–294.

Digges, Dudley, ed., *The Compleat Ambassador, or Two Treaties of the Intended Marriage of Queen Elizabeth of glorious memory comprised in Letters of Negociation of sir Francis Walsingham*, London, 1655.

Discours du Roy Henry troisiesme a un personnage d'honneur et de qualité, estant près de Sa Majesté, des causes et motifs de la Sainct Barthelemy, in *Mémoires d'Estat* de Nicolas de Neufville, seigneur de Villeroy (Paris, 1623), pp. 68–69, reprinted in Claude Petitot, ed., *Collection de mémoires relatifs à l'histoire de France*, 1st series, vol. 44 (Paris, 1824), pp. 496–510.

Discours merveilleux de la vie, actions et déportements de Catherine de Médicis [1575 and 1576], ed. Nicole Cazauran, Geneva, 1995.

Discours politiques des diverses puissances establies de Dieu au monde, du gouvernement legitime d'icelles, et de ceux qui y sont assujettis, published in Simon Goulart, *Mémoires de l'Estat de France sous Charles neuviesme*, 2ᵉ ed. (Middleburg, 1578), vol. 3, fols 203v–296r.

Discours sur la mort de Gaspart de Coligny qui fut admiral de France, by I. S. P., Paris, 1572.

Dorat, Jean, *Œuvres poétiques*, ed. Charles Marty-Laveaux, Paris, 1875, reprint Geneva, 1974.

[Du Faur de Pibrac, Guy], *Traduction d'une Epistre latine d'un excellent personnage de ce Royaume*, Paris, 1573.

Du Faur de Pibrac, Guy, *Les Quatrains. Les Plaisirs de la vie rustique et autres poésies*, ed. Loris Petris, Geneva, 2004.

[Du Haillan, Bernard de Girard, seigneur], *Discours sur les causes de l'execution faicte es personnes de ceux qui avoyent conjuré contre le Roy et son Estat*, Paris, 1572.

Du Part, Antoine, *Déploration de la France sur le trespas du Tres Chrestien Roy Charles IX*, Paris, 1574.

Fabre, Pierre, *Response au cruel et pernicieux conseil de Pierre Charpentier, chiquaneur, tendant à fin d'empescher la paix et nous laisser la guerre, traitté dans lequel on apprendra en quel cas il est permis à l'homme chrestien de porter les armes. Traduit du latin*, n.p., n.d. [1575].

Gachard, Louis, *La Bibliothèque nationale à Paris. Notices et extraits des manuscrits qui concernent l'histoire de Belgique*, 2 vols, Brussels, 1875–77.

Gaches, Jacques, *Mémoires sur les guerres de religion à Castres et dans le Languedoc, 1555–1610*, ed. Charles Pradel, Paris, 1879 (reprint Geneva, 1970).

Garrisson, Janine, ed., *L'édit de Nantes*, Biarritz, 1997.

Gassot, Jules, *Sommaire Mémorial (1555–1623)*, ed. Pierre Champion, Paris, 1934.

Geizkofler, Luc, *Mémoires de Luc Geizkofler, tyrolien (1550–1620)*, ed. Edouard Fick, Geneva, 1892.

[Gentillet, Innocent], *Briève Remonstrance à la noblesse de France sur le faict de la Déclaration de Monseigneur le duc d'Alençon*, n. p., 1576.

Gentillet, Innocent, *Discours sur les moyens de bien gouverner et maintenir en bonne paix un Royaume ou autre Principauté [...] contre Nicolas Machiavel Florentin*, 1576, ed. C. Edward Rathé, Geneva, 1968.

Goulart, Simon, ed., *Mémoires de l'Estat de France sous Charles neuviesme*, 2ᵉ ed., 3 vols, Middleburg, 1578.

Haton, Claude, *Mémoires*, ed. Laurent Bourquin, 4 vols, Paris, 2001–7.

[Hotman, François], *De furoribus gallicis, horrenda et indigna amiralii Castillionei, nobilium atque illustrium virorum caede, scelerata ac inaudita piorum strage passim edita per complures civitates [...] Ernesto Varamundo Frisio auctore*, Edinbugh 1573; anonymous French trans., *Histoire des massacres et horribles cruautez commises en la personne de Messire Gaspar de Colligny et autres seigneurs gentils-hommes, le 24 jour d'aoust 1572 et autres suivans. Traduite en françois et augmentée de quelque particularitez omises en l'exemplaire latin*, n.p., 1573.

[Hotman, François], *Gasparis Colinii Castellonii, magni quondam Franciae amiralii, vita*, n.p., 1575; anonymous French trans., *La Vie de messire Gaspar de Colligny, seigneur de Chastillon, admiral de France*, Leiden, 1643, ed. Émile Telle, Geneva, 1987.

Hotman, François, *Francogallia*, n.p., ed. Ralph Giesey and John Salmon, Cambridge, 1972; French trans. attributed to Simon Goulart, *La Gaule françoise de François Hotman jurisconsulte*, Cologne, 1574, ed. Antoine Leca, Aix-Marseille, 1991.

Jeannin, Pierre, *Les Négociations de Monsieur le président Jeannin*, Paris, 1656.

Kervyn de Lettenhove, Joseph, ed., *Documents inédits relatifs à l'histoire du xviᵉ siècle*, Brussels, 1883.

L'Estoile, Pierre de, *Mémoires pour servir à l'histoire de France depuis 1515 jusqu'en 1574*, ed. André Martin, as appendix to l'Estoile, *Journal pour le règne de Henri IV et le début du règne de Louis XIII*, Paris, Gallimard, 1960, pp. 447–483.

—, *Registre-Journal du règne de Henri III*, ed. Madeleine Lazard and Gilbert Schrenck, 6 vols, Geneva, 1992–2003.

L'Histoire de la mort que le R. P. Edmond Campion, Prestre de la compagnie du nom de Jesus, et d'autres ont souffert en Angleterre pour la foy Catholique et Romaine, Paris, 1582.

L'Hospital, Michel, *Discours pour la majorité de Charles IX et trois autres discours*, ed. Robert Descimon, Paris, 1993.

—, *Œuvres complètes*, ed. Pierre Joseph Spiridion Duféy, 5 vols, Paris, 1824–36, reprint Geneva, 1968.

La Ferrière, Hector de, *Le XVIᵉ siècle et les Valois, d'après les documents inédits du British Museum et du Record Office*, Paris, 1879, p. 419.

La Fosse, Jehan de, *Les 'Mémoires' d'un curé de Paris (1557–1590)*, ed. Marc Venard, Geneva, 2004.

La France-Turquie, c'est-à-dire conseils et moyens tenus par les ennemis de la Couronne de France pour reduire le royaume en tel estat que la tyrannie turquesque, Orléans, 1576. (This collection contains the *L'Antipharmaque du chevalier Poncet* [Paris, 1575], and the *Lunettes de christal de roche par lesquels on veoyt clairement le chemin tenu pour subjuguer la France a mesme obeissance que la Turquie*, n.p., n.d.)

La Huguerye, Michel, *Mémoires inédits 1570–1602*, ed. Alphonse de Ruble, 3 vols, Paris, 1877–80.

La Noue, François de, *Discours politiques et militaires*, ed. F. E. Sutcliffe, Geneva, 1967.

La Saint-Barthélemy devant le Sénat de Venise. Relations des ambassadeurs Giovanni Michiel et Sigismondo Cavalli, published by William Martin, Paris, 1872.

Le Politique: Dialogue traitant de la puissance, authorité et du devoir des Princes: des divers gouvernement: jusques où l'on doit supporter la tyrannie: si en une oppression extreme il est loisible aux sujets de prendre les armes pour defendre leur vie et liberté: quand, par qui, et par quel moyen cela se peut et doit faire, published by Simon Goulart, *Mémoires de l'Estat de France sous Charles neuviesme*, 2ᵉ ed. (Middleburg, 1578), vol. 3, fols 61r–116v.

Le Réveille-Matin des François et de leurs voisins, composé par Eusèbe Philadephe Cosmopolite en forme de dialogues, 2 vols, Edinburgh, 1574; facsimile reprint, Paris, 1977.

Le Roy, Louis, *Les Politiques d'Aristote. Traduictes de grec en françois, avec expositions prises des meilleurs auteurs, specialement d'Aristote mesme, et de Platon conferez ensemble*, Paris, 1568.

Le Trespas et obseques du Treschrestien Roy de France, Charles neufiesme de ce nom, Lyon, 1574.

Le Vray Discours des derniers propos memorables et trespas du feu Roy de tres bonne memoire Charles neufiesme, Paris, 1574.

Les Regretz et lamentations de tresillustre et vertueuse princesse Elisabeth d'Autriche sur la mort et trespas du Roy Charles neufiesme son espoux, n'agueres decedé. Par A. de la T. D., Paris, 1574.

Lettres de Catherine de Medicis, ed. Hector de La Ferrière and Gustave Baguenault de Puchesse, 10 vols, Paris, 1880–1909.

Lettres de Charles IX à M. de Fourquevaux, ambassadeur en Espagne, 1565–1572, ed. Charles Douais, Montpellier, 1897.

Lettres du cardinal Charles de Lorraine (1525–-1574), ed. Daniel Cuisiat, Geneva, 1998.

Lettres inédites de Jacques Faye et de Charles Faye, ed. Eugène Halphen, Paris, 1880.

Marguerite de Valois, *Correspondance*, ed. Éliane Viennot, Paris, 1998.

—, *Mémoires et autres écrits*, ed. Éliane Viennot, Paris, 1999.

Memoires de la troisieme guerre civile, 1576, published in Simon Goulart, *Mémoires de l'Estat de France sous Charles neuviesme*, 2ᵉ ed., Middleburg, 1578, vol. 3.

Mémoires des occasions de la guerre, appellée Le Bien-Public, rapportez à l'estat de la guerre présente, n. p., 1567.

Mémoires et instructions pour les ambassadeurs, ou lettres et négociations de Walsingham, ministre et secrétaire d'État sous Élisabeth, reine d'Angleterre, traduit de l'anglois, Amsterdam, 1700.

Mergey, Jean de, *Mémoires*, ed. Michaud and Poujoulat, *Mémoires pour servir à l'histoire de France*, vol. 9 (Paris, 1838), pp. 557–580.

Mieck, Ilja, ed., *Toleranzdikt und Bartholomäusnacht. Französiche Politik und europäische Diplomatie, 1570–1572*, Göttingen, 1969.

Monluc, Blaise de, *Commentaires, 1521–1576*, ed. Paul Courteault, Paris, 1962.

[Monluc, Jean de], *Vera et brevis descriptio tumultus postremi Gallici Lutetiani*, Cracow, 1573.

Monluc, Jean de, *Harangue faicte et prononcée de la part du Roy Très-Chrestien le dixième jour du mois d'avril 1573*, Paris, 1573.

—, *Défense pour maintenir le tresillustre Duc d'Anjou contre les calomnies de quelques malveillans*, in Simon Goulart, *Mémoires de l'Estat de France sous Charles neuviesme*, 2ᵉ ed. (Middleburg, 1578), vol. 2, fols 61v–69v.

Montaigne, Michel de, *Les Essais*, ed. Pierre Villey, 3 vols, Paris, 1922–23; reprint Paris, 1988.

Négociations diplomatiques de la France avec la Toscane, ed. Abel Desjardins, 6 vols, Paris, 1859–86.

Pape, Jacques, *Mémoires de Jacques Pape, seigneur de Saint-Auban*, ed. Michaud and Poujoulat, Paris, vol. 11 (Paris, 1838), pp. 497–514.

Pasquier, Étienne, *Les Lettres*, in *Œuvres* (Amsterdam, 1723), vol. 2, reprint Geneva, 1971.

—, *Lettres historiques pour les années 1556–1594*, ed. Dorothy Thickett, Geneva, 1966.

—, *Les Recherches de la France*, ed. Marie-Madeleine Fragonard and François Roudaut, 3 vols, Paris, 1996.

Pithou de Chamgobert, Nicolas, *Chronique de Troyes et de la Champagne (1524–1594)*, ed. Pierre-Eugène Leroy, 3 vols, Reims, 1998–2000.

Portes, François, *Response de François Portus Candiot aux lettres diffamatoires de Pierre Charpentier advocat. Pour l'innocence des fidèles serviteurs de Dieu et obeissans subjets du Roy, massacrez le 24. jour d'Aoust 1572, appellez factieux par ce plaidereau. Traducte nouvellement de latin en françois*, n.p., 1574.

Recueil des choses memorables avenues en France sous le regne de Henri II, François II, Charles IX, Henri III et Henri IV [sometimes attributed to Jean de Serres, but more probably to Simon Goulart], 1595; 2ᵉ ed., n.p., 1598.

Recueil général des anciennes lois françaises, ed. F. A. Isambert, A. J. Jourdan and Decrusy, 29 vols (Paris, 1821–33), vol. 14 (July 1559–May 1574).

Registres des délibérations du Bureau de la Ville de Paris, 15 vols (Paris, 1883–1921); vol. 6, *1568–1572*, ed. Paul Guérin [1891], and vol. 7, *1572–1576*, ed. François Bonnardot, [1893].

[Régnier de la Planche, Louis], *Histoire de l'Estat de France, tant de la république que de la religion, sous le règne de François II* (1576), ed. Jean-Alexandre Buchon (Paris, 1836), pp. 203–421.

'Relation de la journée de la Saint-Barthélemy; manuscrit trouvé dans les archives épiscopales de Wiener-Neustadt (Autriche)', *Bulletin des sciences historiques, antiquité, philologie*, 6 (1826), pp. 226–231.

Relation du massacre de la Saint-Barthélemy (from Simon Goulart, *Mémoires de l'Estat de France sous Charles neufiesme* vol. 1), in Louis Cimber and Charles Danjou, eds, *Archives curieuses de l'histoire de France*, 1st series, vol. 7 (Paris, 1835), pp. 1–76.

Résolution claire et facile sur la question tant de fois faicte de la prise des armes par les inférieurs, Bâle, 1575; expanded edition, Reims, 1577.

Response de Stanislaus Elvidius [Joachim Camerarius?] *a l'epistre d'un certain excellent personnage touchant les affaires de France*, 1573, published by Simon Goulart, *Mémoires de l'Estat de France sous Charles neuviesme*, 2ᵉ ed. (Middleburg, 1578), vol. 1, fols 636r–655r.

Response de Wolfgang Prisbachius polonois à une harangue soustenant les massacres et brigandages commis en France, French trans. of Latin original published in La Rochelle, 1573, published by Simon Goulart, *Mémoires de l'Estat de France sous Charles neuviesme*, 2ᵉ ed. (Middleburg, 1578), vol. 2, fols 28v–47v.

Response de Zacharie Furnesterus, soustenant l'innocence et justice de tant de milliers de personnes massacrées au royaume de France, French trans. of original Latin published in 1573, published by Simon Goulart, *Mémoires de l'Estat de France sous Charles neuviesme*, 2ᵉ ed. (Middleburg,1578), vol. 2, fols 70r–95r.

Reuss, Rodolphe, ed., 'Un nouveau récit de la Saint-Barthélemy par un bourgeois de Strasbourg', *BSHPF*, 22 (1873), pp. 374–381.

Rigal, Jean-Louis, ed., *Mémoires d'un calviniste de Millau* (*Archives historiques du Rouergue*, vol. 2), Rodez, 1911.

Ronsard, Pierre de, *Le Tombeau du feu Roy Tres-Chrestien Charles IX, prince tres-debonnaire, tres-vertueux et tres-eloquent*, Paris, n. d. (1574).

—, *Discours des misères de ce temps* et *Continuation du Discours des misères de ce temps*, in *Œuvres complètes*, ed. Jean Céard, Daniel Ménager and Michel Simonin (Paris, 1994), pp. 991–1006.

Sassetti, Tomasso, *Brieve Raccontamiento del gran macello fatto nella città di Parigi il vigesimo quarto giorno d'agosto*, published by John Tedeschi, in Alfred Soman, ed., *The Massacre of St. Bartholomew. Reappraisals and documents* (La Haye, 1974), pp. 112–152.

Satyre Ménippée, ou vertu du Catholicon d'Espagne, ed. Charles Read, Paris, Flammarion, 1892.

Saulx-Tavannes, Jean de, *Mémoires de Gaspard de Saulx-Tavannes*, ed. Michaud and Poujoulat, vol. 8 (Paris, 1838), pp. 19–434.

Serres, Jean de, *Commentariorum de statu religionis et reipublicae in regno Galliae*, 1571–72 (n. p); expanded edition 1575, 3 parts in one vol.

Sorbin, Arnaud, *Histoire contenant un abrégé de la vie, mœurs, et vertus du Roy Tres-chrestien et debonnaire Charles IX, vrayement piteux, propugnateur de la Foy Catholique et amateur des bons esprits*, Paris, 1574.

—, *Le Vray resveille-Matin des calvinistes et publicains François: où est amplement discouru de l'auctorité des Princes, et du devoir des sujets envers eux*, Paris, 1576.

—, *Oraison funebre du tres hault, puissant et tres chrestien Roy de France, Charles IX, piteux et debonnaire, propugnateur de la Foy Catholique et amateur des bons esprits, prononcée en l'Eglise Nostre-Dame en Paris, le XII. de juillet M.D.LXXIIII*, Paris, 1574.

Stegmann, André, ed., *Edits des guerres de Religion*, Paris, 1979.

Sully, Maximilien de Béthune, duc de, *Œconomies royales*, eds David Buisseret and Bernard Barbiche, 2 vols, Paris, 1970–88.

Sureau, Hugues, dit des Rosiers, *Confession et recognoissance de Hugues Sureau dict du Rosier touchant sa cheute en la Papauté et les horribles scandales par luy commis*, Heidelberg, 1573.

Syrueilh, François de, *Journal, 1568–1585, Archives historiques du département de la Gironde*, 13 (1871–72), pp. 244–357.

Taix, Guillaume de, *Journal de Guillaume de Taix*, published by Lalourcé and Duval, *Recueil des pièces originales et authentiques concernant la tenue des États généraux* (Paris, 1789), vol. 2, pp. 269–271.

Thou, Jacques-Auguste, *Histoire universelle depuis 1543 jusqu'en 1607, traduite sur l'edition latine de Londres*, 16 vols, London, 1734.

—, *Mémoires de Jacques-Auguste de Thou, depuis 1553 jusqu'en 1601*, ed. Claude Petitot, vol. 38, Paris, 1823.

Tocsain contre les massacreurs (1577), in Louis Cimber and Charles Danjou, eds, *Archives curieuses de l'histoire de France*, 1st series, vol. 7 (Paris, 1835), pp. 77–133.

Touchard, Jean, *Allegresse chrestienne de l'heureux succès des guerres de ce Royaulme et de la justice de Dieu contre les rebelles au Roy*, Paris, 1572.

Turenne, Henri de La Tour d'Auvergne, vicomte, later duc de Bouillon, *Mémoires*, ed. Gustave Baguenault de Puchesse, Paris, 1901.

Verstegan, Richard, *Théâtre des cruautés des hérétiques de notre temps* [1587], ed. Frank Lestringant, Paris, 1995.

Vigor, Simon, *Sermons catholiques sur les Dimenches et festes depuis l'octave de Pasques jusques à l'Advent*, 2 vols, Paris, 1587.

Vindiciae contra tyrannos: sive, de Principis in Populum, Populique in Principem, legitima potestate, Stephano Junio Bruto Celta auctore, Edinburgh, 1579. Anonymous French trans., *De la puissance legitime du Prince sur le peuple et du peuple sur le Prince*, n.p. There is a critical ed. by Arlette Jouanna, Jean Perrin, Marguerite Soulié, André Tournon and Henri Weber, Geneva, 1979.

Viret, Pierre Viret, *Le Monde à l'empire et le monde démoniacle*, Geneva, 1550; 1561 edition also Geneva.

Voisin de la Popelinière, Henri Lancelot, *L'Histoire de France, enrichie des plus notables occurrances survenues ez provinces de l'Europe et pays voisins, depuis l'an 1550 jusques à ces temps*, 2 vols, n.p., 1581.

Weiss, Nathanël, 'L'Amiral et la Saint-Barthélemy, lettres et pièces inédites (1572)', *BSHPF*, 36 (1887), pp. 412–418.

—, 'La Saint-Barthélemy. Nouveaux textes et notes bibliographiques', *BSHPF*, 43, (1894), pp. 426–444.

Secondary works

Anon., 'Les victimes de la Saint-Barthélemy à Paris. Essai d'une topographie et d'une nomenclature des massacres d'après les documents contemporains', *BSHPF*, 10 (1860), pp. 34–44.

Acerra, Martine and Martinière, Guy, eds, *Coligny, les protestants et la mer*, Paris, 1997.

L'Amiral de Coligny et son temps, Paris, 1974.

Angelo, Vladimir, *Les Curés de Paris au xvie siècle*, Paris, 2005.

Babelon, Jean-Pierre, *Henri IV*, Paris, 1982.

Baguenault de la Puchesse, Gustave, *Jean de Morvillier, évêque d'Orléans, garde des sceaux de France*, Paris, 1870.

Balsamo, Jean, *Les Rencontres des Muses: italianisme et anti-italianisme dans les lettres françaises de la fin du xvie siècle*, Geneva, 1992.

Baulant, Michèle and Meuvret, Jean, *Prix des céréales extraits de la mercuriale de Paris (1520–1698)*, Paris, 1960, vol. 1.

Baury, Roger, 'Célébration de la paix de Vervins et propagande royale', in Jean-François Labourdette, Jean-Pierre Poussou and Marie-Catherine Vignal, eds, *Le Traité de Vervins* (Paris, 2000), pp. 347–372.

Benedict, Philip, 'The Saint Bartholomew's massacres in the provinces', *The Historical Journal*, 21 (1978), pp. 205–225.

—, *Rouen during the wars of religion*, Cambridge, 1981.

—, *The Huguenot population of France, 1600–1685. The demographic fate and customs of a religious minority*, Philadelphia, Transactions of the American Philosophical Society, 1991.

Boltanski, Ariane, *Les Ducs de Nevers et l'état royal. Genèse d'un compromis (vers 1550–vers 1620)*, Geneva, 2006.

Bordier, Henri-Léonard, *La Saint-Barthélemy et la critique moderne*, Geneva, 1879.

Boucher, Jacqueline, *La Cour de Henri III*, Rennes, 1986.

—, *Société et mentalités autour de Henri III*, Paris, 2007.

Bourgeon, Jean-Louis, 'Les légendes ont la vie dure: à propos de la Saint-Barthélemy et de quelques livres récents', *RHMC*, 34 (1987), pp. 102–116.

—, 'Une source sur la Saint-Barthélemy: l'*Histoire de Monsieur de Thou* relue et décryptée', *BSHPF*, 124 (1988), pp. 499–537.

—, 'Pour une histoire, enfin, de la Saint-Barthélemy', *RH*, 282 (1989), pp. 83–142

—, 'La Fronde parlementaire à la veille de la Saint-Barthélemy', *Bibliothèque de l'Ecole des chartes*, 148 (1990), pp. 17–89.

—, *L'Assassinat de Coligny*, Geneva, 1992.

—, 'Quand la foi était révolutionnaire: les sermons d'un curé parisien, Simon Vigor, en 1570–1572', in *Mélanges offerts à Pierre Chaunu. La vie, la mort, la foi, le temps* (Paris, 1993), pp. 471–484.

—, *Charles IX devant la Saint-Barthélemy*, Geneva, 1995.

Bourquin, Laurent, *Noblesse seconde et pouvoir en Champagne aux xvie et xviie siècles*, Paris, 1994.

Braudel, Fernand, *La Mediterranée et le monde mediterranéen à l'époque de Philippe II*, 2nd ed., 2 vols, Paris 1966. English trans. *The Mediterranean and the mediterranean world in the age of Philip II*, 2 vols, London, 1973.

Brunet, Serge, 'Anatomie des réseaux ligueurs dans le Sud-Ouest de la France (vers 1562–vers 1610)', in Nicole Lemaître, ed., *Religion et politique dans les sociétés du Midi* (Paris, 2002), pp. 153–191.

—, *De l'Espagnol dedans le ventre!' Les catholiques du Sud-Ouest de la France face à la Réforme (vers 1540–1589)*, Paris, 2007.

Carroll, Stuart, *Noble power during the wars of religion. The Guise affinity and the Catholic cause in Normandy*, Cambridge, 1998.

Cassan, Michel, *Le Temps des guerres de religion. Le cas du Limousin (vers 1530–vers 1630)*, Paris, 1996.

Cazauran, Nicole, 'Échos d'un massacre', in Marguerite Soulié and Robert Aulotte, eds, *La Littérature de la Renaissance. Mélanges d'histoire et de critique littéraire offerts à Henri Weber* (Geneva, 1984), pp. 239–261.

Céard, Jean, 'Les visages de la royauté en France', in Emmanuel Le Roy Ladurie, ed., *Les Monarchies* (Paris, 1986), pp. 73–89.

Champion, Pierre, *Charles IX. La France et le contrôle de l'Espagne*, 2 vols, Paris, 1939.

Châtellier, Louis, *Le Catholicisme en France, 1500–1650*, vol. 1: *le xvie siècle*, Paris, 1995.

Chaunu, Pierre, 'L'État', in Fernand Braudel and Ernest Labrousse, eds, *Histoire économique et sociale de la France*, vol. 1 (Paris, 1977), tome I, pp. 9–228.

Chevallier, Pierre, *Henri III*, Paris, 1985.

Christin, Olivier, *Une révolution symbolique. L'iconoclasme huguenot et la reconstruction catholique*, Paris, 1991.

—, *La Paix de religion. L'autonomisation de la raison politique au xvie siècle*, Paris, 1997.

—, 'Amis, frères et concitoyens. Ceux qui refusèrent la Saint-Barthélemy (1572)', *Cahiers de la Villa Gillet*, 11 (Sept., 2000), pp. 71–94.

Christol, Marguerite, 'La dépouille de Gaspard de Coligny', *BSHPF*, 111 (1965), pp. 136–140.

Church, William Farr, *Constitutional thought in sixteenth-century France*, Cambridge, Mass., 1941.

Cloulas, Ivan, *Henri II*, Paris, 1985.

—, *Catherine de Medicis*, Paris, 1979.

Cocula, Anne-Marie, *Brantôme. Amour et gloire au temps des Valois*, Paris, 1986.

—, 'Regard sur les événements nocturnes des guerres de religion', in Dominique Bertrand, ed., *Penser la nuit, xve–xviie siècles* (Paris, 2003), pp. 464–485.

Collins, James B., 'La guerre de la Ligue et le bien public', in Jean-François Labourdette, Jean-Pierre Poussou and Marie-Catherine Vignal, eds, *Le Traité de Vervins* (Paris, 2000), pp. 81–95.

Constant, Jean-Marie, *Les Guise*, Paris, 1984.

—, *Les Français pendant les guerres de religion*, Paris, 2002.

Cornette, Joël, *Le Roi de guerre. Essai sur la souveraineté dans la France du grand siècle*, Paris, 1993.

Cosandey, Fanny and Descimon, Robert, *L'Absolutisme en France. Histoire et historiographie*, Paris, 2002.

Crété, Liliane, *Coligny*, Paris, 1985.

Crouzet, Denis, *Les Guerriers de Dieu. La violence au temps des troubles de religion, vers 1525–vers 1610*, 2 vols, Seyssel, 1990.

—, 'Désir de mort et puissance absolue de Charles VIII à Henri IV', *Revue de Synthèse*, (1991), pp. 423–441.

—, *La Nuit de la Saint-Barthélemy. Un rêve perdu de la Renaissance*, Paris, 1994.

—, 'Charles IX, ou le roi sanglant malgré lui?', *BSHPF* (1995), pp. 323–339.

—, 'Capital identitaire et engagement religieux: aux origines de l'engagement militant de la maison de Guise, ou le tournant des années 1524–1525', in Joël Fouilleron, Guy Le Thiec and Henri Michel, eds, *Sociétés et idéologies des Temps modernes. Hommage à Arlette Jouanna*, 2 vols (Montpellier, 1996), vol. 2, pp. 573–589.

—, 'La nuit de la Saint-Barthélemy: confirmations et compléments', in Chantal Grell and Arnaud Ramière de Fortanier, eds, *Le Second ordre: l'idéal nobiliaire. Hommage à Ellery Schalk* (Paris, 1999), pp. 55–81.

—, *La Sagesse et le malheur. Michel de L'Hospital, chancelier de France*, Seyssel, 2002.

—, 'Le devoir d'obéissance à Dieu: imaginaire du pouvoir royal', *Nouvelle Revue du XVIe Siècle*, 21 (2004), pp. 19–47 (special thematic issue: *Métaphysique et politique de l'obéissance dans la France du xvie siècle*), pp. 19–47.

—, *Le Haut Cœur de Catherine de Medicis. Une raison politique aux temps de la Saint-Barthélemy*, Paris, 2005.

Dareste, Rodolphe, 'François Hotman. Sa vie et sa correspondance', *RH*, 2 (1876), pp. 1–59 and 367–435.

Daubresse, Sylvie, *Le Parlement de Paris ou la Voix de la raison (1559–1589)*, Geneva, 2005.

Daussy, Hugues, *Les Huguenots et le roi. Le combat politique de Philippe Duplessis-Mornay*, Geneva, 2002.

Davies, Joan Margaret, 'Languedoc and its governeur. Henri de Montmorency-Damville, 1563–1589', unpublished Ph.D dissertation, University of London, 1974.

Davis, Natalie Zemon, *Society and culture in early modern France*, Stanford, Calif., 1975.

Decrue, Francis, *Le Parti des politiques au lendemain de la Saint-Barthélemy*, Paris, 1892.

Delaborde, Jules, *Gaspard de Coligny, amiral de France*, 3 vols, Paris, 1879–82.

Delumeau, Jean, *Le Péché et la peur*, Paris, 1983.

—, *Rassurer et protéger*, Paris, 1989.

Delumeau, Jean, and Wanegffelen, Thierry, *Naissance et affirmation de la Réforme*, 8e ed., Paris, 1997.

Denis, Anne, 'La Saint-Barthélemy vue et jugée par les Italiens', in Danielle Boillet and Corinne Lucas-Fiorato, eds, *L'Actualité et sa mise en écriture dans l'Italie de la Renaissance* (Paris, Centre interuniversitaire de recherches sur la Renaissance italienne, vol. 26, 2005), pp. 202–225.

Descimon, Robert, 'Solidarité communautaire et sociabilité armée: les compagnies de la milice bourgeoise à Paris (xvie–xviie siècles)', in Françoise Thélamon, ed., *Sociabilité, pouvoirs et société* (Rouen, 1987), pp. 599–610.

—, 'Paris on the eve of Saint Bartholomew: Taxation, privilege and social geography', in Philip Benedict, ed., *Cities and social change in early modern France* (London, 1989), pp. 69–104.

Diefendorf, Barbara, *Paris city councillors in the sixteenth century: the politics of patrimony*, Princeton, 1983.

—, 'Prologue to a massacre: popular unrest in Paris, 1557–1572', *American Historical Review*, 90 (1985), pp. 1067–91.

—, 'Les divisions religieuses dans les familles parisiennes avant la Saint-Barthélemy', *HES*, 7 (1988), pp. 55–77.

—, *Beneath the cross. Catholics and Huguenots in sixteenth-century Paris*, New York and Oxford, 1991.

—, 'La Saint-Barthélemy et la bourgeoisie parisienne', *HES*, 17 (1998), pp. 341–352.

—, *The Saint Bartholomew's Day massacre. A brief history with documents*, Boston and New York, 2009.

Dubost, Jean-François, *La France italienne, xvie–xviie siècle*, Paris, 1997.

Dufour, Alain, 'Le colloque de Poissy', in *Mélanges d'histoire du xvie siècle offerts à Henri Meylan* (Geneva, 1970), pp. 127–137.

—, *Théodore de Bèze, poète et théologien*, Geneva, 2006.

El Kenz, David, *Les Bûchers du roi. La culture protestante des martyrs (1523–1572)*, Seyssel, 1997.

—, 'La victime catholique au temps des guerres de religion. La sacralisation du prêtre', in Benoît Garnot, ed., *Les Victimes, des oubliées de l'Histoire?* (Rennes, 2000), pp. 192–199.

—, 'La Saint-Barthélemy à Dijon: un non-événement?', *Annales de Bourgogne*, 74 (2002), pp. 139–157.

—, 'Les usages subversifs du martyre dans la France des troubles de religion: de la parole au geste', *Revue des sciences humaines*, 269 (2003) [*Martyrs et martyrologes*, eds Frank Lestringant and Pierre-François Moreau], pp. 33–51.

El Kenz, David, ed., *Le Massacre, objet d'histoire*, Paris, 2005.

Engammare, Max, *L'Ordre du temps. L'invention de la ponctualité au xvie siècle*, Geneva, 2004.

Erlanger, Philippe, *Le Massacre de la Saint-Barthélemy*, Paris, 1960. English trans. *The Saint Bartholomew's night*, London 1962.

Fazy, Henri, *La Saint-Barthélemy et Genève, étude historique* (*Mémoires de l'Institut national genevois*, vol. 14). Geneva, 1879.

Foa, Jérémie, 'Making peace: the commissions for enforcing the pacification edicts in the reign of Charles IX (1560–1574)', *French History*, 18 (2004), pp. 256–274.

Forestié, Edouard, *Un Capitaine gascon du xvie siècle: Corbeyran de Cardaillac-Sarlabous*, Paris, 1897.

Forsyth Elliott, Christopher, *La Justice de Dieu. Les Tragiques d'Agrippa d'Aubigné et la Réforme protestante en France au xvie siècle*, Paris, 2005.

Fragonard, Marie-Madeleine, 'L'établissement de la raison d'état et la Saint-Barthélemy', in *Miroirs de la Raison d'état (Cahiers de du Centre de recherches historiques*, no 20 1998), pp. 49–65.

—, *La Pensée religieuse d'Agrippa d'Aubigné et son expression*, 1981, rev. ed., Paris, 2004.

Froeschlé-Chopard, Marie-Hélène, *Dieu pour tous et Dieu pour soi. Histoire des confréries et de leurs images à l'époque moderne*, Paris, 2007.

Garrisson, Janine, *Tocsin pour un massacre, ou la saison des Saint-Barthélemy*, Paris, 1968.

—, *La Saint-Barthélemy*, Paris, 1987.

—, *Protestants du Midi, 1559–1598*, Toulouse, 1980, reprint. 1991.

—, *Les Derniers Valois*, Paris, 2001.

Gauchet, Marcel, *Le Désenchantement du monde: une histoire politique de la religion*, Paris, 1985. English trans., *The Disenchantment of the world*, Princeton, 1997.

Gelderen, Martin van, *The Political thought of the Dutch revolt, 1555–1590*, Cambridge, 1992.

Germa-Romann, Hélène, *Du 'bel mourir' au 'bien mourir'. Le sentiment de la mort chez les gentilshommes français (1515–1643)*, Geneva, 2001.

Gigon, Stéphane-Claude, *La Troisième guerre de religion. Jarnac-Moncontour (1568–1569)*, Paris, 1911.

Girard, René, *La Violence et le Sacré*, Paris, 1972. English trans., *Violence and the sacred*, Baltimore, 1977.

Greengrass, Mark, 'War, politics and religion in Languedoc during the government of Henri de Montmorency-Damville (1574–1610)', unpublished D.Phil dissertation, University of Oxford, 1979.

—, 'Functions and limits of political clientelism in France before Cardinal Richelieu', in Neithard Bulst, Robert Descimon and Alain Guerreau, eds, *L'État ou le roi. Les fondations de la modernité monarchique en France (xive–xviie siècles)* (Paris, 1996), pp. 69–82.

—, 'Amnistie et oubliance: un discours politique autour des édits de pacification pendant les guerres de religion', in Paul Mironneau and Isabelle Péray-Clottes, eds, *Paix des armes, paix des âmes* (Paris, 2000), pp. 113–123.

—, 'Pluralism and equality: the peace of Monsieur, May 1576', in Keith Cameron, Mark Greengrass and Penny Roberts, eds, *The Adventure of religious pluralism in early modern France* (Bern, 2000), pp. 45–63.

Greffe, Florence and Lothe, José, *La vie, les livres et les lectures de Pierre de L'Estoile*, Paris, 2004.

Halévi, Ran, 'Le testament de la royauté. L'éducation politique de Louis XVI', in Ran Halévi, ed., *Le Savoir du Prince* (Paris, 2002), pp. 311–361.

Haran, Alexandre Y., *Le Lys et le globe: messianisme dynastique et rêve impérial en France aux xvie et xviie siècles*, Seyssel, 2000.

Hauser, Henri, *François de La Noue*, Paris, 1892.

—, 'Le père Edmond Auger et le massacre de Bordeaux, 1572', BSHPF, 60 (1911), pp. 289–306.

—, *Les Sources de l'histoire de France, xvie siècle*, 4 vols (Paris, 1912), vol. 3, *Les guerres de Religion (1559–1589)*.

Heller, Henry, *Anti-Italianism in sixteenth-century France*, Toronto, 2002.

Higman, Francis, *La Diffusion de la Réforme en France, 1520–1565*, Geneva, 1992.

Hillairet, Jacques, *Dictionnaire historique des rues de Paris*, 2 vols, 10th ed., Paris, 1997.

Holt, Mack P., *The Duke of Anjou and the politique struggle during the wars of religion*, Cambridge, 1986.

—, 'Attitudes of the French nobility at the Estates-General of 1576', SCJ, 18 (1987), pp. 489–504.

—, *The French wars of religion, 1562–1629*, Cambridge, 1995.

Huchard, Cécile, *D'Encre et de sang. Simon Goulart et la Saint-Barthélemy*, Paris, 2007.

Jacquiot, Josèphe, 'Medailles et jetons commémorant la Saint-Barthélemy', *Revue d'histoire littéraire de la France* (1973), pp. 784–793.

Jouanna, Arlette, *Le Devoir de révolte. La noblesse française et la gestation de l'État moderne, 1559–1661*, Paris, 1989.

—, 'Être "bon Français" au temps des guerres de religion: du citoyen au sujet', in

Ouzi Élyada and Jacques Le Brun, eds, *Conflits politiques, controverses religieuses. Essais d'histoire européennes aux 16ᵉ–18ᵉ siècles* (Paris, 2002), pp. 19–32.

—, '"Capituler avec son prince": la question de la contractualisation de la loi au xviᵉ siècle', in Paul-Alexis Mellet, ed., *'Et de sa bouche sortait un glaive.' Les monarchomaques au xviᵉ siècle* (Geneva, 2006), pp. 131–143.

Jouanna, Arlette, Boucher, Jacqueline, Biloghi, Dominique and Le Thiec, Guy, *Histoire et dictionnaire des guerres de religion*, Paris, 1998.

Joutard, Philippe, Estèbe [Garrison], Janine, Labrousse, Élisabeth and Lecuir, Jean, *La Saint-Barthélemy ou les résonances d'un massacre*, Neuchâtel, 1976.

Kantorowicz, Ernst, *The King's two bodies. A study in medieval political theology*, Princeton, 1957. French trans., *Les Deux corps du roi. Essai sur la théologie politique au Moyen Âge*, Paris, 1989.

Kelley, Donald R., *The Beginning of ideology: Consciousness and society in the French reformation*, Cambridge, 1981.

Kervyn de Lettenhove, Joseph, *Les Huguenots et les gueux*, 6 vols, Bruges, 1883–85.

Kingdon, Robert M., *Myths about the St. Bartholomew's day massacres, 1572–1576*, Cambridge, Mass., 1988.

—, *Church and society in Reformation Europe*, London, 1985.

Knecht, Robert Jean, *Catherine de' Medici*, London, 1998. French trans., *Catherine de Medicis (1519–1589)*, Brussels, 2003.

—, *The French civil wars, 1562–1598*, Harlow, 2000.

Konnert, Mark, *Civic agendas as religious passion: Châlons-sur-Marne during the French wars of religion*, Kirksville, Miss., 1997.

—, 'La tolérance religieuse en Europe aux xviᵉ et xviiᵉ siècles. Une approche issue de la psychologie sociale et de la sociologie', in Thierry Wanegffelen, ed., *De Michel de L'Hospital à l'edit de Nantes. Politique et religion face aux églises* (Clermont-Ferrand, 2002), pp. 97–113.

Krynen, Jacques, *L'Empire du roi. Idées et croyances politiques en France, xiiiᵉ–xvᵉ siècle*, Paris, 1993.

La Ferrière, Hector de, 'Les dernières conspirations du règne de Charles IX', *Revue des questions historiques*, 48 (1890), pp. 421–470.

—, *La Saint-Barthélemy, la veille, le jour, le lendemain*, Paris, 1892.

Lazard, Madeleine, *Pierre de Bourdeille, seigneur de Brantôme*, Paris, 1995.

Le Gall, Jean-Marie, *Le Mythe de Saint Denis entre Renaissance et Révolution*, Seyssel, 2007.

Le Roux, Nicolas, *La Faveur du roi. Mignons et courtisans au temps des derniers Valois (vers 1547–vers 1589)*, Seyssel, 2000.

—, 'La Saint-Barthélemy des Italiens n'aura pas lieu: un discours envoyé à Catherine de Medicis en 1573', in Bernard Barbiche, Jean-Pierre Poussou and Alain Tallon, eds, *Pouvoirs, contestations et comportements dans l'Europe moderne. Mélanges en l'honneur du professeur Yves-Marie Bercé* (Paris, 2005), pp. 165–183.

—, *Un Régicide au nom de Dieu. L'Assassinat d'Henri III*, Paris, 2006.

—, *Les Guerres de religion, 1559–1629*, Paris, 2009.

Le Roy Ladurie, Emmanuel, *L'État royal de Louis XII à Henri IV, 1460–1610*, Paris, 1987. English trans., *The Royal French state 1460–1610*, Oxford, 1994.

Lecoq, Anne-Marie, *François 1ᵉʳ imaginaire*, Paris, 1987.

Lemaitre, Nicole, *Saint Pie V*, Paris, 1994.

Lestringant, Frank, *Agrippa d'Aubigné. Les Tragiques*, Paris, 1986.

—, *La Cause des martyrs dans les Tragiques d'Agrippa d'Aubigné*, Mont-de-Marsan, 1991.

—, *Lumière des martyrs. Essai sur le martyre au siècle des réformes*, Paris, 2004.

Levene, Mark and Roberts, Penny, eds, *The massacre in history*, New York, 1999.

Manesch, Scott M., *Theodore Beza and the quest for peace in France, 1572–1598*, Leiden, 2000.

Mariéjol, Jean-H., *La Réforme et la Ligue. L'edit de Nantes (1559–1598)* (*Histoire de France des origines à la Révolution*, ed. Ernest Lavisse, vol. 6), Paris, 1904, reprint Paris, 1983.

Mastellone, Salvo, *Venalità e machiavellismo in Francia, 1572–1610: all'origine della mentalità politica borghese*, Florence, 1972.

Mellet, Paul-Alexis, ed., *'Et de sa bouche sortait un glaive.' Les monarchomaques au xvie siècle*, Geneva, 2006.

—, *Les Traités monarchomaques. Confusion des temps, résistance armée et monarchie parfaite (1560–1600)*, Geneva, 2007.

Mieck, Ilja, 'Die Bartholomäusnacht als Forschungsproblem: Kritische Bestandsaufnahme und neue Aspekte', *Historische Zeitschrift*, 216 (1973), pp. 73–110.

Monod, Henri, 'Un document sur la Saint-Barthélemy', *Revue de Paris*, 4 (1908), pp. 770–794.

—, 'La version du duc d'Anjou sur la Saint-Barthélemy', *RH*, 101 (1909), pp. 316–325.

Mousnier, Roland, *L'Assassinat d'Henri IV. Le problème du tyrannicide et l'affermissement de la monarchie absolue*, Paris, 1964.

Muchembled, Robert, *Passions de femmes au temps de la reine Margot, 1553–1615*, Paris, 2003.

Nakam, Géralde, *Au lendemain de la Saint-Barthélemy. Jean de Léry, Histoire memorable du siège de Sancerre*, Paris, 1975.

—, *Les Essais de Montaigne, miroir et procès de leur temps. Témoignage historique et création littéraire*, revised ed., Paris, 2001.

—, 'Le rire de Coligny', in Géralde Nakam, *Chemins de la Renaissance* (Paris, 2005), pp. 193–212.

Nicollier, Béatrice, *Hubert Languet, 1518–1581. Un réseau politique international, de Melanchthon à Guillaume d'Orange*, Geneva, 1995.

Noailles, Emmanuel de, *Henri de Valois et la Pologne en 1572*, 2 vols, Paris, 1867.

Pablo, Jean de, 'Contribution à l'étude de l'histoire des institutions militaires huguenots. II. L'armée huguenote entre 1562 et 1573', *Archiv für Reformationgeschichte*, 48 (1957), pp. 192–216.

Paz, Julián, *Archivo general de Simancas. Catálogo IV. Secretaría de Estado (Capitulaciones con Francia y negociaciones diplomáticas de los embajadores de España en aquella corte, seguido de un serie cronologica de éstos)*, vol. 1 (1225–1714), Madrid, 1814.

Peschot, Bernard, 'Alexandre de Bessot de Lamothe (1823–1897) et les protestants du Midi', in Joël Fouilleron and Henri Michel, eds, *Mélanges Michel Péronnet*, vol. 2, *La Réforme*, (Montpellier, 2003), pp. 313–332.

Petris, Loris, *La Plume et la Tribune. Michel de L'Hospital et ses discours (1559–*

1562), Geneva, 2002.

Picot, Georges, *Histoire des États généraux*, 2ᵉ ed., 3 vols, Paris, 1888.

Pineaux, Jacques, *La Poésie des protestants de langue française (1559–1598)*, Paris, 1971.

Poncet, Olivier, *Pomponne de Bellièvre (1529–1607). Un homme d'état au temps des guerres de religion*, Paris, 1998.

Poujol, Jacques, 'Étymologies légendaires des mots France et Gaule pendant la Renaissance', *Publications of the Modern Language Association of America*, 72 (1957), pp. 900–914.

Pradel, Charles, 'Un marchand de Paris au xviᵉ siècle (1560–1588)', *Mémoires de l'Académie des sciences, inscriptions et belles-lettres de Toulouse*, 9th series, vol. 1 (Toulouse, 1889), pp. 327–351; vol. 2 (1890), pp. 390–427.

Renoux-Zagamé, Marie-France, 'Du juge-prêtre au roi-idole. Droit divin et constitution de l'état dans la pensée juridique française à l'aube des Temps modernes', in Jean-Louis Thireau, ed., *Le Droit entre laïcisation et néo-sacralisation* (Paris, 1997), pp. 143–186.

Richet, Denis, 'Aspects socioculturels des conflits religieux à Paris dans la seconde moitié du xviᵉ siècle', *De la Réforme à la Révolution. Études sur la France moderne* (Paris, 1991), pp. 15–51.

Roberts, Penny, *A City in conflict. Troyes during the French wars of religion*, Manchester, 1996.

Roelker, Nancy Lyman, *One king, one faith. The Parlement of Paris and the religious reformations of the sixteenth century*, Berkeley, 1996.

—, *Queen of Navarre. Jeanne d'Albret 1528–1572*, Cambridge, Mass., 1968. French trans. *Jeanne d'Albret, reine de Navarre, 1528–1572*, Paris, 1979.

Romier, Lucien, 'La Saint-Barthélemy. Les événements de Rome et la préméditation du massacre', *Revue du seizième siècle*, 1 (1913), pp. 529–560.

Root, Hilton, *La construction de l'État moderne en Europe. La France et l'Angleterre*, Paris, 1994.

Samaran, Charles, 'Un humaniste italien, Guido Lolgi, témoin de la Saint-Barthélemy', *Studi in onore di Ricardo Filangeri* (Naples, 1959), vol. 2, pp. 397–404.

Sémelin, Jacques, 'Analyser le massacre. Réflexions comparatives', *Questions de recherches/Research in question*, 7 (Sept. 2002), pp. 1–42. Also available in electronic form at http://www.ceri-sciences-po.org.

—, *Purifier et détruire. Usages politiques des massacres et génocides*, Paris, 2005.

Senellart, Michel, *Machiavélisme et raison d'Etat*, Paris, 1989.

Simonin, Michel, *Pierre de Ronsard*, Paris, 1990.

—, *Vivre de sa plume au xviᵉ siècle, ou la carrière de François de Belleforest*, Geneva, 1992.

—, *Charles IX*, Paris, 1995.

Smith, Marc, 'Familiarité française et politesse italienne au xviᵉ siècle. Les diplomates italiens juges des manières de la cour des Valois', *RHD* 102 (1988), pp. 193–232.

Solnon, Jean-François, *Catherine de Médicis*, Paris, 2003.

Soman, Alfred, ed., *The Massacre of St. Bartholomew. Reappraisals and documents*,

The Hague, 1974.

Soulié, Marguerite, 'La Saint-Barthélemy et la réflexion sur le pouvoir', in Franco Simone, ed., *Culture et politique en France à l'époque de l'humanisme et de la Renaissance* (Turin, 1974), pp. 413–425.

—, *L'Inspiration biblique dans la poésie religieuse d'Agrippa d'Aubigné*, Paris, 1977.

Souriac, Pierre-Jean, *Une guerre civile. Affrontements religieux et militaires dans le Midi toulousain, 1562–1596*, Seyssel, 2008.

Sutherland, N. M., *The Massacre of St Bartholomew and the European conflict 1559–1572*, London, 1973.

—, *The Huguenot struggle for recognition*, New Haven and London, 1980.

—, 'Le massacre de la Saint-Barthélemy: la valeur des témoignages et leur interprétation', *RHMC*, 38 (1991), pp. 529–554.

Sypher, Wylie, '"Faisant ce qu'il leur vient à plaisir": The image of protestantism in French Catholic polemic on the eve of the religious wars', *SCJ*, 11 (1980), pp. 59–84.

Tallon, Alain, *La France et le concile de Trente*, Rome, 1997.

—, *Conscience nationale et sentiment religieux en France au xvie siècle*, Paris, 2002.

Taylor, Larissa Juliet, *Heresy and orthodoxy in sixteenth-century Paris. François Le Picart and the beginnings of the Catholic Reformation*, Leiden, 1999.

Thuau, Étienne, *Raison d'état et pensée politique à l'époque de Richelieu*, Athens, 1966, reprint Paris, 2000.

Tournon, André, 'La poétique du témoignage dans *Les Tragiques* d'Agrippa d'Aubigné', in Olivier Pot, ed., *Poétiques d'Aubigné* (Geneva, 1999), pp. 135–146.

Turchetti, Mario, *Concordia o tolleranza? François Bauduin (1520–1573) e i 'moyenneurs'*, Geneva, 1984.

—, *Tyrannie et tyrannicide de l'Antiquité à nos jours*, Paris, 2001.

—, 'L'arrière-plan politique de l'edit de Nantes, avec un aperçu de l'anonyme *De la concorde de l'Estat par l'observation des Edicts de pacification*', in Michel Grandjean and Bernard Roussel, eds, *Coexister dans l'intolérance. L'edit de Nantes (1598)*, (Geneva, 1998), pp. 93–114.

Vasquez de Prada, Valentin, *Felipe II y Francia. Política, religión y razón de Estado*, Pamplona, 2004.

Venard, Marc, 'La présentation de la Saint-Barthélemy aux Polonais en vue de l'élection d'Henri de Valois', in *Les Contacts religieux franco-polonais du Moyen-Âge à nos jours* (Paris, 1985), pp. 116–127.

—, 'Arrêtez le massacre!', *RHMC*, 39 (1992), pp. 645–661.

—, *Réforme protestante, Réforme catholique dans la province d'Avignon, xvie siècle*, Paris, 1993.

Viennot, Éliane, *Marguerite de Valois. Histoire d'une femme, histoire d'un mythe*, Paris, 1993.

—, 'À propos de la Saint-Barthélemy et des *Mémoires* de Marguerite de Valois', *Revue d'Histoire Littéraire de la France* (Sept.–Oct. 1996), pp. 894–917.

Vivanti, Corrado, *Lotta politica e pace religiosa in Francia tra Cinque e Seicento*, Turin 1963. French trans., *Guerre civile et paix religieuse dans la France d'Henri IV*, Paris, 2006.

Wanegffelen, Thierry, *Ni Rome ni Genève. Des fidèles entre deux chaires en France au xvie siècle*, Paris, 1997.

—, *Catherine de Medicis. Le pouvoir au féminin*, Paris, 2005.

Weiss, Nathanaël, 'La Seine et le nombre des victimes parisiennes de la Saint-Barthélemy', *BSHPF*, 46 (1897), pp. 474–481.

Wood, James B., 'The Royal army during the wars of religion, 1559–1576', in Mack P. Holt, ed., *Society and institutions in early modern France* (Athens, Georgia, 1991), pp. 1–35.

—, *The King's army. Warfare, soldiers and society during the wars of religion in France, 1562–1576*, Cambridge, 1996.

Yardeni, Myriam, *La Conscience nationale en France pendant les guerres de religion (1559–1598)*, Paris-Brussels, 1971.

Yates, Frances A., *Astraea. The imperial theme in the sixteenth century*. London 1975. French trans., *Astrée. Le symbolisme impérial au xvie siècle*, Paris, 1989.

—, *The French academies of the sixteenth century*, London, 1947. French trans., *Les Académies en France au xvie siècle*, Paris, 1996.

INDEX

CPSIA information can be obtained at www.ICGtesting.com
Printed in the USA
BVOW05s1956170515

400333BV00002B/6/P